STUDIES IN PUBLIC COMMUNICATION

THE LANGUAGES OF COMMUNICATION

A Logical and Psychological Examination

by

GEORGE N. GORDON

COMMUNICATION ARTS BOOKS

HASTINGS HOUSE, PUBLISHERS • NEW YORK

BF
455
G6

First Edition

Published simultaneously in Canada by
Saunders, of Toronto, Ltd. Don Mills, Ontario

SBN: 8038-4262-7

Library of Congress Catalog Card Number: 74-77349

DESIGNED BY AL LICHTENBERG
PRINTED IN THE UNITED STATES OF AMERICA

For Diane Ellen Gordon
Harry Charles Gordon
Jennifer Cary Gordon

with love.

CONTENTS

Part Four
QUALITIES OF COMMUNICATION

Part Five
INSTRUMENTS OF COMMUNICATION

Part Six
THE FUTURE OF COMMUNICATIONS

PREFACE

EVERYTHING HUMAN beings do may, one way or another, be subsumed under the general heading of "communications."

Dr. Jurgen Ruesch, a psychiatrist whose interests extend to matters of this kind, say that there are forty discrete approaches to communication, ranging from those which apply to mathematics and engineering to interior decorating and parlor games. While he includes psychophysiology, neuro-psychology and psychopharmacology, Ruesch treads lightly on sexual relations as a variety of communication, and he manages to isolate a mere ten more within the fine and useful arts. Speculation, therefore, that five more categories might be added to his list is not out of order here.

Ruesch is right in the all-inclusive proclivity of his approach. Because the topic creeps into almost every corner of modern epistemology, a "communications expert" is likely to be any one of a number of different sorts of persons. His orientation may be scientific or artistic, mathematical or literary, biological or political, or merely "theoretical" or "practical" or "eclectic," in the loose ways that these terms are used today. He may, in the words of Wilde's Lady Bracknell, "know either everything or nothing."

The subject of "communications" is therefore not a single discipline in our present intellectual universe. It is rather the *quality of certain relationships through time,* speculations about which have been recently thrust onto the workbenches of modern scholars in considerable number, due mostly to the development of new instruments of technology. They have accomplished two ends. First, they have rearranged during the past century the quantitative and qualitative interactions of human senders and receivers of communications in drastic measure. Second, they have spawned new instruments of analysis for forms of communication which have been carried out for millions of years and which do not necessarily include human beings in their functions.

When one speaks of communications, he is therefore referring to an overriding phenomenon which is applicable to all facets and conditions of life, even the most basal. Certainly the pathologists who are rewinding the riddles of the bio-chemistry of the genetic origins of life are studying communications. So are the students in a still-life painting class at a school of fine arts. Their interests are bound, in this period of intense and bewildering specialization, mainly by curiosity in common, expressed in science and art, concerning those particular cause and effect relationships which we refer to as "communications." This curiosity bespeaks a modern attitude that has caused us to transcend conventional disciplinary studies and created a new filing cabinet (or waste basket) of "communications' problems." A common disposition has been therefore translated, at least by the authors of university bulletins, into a field of study without a discipline.

This attitude having been identified in contemporary discourse, various experts followed it with some of the essays and books quoted in this volume, among others, and, of course, finally with numerous anthologies. Theories of communications (and communications' theorists) came next, some with highly productive and relevant by-products of established disciplines—and some with colorful moonshine. The latter sort have recently captured the public's fancy for reasons that will be examined subsequently. They have in no way dulled the edge of integrity that more modest and honest scientists, critics and artists in this "field" have honed for it during the first two generations of its life. This is the point at which we arrive for our study of communications today in the chapters to come.

To attempt a survey of *all* the ways in which communications occur— if only to discover how they are similar or different—would be next to impossible. This work would run to several volumes, and it is doubtful that any one author (or team of authors) might conceivably muster a catholic enough grasp of all the relevant material they would have to report. This is the major trouble with most of the extant anthologies on the topic: the author or authors rarely share between them an encyclopedic enough grasp of the subjects they desire to cover in order effectively to separate wheat from chaff. Only when their selections are confined to realistic perimeters (for instance, technological communication or linguistic communication) are the articles they choose likely to give the reader anything like a balanced view of such complex phenomena as those almost invariably involved in the disciplines germane to the study of even one facet of communications.

This volume is certainly not an encyclopedia. Nor is it an anthology, except insofar as most of the ideas presented here have been picked from brains other than the author's. This book is meant to serve as a general introduction to the major problems which face (and will continue to face) the student concerned with the currencies we employ for communications; in other words, their languages.

Faced with vast and, at times, seemingly insurmountable confusions in the basic determinations of what these languages are or how they may be articulated for analysis, the present volume approaches them from what is an as yet untried and, hopefully, clearer direction than to examine them in their contexts as discrete disciplines. The order and nature of this arrangement, while new, was distilled, as the reader will note, from freely available current speculation concerning the inter-disciplinary philosophy of communications, what little there has been of it of more than transient interest.

The method of treatment should be clear from an examination of the Table of Contents. The analysis centers upon an initial differentiation assumed—and defended—between the logics and psychologics of the languages. We are therefore able, throughout the entire volume, to view from at least two perspectives, loosely an aesthetic and a functional viewpoint, what these languages are and how they operate. Our discussion subsequently moves to a discussion of symbols, because most languages of communications draw heavily upon the symbolic process for the mediation of meaning X between individuals and cultures.

The next problem treated is the one likely to give the reader his severest qualms, just as they are offered with the author's greatest humility. This section centers on a redefinition of the so-called "media," the most confusing aspect, in the opinion of many, of present attempts at studying communication processes. First, the suggestion is offered that far fewer "media" than current conventional wisdom accepts, in fact, operate in our numerous communication procedures. Second, a defense is offered for the differentiation of a *medium* of communication from an *instrument* (or *device*) of communication, solely in the interests of clarity and relevance to currently profitable methods of analysis.

Having drawn lines for inquiry into *what* the languages of communication are, we are next concerned with *how they work*, those qualities which give them their distinction and, sometimes, elevate them to the status of art. Cognitive, emotive, stylistic and intentional factors provide the focus of these discussions, as well as a consideration of what may be one of the most significant qualitative element of all: humor. In fact, the reader will note the author's temerity in offering, perhaps unwisely, a section of speculation concerning why people laugh and how laughter is communicated.

At this point, an approach is made to the topic that frequently fills entire books and series of books: the technologies of communications, from the invention, hundreds of years ago, of central perspective in painting to the present gadgetry of television and radio. Our emphasis is mainly upon *devices*: instruments for transmitting sound and printed words, pictures (on canvas, paper and/or screens) that stand still, move, and talk, and similar fascinating technological stepchildren of the age of science.

Last, an attempt is made to evaluate the ways in which the languages of communications relate to a phenomenon usually identified as "mass culture," a quantitative and qualitative novelty of discourse that seems to accompany certain political and technical developments of modern life. The final chapter contains a number of predictions that may be of especial interest to those artists and educators who have had the patience to follow the arguments and, undoubtedly, prejudices in the rest of the volume to their finish.

This book purports to offer no revolutions in theory or practice. Nor does it represent the author's systematic attempts to isolate outstanding and certain specific "problems" concerning communications which may be "solved" scientifically or theoretically, either intentionally or in the course of allied speculations. It evolved simply from the need of one university teacher to find a suitable language for himself with which to communicate with a number of graduate students, most of them highly motivated to understand better their own professional endeavors, who were (and still are) artists, technicians and communicators of various types, actively engaged in the dissemination of thoughts and feelings to others. These students themselves, in many ways, wrote this volume by virtue of their constant demands for satisfactory insights and explanations untainted by doctrines, mystiques or assumptions. The author's gratitude to them is limitless.

Others also bear responsibilities for the virtues of the chapters that follow, if virtues they possess. The writer worked as student and colleague for thirteen years with Charles A. Siepmann. His brilliant critical sense, analytic acumen, and individuality of vision are matters of record. Their example led to most of the inquiries into the topics about which this volume is concerned. While Professor Siepmann would probably disagree with a good number of the notions expressed in these pages (and fault their creator for his ineptitude in expressing them), a personal and professional debt that will never be properly repaid is at least entered here in the ledger.

Examples provided by other colleagues and teachers had much to do with both the method and substance of the coming chapters, among them Constance Welch and the late Walter Prichard Eaton at the Yale Drama School, William Sears and the late Fred Blanchard at New York University and many, many more, including the co-authors of previous books, particularly Irving Falk and John Mulholland, both of whom have done much to temper the writer in the heat of experience.

Preparing a manuscript for publication is always taxing, but the present volume has been unusually difficult. Sally McCarthy, Sue Sternberg and Mary Brophy were, in various ways, involved in typing it, but Edna Bartlett and Harriet Griffith are mainly responsible for its final preparation and dealing patiently with the writer's neuroses concerning fires and earthquakes. Whether she likes it or not, Helen Wallace's criticisms of the first draft were invaluable in subsequent revisions, and she has earned both the author's gratitude and respect. Russell Neale of Hastings House, as he has in the past, provided the invaluable sustained interest that was essential in turning an intellectual adventure into a book. Without his help, the writer would never have gotten beyond this Preface.

But he did, and the pages that follow are the author's sole responsibility. Their irrelevancies, gaucheries and errors are his fault and must not be blamed on teachers, friends or publishers. From this point on, reader and writer are involved with one-way communication by means of the medium of narrative employing the instrument of printed words. I trust that the time and effort of neither will have been wasted!

Forest Hills, New York

February, 1969

INTRODUCTION

AT MID-CENTURY, Crane Brinton hopefully could observe that the price we pay for an essentially enlightened and democratic progress would seem to be multanimity, and "even a degree of alienation." There is always the possibility, he concluded, "that the price may be too high, beyond our resources. But there is equally a possibility that we can pay it; we have certainly paid large installments already." Less than two decades later, pessimism gathers force. Yielding to the fears of nuclear holocaust and to that threat of massive ecological imbalance posed by a runaway population curve, not a few of our leading thinkers are now prepared to declare the grand experiment of democratic Enlightenment a bankrupt failure, and cancel payment.

It is regrettable that so many of our intelligentsia are beginning not only to condone, but actively to propagate notions of a complete biological and psychological overhaul of a sick, entrapped and inflexible *homo maniacus*. If we accept recent testimony, the "old" man is gone—abandoned by Koestler as a biological freak and assigned by McLuhan to a media-induced primitive state of pre-rationality. Man's potentialities for growth are reduced by some to a series of probability levels, and many of his heretofore tolerable thoughts and actions are condemned by others as psychosocial aberrations which must be corrected by the controlled, efficient restructuring of his "total environment." In the pessimist's world of the future, multanimity will have no place, and "the general good" will be the only acceptable version of human progress.

Amidst the growing defeatism, confusion and demand for "mutation," those possibilities for human change which rely upon that traditional aspect of interaction called *communication* are being either ignored or dismissed as useless unless more fundamental alterations in man's physical and psychic make-up are first effected. Only when the more pessimistic of our thinkers are asked why the typical man in Western societies continues to cling to what they consider irrational faiths and illogical attitudes is the "problem" of communication touched upon, and then only in such manner as to confirm past failures.

The lessons of history are, after all, quite clear. According to the conventional wisdom, the reason the masses cannot be moved to face the demands of our century is that they cannot be brought to care or think deeply enough about their own destiny. Exploited, manipulated, misinformed (or uninformed) by those who have power over our symbol-producing institutions and machinery, 20th-century man is gripped by a sense of helpless fatalism. Until now (continues the pessimist's argument), civilization has —generally for the worse—been able to offset this *anomie* with occasional strong doses of manufactured "purpose." But alienation is now too pervasive —and threat to the entire species too real—to allow men to continue in pursuit of that cheap faith which says "things will get better if we try to make them better." Man is in fact immobile, incapable of using his vaunted powers of communication to create any kind of order and progress, and trapped by his increasingly useless symbols.

Fortunately, another view of the potentials of human communication is open to us—a view predicated upon the more optimistic and, I believe, more accurate assumption that modern man's true perception of his world is entirely unrelated to what our despairing theorists suppose it to be. The degree of alienation felt by the citizens in Western societies is, after all, a positive by-product of an equally positive force—the increasing understanding of the fact of multanimity. If a single deep-flowing trend in Western man's response to his fellow-beings since mid-century can be discerned, it is his *acceptance* of the significance and value of diversity in human make-up. More than at any point in history, the "average" man is inclined to forbearance, to recognition of other's needs, and to the common qualities of humanness which extend beyond mere animal function. This acceptance, it may be noted, is a direct result of his capacity to generate self-change through *communicative* acts and processes—and to employ a wondrous technology of dissemination to extend and enlarge this capacity.

What the conventional wisdom cannot admit, of course, is that the moral, intellectual, philosophical, political and scientific world-views posed by his intellectual betters are indeed being communicated—at one level or another and in one form or another—to the most lowly in our civilization. Questions of good and evil, right and wrong, justice and tyranny, freedom and slavery, sanity and insanity, order and chaos, have been re-worked into all communicative symbol-systems, recast in all communicative media, and re-transmitted by all of our instruments of dissemination. Further, these images are not only perceived, but *comprehended*, by the great majority.

Yet the pessimist continues to dismiss what he holds to be an apparent unconcern with serious questions among the "average" in this civilization as a foreboding state of *verfremdung*. This is the initial error which leads many thinkers to such dark conclusions and sweeping proposals for bio-chemical and psycho-social mutation controls upon man's inner and outer environments. For comprehension does not imply acceptance, and it must therefore be concluded that the most significant failures in human communication in this century occur neither in the interaction between political entities nor between common men. In their efforts to preserve or extend whatever they value, the assumptions and actions of both often become unreasoning and brutal, yet these "breakdowns" imperil mankind less than the inability of many of the best-trained, most sensitive and perceptive minds of this age to evaluate the needs and aspirations of great numbers of their fellows *in any other than negative terms.*

We are aware that an endless stream of messages flows "downward" from the towers of science and the arts to the mass of society, but analysis of this flow in light of the simplest model of the communications process will reveal that many of these messages are hardly perceived as they were intended. This condition obtains neither because the greater number in society are intellectually incapable of understanding the content nor because they are denied exposure to it. Rather, most members of Western societies are unable to accept the connotation underlying an increasing number of such messages—*that it is useless to continue in their present state.* The typical human being can be told many things that will encourage him to change, but he cannot be told that he has reached his limits and must, in effect, *stop becoming.* If he *could* accept that message he would stop being human, and there would be no reason for any telling of anything.

Bronowski reminds us that the values by which we are to survive are not rules for just and unjust conduct, but are those "deeper illuminations in whose light justice and injustice, good and evil, means and ends are seen in fearful sharpness of outline." Such illuminations have been provided for us in the past, and there must be reason for us to hope that mankind—given freedom from enforced and artificial controls upon his brain as well as his mind, will continue in his struggle to bring himself into the light.

Perhaps the pessimists are right, in which case *Studies in Public Communication* may well evolve into a series of volumes devoted to cellular structure, chemical formulae and animal behavior. But whether the more despairing of our thinkers, artists and scientists come to terms with man-as-he-is or not, others among their peers hopefully will continue to equate man-as-he-is with man-as-he-must-be, proceed in their attempts to understand and evaluate the pitfalls and possibilities of man's communicative acts and processes, and refrain from assigning blanket guilt. If such world-views were not expressed, it is indeed possible that total *anomie* would result.

The optimistic view, then, is in itself an act of faith. That faith is represented in this volume by Dr. Gordon's stimulating and positive effort to bring still another fresh, independent and systematic view to the languages which man employs as he engages in the human dialogue.

A. WILLIAM BLUEM, Ph.D.
General Editor: *Studies in Public Communication*
Newhouse Communication Center, Syracuse University

My general thesis is that many of the communication diffi-culties between persons are the by-product of communication barriers *within* the person; and that communication between the person and the world, to and fro, depends largely on their iso-morphism (*i.e.*, similarity of structure or form); that the world can communicate to a person only that of which he is worthy, that which he deserves or is "up to"; that to a large extent, he can receive from the world, and give to the world, only that which he himself is. As Georg Lichtenberg said of a certain book, "Such works are like mirrors; if an ape peeps in, no apostle will look out."

ABRAHAM H. MASLOW

Mutual understanding is the result of maximal communi-cation through mutual empathy. It can approximately be reached through means of manifold tools of communication, of which semantic language is only one.

JOOST A. M. MEERLOO

Part One

LOGICS AND PSYCHOLOGICS OF COMMUNICATION

Chapter 1

THE LOGICS
OF COMMUNICATIONS

I F THIS BOOK has a villain, it is the ghost of what is known as the "mind-body problem," a question drawn from philosophy, in the words of Ludwig von Bertalanffy, one of the oldest, "tossed around for centuries and disputed by the most illustrious minds in vain." [1]

René Descartes was and is the most eloquent spokesman in all of literature for this viewpoint, one that is continually demolished by philosophical cleverness but hovers not only over the intellectual argument of the modern world but the division of the concept of "communications" into viable "logics" and "psychologics" in this and the following chapter. As von Bertalanffy notes, "public" (or shared) perceptions of events and private (or mental) experiences still constitute the two major classes of descriptive phenomena available either in common talk or specialized reporting. "As a matter of fact," says he, "the Cartesian dualism is still with us and at the basis of our thinking in neurophysiology, psychology, psychiatry and related fields." [2] It also provides a basis for other, less subjectively oriented scientists, less by virtue, frequently, of what they report to us in their journals than by what they disregard.

Briefly, as von Bertalanffy has stated:

> . . . the Cartesian dualism between material things and conscious ego is not a primordial or elementary datum, but results from a long evaluation and development. Other sorts of awareness exist and cannot be dismissed as illusory. On the other hand, the dualism between the material brain and immaterial mind (to which the dualism boils down) is a conceptualization that has historically developed, and is not the only one possible or necessarily the best one. As a matter of fact, *the classic conceptualiza-*

---

[1] "The Mind-Body Problem: A New View," *Psychosomatic Medicine*, XXIV (1964), quoted in Floyd W. Matson and Ashley Montagu (eds.), *The Human Dialogue* (New York: The Free Press, 1967), p. 224.
[2] *Ibid.*, p. 227.

tion of matter and mind, res extensa and res cogitans, no longer correspond to available knowledge. We should not discuss the mind-body problem in terms of seventeenth century physics, but must reconsider it in the light of contemporary physics, biology and behavioral and other sciences.[3]

This is, of course, precisely the intent of this first part of the book, insofar as this classical problem still bears upon the considered analysis of the content, mediums and devices of communication in contemporary civilization.

The Quality of Duality

Gilbert Ryle[4] and the modern English linguistic philosophers handle what he calls the "Cartesian Myth" with British dispatch. Ryle and his followers reduce to mere conveniences the powerful descriptive force once filled by the formerly lusty "official doctrine" of philosophy, as the linguistic philosophers call it. Ryle construes Descartes' thinking as demonstrating a split between two separate aspects of life, certain portions of which are external and belong to the physical word, other aspects of which are mental or internal.[5] They are, to him, irreconcilable and incompatible data and therefore absurd as a "dualism."

Ryle tries to create a whole system of analysis which appears to be more linguistic and external than synthetic or mental. His argument concerns *nothing but* mind or matter—it is sometimes difficult to tell which. He even, by way of pyrotechnical display of literary ingenuity, dispenses with all of modern psychology in a dozen pages.[6] As a result, the non-Oxfordian is left wondering what the price of discarding Descartes' duality is! Dr. Johnson activated his gouty foot by kicking a curbstone in refutation of Bishop Berkeley's contention that matter did not exist without mind. Ryle appears to cut off a leg in order to demonstrate that he does not have a sore toe.

Warnock, a sympathetic member of the British school of linguists snatches the problem of duality from Ryle's grasp with the observation[7] that Ryle's attempt—or any attempt—to reduce the dualism between physical events and states of mind inevitably constructs a merely *descriptive* view of life processes, similar to Pavlov's or Watson's[8] psychologies of behavior, both familiar in outline fashion to most of us. Thus does their attempt destroy the dual proposition of the famous sentence "I think; there-

[3] *Ibid.*, p. 228, (italics and parenthetical note added).
[4] Gilbert Ryle, *The Concept of Mind* (New York: Barnes and Noble, Inc. 1941).
[5] *Ibid.*, p. 12.
[6] *Ibid.*, pp. 319–330.
[7] G. J. Warnock, *English Philosophy Since 1900* (London: Oxford University Press, 1958), pp. 99–102 (italics added).
[8] The contributions of both to the psychologics of communication will be considered in Chapter II.

fore I am" by reducing it to the absurd (but true) statement "I am." Thinking has passed from the scene.

In Ciceronion rhetoric, Warnock also observes that Ryle's efforts at destroying the "mental ghost" (the metaphorical "mind") is perverse and quixotic when directed against Descartes. It is true, observes he, that Descartes was the first mind-body philosopher in the modern mode, but Warnock slyly observes (like von Bertalanffy) that Ryle's *bete noire* goes "through a rough genealogy (which) might be traced further back through many theories as far at least as Plato." [9]

We "find in our *language*" says Warnock, "many idioms suggestive of such a theory," [10] giving Ryle and his followers the right to discard Descartes. So it does. And in the construction of today's British linguists (stimulated originally by the writings of Ludwig Wittgenstein) the elimination of duality—leaving verbal constructions where once the world of thinking men had been—may signify the "coming" philosophy of our century, simply because man is separated neither from his thought nor his actions but is taken whole on the face of what he says about himself.

Attention is called to the tidy position of the British linguistics to clarify a major point concerning the discussion which follows. Other examples might have been taken from the doctrines of General Semantics, Gestalt Psychology, Logical Positivism (in its non-linguistic phase), various theological principles or even concepts of art. What they all illustrate, the Linguistics more aptly and sensitively than others, is the powerful current of *modern* skepticism concerning the *natural* duality of mind and body. The words "modern" and "natural" have been chosen with care and are based upon the argument offered by J. Bronowski in the essay which preceeds the published edition of his radio play, *The Face of Violence*,[11] an argument demonstrating the naturalness and modernity of these ideas.

Bronowski demonstrates that the *ancient* myth-ridden mind which created the concept of the sphinx was indeed fully aware of the dualism between mind and body, although capable of expressing it in one way only: the *natural* way. It did not choose one sphinx or one period of time, but many sphinxes over many eras. The one that remains at Giza today is only "a dear little kitten of a Sphinx" in Shaw's words, but she, he, or it, reminds us that man has confronted his universal problems in dual terms since antiquity.

---

9 *Ibid.*, p. 102.
10 *Loc. cit.*
11 J. Bronowski, *The Face of Violence* (New York: George Braziller, 1955), pp. 9–62. Bronowski's drama, adopted for the stage by a skilled writer, would provide a remarkably entertaining example of a powerful historical and philosophical communication translated into emotional impersonations which will be discussed in Chapter 15, that is, should the actors be able to capture the timeless quality of its none-too-reassuring theme.

The sphinx is the animal with the brain and potential for reasoning of a man. It communicates to us, with little distortion or extrapolation, the primitive insight which distinguished the poles between thought and action, body and mind, essence and existence—and, in contemporary terms, between logic and psychologic.

Upon the correctness and adequacy of this primitive and classical observation, the considerations which follow depend. Our discussion will include a number of hueristic starting points for the study of the logics and psychologics of communication, including those labeled with so up-to-date and satisfying a rubic as "interdisciplinary." [12]

No claim, however, is herein put forward that there is but one choice between any of numerous holistic views of communications and the mind-body one which will shortly be proposed. Of course, each may contain what John Stuart Mill once called "a portion of the truth" in a comfortable age when it was easier to tell the truth from error than it is today. Hegelian and other theorists of process sometimes deny that substantive premises like those discussed above are necessary analytically under all conditions, especially Freudian or Marxian Hegelians. At least one neo-Hegelian "expert" on communictions media[13] has achieved riches and fame on the basis of a claim of this nature: namely, that the medium (of communication) is the message.

That Understanding Media[14] became a "best seller" of its kind is a clear indication of deep interest in and deeper misunderstandings of communications in their most elemental constructions: mind and body, medium and response or, more precisely, logic and psychologic. The problem of understanding these mediums is not one of differentiating messages from mediums, as McLuhan appears to believe, but of relating them to the problem of duality.

What the brilliant, charming McLuhan has, to his credit, accomplished is to draw the attention of many to questions posed by the processes through which communications occur. And he has answered in terms of

[12] The choice is made even in the face of the seemingly indisputably rewarding cybernetic attempts to quantify and schematize communications processes in an objective scientific matrix which regards the duality of mind and body as more or less beside the point. Cybernetic objectivity, for instance, theoretically precludes the development of a rich psychologic of the languages of communication. Norbert Weiner's seminal book Cybernetics (New York: John Wiley and Sons, Inc., 1948), is, however, suggested for study of language in either its logical or psychological phases. He qualifies a number of processes in communication (what is commonly called "feedback," for instance), to give insight into their complexities in communication more artful and sophisticated than those employed in cybernetic models alone.
[13] Because its recent misuse appears to have damaged its meaning, the word media will not be used in this book. The plural of "medium" will be signified by the word "mediums."
[14] Marshall McLuhan, Understanding Media (New York: McGraw-Hill Book Company, 1964), is the book which gave McLuhan his present eminence. Students of the languages of communication will expose themselves to McLuhan's ruminations with profit.

seemingly satisfactory categories of analysis: medium and message. The content are wrong but his method is correct. A two-pronged response to the question of how man communicates is inevitable. All of our activities occur in frameworks which are, like it or not, either demonstrable in physical environment or components of our peculiar methods of perceiving the worlds around us.

The Quality of Logic

The Aristotelian notion of logic was one of many instrumentalities for speculation discovered in the ancient world.[15] Recall that the Phoenicians, Egyptians, Greeks and Romans had by the Christian Era evolved nearly *all* of the commercial, economic, social, political, philosophical modes of inquiry that anyone has yet produced to this day—save one or two. (The vitality of these one or two entitle us to term the period from the seventeenth century to the present "modern"). Contemporary societies replay endless themes on forms of civilization and styles of living familiar to one or another culture in the ancient world. There societies experienced many thousands of years of interactive experimentation with one another, remarkable developments considering their primitive methods of transporting men and messages.

The Aristotelian concept of logic is only slightly less vital today than it was 2,500 years ago, despite its treatment at the hands of science and technology. Deductive reasoning received its first direct challenge in the English language in Bacon's *Novum Organum,* and the pathway from Bacon to the growth of science and the era of invention is clear. Bacon regarded the Aristotelian deductive tradition as reactionary mischief, although his debt to Greek and Roman (as opposed to medieval theological) teaching was acknowledged and insistent in his argument.

What repelled the liberated scholars of the Renaissance was the suspicious number of "given" factors in Aristotle's numerous systems of biology, ethics and physics—as well as his system of logic. Deduction, working from general concepts to specifics, as in syllogistic reason, begged the *truth* of its postulates. Semantics, or some other method of linguistic analysis of the adequacy of language, may therefore maintain or destroy the truth of *any* Aristotelian syllogism.

The newer inductive reasoning, however, apparently took *nothing* as given, and there lay its attraction for the objectives of science. Men like Bacon may indeed have been thinkers ahead of their time, but their dis-contents seem today inevitable. To deduction they brought the essential elements of empirical research. First, they were skeptical of all general concepts on any but certain theological issues. Secondly, they began a tradition

[15] See the section on Aristotle in Rex Warner's *The Greek Philosophers* (New York: Mentor Books, 1958), pp. 108–138, especially pp. 112–113. Warner's trip through antiquity is rapid and pungent.

of uninvolved experimentation that ran counter to the clean, cerebral perfection formerly ascribed to Greek thought, geometry, architecture and art that was cherished by the neoclassicists in European universities. Arthur Koestler's observations on these tendencies as they affected one of these inductive scientists, Galileo in particular, has a familar contemporary ring. He writes:

> There existed a powerful body of men whose hostility to Galileo never abated: the Aristotelians at the universities. The inertia of the human mind and its resistance to innovation are most clearly demonstrated not, as one might expect, by the ignorant mass—which is easily swayed once its imagination is caught—but by professionals with a vested interest in tradition and a monopoly on learning. Innovation is a twofold threat to academic mediocrities: it endangers their oracular authority, and it evokes the deeper fear that their whole, laboriously constructed intellectual edifice might collapse.[16]

Suspicions, however, of the demise of Aristotelian logic as a method of obtaining knowledge at the hands of the newly risen scientific men were unwarranted. Both common and uncommon men are not freely disposed to discard methods of ratiocination, however discredited, as long as they work.

The Longevity of Logic

How and why did Aristotle's logic survive? The means for its transmission over the centuries has resided in numerous exponents and popularizers of "deduction" and "logic" for what were apparently practical purposes. In fact, most of them were literary figures rather than pragmatic men who were likely to be scientists or technologists. One of the greatest in recent times was the legendary Sherlock Holmes and his offspring: the British literary tradition of mystery stories.

Why Aristotle's logic survived has already been explained superficially above. Examination of one of the better books available on the use of "fallacy" in argument discloses the utilitarian value of Aristotelian logic in debate and propaganda passed down to the modern world.[17] Such books usually begin with an explanatory section on Aristotelian deduction, not to demonstrate shortcomings in the face of problems requiring a skeptical-empirical approach, but rather how to *use* these constructions to win argu-

---

[16] Arthur Koestler, *The Sleepwalkers* (New York: The Macmillan Company, 1959), p. 427. Koestler's book has been cited here as an interesting study of the end of Aristotelian and neo-classical thinking in Europe. Koestler would, however, challenge the assertion above that as deduction died empiricism and science followed in anything like an orderly manner. The book is recommended reading to anyone who cherishes the belief that modern science was formed in the crucible of rationality. Koestler's study of Tycho, Kepler, Copernicus, Galileo and Newton emphasizes the degrees to which good luck, mistakes and lucky bungling opened the doors—quite by accident—of modern scientific inquiry. Hence the title.

[17] For example, W. Ward Fearnside and William B. Holther, *Fallacy, The Counterfeit of Argument* (Englewood Cliffs, N.J.: Prentice Hall, Inc., 1959.)

ments or to punch holes in those of others. They are debator's tools, advertisers' *impedimenta*, rhetorical devices, as useful to us as to the countless generations who once accepted them as the *only* immediate and adequate way of achieving truth, short of consultation with gods.[18]

Modern concepts of "logic" are clarified in the Introduction to one such volume. "The processes of logic," write the authors "are rather like those of a machine, and the logical fallacies show a clear misfunctioning of forms designed to go smoothly and produce valid arguments." [19] Note that the *argument* (not its truth, relevance to life or function) is all important, as it is to a debater, advertiser or candidate for public office. For the latter, the "campaign promise" frequently has nothing to do with the candidate's probable course of action (if elected), just as the most interesting debates are frequently incapable of affecting reality.

Recall also that inductive empiricism, built on a structure of skepticism, maintains that *all* possibilities for the discovery of "truth" are possible, including the possibility that the inductive method itself is incorrect or inadequate and that deduction—Aristotle's logic—is sometimes superior. An empiricist like Bacon maintained, for instance, that certain theological generalizations stood apart from his science. A modern physicist might introduce moral caveats into his inductive agenda (by way of generalizations) that would limit his empirical behavior with radioactive cobalt or some other material that might blow up the world. Many, perhaps all, inductive systems hold certain generalizations *a priori* to be applied in deductive fashion to the process of induction, or else the inductions themselves would not exist nor would anybody bother to articulate them!

Remember also that existential philosophers challenge these particular generalizations quite successfully, and therefore bring much skepticism to *all* inductive or scientifically oriented ways of thought, and the application of empiricism, skepticism, experimentalism and all types of positivism to the full range of modern life and mind.[20] The specific "given" in existential philosophy is the existence of the philosopher: man thinking and standing for the human condition. The heroes, therefore, of existential novelists and playwrights are isolated men, dramatizing the primacy, morbidity and alienation of existence tempered by brief and unsatisfactory contacts with others. They are modern counterparts of the classical Aristotelian "logician" or Descartes' "thinking man" who *is* because he *thinks*. The modern

18 The main break with the Aristotelian tradition that one finds in modern "logic" books is the introduction of psychological trickery to debate, probably familiar to Aristotle's followers but which he was unable to classify as "logic." Aristotle does concern himself with psychological factors in discourse (particularly narrative) in his *Poetics* (See chapter 8.)
19 Fearnside and Holther, p. 4.
20 In these terms, the British linguists described above following Wittgenstein are also positivists, limiting their particular inductions to what is *said* about living rather than what is *done* about it. Therefore they remain at odds in most respects with the highly contemporary existentialists.

coloration is given the existentialist because his *mood* is usually contemporary (and gloomy); he is suspicious of the value of positivistic-induction (meaning science and technology to most of us) because of his strange negative *faith*, which is at once logical and nihilistic.[21]

William Barrett, an existentialist himself, shows clearly why the sword of inductive reasoning cannot slay the dragon of deductive logic. Positivism, the philosophy of induction:

> . . . takes as its central fact what is undoubtedly the central fact distinguishing our civilization from all others—science; but it goes on from this to take science as the ultimate ruler of human life. . . . Positivist man is a curious creature who dwells on a tiny island of light composed of what he finds scientifically "meaningful," while the whole surrounding area in which ordinary men live from day to day and have their dealings with other men is consigned to the outer darkness of the "meaningless." Positivism has simply accepted the fractional being of modern man and erected a philosophy to intensify it. Existentialism . . . has attempted instead to gather all the elements of human reality into a total picture of man.[22]

Note, however, that deductive logic cleaves from inductive empiricism in many ways other than existentialism in philosophy. The existentialist-positivist controversy has been chosen above because it so clearly demonstrates (and in so familiar a context) the durable qualities which Aristotelian logic has displayed in its nearly two and one half millenium history and why it applies directly and with continual insistence to the languages of communication.

The Rape of Logic

If deductive logic has become increasingly suspect during the past century, this has occurred neither at the hands of the natural scientists or poetic-philosophers. It is rather the behavior scientists who, in common with the empiricist, have turned their backs on generalization and given truths,[23] but unlike him, refused to relinquish his claims upon the device of

---

[21] Camus' *The Stranger* is the embodment of this gloomy logician. (The book is available in many editions in French and English; it seems gloomier in French.) Note that this non-hero displays all the qualities that a good inductive reasoner would not. He does not even start the first step of the scientific method: the isolation of the problem at hand so that it can be observed and tested. Instead, he *lives* his alienation, suffering through application of the generalizations that life has provided.

[22] William A. Barrett, *Irrational Man* (New York: Doubleday Anchor Books, 1958), p. 19.

[23] A sarcastic critic of these behavior scientists might claim that they turned their backs upon truths given by the wrong people. When generalizations were offered by men like William James, Sigmund Freud or James Rush they proved—and still prove—to be far less skeptical than their brother natural scientists. "Givens" abound like weeds in all the behavior and social sciences, but they are of little concern to the present defense of deduction, even though they are indispensible to the conduct of the social sciences themselves. Notice, however, the naïve approach—as inductive reasoning—of

logic for the instrumentation of thought one jot or tittle! Deduction (or by-products of the deductive method) have been simply far too valuable tools. In order to have his conceptual cake and eat it also, philosophers and medical men originated the concept of "psycho-logic," a fusion of deduction as a mode of apprehension first, and application of thought and induction as a method of empirically viewing reality second.[24] A formidable step, but one which brought little cheer to logicians and remains the source of confusion to inductive empiricists.

Psychologic's main curiosity is that it is a method of observing and reporting, at most, an extremely limited part of the spectrum of events that occur in the universe—including those that human beings *think* happen to them. *All* methods of observation and reporting are in some manner limited, but the limits of the application of psychologics are far greater than those of logic, held as they are to the observation of the behavior of (mostly) men and animals and to speculations about why they behave as they do.

Psychologics Versus Logics

The temptation is great to regard psychologics as a compromise of course down the "middle of the road" between deductive logic and empirical induction. This concept, however, is too neat and pat to satisfy psychologists (who usually emphasize the scientific aspect of their discipline) or philosophers (who emphasize the lack of inductive rigor in this applied science). We shall deal with the exact nature of psychologics in the next chapter and demonstrate other shortcomings in the "compromise" approach to psychologics.

(For the present, we need merely to contrast psychologics with logics sufficiently to clarify how they bear upon the dual nature of the languages of communication as we shall examine them in this book. It is sufficient to note here the more or less self-evident proposition that there exist characteristics of psychologics noticeably *different from* those of logics. Further discussion of psychologics in this chapter will henceforth include only those observations necessary to demonstrate these differences.)

First, psychologics do *not* stem from given generalizations which are understood to be derived from nature or generated as part of culture. Psychological generalizations in the deductive mode are usually formulated

Peter L. Berger, *Invitation to Sociology* (New York: Doubleday and Company, Inc., 1963), a lucid and honest elementary statement of sociology's nature and function. Pp. 151–186 are particularly revealing of the sociologist's hydraheaded perspective concerning deduction and induction, particularly the revealing statement of faith on p. 161.
24 In the same manner the *logos* or "reason" of things has been for eons associated with systems that have the "inevitable and predictable" elements (to quote Webster) built into them. "Physiologic," "chronologic" and even such terms as "scatologic" have, in common with the term "psychologic," the empirical and orderly articulation of a system in the world we perceive that allows us to impose an orderly mode of thinking upon it.

from "givens" discovered by one of two means: revelation or insight. They are formulated as "theories" or "hypotheses," grist for the mill of subsequent inductive testing and proof for truth.

Second, since they are functions of the behavior of organisms, and these organisms are endowed with what we call "life," these generalizations tend to become increasingly difficult to articulate, particularly as the complexity of the organisms increases. Accordingly, these descriptions tend to vary greatly through time and over space.[25] What is missing from most psychological generalizations is the universality and timelessness that is achieved easily by the application of logics to even highly complex problems. Psychologics tend to be subjective; logics strive towards greater objectivity, although the former be elegant and profound and the latter be obvious enough for a child to comprehend. Neither, in practice, invariably reach their goals.

Third, the data of psychologics are usually mediated to the observer through a thicker forest of symbols, emotions, motivations, and what are sometimes called "instincts" than are the data of logics. Deductive logic, in the strict application of generalities to observable phenomena, regards the world more or less as it looks, things and people more or less as they seem to be. To a logician, a circle is a circle; to a psychologist it may be many things, depending upon number of factors. To a logician, when a man says he is happy, this is a truth or a lie; to a psychologist it may be neither a truth nor a lie, but a clue, or a symbol portending many possibilities. Truth and falsehood may, for him, be irrelevent.

The Uses of Logic

The role of logic, therefore, in the description and analysis of the languages of communication, is associated fundamentally with the *aesthetic* of a particular language. This role would be invariable were the term "aesthetic" confined to its dictionary definition, the "philosophy of the beautiful," and were the concept of philosophy to be drawn from the Middle Ages. Unfortunately, the contemporary idea of aesthetics is frequently associated with (and obscured by) its association with phrases like "aesthetic emotion" or "aesthetic attitude." "Emotions" and "attitudes" transcend the limits of logical analysis.

This problem has been recognized by Susanne K. Langer, who apparently is content to settle for the notion that "rightness and necessity" dictate a logical framework for the development of an aesthetic—in other words, a deductive philosophy of the beautiful: a logic.

"Certainly 'rightness and necessity,'" she writes, "are properties with philosophical implications, and the perception of them a more telling inci-

---

[25] The cross cultural phenomenon in psychology itself is simple to observe in the various differential styles of psychological history and research in the various countries where the field developed.

dent than an inexplicable emotion. To recognize that something is right and necessary is a rational act, no matter how spontaneous and immediate the recognition may be; it points to an intellectual principle in artistic judgment. . . ." [26]

Langer cannot, however, maintain for long the notion that aesthetics are entirely a logical construct; again and again, she is faced with psychologics of "attitudes" or "emotions," and she is frequently busy, following John Dewey, weaving in and out reactively from the work of art she discusses to the perspective of the viewer and back again to the object.[27]

Because her concern is art rather than communication,[28] Langer rarely appears eager to separate the logical and psychological modes from the music, paintings, dances and dramas she scrutinizes in her works. They would lose their value as criticism which depends largely upon Langer's refined senses of apprehension opposed to her observations of consumer (or audience) reaction. The art critic must be *conscious* of the difference in logical and psychological modes. He is also aware that he cannot apply any logical standard of aesthetics to a work of art without introducing complicating psychologics.

We must, therefore, construct a definition of the logics of communication, mindful of what appears to be a major critical inadequacy. But for purposes of definition alone, it will shortly provide us with a conception of *one* aspect of the communications process otherwise difficult to isolate and discuss.[29]

Accordingly: *the languages of communications, in their logical phases, reflect certain rules of order in the dissemination of sound, sights or actions which are commonly meaningful to two or more people acting as both senders and receivers.*[30] In other words, this construction of the logics of the

---

[26] Susanne K. Langer, *Feeling and Form* (New York: Charles Scribner's Sons, 1953), p. 33.
[27] *Ibid.*, pp. 397–98.
[28] Langer's concept of art *includes* much data relating to communication. In her works she has, however, ordered these observations according to the needs of an art critic rather than as a student of communications. In this volume, her trenchant observations of these matters, particularly those involving symbolism, will be drawn upon as needed by the author.
[29] Similar definitions of facets of communication have, of course, been attempted. "Who says what to whom with what effect and how?" *comes close* to being a true and useful definition of one *process* of communication. Since logical and psychological factors are involved in this kind of inclusive definition, we are not likely to see a better one emerge for its limited functions in the near future. All such attempts deal with selected aspects of communication at best. See John B. Newman, "A Rationale for a Definition of Communication," in Alfred G. Smith (ed.), *Communication and Culture* (New York: Holt, Rinehart and Winston, 1966), pp. 55–63.
[30] Since the *absence* of such rules of order would be part of the logical content of the communication (the way a missing finger communicates a message about a human hand: one finger never grew or has been severed), this statement may apply to abstract designs, atonal music, or even to paintings executed by apes—as long as the painting is *shown* by a man to another man and not by ape to ape. Two apes might be capable of

language of communication might describe the *aesthetic* of that communication, were that aesthetic construed entirely logically, and were matters of "emotion," "attitude" and other *psychologics* (and/or purely subjective factors) excluded. What is important to a clear perception of the logics of communication is the articulation of an agreed starting point, a point of reference or even a set of standards by which all communications will therefore be amenable both to quantification and qualification in a systematic manner according to some rational criterion or criteria.

Testing for Logic

Must the test for logic always be a matter of deduction, as implied above, or may empirical scientific investigations of the logic of communications be made as well or instead of a deduction?

This question does not yield an easy answer. When we introduce any manner of inductive problem solving to our analysis of any kind of communication we are dealing with data which *might* concern psychologics rather than or in addition to logics. If so, we have therefore lost the precise instrument of logic and logic alone by which communication and its languages may be analyzed.

For instance, in David Berlo's interesting book on communication,[31] the author frequently appears on the verge of this discovery, but, because he has chosen to review variously entirely different aspects (both logical and psychological) of communication as if they were all part of *one* process, he misses the idea. One simple example is his citation of Aristotle's observation that there are three ingredients to the communication "process": the speaker, the speech and the audience.[32]

As recorded by Berlo, the statement is satisfactory logically. But is it used logically? By the end of the chapter it has been transmuted somehow into a psychological process consisting of five elements (from "source" to "receiver"), not only involving vaguely articulated concepts of "coding" and "decoding" messages but also hypothesizing about the manner in which the human nervous system operates.[33] Berlo even tells the reader what psychological operations he is experiencing while reading his prose! "The message is transmitted to the medium of a book," he writes, "by means of light waves." Your eye is the decoder. (Many psychologists of perception

---

psychological communication in this manner, but observers report their logical proclivities are limited.

[31] David Berlo, *The Process of Communication* (New York: Holt, Rinehart and Winston, 1960). Berlo's main problem is that he attempts to subject empirical data of communication in its many historical forms (its manifestations as information, meaning and art), to logical and psychological scrutiny simultaneously. In the degree that he succeeds in one of this multitude of tasks, he fails at the others. For example, when he talks about art, he is a poor scientist and vice versa. When he is an historian, he fails as a sociologist and vice versa.

[32] *Ibid.*, p. 29.

[33] *Ibid.*, p. 30–38.

doubt this.) It receives the message, decodes it, retranslates it into a nervous impulse and sends it to your central nervous system. Your central nervous system is the receiver. As you read, you will make responses to the book.[34]

Dr. Berlo's words here may or may not make physiological or psychological sense.[35] Their accuracy is irrelevant to a subsequent misuse of the simple logical "given" from Aristotle that, logically, three elements are needed for communication: a speaker, a speech and an audience. Each is indispensable to the process of communication, and, if any *one* is missing, communication cannot result. Should we wish to generalize Aristotle's idea further to cover communication other than speech, note the following diagram:

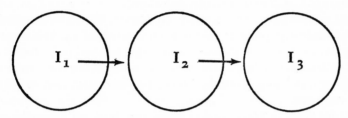

What is illustrated here is that a 1) man with an Idea, 2) speaks through an Instrument, and 3) acts upon an Individual (or group)—the general equivalents of Aristotle's 1) speaker, 2) speech and 3) audience, but extended to cover non-verbal communications.

Now it is possible to fill columns of data, arrived at empirically, or by hunch, or by minute measurement, to describe qualitatively and quantitatively points 1), 2) and 3) without *once* necessarily making a statement of a distinctive psychological nature. Numerous relatively objective and well known methods of research utilizing such instruments as tape recordings or films, and drawing upon various methods of content analysis, may yield much information about the man with the Idea, the instrument he uses or the subject's reactions to them. If he spoke verbally, for instance, did he speak in a high or low pitched voice, quickly or slowly? How high? How low? How quickly? How slowly? Was his voice amplified? To what degree?

---

[34] *Ibid.*, p. 33.

[35] I am under the impression from a limited study of the psycho-biological aspects of perception that they do not. The interested reader is referred to R. L. Gregory, *Eye and Brain* (New York: World University Library; McGraw-Hill Book Company, 1966), pp. 34–71 for two chapters, well written for the layman, on how the human eye and brain seem to work. Gregory's book is useful to those who may accept simple mechanistic analogies in descriptions of the complex subject of human perception and who are inclined, for instance, to consider the human nervous system as something like a telephone network.

See also the discussion of the unsolved problems of this aspect of visual perception by James J. Gibson, "A Theory of Pictorial Perception," in Gyorgy Kepes (ed.), *Sign, Image, Symbol* (New York: George Braziller, 1966), pp. 92–107, but especially the problem stated on p. 104.

We also can observe the reactions of the audience by crudely "counting the laughs," or employing questionnaires, tests or any one of a number of *logical* devices. The results of the investigation will *not* yield psychological statements. Aristotle's original seemingly self-evident observation has expanded our logical command of the analysis of an act of communication, making it useful or useless depending upon how it is used. Whatever psychological insights we may have gathered along the way are gratuitous—and probably unreliable.

Applications of logic to communications require numerous kinds of reliable information to establish valid categories of inquiry (which may be inductively or deductively derived). They may be developed by applying further general principles to those already provided.[36]

When one moves (unsuspectingly or deliberately) away from the logical mode of communication analysis into the psychological, as Berlo has done, the result will be an attempt to relate incompatibles. This is the great *non sequitur* in the lion's share of communication "analysis" today: drawing psychological conclusions from logical premises and vice versa. This tendency is little worse than the logical question once asked on the burlesque stage, "Who are you working for?" to which the psychologically valid answer is made, "The same gang; the wife and kids!"

We may next state a number of further elementary propositions if our characterization of logic in communications is to be of use to us in the pages to come, self-evident as they may seem.

The appropriate logical question to bring to all communications—including what is called "a work of art"—is: "How logical is it?" In other words, how does the communication at hand obey or disobey conventional rigors of order which may, by consensus, be brought to it? What is its function, and does the communication appear, given the data available, to be capable of making its point? Is it articulated in such a way that it may possibly be communicated to another individual? Simple questions that are often difficult to answer!

A test of some kind for the logical qualities of every communication made between sentient protoplasms can be given—from the degree of one's repulsion at the smell of a skunk to a child's vocal responses to a thriller on commercial television. Holding the test to rigorous measures of quantity and/or quality is the ubiquitous problem we shall have to attempt to solve *ad hoc* each time it arises (as it must) in the pages to come.

[36] Applying the principles of Aristotle's Poetics to the modern drama requires such development of generalizations. See Barrett H. Clark (ed.), *European Theories of the Drama* (New York: Crown Publishers, 1947.) On pp. 4–24 the principles are presented in translation from Aristotle. On pp. 529–536 appear sections from Eugene O'Neill's notes illustrating the logical application of the "givens" in the poetics to the "givens" in the American theatre in the nineteen-twenties along with the historical factors that led O'Neill to the composition of *Mourning Becomes Electra*. There *appears* to be nothing inductive in O'Neill's method of playwriting in its conceptual states—if we can trust his diary.

Strictly logical analysis of the languages of communication is a prior condition for understanding them, their role in our society and their uses and misuses. How rarely is it attempted, for instance, in critical literature! Logic, naturally, tells us only a part of the whole story. It tells us almost nothing about the measure of sensitivity and skill a photographer brings to his camera or the particular viewpoint of a subject he chooses finally to commit to photographic paper. These are mainly psychological matters. And when one reports that yesterday he had his picture taken, he is not telling you *much*. But this logical report *may be* as much as you want (or need) to know!

Conclusion

Thinkers since antiquity have observed that man's experiences tend to yield to a dual mode of apprehension and, subsequently, description. Contemporary scholars of various schools have attempted to deny this duality and have even indicted it as the fatal flaw in all philosophy. They have tried various ways of unifying the two modes, while others have split them into further fragments. All, for their own (and usually rhetorical) purposes, have been reasonably successful, in that their reconstructions have "worked." They have explained the nature of certain linguistic, historical or other phenomena to their own satisfactions.

The logical mode of deductive reasoning was one aspect of a dual system discovered relatively early in our western tradition. Almost from the moment of its birth, it was opposed: first by an informal "school" of empirical dissenters who preferred to trust what they saw, felt and tasted to the "truths" that the deductive employment of generalizations produced. It was not until the end of Europe's dark ages, however, that the modern concept of science gave new power to the inductive method of inquiry.

Inductive principles took men far into the study of the world around them, but it left in its wake an unavoidable confusion in styles of thought. These styles, basically the differences between deduction and inductive-empirical observation, have been called, for purposes of this book, "logics" and "psychologics" for reasons clarified in this chapter. We shall apply them shortly to observations of how and why the languages of communications were developed and how they function.

Three hundred years ago, in fact, Pascal observed that there were two different ways in which men seemed to conjecture. One he called "geometric" or scientific, by which one speculated, employing *few* difficult principles, far removed from daily life but apparently applicable to all phenomena. The other he characterized as the "subtle mind" which observed and reacted to multitudes of fine data derived from the innumerable ongoing experiences of living.

"When these scientists," wrote Pascal "want to deal geometrically with these matters of finesse, beginning with definitions and going on to principles, they make themselves ridiculous, for such is not the way to reason in those cases—not because the mind does not proceed by reasons, but because it does this tacitly, naturally, artlessly." [37]

When many of us desire to deal logically with matters of a primarily psychological nature, we are equally at a loss. The blunt instrument of our generalizations is not capable of so "subtle" a task. For example, no general principle yet evolved provides the individual with much satisfactory insight into why and how he falls in or out of love. The problem is not one of logic. It is psychological. We would be equally ridiculous, should we apply our psychological finesse by means of our "tacit, natural and artful" empiricism to the solution of a logical challenge. Removing a boulder from a dirt road requires a strong arm, a crowbar, a mallet and a few simple general principles of gravity and leverage. The next logical move is to get to work.

This chapter has centered on the necessity for a few satisfactory general principles to deal adequately with the logics of the mediums of communication which are hopefully contained in the discussions to come.

[37] Quoted in Jacques Barzun, *The House of Intellect* (New York: Harper and Brothers, Publishers, 1959), pp. 247–248.

Chapter 2

THE PSYCHOLOGICS
OF COMMUNICATIONS

W<small>EBSTER</small> provides us with the noun "psychology" and the adjective "psychological." "Psychologic" appears not to be needed by our language, so familiar have the other terms become and so popularly understood are their meanings.[1]

Hardly a popular book—from the best to the worst—on any aspect of mind-life does not begin with a statement that the *term* "psychology" is misunderstood by the general public, and sometimes psychologists themselves.[2] What the author proceeds to do thereafter is clarify the situation by offering *his* peculiar or original construction of the term. His fundamental premises may lean largely on statistical evidence, theory, or informal observations made in a laboratory or clinic. They are frequently offered as *the* major significant constructions of the sciences of behavior and mind.

---

[1] According to Webster's *Collegiate Dictionary*, the prefix "psyche" is related in its *first* definition to the Greek term meaning "breath" or "soul." After this, the fifty or so terms and words using the root ignore the classical origins of psychology in philosophy, except in so far as psychology has been confronted during the past century with philosophers' problems (as in "psychological hedonism"). The word "psycho" itself is defined to describe "a victim of a severe mental or emotional disorder," synonymous with "madman." Far more evident in this "popular" dictionary is the relatively recent relationship of the prefix "psych-" with "psychic phenomenon," defined as unnatural forces like spirits and ghosts. Language appears to follow culture here in its imputation of sorcery and magic to the study of "psychology."

[2] Some of these works tend to clear up the situation either by their razor sharp delineation of a single aspect of psychological progress, as in A. A. Roback's highly recommended *A History of American Psychology* (New York: Collier Books, 1964), which is, as the title infers, a genuine historical study of an aspect of behavior science (mostly at Harvard) or such all-inclusive works as H. J. Eysenck's books in the British Pelican Series starting with *Uses and Abuses of Psychology* (London: Penguin Books, 1953). The latter author devotes himself *entirely* to the clarification of the role of psychology in science and life, attempting to free himself from doctrine to the degree that his ecclecticism may appear doctrinaire.

19

Psychologics Today

Legitimate reasons for this apparent confusion center on the frequent observation that psychology is a relatively young science. Sigmund Freud, the first giant of psychological theory, was a Victorian chronologically as well as temperamently and educationally. The vigor of his rebellions against the manners of his age parallels other and equally violent protests by other contemporary giants against other accepted norms in art, literature and politics. Victorianism is still notable in many aspects of present culture. If Victorian intellectual rebellions of any sort still seem peculiarly modern, one must remember that styles of living appear to change faster than styles of thinking, and Victorian history is relatively recent history.

Certain philosophical roots of psychology, however, extend back to the beginnings of the scientific era, to men like Bacon himself who could not, of course, distinguish clearly between mental and physical phenomena in the seventeenth century. Nor, for many years, could other natural scientists. Logics and psychologics were one—due in most part to the inability of early scientists (until roughly the first part of the nineteenth century) to differentiate clearly between events *external* to themselves and processes which were happening to their own sense organs as they perceived these events.[3] Their interests, nevertheless, ran high in describing and explaining phenomena of mind and behavior.

The earliest psychologists were inevitably also philosophers, and we read them today mostly for their contributions to the development of Western philosophy. Intellects as varied as those of Rousseau, Swift, Samuel Johnson, John Stuart Mill, Voltaire, Emerson and even Descartes contributed much to the development of the wide spectrum of modern psychological thinking in its numerous schools.[4] Scientists, physicians and philosophers of the nineteenth century before Freud attempted to pull together these crude speculations and curiosities of behavior (like hypnotism and visible symptoms of neuroses) into a semi-science at least as well-ordered and methodical as biology at that time.

These nineteenth century pioneers of psychology are eclipsed by the later genius of Freud and were far less colorful. They range from experimentalists like Charcot and Janet to medical psychologists like Alzheimer

---

[3] The problem still affects certain aspects of scientific life and will be discussed subsequently.

[4] G. B. Levitus (ed.) in *The World of Psychology* (New York: George Braziller, 2 volumes, 1963), identifies writers as diverse as Plato, St. Augustine and Cicero as contributors to modern psychology in a lengthy series of essays. Before the introduction of the scientific method, of course, all psychology was empirical and/or speculative as well as subjective—like physics, chemistry (alchemy) and medicine. Most of it was heavily laced with remarkable wisdom, and even Aristotle the father of logic, almost invariably chose to illustrate his logical principles with behavioral or attitudinal "truths" he had observed in life around him.

and Korsakov and Breuer, to the positivistic philosopher, Ernst Mach, who was instrumental in producing the very matrix of concept in which Freud's theories of the unconscious took shape.[5]

During this same period, Freud in Europe and William James in America approached the subject of behavior and its relation to mind from entirely different points of view. They provide an interesting contrast, illustrative of early definitive problems in psychology which are still with us. For instance, Freud's orientation to the source of emotion was organically motivated: people *felt* because of various mechanisms inside themselves interacting with an environment and yielding a resultant emotion. James viewed emotion from the opposite vantage point. One reacted to a simulus, and emotion was felt as the result of how one behaved—as the result of a reaction. Freud assumed that one felt "afraid," for example, because of dispositions inside him which were usually activated by certain specific environmental forces. James assumed that he felt fear because he had reacted previously in a specific neurological and muscular manner to what he perceived as a "fear arousing stimulus" in the environment.[6]

In spite of "chicken and egg" differences of this sort, however, both psychologists had much in common and in their speculations the traditions of American psychology developed in the early part of this century. Both men were in great measure scientists, or at least both borrowed from science its skeptical stance, its experimental method, and its proclivity towards *inductive reasoning.*

As noted in the previous chapter, inductive thinking invariably leads to generalizations of some psychological value; that is, some sorts of reliable *conclusions* concerning a facet of the observable world. Modern psychology may therefore be said to have been born with the invention of inductive science. But James and Freud were probably among the first men in our tradition to venture responsibly first, beyond the mere matter of descriptive *behavior* and into theories of *motivation* and second, to dare to study the problem of *mind* as conceptually discrete from the behavior of the total organism. This gave them further power to attempt explanations of human

[5] The writer is indebted for much of what he understands about developments of nineteenth century psychology to his former colleague and friend, Dr. John Sullivan. See his award winning article "From Breuer to Freud," *Psychoanalysis and Psychoanalytic Review*, Summer, 1959, pp. 69–90.

See also Gordon W. Allport, "Psychological Models for Guidance," *Harvard Educational Review*, XXXII (1962), pp. 373–381 for an interesting discussion of the relation of positivism to various types of psychological activity in practice today.

[6] The difference between the two theories of emotion is simple to comprehend considering the data from which they were derived. Freud based his observations on what he had learned in his clinic; James studied the behavior of actors in his time, many of whom were influenced by various acting methods which posited that if an actor assumed a pose he would feel emotion associated with it. Freud's assumptions pervade most of his works. James' theory of emotion is clarified in *Psychology, The Briefer Course* (New York: Harper and Row, Publishers, 1961), pp. 240–257.

behavior, not only in its individual but its *collective* manifestations also. These contributions will be examined further in Chapter 10, where problems of collective communications phenomena will be discussed.

In short, the intellectual breakthrough of the Victorian theorists left the legacy of a "modern" psychological mode of apprehension of reality, rather than a pat all-purpose set of explanations or principles of it. Because it serves as a style of thought, Freudians, behaviorists, Jungians, philosophically and medically oriented psychologists survive side by side today in universities with a minimum of intellectual friction. One tends his rats while another studies Biblical psalms for their symbolic content, and yet both agree that behavior may be studied through the inductive method of thought, and both agree that in the concept of "mind" one might possibly explain curiosities of perception, feeling, and ultimately behavior, inductively.

This mode of thinking is peculiarly post-Victorian and modern. The concerns of psychology were once, not long ago, primarily ultimate concerns of gods, the fates and furies. They remain today, in fact, within the domain of the supernatural throughout most of the world, if we look to the judgments, opinions and ideas of most Western and Eastern men. For centuries, logical axioms concerning bodily "humors" were deductively applied to explain *all* types of behavior in and out of madhouses. Humors, being god-given, were—and are—impossible to control.

The humors are still with us. One cannot disregard elements of predestination in the theories of Cesare Lombroso, Ernest Hooton, William H. Sheldon and/or Ernst Kretschmer and at the same time accept their utility (to anthropologists probably more than to psychologists). They are examples of thinking cast in the inductive, scientific, and psychological mold, with strong ancient, deductive accents.[7] The work of these scientists, irrespective of the adequacy of their theories, represent a strange but infuriating blend of primitive deduction concerning personality with modern methods of inductive reasoning, but we can at least admire their ingenious applications of the psychological style of analysis.

In the United States, differently oriented psychologists and teachers have devoted their energies to therapy, testing, theory (including learning theory) articulation and modification, experimentation and eclectic teaching,[8] roughly in that order. A few of them employ their psychological perspective of life to investigate other disciplines, usually History, Art or Literature. It is this latter function of psychology's *Zeitgeist* in our society that will be hopefully employed in this book to examine the languages of communications where and when matters of human behavior and mind-life are

[7] See Ellsworth Huntington, *Mainsprings of Civilization* (New York: The New American Library, 1959), pp. 56–58.
[8] Not all teachers of psychology are eclectic. Many use their classes for group therapy, testing, experimentation, or as propaganda forums for theories old and new, as well as the teaching of therapeutic procedures *and* for teaching psychology.

of prior (or sole) concern to the question of how or why men are communicating (or failing to communicate) with each other.

Psychological Conditions for Communication

We have seen how the logics of communication—under given circumstances—yield prior conditions for the statement and reception of a message and that an appreciation of this logic was probably ancient knowledge at the time of Aristotle.

That psychologics are also involved in communication is a more recent insight and followed hard upon the innovations in thought which James had developed and Freud subsequently brought with him to the United States before World War I. An interest in the psychologics of communications centers on the conditions involved in communicating as opposed to an interest primarily in the communication process itself. In other words, logics are concerned with the nature of communications and the various mediums and instruments involved; psychologics center on *how* and *why* communications occur as they do (considering, naturally, the conditions of reception and the nature of the mediums involved). Using our diagram from Aristotle in the previous chapter, it is possible to schematize the difference between logics and psychologics of communication as follows:

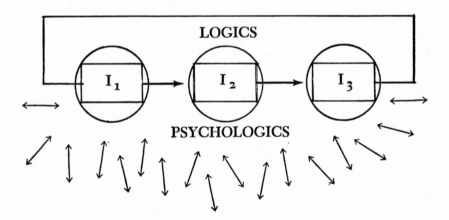

The logics are constant modifiers of the constructual pattern of the communications act (or process) which Aristotle described. Psychologics, on the other hand, are concerned with less concrete conditional factors. They relate to the same logical act (or process) but act upon, and are influenced by, any number of possible components of the environment, or any peculiarities discernable either in the Idea (or communicator), the Instrument (or medium)[9] or the Individual(s) receiving the message. This dia-

[9] Mediums here are specifically meant to refer to the forms of communication as re-

gram is intended to illustrate that, while logics and psychologics of communication relate to the same data, they do so in entirely different manners.
One (logics) is kept within a strict perimeter, the other (psychologics)
functions as a continual interchange of forces, moving into and taken out
of the environmental setting of the communication act.

That the focus of much interest at present in popular literature of
communications is upon these psychologics is not surprising. We must consider broadly the shift in what we believe to be authentic sources of knowledge in the modern world. We have moved from a reliance upon deductive
truths applied to life to a belief in empirical, inductive examination of our
environment. Our examinations may be "scientific" in the fullest Baconian
sense of the word. They may be complex or simple, or qualitative or quantitative. They may derive from many different types of data.

The method by which these examinations are made is irrelevant to
whether they are logical or psychological. So far as the process of communication is concerned, it is necessary only to determine whether these statements satisfy the rigors of logic (specified in the previous chapter), or
whether they are inductive-empirical statements describing the conditions
of communications and how they affect certain individuals, human or animal.[10] If they are of the former quality, they are logical. If they appear to be
the latter types of observations, they are psychological.

If our criteria for the psychologics of communications are less precise
than those of the logics, we have stumbled upon the inevitable consequence of the perspective of psychology. We are often told that "psychology is not yet an exact science," and therefore we must not expect it to clear
up all the mysteries in its domain in quite the manner of physics or chemistry. In fact, however, psychology is a *most* exact science—more exact in
some respects than the natural sciences. Its precision lies in the way it
measures and articulates the variables which it isolates in human behavior
and in reporting and interpreting symbolic components of that behavior. It
is not at its rigorous best in immediately *utilizing* these data to change behavior or to modify the conditions under which it occurs.

In our study of communications, we must bear down strongly upon the

---

defined in Chapters 7, 8, 9 and 10, where the nature of each is contingent upon its
psychological function.

[10] Considerable speculation exists on communications between man and animals and
between animals, where apparent logics and psychologics are involved in the process.
These statements therefore cannot be limited in their present form to *people*. Animals
seem frequently to be impelled to various behaviors by a logic far more rigorous than
those that men employ. There is also a psychology of animals—which unfortunately
does not seem to correspond regularly to the degree of advancement or complexity of
the organism, or its brain size, or the elegance of its nervous system. In other words,
the sophistication of an animal's psychology is *not* a direct correlative of how much its
species resembles a human being. We find, for instance, closer analogies to the political
behaviors of human beings among certain types of fish than among the higher apes.
See Konrad Lorenz, *On Aggression* (New York: Harcourt, Brace and World, Inc.,
1963), pp. 145–146.

psychological aspects of the communication which are most reliable; that is, the measurement and description of the conditions under which a particular communication is occuring under given circumstances at a specific time. When communications are approached from this perspective, there is little question as to whether the logical or psychological mode of discourse is being emphasized.

Conditions for communications (two-way arrows in the diagram above) may of course originate from a great number of sources. They are all functions of the behaviors, mind sets and dispositions of individuals involved in communicating. These factors, of course, are the results of the psychological natures as they relate to the flow of the environment. Let us call these "conditions of communication" and examine their major factors.

Conditions of Perception

I. A. Richards provides us with a clear description of the psychologics of communication in his well known series of essays on literary criticism.[11] Writes Richards:

> Communication, takes place when one mind so acts upon its environment that another mind is influenced, and in that other mind an experience occurs which is like the experience in the first mind, and is caused in part by that experience. Communication is evidently a complicated affair and capable of degrees in at least two respects. The two experiences may be more or less similiar, and the second may be more or less dependent on the first.[12]

Whether Richards did or did not intend this description as primarily a *psychological* statement is irrelevant. The observation obviously demonstrates little logical rigor. We have no indication of what is happening in A's mind, nor do we have any indication of the medium or instrument which communicates the experiences between A and B. We are, however, provided with a fundamental and clear description of the psychologics of communication (minus a reference, of course, to the psychologics of the medium and communication techniques involved), offering a number of possibilities for examination.

Certain obvious factors or conditions influence the likelihood of A's mind acting upon B's, upon the similarity of the experiences and upon the degree of dependency they exhibit, one upon the other. It is possible to

[11] I. A. Richards, *Principles of Literary Criticism* (New York: Harcourt Brace and Company, 1947).
[12] *Ibid.*, p. 177. The main problem in Richards' brilliant discussions of problems of art and value seem to center upon his apparent disregard of the discrete logics and psychologics of criticism. Richards' evaluations tend to be psychological. Yet he is continually aware that a logic of communication must be employed somehow as a reference for his psychological observations. He appears to imply that this logic is found in the "apparent meanings" or "common sense" interpretations of art. In fact, such obvious meanings may be far from logical. The result is that Richards' criticisms seem frequently to lean on interpretations of poetry (particularly) to which he alone is privy.

examine them without knowing the nature of A's information, the receptivity of B's mind or the nature of the instrument used. We need presume merely *that some sort of communication has taken place* and have no need, from a psychological perspective, to know what it is. To answer these questions we would be forced to consider irrelevant logical issues noted in Chapter I which have nothing to do with the process as Richards describes it.

First, there are general psychological and physical factors which must be considered relative to the action of both minds which communication is likely to elicit. Germane to the psychologics of communication are such seemingly trivial or unrelated matters as air temperature, degree of outside noise, static,[13] the phrasing of the communication itself, visibility, and numerous other factors in the environment, external to the communicators. All are elements of psychological interest.

Second, we must consider the complex matter of the internal state of the communicating individuals' perceptive processes, factors of which they themselves may not be directly and immediately aware. The social, cultural and educational development of the communicants, their degree of motivation for understanding or misunderstanding and perhaps whether to act upon the communication, as well as the inherent limitations of their perceptions[14] are involved. Among the usually non-conscious elements which bear upon the psychologics of communications are also the sender's and receiver's degree of receptivity to the vocabulary, symbols,[15] memories of past activities, prior experiences with communications of this sort, general and specific antagonisms, frustrations and appetencies, to say nothing of factors like the disposition of digestive systems, blood pressure and oxygen metabolism rates. In discussing the psychologics of communication, accordingly, we may make a surprising number of meaningful statements concerning the nature of a given communication (or about the communication process) *without information concerning either what is being communicated or even the medium and instrument that are employed.* Because the focus of psychologics is centered so directly upon behavior and mind rather than cognitive or emotional content, factors which might influence (that is clarify or distort) the communication process are of primary interest from this perspective. That the medium or an instrument of communication appears to be irrelevant in these general considerations, in no way implies that it

[13] The condition of psychological "entropy," related to the concept of static, will be considered further in Chapter 3.
[14] Color blindness and tone deafness are problems that hang somewhere in the shadow world between logics and pyschologics in the process of communication. Since the chances are slight that all the individuals involved in the disseminaton of any communication to a small group—to say nothing of *mass* communications—might be color blind or tone deaf, let us consider it a psychological rather than a logical determinant of communication which it might be in a society of color blind and tone deaf people. For a terse discussion of color blindness, see Gregory, *op. cit.*, pp. 126–129.
[15] See Part Two.

may not be extremely significant in the modification of perceptions at times. But their central influence bears, as we shall see, upon *how communications operate* in their *logical* phases.[16] The medium or the technological instrument used to disseminate the communication are *never*, however, the *sole* object of logical attention. They constitute two of *many* self-evident psychological forces involved in all communications between any organisms. The medium and the instrument's primary functions are the self-evident tasks of providing an appropriate conduit for messages between senders and receivers. |

The Illogical Science

Psychological interpretations of an event are often judged to be looser, more humanistic and therefore "warmer" than a "cold" logical report of the same event. That such interpretations of logic and psychologic are spurious is beside our point; that they are generally *accepted* is characteristic of some of our contemporary attitudes towards thought itself.

The logician of communications maintains a formidable cognitive advantage over the psychologist in the field by virtue of the ease, sureness and elegance with which the former may operate. One assumes correctly, therefore, that the most ubiquitous type of communications' analysis today would be an analysis of the deterministic forces in discourse which are general logical matters. William Empson refers to the *logical* critic of letters when he states, "In wishing to apply verbal analysis to poetry the position of a critic is like that of a scientist wishing to apply determinism to the world. It may not be valid everywhere; though it may be valid everywhere it may not explain everything; but in so far as he is to do any work he must assume it is valid where he is working, and will explain what he is trying to explain." [17]

Empson defines for us precisely the logician's advantage in communication's analysis: his basic assumption of deterministic forces which are required antecedent to the logical structures by which communications are analyzed. Empson himself, interestingly, expresses a passing preference for psychological analysis of communications when he writes, "I must confess I find the crudity and latent fallacy of a psychologist discussing verses that he does not enjoy less disagreeable than the blurred and tasteless refusal to make statements of an aesthete (read "logician") who conceives himself only to be interested in Taste." [18]

Empson, with his enormous command of critical insights into English

[16] Logics and psychologics of communications naturally influence *one another* in various degrees under different circumstances. One logical factor, for instance, concerning any communication is exactly what we may discover with certainty about its psychological value; one matter of psychological significance is likewise how the logics of communication operate of and by themselves and the function they perform in perception.

[17] William Empson, *Seven Types of Ambiguity* (New York: Meridan Books, 1955), p. 22.

[18] *Ibid.*, p. 15.

literature, has neglected to note in this latter revealing statement that an aesthete or logician of communications would best be advised to eschew entirely a discussion of the problem of "taste." "Taste," in its active or reactive phases (from the sensitivity of the human intellectual palate to the articulation of a concept of "tastelessness"), is a psychological matter. Nor need one interested primarily in this psychological mode of communication necessarily "not enjoy" the "verses" he studies. Within the psychological parameters of analysis one discovers much room for enjoyment. Although some psychologists of Empson's acquaintance may seem to *prefer* to *discuss* communications rather than *enjoy* them, there is no reason for them not to take pleasure in them, even if their psychological involvement in life leads them on to such humorless paths as those followed by psychoanalytically oriented literary critics.

Analysis in the logical mode might more likely be coupled with a lack of enjoyment than that which deals in psychologics. The logician, as we shall see, must maintain an uncomfortable and rigid posture in his consistent analysis of the multitude of complexities involved in communications. In boiling them down to generalizations adequate to explain the success or failure of any communication, they may frequently be rendered as dull as ditch water.[19]

The main reason to consider the psychological mode of communication an "illogical science" is that it lacks an external referent for psychological judgments, except by recourse to other or more general psychological assumptions. In great measure, this illogical caveat applies to *all* science. It is one reason that the logical but pre-scientific era is considered by some historians to have been intellectually more "comfortable" than our scientific age. In the world of deductive analysis, *all* data could eventually be referred to one or another of the copious generalizations from which inquiry sprang. Here was a closed system which was neatly exploded by the invention of science.

The logics of communication as well still display some characteristics of these closed systems, as we have shown in Chapter 1. When logical statements are adequately made about any type of communication, they are made once and for all. Logicians may disagree about the aptness or cleverness with which they are applied. But disagreement ideally yields a more formal, exact, logical truth than before, reinforcing the value of the generalization from which it sprang.[20]

[19] Empson, a remarkable logician, has located seven types of ambiguity in English literature, and has provided copious illustrations of each in his book. It is an important document for anyone concerned with the protean nature of the logics of communication and many of the ironies one discovers in *all* logic. That he is as suspicious of psychologics as his contemporary Richards (writing on a similar subject) was fond of them is illustrative of how different temperaments face similar problems of communication in different ways.

[20] One instance of this reenforcement is the case that Empson makes for the power of ambiguity. Because of his patient application of the concept to centuries of English

Psychologics, on the other hand, do not operate in a closed system. Like all inductive propositions, therefore, they cannot forever be referred to more adequate generalizations. The physicist, for instance, when pressed, must ultimately assume an expanding universe, a residue of energy, a time-space dimension (or all three) if he is going to insist upon continued inductive examination of the universe. A biologist, likewise, must end up in an organic, chemical never-never-land if he is going to follow all the inductive evidence of life around him in the direction of its roots.

Another enigma faces the psychological study of communications. It emerged originally from the physical theory but has much wider range of application.[21] Usually associated with the name of Werner von Heisenberg, it is called "the principle of uncertainty" or "indeterminacy" which casts doubt on inductively originated causal conclusions in *all* scientific procedures, including (or especially) those by which psychological data are gathered. It also limits the range of absolute predictability of certain particles in nature, particularly those which are very small or very large.

(As Jacques Barzun has noted,[22] the principle has been employed to support no end of theological and philosophical arguments—particularly on the part of those who want to resolve the contradiction between science and religion—to the degree that it is no longer either disturbing to the progress of science or interesting to spiritual phenomena.)

The uncertainty principle, particularly as it applies to the inevitable distortion of all empiricism *because* it is observed knowledge, is simply one *more* problem in delineating lucid ground rules for the study of the psychologics of communication. It probably affects, as well, the labors of most behavior scientists in the employment of the inductive method of problem solving.

Delineation, therefore, of strict criteria for the study of the psychologics of communications is far more difficult than the construction of our "non-definition" for their logics. The art (sic) of the derivation of adequate inductive techniques for the study of behavior of the human mind are not so much in their infancy (as is often claimed), but in late adolescence, a time of life usually characterized by a confusion of the many possibilities which life holds for the individual. The analogy need be pressed no further. The present incompatabilities in the modern psychological fraternity—with its strange mixture of empiricism, grand theory, medical techniques, and

literature, he has given the idea of ambiguity itself far more power, importance and stability than it previously had. The validity of the generalization that ambiguity is a highly significant quality in literature lies now almost beyond logical dispute.

[21] J. W. N. Sullivan, *The Limitations of Science* (New York: The New American Library, 1952), pp. 69–72, 148.

[22] Jacques Barzun, *Science: The Glorious Entertainment* (New York: Harper and Row, 1964), p. 63. Barzun's book is unnecessarily brutal to the principles of inductive science, but is quite fair in its indictment of our unwarranted worship of scientists, our misunderstanding of scientific methodology and spirit, and our near fatal confusion between science and technology.

plethora of statistical data—are no more bewildering than those which faced the science of biology a century ago, as previously observed.

The necessities for the clarification of as many principles as possible of the psychologics of communication should appear justified by the nature of our task in describing as clearly as possible what the languages of communication are and how they work. Were our psychologics dependent upon one or another particular school of psychological theory, this problem would be less difficult than it is, but the reader sees (hopefully) why this dependence would merely be the substitution of a pseudologic for a psychologic.[23]

The Question of Psychologic Truth

How may we then formulate a psychological description of the communications process when no common or invariable references exist in the minds of the people who are communicating with each other? The problem seems insurmountable. Should a theatregoer, for instance, laugh uproariously at a beautiful production of *Hamlet,* there is little to be done about it—except possibly to request him to leave the theatre lest he disturb the audience. Even this amenity might be difficult to perform because, as a paying theatregoer, he maintains—theoretically—the right to react to a performance in any way he desires, within limits. We could not object to his laughter at *The Merry Wives of Windsor!* Nor might his tears at the latter production be quite as offensive as his mirth at *Hamlet.*

The psychological correctness of his position is both obvious and painful—painful, that is, to our *logical* sensibilities. What he has provided for us is a psychological reaction against which we are powerless. We are theoretically quite helpless in the face of his laughter: as helpless as if he told us that he abhors lemon cake, or adores mud turtles, or that he is compelled to smoke eighty cigarettes a day!

All of these statements (and our theatregoer's laughter) are *psychological truths,* but they are also *logical anomalies.* Suppose we maintain that no one in his right mind would laugh at Hamlet! We may be correct, begging the question of what constitutes "right mind," but our statement above does not prevent *one man* or *a thousand teenagers* from actually laughing at Hamlet—*and both one man and thousands of teenagers have laughed at a fine production of Hamlet recently in the city where this is being written.* This is both an historical *and* a psychological *truth,* as illogical as it may seem.

The claim might be made that this bizarre reaction resulted from some aberration, individual or collective, in the perception of individuals watching

---

[23] In the coming chapters we shall not hesitate to relate generalizations drawn from the ideas of behavior scientists (and aestheticians, historians, economists, biologists and others) of various schools to the mediums and instruments of communications for the purpose of examining the resultant *logical* ideas of such juxtapositions. These generalizations (or theories) make poor starting points for examining the psychologics of communications, however.

the performance. Perhaps. Or we may indict our culture and modern educa-tion with a generalization that many people, especially the young, react *en masse* strongly and strangely to certain stimuli.[24] Logical criteria, in other words, are useless to analyze the situation. The matter demands the applica-tion of psychological criteria for an empirical-inductive analysis of the be-haviors involved and the test of numerous hypotheses which might possibly explain them.

Psychologics do not apply merely to aberrant aspects of communica-tions like this one, of course, but to *all* communication processes, as the diagram on page 23 indicates. In abberant situations, however, the unimpor-tance of logic and the power of psychologic is underscored, just as the re-verse obtains: psychological significances of certain kinds of communica-tions (the address on a letter sent fourth class mail, for instance) may be almost non-existent, while the logics of the communication (centering in this case on how people are identified and located by technology in a society of millions) may be rich enough with data in the logical mode to fill a book. The scale from logic to psychologic may move in either direction and may tilt at many angles.

To isolate a *single* psychological truth is difficult in all human enter-prises, which is to say in *nearly* all enterprises of interest to *us*. Most reli-able, demonstrable psychological truths at present tend to concern re-sponses to specific stimuli governed in great measure by the autonomic nervous system operating without the intervention of directive conscious-ness. The psychologics of communication are more difficult to isolate be- cause of the mediating factors between sender, medium and receiver, many of which are related to thought and/or emotions or feelings. These latter factors rarely display consistency and are difficult to measure, either quanti-tatively or qualitatively. We are not stopped, however, from trying.

One is exposed to statements of proposed psychological truths in re-gard to communications from individuals as different, one from the other, as college professors and sideshow barkers. Each is presumably offering the specific "truth" that satisfies his needs for the type of communication he experiences. There is little chance, however, that he has discovered one single universally applicable psychological principle concerning how men communicate!

Conclusion

The search for an orientation to the psychologics of communication which will be of use to us in the chapters to follow must involve the follow-ing two considerations in order to permit the formulation of meaningful statements in a psychological mode about communications.

[24] This premise is by no means taken for granted, in spite of the weight of opinion one can find behind it. The "decline of culture" in our society implied here is a topic re-served for qualified discussion in Chapters 19 and 20.

First, we must determine the relationship of the logical mode of analysis to the psychological mode. In what measure do they coordinate? In the case of the individual who laughs at *Hamlet,* a logical analysis of the conditions of a performance and an examination of the spectator by means of various instruments will give us much material for conjecture concerning the behavior of our subject and his relationship to the psychologics of the communication process involved in the incident. The observation produced by this comparison, along with other observations, may yield for us insights into how the languages of communication are speaking to a certain individual under a given set of circumstances. The reaction of another audience to another performance of the same play will provide us with further information of a psychological nature into what was at one time called "audience psychology." These observations, held now against the logic of an occasion (a performance of a play in a theatre), should produce valuable empirical data for the student of communications.

Secondly, we can study the psychologics of any communication or set of communications to answer specific relevant questions. What does the *community* of response reveal to us about common psychologics of any *single* group in the population? What, for instance, does the supposed popularity of the book *The Lord of the Flies* among college students reveal to us about college students—if anything? What do discoverable divergences demonstrate? For example, what psychological factors make certain easily identifiable advertising appeals more or less attractive to Negroes than to whites? And lastly, we can question what the psychologics of any *one* individual's response to a given communication may reveal about *him* or *her?*

Logics and psychologics together are therefore both rigorous but flexible instruments for explaining, to a degree, how communications work and also why they *may* not work.

Chapter 3

WHY COMMUNICATIONS FAIL

COMMUNICATION failures are frequently associated with individual and social abberations or disasters. Such assumptions are not warranted, nor does the failure of a given communication constitute a value statement about it. The United States, for instance, has fought its major wars *against* people with whom it communicated quite well, nations similar to the U.S.A. in many ways and which, generally speaking, we understood and understood us.[1] Clear channels of communication, in these instances, enhanced the opportunity for numerous antagonisms to grow into the tragedy of warfare. Successful communication may mean the successful promulgation of disasters of many kinds and has nothing to do with the psychological or material welfare of the organisms communicating. Successful communications, it is sometimes assumed by the naïve, guarantee the solution of so-called "misunderstandings" which may generate the major problems of society. That numerous members of our academic community have accepted this sly canard is unfortunate. It is particularly disturbing when the assumption is disguised by the rubric "Human Relations" or another term from the lexicon of contemporary Sociology or General Semantics.[2]

---

[1] Our major enemies in Europe have been the British, the Spaniards, ourselves (in the Civil War), and the Germans. The latter nation may have been intellectually closer to the U.S.A. in matters of education and technology than even our mother country (and first enemy) Britain. In Asia, our main enemy has been Japan, a nation so "western" it even indulges in our national sport, baseball. By the time Russia had become an industrial empire and shared many traits in common with us, we were fighting a "cold war" against her.

[2] A lengthy reading list might be given here, but one book edited by S. I. Hayakawa (ed.), *Our Language and Our World* (New York: Harper and Brothers, 1958), is sufficient. It contains the best articles from the magazine "ETC: A Review of General Semantics," pieces written by social scientists, critics and others reflecting the view noted above. The entire movement of General Semantics reflects indefatigable American optimism towards solving collective social and psychological problems in the face of years of

33

Success or failure in communications is independent of value, except insofar as we understand that an objective has or has not been achieved. A telephone that does not answer, a message that is misunderstood, a poem that is misinterpreted are never indications of a breakdown in any "natural" process. Elaborate warning systems which may communicate (after scrutiny by many protective devices) instructions to explode a nuclear bomb have been built for the purpose (both in the U.S.A. and elsewhere) *of never being used.* They themselves act, in their logical phases, as psychological deterrents to their own employment—or let us hope that they do. That they may eventually serve little logical *purpose* is clear (particularly to those who enjoyed the film or book, *Dr. Strangelove*), but the psychologics of such systems exert power upon the "non-communicators" who are entrusted with the difficult responsibility of "not communicating" by means of them.

The failure of communication is not inevitable when a system is designed *not* to be used to communicate or when communication *appears* unlikely. No generalization applies here, except that when the logics of communication hold a potential for a message to be transmitted, it *may* be, although all the psychological forces at the command of the communicator be brought to bear against it. An example might well be the way that evidence which one is trying to withhold is "seen through" by an alert police investigator, a lie detector or even a clever "fortune teller." Circumstantial evidence is frequently just such kind of inevitable communication.

In theory, therefore, it is not difficult to understand why all communication "systems" contain the potential of working—if all factors involved in their transmission and reception are put into working order. A fundamental physical principle dictates that, once an environment has been disturbed, an exchange of energy has occurred which is reversible only by executing another change of energy. All messages of any kind (and every message of all kinds) are disturbances of energy in the environment which *might* be received by an appropriate sentient organism, were that organism present and properly tuned to detect that particular energy change.[3]

We have not the right to affirm that *psychologically* there might not be multitudes of forces which may interfere with the *logical potential* of a communication and stop it before it starts. We do this when we turn off a radio, hold our hands over our ears, or close our eyes to blind ourselves to a disturbing sight, or when we purposely misunderstand what we may be

---

worsening failure at the advice of "schools" of analysis and social amelioration—like General Semantics.

[3] The Berkelian problem inherent here of whether a communication whose meaning cannot be received is in fact a communication at all is a speculative concern discussed in conjunction with relevant basic problems in J. R. Pierce, *Symbols, Signals and Noise* (New York: Harper and Row, 1961), pp. 107–124, especially pp. 116–123. Pierce's book is a clear explanation of the uses of "information theory," written, for the most part, for the general reader.

afraid of understanding. Theoretically, therefore, failure of communication is by far a greater potential psychological hazard than a logical one.

Redundancy in Communication

All threats to the efficacy of communications are diminished in some measure by the *redundancy* inherent in the process. In response to various obstacles of a psychological origin in man (which apparently threaten chances for successful alteration of environments), nature has seemingly made provisions for a logically oriented device demanding the repetition of previously communicated material, so that it possesses alternative chances of being transmitted from sender to source. Linguists have calculated, for instance, that the English language is about fifty per cent redundant as spoken or written. The quality of my repetition, as I write, motivated by a psychological desire to be understood, leads me in a multitude of subtle ways to redundancy, starting with my very choice of a written means of communication that *a priori* is half redundant.[4]

The ascription above of this psychological tendency (and logical result) to nature rather than to man is explained by the observation of Colby's that "(o)ne may say that life in general, like language, seeks an equilibrium of about fifty per cent redundancy—an equilibrium between the new (unexpected) and the old (predictable); between disorganization and organization."[5] Language, observes Colby, is merely symptomatic of a tendency of all life "in which deviations from the mid-point are checked before getting out of hand in either direction,"[6] allowing therefore both stability and growth. Should the principle of redundancy be operative, therefore, half the time in the logical mode of every communication, it probably also influences, as we shall see, the psychological tendency to *cause* communications to fail.[7]

Communications still fail, redundancy notwithstanding, but it increases, in theory, their chances of success considerably—by *less than* fifty per cent, however, since there is a decrease of likelihood of success in communication with each consecutive repetition, unless all external conditions are changed each time. And, because half of the activity of life appears to be non-redundant, there is much opportunity for failure as attention is turned to novelty. That is, if logics of communication fail to achieve their

---

[4] Most other classical and modern languages are also about 50 per cent redundant, indicating a cross-cultural similarity in psychologics of linguistic communication. See Benjamin Colby's article "Behavioral Redundancy" in Smith, *Culture and Communications*, pp. 367–374.

[5] *Ibid.*, p. 369.

[6] *Loc. cit.*

[7] By way of illustration, suppose one calls another person a "liar," who subsequently stops up his ears and runs away. One can vitiate the psychological attempt to spoil the communication by exercising the logic of redundancy and repeating loudly the word "LIAR" in such a way that it *must* be heard. But the word may still be psychologically rejected, no matter how loud one screams or how many times the word is repeated.

potential to carry their message, or as the psychologics work their apparently arbitrary (but sometimes predictable) mischief in distorting or confusing logics.

Our half-redundant world must be considered when analyzing or predicting the result of any communication. The knuckle of nature does indeed knock twice, or rather one and one-half times. One is reminded of Shaw's observation that "the great Life Force has hit upon the device of the clockmaker's pendulum, and uses the earth for its bob; that the history of each oscillation, which seems as novel to us, the actors, is but the history of the last oscillation repeated." [8]

The question remains as to how we might fare were this redundancy somehow eliminated. Suffice it to note here that the kinds of communication that man makes with computing machines and computers are mostly non-redundant. Might our covert recognition of this fact be one reason for fears we hear expressed of a computerized society? Might they frighten us because they do *not* demonstrate a "natural" proclivity for redundancy? How might we feel were we exposed to a fumbling computer mechanism with fifty per cent redundancy programmed into it? Might we regard it as more "natural" than its more highly efficient brother? [9]

Entropy

Another concept germane to a consideration of communication failure is related to so-called "Information Theory," the study of methods for quantifying regularities in mechanistic systems of communication and, analogously, in language. It is the idea of *entropy*, a peculiarly satisfactory construction for the description of certain of these types of systems, which, under many circumstances, are amenable to precise measurement and statistical manipulation.[10] It may also be applied, as noted above, with considerable profit but in a less precise manner, to the analysis of the known regularities of language.[11]

Entropy may involve many things, relating to the type of system in

[8] George Bernard Shaw, *Man and Superman* (New York: Bantam Books, 1959), p. 140.
[9] The previous two paragraphs have been written with the purpose of demonstrating how redundancy in the presentation of ideas can facilitate certain aspects of communication and enrich or re-enforce their logic as well as enrich them psychologically by "playing with" the possibilities of a simple but challenging observation.
[10] "Redundancy" is likewise a precisely measurable factor in information statistics as it occurs in many kinds of communication systems. It is more familiar as a general concept of rhetoric than entropy which, until recently, referred usually to a property of highly regular physical systems. The entropy of a system is a degree of probability within that system that the variables are distributed in a certain way; the less regularity or order in a system, the more entropy. The idea derives from the principle of the conservation of energy (the first law of thermodynamics) and applies, it appears, to all matter and probably to all discovered and undiscovered logics of all communication.
[11] Joshua Whatmough, *Language, A Modern Synthesis* (New York: The New American Library, 1956), pp. 179–197. The clarification of the mechanics of language in this survey is comparatively lucid when held up against many other "simple" descriptions in the science of philology.

which it occurs and to which particular era in modern scientific thought it refers.[12] The notion seeming to remain constant, however, is that of "random disorder": the tendency which all systems display to fall apart. As a logical idea, entropy is the degree of possibility of disorder that one might discover in *any* system. In communications, it is usually understood as *the degree of loss of information*—or the *probability* of such a loss—in the verbal or written modes, from speaker to listener or listeners. That this probability may often be expressed numerically is an interesting, if not invariably relevant, matter to the logics of the languages of communication. Much research, however, has recently delineated in numerical forms the precise degree of entropy in many communication systems. These forms appear, again logically, to be indices of the exact *efficiency* of communication or of the language used to achieve it—information frequently of greater interest than utility.

Logical Entropy

Without resorting to the apparent respectability that statistics often lend to discourse, this precision may be illustrated by two person-to-person communication situations where the degree of entropy relates entirely to the language used.

The first might be the example of a college freshman listening to a paragraph of Chinese history read in the Mandarin dialect. Grant that he is completely ignorant of the Chinese language but is well versed in English. Systematically, therefore, the meaning of any single word he hears *might* be the meaning of *any* word in the English dictionary. The paragraph he hears might mean almost anything; one might confidently take any odds against his translation of it being more accurate than chance alone permits. The entropy of the system is extremely high, and the efficiency of the system is about zero.

(Note that we have discounted the psychologics of the communication which would certainly be involved in the occasion. Our reader might end up laughing or crying—or certain contextual clues of the performance might permit our poor subject to make an enlightened guess as to the meaning of the Mandarin selection. These, and many other possibilities, are all germane to the psychological, rather than logical, considerations of entropy.)

At the other logical extreme, where entropy might be least, let us consider what happens when one talks to himself, as many of us do, when we speak to inanimate objects like hammers, pencil points, and unpaid bills or to numerous quasi-anthromorphic objects like cats and dogs. When one considers the logical nature of these occasions—that we are talking to our-

12 Concepts of energy and the possibilities for the transmutation and order thereof have naturally traveled a great distance from Isaac Newton's stable physical universe to the modern period of nuclear exploration, where the borders between matter and energy have themselves been redefined.

selves and not to hammers, pencils, cats, or dogs—entropy drops to about zero, and the system is absolutely efficient in logical and psychological content.

Note that we have here an *apparently* efficient, but absolutely useless, communications system. Logically, this is true, and talking to one's self appears to accomplish nothing. Psychologically, another construction applies to this eccentricity as one releases energy, satisfies tensions and performs numerous salubrious functions. Popularly, talking to oneself is considered symptomatic of derangement, but, because so many supposedly "sane" people do it (and for this reason only), it is a fair assumption that it is not a sign of sickness unless combined with other bizarre symptoms.

As we qualify the purely logical concept of entropy, it is possible to equate the concept with the more generally understood idea of *static*. Many of us think of static as an audio phenomenon in radio broadcasting and as a visual annoyance on television receivers. It is, accordingly, not difficult to generalize our conceptions of static to other technological instruments of communication and then to non-technological devices like a written note, an illegible scrawl, or the inaudible recitation of a poem. Static is a kind of roughly predictable interference with the accomplishment of satisfactory communication. From the general principle of entropy, we may predict the logical degree of probability of failure or success of attempted communications, all factors being measurable.

In regard to human communications, where *few* factors are measurable, we have already made the assumption that logical statements concerning the degree of failure or success of communications due to the effects of entropy may at best be roughly calculated. They can, at least, be described as the *likelihood that a given communication will accomplish its objective*.

Psychological Entropy

What we more often cannot diagnose accurately is the degree of psychological entropy involved in any communication. Variability of factors in sending and receiving messages of even the simplest type appear nearly as unpredictable as the system of extraordinarily high entropy which produces snowflakes.

Psychologics of entropy involve the same kinds of variabilities, regardless of how precisely information theorists have to date defined, measured, predicted or even controlled the logical elements of communication. And this is where the familiar communication models, like those of Shannon and Weaver,[13] are bled of their precision and subsequently lose their value. They are suspect as mechanical and logical formulations of communication processes in the degree to which psychologics become increasingly involved with their components.

[13] See Claude E. Shannon and Warren Weaver, *The Mathematical Theory of Communication* (Urbana, Ill.: University of Illinois Press, 1949).

If one is able to picture communication in the logical mode entirely from men to men, or from a man made system (a government, for instance) to another man made system, the mathematical models of the process are indeed significant. To the extent that psychologics are involved, a mathematical model is useless—as useless as a photograph of a man would be in giving us an idea of his behavior. (The picture might show us that he had neither arms nor legs, for instance, but the photograph might turn out to be misleading for many reasons.) Mathematical models, accordingly, of man-oriented communications may likewise be similarly misleading when applied to his games, wars, dreams, and aspirations.[14]

The psychological limitation is particularly important in the consideration of entropy, because this particular probability concept has, like redundancy, been borrowed from a highly rigorous and logical empirical science, the study of physical properties of matter as expressed in the abstract language of mathematics.

Many analysts of communication handle the concept of psychological entropy by ignoring it, pretending it does not exist and subsuming its manifestations to some other qualities of psychologics of communication, like previous conditioning or repression. Entropy is not a familiar psychological term, but it is all too commonly observed in the psychological aspects of communications involving humans.[15]

Most so-called "communication breakdowns" we observe are, of course, functions of psychological entropy. Examples of them are all around us. They are explainable *only* in psychological terms. One individual thought an advertisement for a film called "Fire Under Her Skin" said "Fur Under Her Skin." (She blamed the print in the newspaper which was perfectly clear.) The Russian delegate at the U.N. misinterprets vague hos-

---

[14] See Anatol Rapoport, *Fights, Games and Debates* (Ann Arbor: The University of Michigan Press, 1960), for a clear example of how the logic of mathematic models can be moved from their application to the inanimate world (like cards and dice) to games (which differentially involve psychological factors) to epidemics, to debates, to linguistics, to social problems and eventually to international hostility. Not content with his ingenious analysis of the logical world, Rapoport communicates considerable amusement to the psychological-theatrically sophisticated reader when he applies his model to the "showdown" between Othello and Desdemona. One clever mathematician appears to have missed the psychological value of the theatrical medium of communication, and displays, as a writer, at least, little insight concerning feminine nature. (See *ibid.*, pp. 234–242.) Rapoport *does* frequently and generously note the kind of limits to which his logical devices are subject, even as he exceeds them.

[15] The most simple explanation of psychological entropy is facile utilization of Freudian symbology to demonstrate how non-conscious mechanisms handle tension provoking stimuli, as in the so-called "Freudian slip." Explanations which tell us, in effect, that we misunderstand communications because we do not *want* to confront them are not explanations at all. The problem, as Freud himself carefully observed many times, is less *what* we misinterpret than *why* we misinterpret in the first place. See "Mistakes in Speech" in Sigmund Freud, *The Basic Writings of Sigmund Freud* (New York: The Modern Library, 1938), pp. 69–86. All of the materials in Book I, "Psychopathology of Everyday Life," are useful as primers for understanding this all too frequently simplified facet of the psychologics of communications.

tile remarks by the American delegate (in translation) as an "ultimatum." Sometimes this sort of event is a logical political ploy; more often it is the result of psychological entropy due to a system of translation from English to Russian over a telephone system. A story is told about the group of old-timers discussing whether ghosts exist. One codger claimed he had not only seen one but had had sexual relations with it. When questioned further and the psychological entropy had cleared, his retort was "Oh, I misunderstood. I thought you said a *goat!*" And so forth.

The Uses and Abuses of Entropy

Searching out causes for much logical entropy need not strain our imagination, although entropy in communications may be difficult to eliminate from our lives. Redundancy tends naturally to operate against entropy in communications, as it does in all of nature. But just as redundancy's logical force in encouraging the natural world into novel arrangements of the environment is limited by a conservative tendency, so is its organizing, entropy-reducing power modified by a continual trend towards disorganization.

Efforts of most communicators are directed to reducing, as far as possible, the effects of entropy, unless their communication is *designed* to be misunderstood for some reason. Or, it is possible to employ entropy for producing merely a field of some kind of familiar static, much as a jamming mechanism in international broadcasting operates at a level of almost complete entropy. The final paragraph of many political speeches (containing appeals to "God and country," confidence in the "wisdom of the people" and "the grand heritage of democracy") is also just so much logical static hardly even functioning as a punctuation mark. The "double talk" act of the late comic, Al Kelly, was intentional linguistic entropy employed for amusement.

The tendency of most communicators is to attempt to bring the level of logical entropy down as far as possible. Differential vocabularies of different people, confusion of symbols, mistakes in transmission and outside "interference" contribute to the difficulty of the task. Were we able to create a human communications system in which logical entropy was entirely absent—and perhaps we can[16]—we would still be plagued by factors of psychological entropy which would militate against our pains. So it occurs when a reader misunderstands an author's ideas (although the writer has taken meticulous pains to express himself clearly) simply because a cherished bias is attacked, or because a radio next door is distracting him.

Keeping logical entropy at a low level appears deceptively simple. Rea-

[16] The level of logical entropy between the voice (of recording) that reports the time over the telephone and the listener is probably extremely low, when one is told that, at the sound of the tone, the time is exactly 9:53 and 40 seconds. One is not told whether it is A.M. or P.M., however, and should he be confined to a windowless room or drunk or drugged, the degree of entropy would be high.

sonable controls of it are taken as *a priori* assumptions in most of the logical statements, particularly philosophical statements, man makes. Perhaps this accounts for one reason why philosophy often appears impotent to modify behavior, while instruments of lesser entropy, like machine guns and bank drafts, seem so effective.

Low level *logical* entropy philosophy has, of course, attempted to leave little opportunity for the development of *psychological* entropy for centuries—thereby inviting a good deal in practice. Most intelligent men, discouraged and confused by the pains to which the philosophers go to be "understood," merely "turn them off" (as Plato long ago feared[17]), in favor of more satisfying psychological occupations.

Bibles, holy books and other literature of religion contain high levels of logical entropy that have therefore permitted a wide range of psychological "meanings" to emerge, which have satisfied readers in numerous non-logical ways. Because of the arbitrary selection and arrangement of most of this material, it has proven equally satisfactory to wise men and fools of different backgrounds and nationality and, perhaps most important, irrespective of the particular times at which they have read or listened to it.

Scientific and technological systems, of course, with their extremely low levels of logical entropy, have also succeeded in modifying social and individual behavior profoundly. That the levels of entropy of professional discourse in some sciences and many technologies are often higher than many practitioners believe is necessary (forensic medicine being one example), need not be discussed here. It is sufficient to note that science and technology give observers a firm *impression* of a low order of logical entropy —even negative entropy, upon which, one observer claims, "life itself feeds." Psychological entropy accompanying them has, therefore, been generally and correspondingly low (after the first inductive scientists had severed their connections with superstition and witchcraft[18]), although resist-

[17] Jean Giradoux's play, *Tiger at the Gates*, clarifies Plato's point in a low entropy, pseudo-modern context. After the audience is exposed to a countless number of logical, philosophical reasons why the Trojan War should *not* be fought (reasons which are understood clearly by the combatants), they are overridden by the poet's psychological appeals to the people and the disputants themselves.

[18] Science's basic historical conflict with religion was almost immediately apparent to both scientists and followers of religion. The difference in logical entropy between almost any page of Newton's *Principia*, and almost any page of the Old or New Testament was as striking in its own time as a comparison of the Koran with one of the late Norbert Wiener's essays would be in ours. Farsighted religionists have long been aware that God must suffer diminution at the hands of science, just as one school of theology today claims (with philosophical justice) that it is likely that He has been killed entirely by technology. What writers like Harvey Cox in *The Secular City* (New York: The Macmillan Company, 1965), appear to be asking for is religion which communicates at the same level of logical entropy as science or technology. Whether such religion might still be "spiritual" (in the sense that Western man understands the term) is open to doubt. If it may not, then Cox has made a good case, for the death—or impending death—of God, far better than those who presently laugh at the so-called "God is dead" movement realize.

ance to scientific "knowledge" and technological "progress" has never been lacking, for two reasons. Either men have so misunderstood their own disciplines so as to impute to them greater degrees of logical entropy than they really displayed, or they have recognized the actual entropy in supposedly "true" scientific statements and "beneficial" technological programs—low, but nevertheless significant; crucial if ignored. Both of these factors have caused the psychological entropy that has existed (and exists today) towards public pronouncements of scientists and technologists, including our technologists of power and finance.[19]

Sources of Entropy

In the vast number of technologies (or systems) which are presently functioning in our society, sources and the probability of degrees of entropy are not difficult to locate, so long as they are studied in the logical mode. They are variably difficult to eliminate, depending upon the degree of potential stability of the system at hand, which is not always possible to determine except by extended periods of observation. They are only discovered after an orderly search—frequently mathematical in nature—has unearthed that portion or portions of the process where random behaviors are likely to occur and relationships may be stabilized. Since logical entropy is a definite proportional probability of the efficient operation of the rest of any system, it is always theoretically locatable, if not correctable.

This is true in all matters involving communications, including the functions of languages themselves. If we are able to create instruments fine enough to describe accurately a linguistic system and make reasonable predictions about its components, we may also predict its degree of entropy.[20]

[19] One excellent example is the Surgeon General's recent report confirming the statements of dozens of researchers on mice and men who have provided "scientific proof" that smoking causes lung cancer, heart failure, and other physical disorders. To quote what it says on every pack of cigarettes sold in the United States today, "Cigarette Smoking May Be Hazardous to Your Health," an understatement in the light of the conclusions of science. Yet cigarette consumption continues to rise. This is because, on the one hand, the scientific proof of tobacco's harmfulness to total health *through* life (not merely related to longevity and degenerative diseases of old age) has *not* been clearly demonstrated, although propagandists for anti-smoking interests communicate as if it has. (Unfortunately, the Surgeon General's conclusions contained greater logical entropy than they should have.) On the other hand, the *genuine* degree of physical damage which cigarettes *might* do to people, as well as the *good* they *might* do them (under certain circumstances), have *not* been published in our market place of thought in low entropy public communications. Instead, we have been flooded with messages of high logical and psychological entropy, ranging on one side from the scare tactics of The American Cancer Society to absurd and irrelevant cigarette commercials on the other. Considering these factors, it is not surprising that so many of us have concluded that it is not after all unwise for us to continue to smoke and take our chances of not living as long as non-smokers. The years we are sacrificing for our temporary enjoyment will, after all, be our last ones, hardly likely to be our best.

[20] Linguists, for instance, have created concepts like *phonemes, morphemes,* and

Certain psychological regularities of human behavior exist as well, and they sometimes also yield relatively high degrees of predictability, but most of these data are limited by the instruments of their discovery: that is, tests or surveys. These devices apparently work well for solving certain psychological (and sociological) problems, and for showing certain kinds of relationships (between intelligence and social class, for instance), but they are obviously only reliable when employed in circumstances similar to those in which the data were gathered originally.

In a clinic or, by means of certain strategies in pseudo-environments set up by behavior scientists, it is possible to replicate certain aspects of these original conditions. This accounts for the reliability[21] of instruments like aptitude tests, personality inventories, and public opinion or attitude questionnaires. As we have seen in Chapter II, it is difficult to insure a similar degree of reliability when examining most psychological factors of communication. They are intricately involved with covert dispositions, almost entirely dependent upon highly variable conditions under which the same communication may be received by different people; or different communications may be received by the same people; or different communications may be received by different people!

Here we have merely *one* set of hazards facing the psychological systematication of just *one* general type of communication, only *superficially* articulated. These difficulties obviously increase in geometric progression as new psychological variables are introduced regarding the people communicating and receiving the communications. Isolating *parts* of the communications process to control variables has, of course, been attempted, but such isolation appears to clarify more profitably the logic of entropy than its psychologic.

Sources of entropy, particularly psychological entropy, may be located in exactly the same place as one's "communicating" environment is developed: the circumstantial and personal conditions of individual growth. Among the many factors which are sources of entropy in the languages of communications, four appear to be particularly worthy of discussion, although none is operationally exclusive of the other. And any or all may be subsumed under other possible categories from different perspectives of analysis:

Culture: More than forty-five years ago the late Edward Sapir pub-

---

graphemes to describe regularities in language so that probability statements about factors like entropy may be formulated about written and spoken words. See Charles E. Osgood and K. V. Wilson, *Some Terms and Associated Measures for Talking about Human Communication* (Urbana, Ill.: University of Illinois, 1961), for examples of how this is accomplished.

21 The term "reliability," of course, refers to similar results obtained when repeating surveys or tests. "Validity" is another yardstick of whether a test or survey relates to what it is supposed to measure, a problem not under discussion here.

lished a series of cultural observations in his book on language,[22] two of which are central to an understanding of cultural entropy concerning, in a broad manner, "why inter-cultural communications fail," and therefore providing reasons for the psychological sources of entropy in such communications.[23]

Sapir exposes two sides of a linguistic coin, each of which has led other scholars to seemingly antagonistic avenues of research; but both are actually complementary from the communications perspective. First, he observes that various languages express most effectively in words those ideas or objects which are most common in each culture. Observing primitive societies, Sapir noticed that every one of them had produced a fully developed language that was arranged by means of syntax, vocabulary and other linguistic devices to communicate most effectively (with the least possible degree of entropy) that which was of prime importance in *that* particular culture. In other words, each language could handle both concrete and abstract ideas in its communications, *dependent upon the state of that culture.*

Simply, he observed that people seem to find ways of saying what they *need* to say.

On the other side of the coin, Sapir made the less well known observation[24] that an individual in any culture with its own language is able to say almost anything in *his* tongue that someone else might say in a different language. His use of words may be highly inefficient or necessarily redundant; his level of entropy might be high; but even the most primitive native of New Guinea is able to describe an atomic missile with a nuclear warhead, although he must employ such circumlocutions as "man make arrow like, big, go boom, kill many people, far away, heavy, made of metal like ring in nose, etc., etc., etc." to describe accurately an idea alien to his culture. Sapir's book itself is filled with just such ideas and concepts (as well as descriptions of concrete objects) familiar to various primitive people which he has no trouble in describing accurately for his readers in English, despite the limitations of the language in which he is writing.

The impositions of culture do not necessarily militate against cross-cultural communication, providing that one is ready to put up with much circumlocution (redundancy) and even more static (entropy) and a low degree of linguistic efficiency to achieve communication.

The relationship of culture to entropy can be found in a synthesis of both of Sapir's observations. Chances of entropy rise as cultural differences

[22] Edward Sapir, *Language: An Introduction to the Study of Speech* (New York: Harcourt Brace and World, Original Copyright: 1921).
[23] One of the most ingenuous recent entries into the field of linguistic anthropology in Edward T. Hall's *The Silent Language* (Greenwich, Conn.: Fawcett Publications, Inc., 1961), particularly Chapters 1–5, pp. 15–98, and Hall's clever map of cultural vocabularies, pp. 174–175.
[24] See *Ibid.*, p. 207–231, especially.

increase, with psychological entropy probably rising a good deal faster and more severely than logical entropy as communications progress. They seem to reach a peak, however, and begin to decline again with psychological entropy in the lead falling fastest and first. This diminution occurs as two people of different cultures perceive their common humanity and common goals, and they estimate the degree of threat one poses versus the other—as well as the amount of profit each may obtain from cross-cultural nexus. Culture is therefore a mercurial source of both logical and psychological entropy, the control of which depends upon the inclinations and motivations of the individuals communicating.

Character: Among the factors which influence logical and psychological entropy is the matter of character, a complex function, naturally, of countless forces in the life of all human communicators. Because the character of an individual is so trenchantly descriptive of his potentials, this factor is included as one possible major component of entropy.

Physical factors like blood pressure, glandular activity and brain capacity are obviously crucial matters in the success or failure of interpersonal communications. Certainly, both logical and psychological entropy diminish as physical growth and maturation occur in individuals, and sometimes they rise as growth turns to degeneration of the organism in the presence of disease or old age.

Characterological factors in men and women (and other living organisms as well), result from forces other than physical ones, however. Physical factors of character, especially those involving movement and stance, are those most immediately noticeable, as clever cartoon caricaturists know. Rather than capture the psychological character of a subject, artists like Hirschfeld and Herblock seize in their drawings the overt physical identifying idiosyncratic features of an individual both in repose and in motion, just as Ben Johnson did in *Volpone* centuries ago by identifying his characters with animals whose physical traits were highly deterministic of their characters.

Experience and Education: A familiar saying runs "As the twig is bent, so grows the tree." What we can learn of value from its simple formulation is that entropy can be *learned*, or, in other words, entropy can be a function of any individual's—or a group's—cumulative experiences.

Many voices, for instance, spoke in many ways to the German people during the nineteen-twenties and thirties, giving them clear warning of the tragedy to come. Still, most of them did not (could not) hear. Educated to fierce nationalism and having experienced defeat in World War I, one voice, however, spoke clearly, and *was* heard. Hitler's firm resolve and clear objectives cut like a knife through the entropy-filled indecisive rhetoric of competing politicians. Psychologically, Hitler's very presence produced negative entropy for many Germans. Logically, even his most ambiguous speeches, filled with vague threats, lies and wild promises, found their marks in minds and hearts tuned to understand them in the crucible of immediate experience and contemporary German history.

Values: The distillate of all the factors affecting entropy is the phenomenon of human value, difficult to define and to measure or predict precisely. Among similar people in a given culture, of given characters, of given degrees of experience and education, individual values will still influence the amount of entropy in their communications.

Into our value structure we mold our degree of maturity, our exposure to circumstances, our limitations in understanding certain types of ideas— to achieve what I. A. Richards calls our individual socially appropriate "stock responses," preconceptions, vulnerabilities, etc. Richards himself notes that in our reactions to communications, "what we *say,* in nine cases out of ten, has nothing to do with the poem (when exposed to this medium), but arises from politeness or spleen or some other social motive." [25]

Certain psychological responses on the overt level may indicate a covert disposition and therefore notify us of how values are assimilated into ourselves. For the reasons Richards cites, many of us may pretend there has been not one bit of logical entropy in a communication to which we have been exposed, although we may not have understood its structure, objective or vocabulary. Yet we lie through our teeth about the nature of the psychological responses we experience to many communications. One is reminded of generations of weary "opera lovers," "music lovers" or "art lovers" who do not patronize opera houses or concert halls or museums because they *want* to, who do not understand what is going on around them (and do not care to), but think they must applaud in appreciation of the Culture to which they are exposed. They are where they are merely because they think they are where they *ought* to be. If they suffer the cruelties of boredom induced by logical and psychological entropy, they are paying a just price for the maintenance of their foolish values.

Conclusion

Success and failure of communications are relative matters, hinging upon the balance of numerous factors relating to the interplay of both logical and psychological elements.

Success and failure of communications are independent of any kind of value; nothing in nature permits the assumption that success at communication is "good" or that any failure is "bad" *per se.* In fact, the reverse might be true under certain logical or psychological circumstances, and pseudophilosophies which posit sure virtue in success at communication operate in controvention of the experience of man.

Ambiguity, entropy and efficiency in communications are simply the

[25] I. A. Richards, *Practical Criticism* (New York: Harcourt Brace and Company, 1954), p. 318. (Italics added.)

ways in which activities involving communications are similar to other systems and are prone to the same kinds of disorders of logic and psychologic. The latter factors are often overlooked or considered irrelevant by Information Theorists and other positivists who create mathematical models to emulate mechanical systems of communications. Powerful forces and counterforces, which may be calculated with fair logical precision but with less psychological precision, keep most communications systems in their various manifestations in a constant state of uncertainty concerning failure and success.

In the search for novelty, companionship and meaning in life, however, human beings have probably succeeded in producing *significant* communications, one with the other, much more of the time than they have failed.

Part Two

SYMBOLS AND COMMUNICATION

Chapter 4

SYMBOLS AND MEN

IN A RECENT BOOK, Kenneth Burke has described the human being as follows:

Man is
the symbol using (symbol-making, symbol-misusing) animal
inventor of the negative (or moralized by the negative)
separated from his natural condition by instruments of his
    own making
goaded by the spirit of hierarchy (or moved by a sense of order)
and rotten with perfection[1]

Burke subsequently defends each of these propositions in a brilliant discourse.[2] The characteristics stem one from the other in proper order and delineate the concept "man" as Burke sees him. If we recognize him as a psychologically determined beast, impelled to a limited degree of harshly determined logical behavior (but aware of his own limits and perversities), we are probably talking about the same type of creature Burke is.

Note that Burke places man's symbol using and abusing characteristics *second* on the list; that is, immediately after he has affirmed man's *essence*. Most contemporary observers agree with him, because modern perspectives of man literally force us to consider the symbol as basic to our fundamental processes of awareness.

In the words of von Bertalanffy, "Man's unique position is based on

---

[1] Kenneth Burke, *Language as Symbolic Action* (Berkeley and Los Angeles: University of California Press, 1966), p. 16. This is a recent collection of essays, poems, papers, criticism and other odds and ends, and comprises a hearteningly lucid collection of Burke's ideas. Since it may be examined almost at random and deals with the entire range of the author's interests, it is especially recommended for readers who may have become discouraged by the density of Burke's more formal books.
[2] Ibid., pp. 3-22.

the dominance of symbols in his life. Except in the immediate satisfaction of biological needs, man lives in a world not of things but of symbols. . . . Symbols can be defined as signs that are freely created, represent some content and are transmitted by tradition. It appears that the characteristics indicated are necessary and sufficient to distinguish symbolism . . . from subhuman forms of behavior." [3]

A. N. Whitehead has demonstrated [4] tersely that knowledge is mediated to the human being either directly (as when one is slapped in the face) or through a symbolic screen (as when one understands the *meaning* of a slap on the face). Whitehead writes: "There is one great difference between symbolism and direct knowledge. Direct experience is infallible. What you have experienced, you have experienced. But symbolism is very fallible, in the sense that it may induce actions, feelings, emotions, and beliefs and things which are mere notions without that exemplification in the world which the symbolism leads us to presuppose." [5]

Human beings in every culture of which man has known have been dependent upon that "world which symbolism leads us to presuppose" for hundreds of thousands of years, but the symbolic world itself has been taken for granted for most of this time; that is, seen as an *extension* of the world of direct experience. A poignant illustration of this fact may be found at the end of the Ingmar Bergman film, *The Virgin Spring.* A father (skilfully played by Max von Sydow) having avenged the rape and brutal murder of his daughter by killing her assassins, raises high his hands, their fingers just touching, to God. We are then told that at the place where he stands a spring began to flow and a great cathedral was built. As the film ends, we see von Sydow from the back, on his toes, head to the heavens, his arms arched, transformed in a human replica of a church. For an instant, a perceptive film maker has given us a glimpse of the architecture of a house of worship *as a symbolic extension of the physical figure of man himself, in excelsis,* praying to his God. He has also illustrated the simplicity (and perhaps inevitability) of the generation of such symbols, and, incidentally, the source of their power.

Symbolic insights of this sort were probably generally taken for granted for thousands of years. Certainly, traditional wisdom did not impel men, before the middle of the last century, to examine their symbol structure in the ways writers like Burke, von Bertalanffy and Whitehead have done in recent times. Many poets and philosophers for centuries, on the other

---

[3] Ludwig von Bertalanffy, "The Tree of Knowledge" in Gyorgy Kepes, *op. cit.,* p. 274.
[4] Alfred North Whitehead, *Symbolism* (New York: The MacMillan Company, 1958), pp. 1–6. Whitehead's concept of symbolism will form the matrix for the discussion of symbolism in society in Chapter V, and therefore will be discussed only briefly here. The author wishes, however, at this point to record his indebtedness to Dr. Joe R. Burnett of the University of Illinois for his patient instruction in Whitehead's thinking while they were colleagues at New York University.
[5] *Ibid.,* p. 6.

hand, seemed frequently impressed by the symbolic "truths" with which
they dealt, but they dared not conjecture that any symbol system—much
less language itself—was likely to be less than an infallible guide to "truth"
when opposed to experience. One hundred years ago—even three generations ago—the following paragraph by Burke would probably have been
considered the work of a deranged mind. Yet, to our senses it is hardly
revolutionary, merely descriptive of what most of us already know. Burke
says:

> Can we bring ourselves to realize . . . just how overwhelmingly
> much of what we mean by "reality" has been built up for us through
> nothing but our symbol systems? Take away our books, and what do we
> know about history, biography, even some things so "down to earth" as
> the positive position of seas and continents? What is our reality for to-
> day (beyond the paper-thin line of our own particular lives) but all this
> clutter of symbols about the past combined with whatever things we know
> mainly through maps, magazines, newspapers and the like about the
> present? In school, as they go from class to class, students turn from
> one idiom to another. The various courses in the curriculum are in effect
> but so many different terminologies. And however important to us is the
> tiny sliver of reality each of us has experienced firsthand, the whole overall
> "picture" is but a construct of our symbol systems. To meditate on this
> fact until one sees its full implications is much like peering over the edge
> of things into an ultimate abyss. And doubtless that's one reason why,
> though man is typically the symbol-using animal, he clings to a kind of
> naïve verbal realism that refuses to realize the full extent of the role
> played by symbolicity in his notions of reality.[6]

Recognition of Symbols

Burke's observation, above, however, *in no way* frees man from the
symbol system in which his own writing and thinking are enmeshed. Nor
are we freed on these pages themselves from the symbolic environment of
the society in which these words are written merely because we are discussing symbols.[7] Knowledge of a symbol system gives one little but psychological power over it. The holiness of a church is not reduced by Bergman's
insight of the extenuation of a religious symbol from the human form. For

[6] Burke, *op. cit.*, p. 5.
[7] Psychological reasons for this phenomenon may elicit considerable speculation. Plato's
allegory of the cave gives us one clue: that men born and raised in an environment of
darkness cannot conceive of sunlight. Carried further, a prisoner is not free to roam at
will, whether or not he is ignorant of the fact that he is imprisoned. His logical condition (of incarceration) is the reality through which he is forced to live, and what he
knows (or does not know) is irrelevant to his condition. It is difficult to say that we
are "imprisoned" by our symbol systems, but in many ways this is how it appears. When
we reach beyond them, our behavior is apt to be regarded as deviant, and we may even
run into trouble with that great symbol of societal order: the law. We are thus impelled by ongoing pressures to continue symbolic cooperations which our society demands
from us.

the religiously inclined, the derivation of such a symbol even enhances its value—should an individual question the "human" purpose for the construction of cathedrals (to God's glory) while men live in hovels. *The Virgin Spring* provides *an answer*, satisfactory to some of us and unsatisfactory to others, but a clear and irrefutable answer. In fact, as we shall see in Chapter V, knowledge of symbols and how they work may serve as an impetus for society to develop methods of utilizing symbol structures for collective and individual therapy. Utilization therefore actually increases the currency and power of symbols in those cultures where many individuals are acutely conscious of the *symbol of symbolism*, as in the West today.

Some communications analysts go to great pains to differentiate between *symbols* and *signs*, conscious of the oddity that signs are understood by non-human animals, while symbols are almost entirely bound to human perceptions. The difference is misleading, primarily because a sign to one individual in one culture may be a symbol to another. Different signs, also, may vary in symbolic value through the history of a single culture. Ashley Montagu has, however, recorded the difference quite succinctly. "A sign is a concrete denoter: it signals 'This is it. Do something about it,'" he writes. "A symbol, on the other hand, is abstract, connotative, contemplative, knowing, knowledgeable. A sign is eternal. A symbol is internal. Signs relate mostly to the world of things, symbols to the world of ideas. A symbol is an abstract meaning of value conferred by those who use it upon anything, tangible or intangible. A sign, on the other hand, is a physical thing which is apprehended as standing for something else." [8]

Can a symbol be more specifically defined? If it can, we are on our way to specifying the symbolic base of the various languages of communication. If it cannot, we are hurled into a mystical discourse where, unfortunately, much current discussion of symbolism (particularly as it applies to the arts) is held. Of many attempts at definition one of the clearest is Susanne K. Langer's short statement, "A symbol is any device where we are enabled to make an abstraction." [9]

Let us examine this deceptively simple sentence. First, "A symbol is a device. . . ." Symbolism is therefore not a medium of communication *but a way in which ideas are transmitted by means of mediums*. Neither is a symbol a unit of language. There exists no "language of symbols" or discourse solely by means of symbols, unless certain specific ideas are lined up (or somehow arranged) and thereafter symbolized in turn.[10] By means of this parade of symbols we are neither creating a symbolic sentence nor con-

---

[8] Ashley Montagu, "Communication, Evolution, Education," in Matson and Montagu, *op. cit.*, p. 446.
[9] Langer, *Feeling and Form*, p. 11.
[10] Certain kinds of surrealistic paintings deal with symbols in this manner, but they *never* articulate a symbolic sentence with linguistic rigor. Each painting, so "loaded" with symbolic material becomes a new *inter*-symbol of new interest in its own right.

structing a meaningful vocabulary of them, but merely arranging a number of simple symbols into one long, complex symbol. We may analyze the components of this complex symbol, but it will lack, *sui generis,* a grammar, a syntax and probably even a clear aesthetic.

The definition continues ". . . whereby we are enabled to make an abstraction." The nature and burden of symbolism are therefore subsumed under considerations of the psychologics of communication. While the logics may be drawn upon in inducing the *history* of a symbol (or a symbol system) and its social function, and it may be amenable to description in the logical mode, the process of symbolism itself is psychological. The fabrication of abstractions stems from our psychological rather than logical proclivities. The activity of symbolism does not, however, preclude logic in communication. Arithmetic, for instance, a highly abstract method of manipulating the environment, is quite logical. The process by which concrete elements are first, translated into abstractions, and second, translated back into concrete entities (arithmetic included) is more likely to involve the psychologics of communication than their logics. The words ". . . we are enabled" in Langer's definition clearly indicates that the process is one of *mind.*

Modern psychological theory deals, therefore, both fully and profitably with the symbolic aspect of man's mind-life. Freud is mainly given both credit and blame for the development of modern schools of symbology and for their influences on so much of our cultural life. Philosophers were, of course, investigating the role of symbols in the lives of men well before Freud, although the focus of their interest was less upon symbolic influences upon neuroses and other behavior disorders than upon letters and art, particularly graphic arts and the theater.

Mordecai Gorelik, noted scene designer and theatrical historian, speculated some years ago that the currents of thought which led to the analysis of symbolism in modern terms began in the period between 1849 and 1869 in the grand visions of Richard Wagner.[11]

First, Wagner was raised in the Germanic theatrical tradition, which had been strongly influenced by Duke Georg of Saxe-Meiningen's non-naturalistic "director's theatre." The Duke had broken with tradition by treating the stage not as a vehicle for individual virtuoso actors or as a platform for well made plots, but as an orchestrated, abstracted *event,* analogous to the musical symphony.

Wagner's imagination was fired by this first *self-consciously symbolic art form* that had been conceived in the West, an art form in which the stage setting, lighting, music and lyrics all were intentionally contrived to "stand for" a totality greater than the sum of the parts. In this self-con-

---

[11] Mordecai Gorelik, *New Theatres for Old* (New York: Samuel French, 1947), pp. 189–190.

scious conceptual arena, Wagner attempted to capture the Teutonic spirit of "folk, blood and soil." [12]

The myths upon which Wagner's operas were based (including the Faust play), were (and remain) some of the most highly charged symbolic material in the folklore of Europe, the result of cultural mysticism centuries old.

What emerged was a theatre of symbolism, "suggestion, vagueness of outline, posteresque light and shadow and, most of all, an impenetrable blending, 'a complex and rhythmic fusion of setting, lights, actors and play.' " [13] Its symbols implied what it did not state directly about Germanic nobility, the perfection of primitivism, and the evils of effete civilization. The theatre, for Wagner, was a vehicle for the expression of those specific symbols which could manipulate his special audience's thoughts and feelings appropriately.[14]

Against this artistic and nationalistic background began the scientific period of "great doubting" during the last half of the past century. Another genius, schooled in Germanic traditions, grasped at the newly enfranchised symbol. Freud discovered an emancipated symbology in middle-European thought, freed from its place in the world of objective reality and located in the basic psychological, universal, human system of perceptions.

Here was Freud's response to the fundamental question posed to him by philosophers of his day: How could he know anything about the workings of the unconscious if the unconscious was, by definition, closed to perception? The most convincing answer was the *symbol*, that by-product of an unconscious human process which had been secretly fueling human consciousness for hundreds of thousands of years without man being aware of it. Wagner had located it in the theatre and had developed a near-religious theory of symbolism to justify the enormity of his dramatic undertakings. Freud's concept was no less heroic. He enshrined the symbol as the *lingua franca* of man's instinctual processes, speaking in its own strangely potent

[12] This was the same mystique one finds in the work of Nietzsche. Hitler utilized it as a progapanda tool years later in his deliberate grasp at potent symbols to capture the loyalty of the German people.

[13] *Ibid.*, p. 190.

[14] Wagner's operas continue to move the vulnerable and to provide podiums for the virtuosity of certain kinds of singers. To some they are as repellant as they are attractive to others, largely, one suspects, because of the relevance of the symbolic manipulation they involve to the value and peculiar (sic) symbol sensitivities of the auditor's. What is curious is not that Germanic symbolism had such power in the theatre, but that the construct of the "Wagnerian type" symbol clings so consistently at present to Middle European-style of thought, even at the hands of so Americanized a thinker as Langer. Her debt to the Germanic fashion of symbolic analysis—especially that of Rudolph Carnap and Ernst Cassirer—is obvious. Note her agreement with Cassirer's basic psychological observation about symbolism: that to the naïve mind it "is not sharply divided into symbol and object, but both tend to unite in a perfectly undifferentiated fusion," as quoted in Susanne K. Langer, *Philosophy in a New Key* (New York: The New American Library, 1948), p. 199. The statement appears to include the conceptual springboard for her own discussion of symbolism, but it might satisfy the most avid Wagnerian.

vocabulary to his patients from the polite middle-class world of old Vienna.

When the American psychologist Clark Hull later attempted to articulate what he hoped would be a valedictory general theory of human behavior, "communicational symbolism . . . the use of symbolism in individual problem solution involving thought and reasoning; . . . social or ritualistic symbolism," [15] headed his list of concerns. The time was now the 1940's. Hull even promised his colleagues a veritable model of symbolism, a "mathematico-deductive" theory which would apply to—and crack the riddles of—virtually every problem known to social science.

Hull himself was an outstanding experimentalist with a bias towards analogies which employed mechanistic explanations in explaining behavior.[16] His strict determinism took for granted a full-blown, clearly articulated concept of symbolism, which had emerged tentatively little more than two generations before from hypotheses of artists, philosophers and psychologists who were trying desperately to interconnect history, mythology and religion with the new sciences of biology and psychology.

The intervening years had seen the growth and spread of the concept of the universality and power of symbols. At the same time, many of the basic religious, mythological (and even nationalistic) objects for which the symbols stood were examined and rejected. Men of the stature of William James[17] and Sir James Frazer[18] were to search the corners of the earth for primitive cultures in order to study the rites of antique religions and their yield of specific symbols and symbol systems which hopefully might appear in similar manifestations in widely different cultures. By implication, they attempted to demonstrate for all time that the Western Judeo-Christian tradition was not exempted by virtue of recency from the same kind of symbolic behaviors in which our ancestors had indulged thousands of years ago.

The universe of symbolism was current, their writings implied, in societies blessed by the revolutions of science, technology and popular government! The professor at Harvard, proud of his liberal status as a Unitarian minister, the "good" Democrat, clubman, golfer and patron of the arts, was united in the new brotherhood of symbols with the Batak of Sumatra. The publication of these discoveries made little difference to the way of life pursued by the natives of Sumatra, but Cambridge, Massachusetts, and similar communities in the Western world, were never to be the same again.

[15] Clark L. Hull, *Principles of Behavior* (New Haven: Yale University Press, 1952), p. 399.
[16] See Clark L. Hull *et al., Mathematico-Deductive Theory of Rote Learning* (New Haven: Yale University Press, 1940), for, at least, statements of the promises offered by Hull's psychological system.
[17] See William James, *Varieties of Religious Experience* (New York: The New American Library, 1958). This classic work was originally published in 1902.
[18] See James G. Frazer, *The Golden Bough* (New York: The Macmillan Company, 1923). The one volume abridged edition is sufficient for readers whose intention is to acquaint themselves with the general range of this remarkable study.

The Ubiquity of Symbols

From a logical frame of reference, George Herbert Mead explains the ubiquity of symbols:

> Thinking always implies a symbol which will call out the same response in another that it calls out in the thinker. Such a symbol is a universal of discourse; it is universal in its character. We always assume the symbol we use is the one which will call out in the other person the same response, provided it is a part of his mechanism of conduct. A person who is saying something is saying *to himself* what he is saying to others; otherwise he does not know what he is thinking about. . . .[19]
>
> The isolation of the symbol, as such, enables one to hold on to . . . given characteristics and to isolate them in their relationship to the object, and consequently in their relationship to the response. It is that, I think, which characterizes our human intelligence to a peculiar degree. We have a set of symbols by means of which we indicate certain characters, and in indicating those characters hold them apart from their immediate environment, and keep simply one relationship clear.[20]

Mead provides us with a clear description of *how* a symbol is formed; *what* it accomplishes everywhere; and *why* observers as logically dissimilar as Hull and Burke place symbols first in importance as an artifact of human endeavor, ahead of fire, the axe or the tribe.

Mead's points apply to the *single* symbol. What about *symbolism*, the *total* process by which symbols are somehow combined into complex and sophisticated formalities and preserved as events called "rites" or as "rituals" or "ceremonies"?

Our explanation must necessarily move from the lucid and relatively simple form of logical analysis to the operation of psychologics. From the psychological reference point, there is no diminution in the sweep, scope or pervasiveness of symbolic activity in the lives of men. What emerges is the degree of the individual's immersion in the universe of symbols, insofar as the *emotional* or *feeling* side of his nature is concerned. We discover amazing elaborations and combinations of symbols which, while rarely satisfying the logics of language, often appear, nevertheless, to satisfy deep human cravings.

Symbols, first and most strikingly, attempt to define, clarify or manage the fundamental enigmas of existence: matters relating to birth, reproduction and death. They appear to unite the role of man with the processes of nature. The ubiquity of symbolism in this context indicates that the psy-

---

[19] Anselm Strauss, *The Social Psychology of George Herbert Mead* (Chicago: The University of Chicago Press, 1956), p. 224 (italics added). Mead notes that dissemblers and actors may be exceptions here, who, in a sense, know *more* than their audience does. An actor, says Mead, is "able to respond to his own gesture in same sense as his audience does."

[20] *Ibid.*, p. 198.

chologics of symbolism go far beyond Mead's explanation of symbolic intercourse, based on sheer (or mere) utility and facility of social communications.

S. Gideon describes these psychological processes thus, comparing them functionally as modern manifestations to their roles in primitive societies:

> Today's symbols are anonymous; they seem to exist for themselves alone, without any direct significance. Yet they are imbued with an inexplicable attraction: the magic of their forms. In a sense, they represent a regenerative or healing process, a flight from technological frenzy. Beside these anonymous symbols or forms without direct significance, age-old symbols from the remote past have been revived and integrated into new contexts . . .[21]
>
> The essential nature of the symbol has always consisted in an urge to express the inherently inexpressible, but in primitive times the crystallization of a concept in the form of a symbol portrayed reality before that reality came to pass. The symbol itself was reality, for it was believed to possess the power of working magic, and thus of directly affecting the course of events: the wish, the prayer or the spell to be fulfilled.[22]

Sometimes symbols are conceived of, however, in so general a psychological sense, that they may refer to *any* so-called "sign" which is a substitute for another "sign," as they are, for instance, by Charles Morris.[23] Under these circumstances, symbolic ideation transcends Burke's poetic definition of man, although Burke does not say that man is the *only* animal that is a symbol user. "Sign" substitution may be seen in the behaviors of apes, hooded rats (trained in laboratories) and other mammals. One may discover it in the colorful habits of hundreds of thousands of species of invertebrates.

Konrad Lorenz clearly differentiates between the kind of symbol evident in the animal kingdom carried on by sign substitution and the kind that man employs in communication. "No means of communication, no learned rituals are ever handed down by tradition in animals. In other words, animals have no culture." [24] Symbols, in Morris' semantic sense, are far more ubiquitous than symbols in the traditional-cultural sense, but they lack utterly an historic or cultural function and their psychological ramifications for the explanation of human communications appear to be nil.

[21] S. Gideon, "Symbolic Expression in Prehistory and in the First High Civilizations," in Kepes, *op. cit.*, p. 79.
[22] *Ibid.*, p. 87.
[23] See Charles Morris, *Signs, Language and Behavior* (New York: George Braziller Inc. 1955), pp. 23–27. Morris is concerned almost entirely with the semantic restrictions upon the use of the word "symbol" and apparently with their function in facilitating psychologically man's control of his environment.
[24] From ON AGGRESSION by Konrad Lorenz, copyright © 1963, by Dr. Borotha-Schoeler Verlag, Wien, Austria; English translation, copyright © 1966 by Konrad Lorenz. All quotes reprinted by permission of Harcourt, Brace & World, Inc.

The difference between the use of symbols individually to enhance meaning and the employment of rites, rituals and ceremonies to perform far more elaborate psychological tasks is small. Because symbolism in any form is *not* itself a medium of communication, it does not lend itself to the kind of distinctive logical and psychological analysis that the mediums permit. Instead, a symbol's psychological power is derived from relationship with specific culture traits. Without them as references, it is meaningless. For instance, the pine tree may be the discrete symbol of winter in the Christmas ceremony as performed in the United States. But the celebration of Christ's birth, with all its religious and materialistic manifestations, is a nearly *total societal* obeisance in our culture, not necessarily confined to religious Christians, but observed by Jews, atheists and others. The American Christmas ceremony entails a complicated set of rituals, the mixture of many individual symbols, psychologically best described by an enumeration of its logics. These logical events appear to contain considerable psychological power in our culture, particularly for children.[25]

Burke differentiates the *symbol* from *symbolism* by treating the former as "scientistic" (or amenable to atomistic and frequently logical analysis). The latter he calls "dramatistic" (or totalities more psychologically oriented), which are captured and communicated in "stories, plays, poems, the rhetoric of oratory and advertising, mythologies, theologies and philosophies after the classic model." [26]

The former may yield to semantic analysis. The latter demands a cultural perspective to be understood. It is developed in "the tribe's way of living (the practical role of symbolism in what anthropologist Malenowski has called 'context of situation'). Such considerations are involved in . . . the 'dramatistic,' stressing language as an aspect of 'action,' that is as 'symbolic action.' " [27] Symbolism, the elaboration of symbols, is therefore primarily an anthropological matter, while discrete symbols, behavioral, logical and/or psychological are perhaps semantic manifestations of the kind discussed previously in the work of Mead, Hull and others.

Because one must employ them in different contexts, however, does not isolate the notion of symbol from symbolism or demand totally exclusive categories for the study of each. It appears merely that the psychologically elaborate process of ceremony is located at one end of a continuum on

---

[25] The same observation may be made, of course, of the totally religious Christmas. The *symbol* of Christ the messiah has been elaborated into a complex ceremony accenting birth, love, peace and benevolence. This ceremony (formulated in an exciting era of intellectual revolt and philosophical activity) appears to offer the masses less psychological satisfaction than the religious-materialist Christmas in America and some parts of Western Europe. In the U.S.S.R. the virtual abolition of the religious Christmas and the preservation of the pagan one appears to have solved contraditions between the two. Possibly the Soviet ceremony absolves the participants of a sense of hypocrisy on the one hand and satisfies yearnings for "old-fashioned" religion on the other.
[26] Burke, *op. cit.*, pp. 44–45.
[27] *Ibid.*, p. 44.

which the single symbol in its logical phase (as shown by Mead) is located at the other.

Burke's "dramatistic approach" must represent the accumulation and interplay of numerous isolated "scientistically" derived atomistic symbols. Experience demonstrates the ease with which we may untangle almost any aspect of "dramatistic" life into its individual symbolic elements, even in a culture with as many complex ceremonies, rites and rituals as ours. Indeed, "symbol-hunting" of many kinds has become an appropriate (and not un-profitable) activity for countless people. "Symbolic criticism" of drama and literature is presently much in vogue. That such criticism is often brought cleverly to bear upon the classics as well as modern works demonstrates the ease with which the complex "dramatistic" symbolic structures may be broken down into their "scientistic" elements.[28]

The Function of Symbols

To ascribe, therefore, discrete psychological and logical functions to symbols and symbolisms is to stumble into an easy but well-worn trap which permits one to "explain" symbols without understanding the role they play in communication.[29] Having differentiated between symbol and symbolism in matters of *kind* rather than complexity and/or *degree*, we are likely to indulge in the kind of "interpretation" and hair-splitting one finds so frequently in the present literature of semantics and in numerous types of language study.

The *social* functions of symbolism will be the concern of the next chapter. We are concerned here with symbols as they relate to individual life or the mind-life of individuals.

Burke offers our first problem, namely the *difference* between *symbolic* reality and *real* reality. Is there any? Burke responds: "Our presence in a room is immediate, but the room's relation to our country as a nation, and beyond that, to international relations and cosmic relations, dissolves into a web of ideas and images through our senses only insofar as the symbol system, that report on them are heard and seen. To mistake this vast tangle of ideas for immediate experience is much more fallacious than to accept a dream as immediate experience." [30]

Burke has identified a concept discussed also by Daniel J. Boorstein,[31] that of the *pseudo-environment* which is made up largely (or entirely) of symbols. This pseudo-environment so influences our patterns of life and thought that we seem to have lost the ability to distinguish between a real

[28] Note particularly of the abundance of Marxist symbolic criticism which was brought to much literature, contemporary and classic, during the nineteen-thirties, as well as the psychoanalytically-oriented middle-class criticism, now so prevalent in fashionable magazines.
[29] See Chapters 7, 8, 9 and 10.
[30] Burke, *op. cit.*, p. 49.
[31] Daniel J. Boorstein, *The Image* (New York: Harper and Row, 1964).

environment and the artificial, symbolic one. While Boorstein extrapolates this idea into the speculative territory of mass culture, he considers this psychological problem a sickness endemic to our entire culture. Perhaps he has exaggerated the symptoms as extravagantly as he has diagnosed the disease, but it *is* difficult to gainsay the hard truth that, when we deal with individuals who cannot recognize the nature of genuine experiences, we are dealing with people who manifest psychoses. It is also as difficult to deny that an uncomfortable amount of such behavior is easily visible in our culture, even in highly exalted circles.

We must remember, however, that we may also find confusions between symbols and reality in many pre-technological societies, and that all throughout history men have, by means of religions, ceremonies, dramas, songs, poems, stories and (especially) the art of philosophy, insulated themselves from the realities of life by the creation of various types of pseudo-environments. It is, one supposes, the mass and homogeneous nature of the contemporary pseudo-environment that disturbs social thinkers like Boorstein.

There appears to be little either startling or upsetting about a certain degree of confusion manifest in *individuals* between symbols and reality. Our nervous systems and brains probably have been conditioned to allow for this peculiarity of perception. One is not aware as he writes that he is using a symbol system. Occasionally one confuses the process of composition with a live discourse and responds accordingly with a vocalized expletive, for instance. But the confusion is momentary, and one exercises a large measure of control over the symbols used in written language.

Is someone who cherishes a religious icon blessed by a spiritual leader unrealistic because he ascribes power to that particular symbol? Consider the many psychoanalysts who keep a framed picture of Freud (or Jung or Reik) in their offices. Note also the tendency to preserve the personal possessions and original documents of men like these and other great scientists. Let us not forget the General Semanticists' reverence for trivia surrounding the life and times of Count Korzybski, or our reactions to a man in a police uniform or a laboratory robe, and our recent passion for naming objects after dead martyrs.

Is, therefore, the confusion between the real and symbolic environment a symptom of individual psychological disturbance, or is it an inevitable manifestation of symbol usage? May it be both?

In severely disturbed people, of course, confusion between symbols and reality reaches bizarre dimensions. That this confusion is less one of *kind* than degree indicates an uncomfortable probability that so-called mental illness is frequently a variant of "normal" behavior in an incompatible environment. Fenichel notes that "schizophrenics, for example, show an intuitive understanding of symbolism. Interpretations of symbols, which neurotics find so difficult to accept in analysis, are made spontaneously and as a matter of course by schizophrenics. Symbolic thinking for them *is not merely a method of distortion but actually their archaic type of thinking.*" [32]

Symbolic confusions in severely disturbed individuals have stimulated close investigations of the pathological aspect of symbol usage. These studies have sired "disciplines" which attempt, vainly many believe, to create a cognitive, logical type of discourse in which continual differentiation between the symbolic environment and reality is demanded. One such system asks us continually to bear in mind, for instance, slogans like "A word is not a thing", or "A map is not a territory", in order to insure the relevance of language to cognition. The "school" of General Semantics[33] is motivated (undoubtedly sincerely) to utilize language precisely and to minimize entropy in communication.

What Semanticists do not take into account—and obscure from their mechanistic perspectives—is that symbols *themselves* are as formidable a part of man's psychological reality as the "things" and "territories," his logical realities, to which discourse is reduced in their system. Meaning is rarely clarified by the compulsion to "define" symbols, be they words, pictures or objects. The subtle potentiality for sophisticated thought and the elaboration of emotion of which man is capable is thereby lost. Language—and communication—is reduced by General Semantics to a relatively crude instrument. It has cleared the "semantic mist", but it has been sterilized also of *nearly the entire spectrum of communications in the psychological mode which our symbol-making capacity permits.*

The value of this spectrum to human communications depends upon the relevant analysis of what symbols stand for and how they function. Perhaps such analysis is impossible to accomplish at present for the major symbols in our culture. It may be a task beyond the capacities of human intellect. It would necessarily start with the assumption that *all symbols are analogues* and that all symbolism is a method of making metaphors of different kinds. These analogues and metaphors are psychologically—but *not* necessarily logically—more *convenient* for most people to handle conceptually than whatever they stood for. Or they make possible—again by

[32] Otto Fenichel, *The Psychoanalytic Theory of Neurosis* (New York: W. W. Norton and Company, Inc., 1945), p. 422. (Italics added.) Fenichel, like most Freudians of his period, tends to regard symbol-making as ego regressive, distortive and pre-logical —a magical antithesis to the "reality principle" and logic. The particular symbols of most interest to therapists are those which neurotic patients frequently employ to deny some aspect of reality and which seem to be generated spontaneously in patient after patient. See *Ibid.*, pp. 48–51.
[33] See the classic, S. I. Hayakawa's *Language in Thought and Action* (New York: Harcourt, Brace and Company, 1949), for a well written, simple and frequently amusing explanation in layman's terms of the General Semanticist's position. The naïveté of the movement is immediately apparent in Hayakawa's discourse, particularly in regard to the treatment of symbols in culture. The book contains, however, numerous valuable common sense observations about language.

analogue—a type of conviction or thought or feeling which would other-wise be impossible to generate without a particular symbol or certain symbol system.

The analogous quality of language is self-evident. Our dictionaries and concepts of "definition" attempt, in complicated ways, to untwine the analogues of words. Critics and teachers battle with the more complicated metaphors enclosed in the symbolism of the elaborations of language. Some kinds of symbols—those identified by Freud, for instance—are believed to allow us to formulate benign analogies and metaphors for repressed or unconscious material which would, according to theory, threaten us too dangerously in raw form. A mystical or religious symbol is an analogue of an historical event, a subjective feeling, or a rite or ritual. An icon is a metaphor that stands for a complex array of events, spiritual inclinations, objects, and other matters of relevance to one particular aspect of psychological life.

The analogous function of *all* symbolism does not diminish either the power or the importance either of that which is symbolized or the symbol itself. In other words, one cannot disparage a symbol (or its power) merely *because* it is a symbol and therefore *only* an analogue of something else. Here we have the "genetic fallacy" which, according to Langer "arises from the historical method in philosophy and criticism: the error of confusing the *origin* of a thing with its *import*. . . ." Langer specifically notes that *"all elementary symbolic forms have their origin in something else than symbolic interest."* [34] One might quarrel with the word *"elementary"*; *complex* symbols also have their origins in elementary symbols, which have their origin in an analogue in the world of reality. The statue of Abraham Lincoln, for instance, in the Lincoln Memorial, is a fairly complex symbol of many qualities that it is believed Lincoln himself *today* stands for. They, in turn, are metaphors of the Lincoln who has been symbolized in the process we call "history." This process is an analogy system based upon reality: the things that really happened to President Lincoln during his lifetime. The part of reality which relates to this analogy system is, in fact, very small—a fraction of what actually occurred to the real Lincoln: president, man, Republican, politician, father, writer, sage and so forth. But it is, as Langer would say, this part which yields the *important* analogues of the symbol structure related to the statue in Washington, D. C., as perceived by most of us.

Much the same (but far more complex) types of analogues and metaphors systems are involved also in artistic and religious symbols. The vision of life which they provide our apprehensions modifies reality (*crude* reality in most cases) into a refined series of metaphors which are at once pleasurable and logically and psychologically valuable experiences.

Will we ever ascertain for certain the "reality" which provided Cer-

[34] Langer, *Philosophy in a New Key*, p. 201. (Italics are Langer's.)

vantes the metaphor he created in the person of *Don Quixote?* Of course not; but we may safely conjecture that the Knight of the Woeful Countenance had some (or many) sorts of equivalent in reality that were economically drawn together into Cervante's metaphorical hero.

All artists (and all saints) speak to us by metaphor. Their symbol systems act as analogues of life, "mirrors of nature," not so much *reflecting* reality as *translating* it into suitable and digestable metaphors.

The mirror facilitates communication in even so abstract an art as music, where the *particular* analogies of musical sounds are usually far less precisely articulated than in other arts. Music has traveled the route from program music to high abstraction. Modern composers, tired of the tenuous analogies in their "art form," began introducing taxicab horns, boat and factory whistles into their compositions to orient them to reality in the same manner that program music once had done. The compass point of musical symbolism then swung to its origin: back to nature that had provided the first chance variations of sounds which a primitive musician, ages ago, had first translated into a musical symbol.

Conclusion

Analogy and metaphor are found in the heart of the communication process. From them, we create symbols that are the instruments by which the languages of communication become possible, and through which we transmit an enormous range of logical and psychological data. Symbols are the keystones of the words used in language, and are therefore fundamental to human thought itself. They are, as many observers have recorded, distinctively human when they arrive at certain degrees of complexity, logically, psychologically or both.

The present era has seen human enquiry into the ubiquity of symbols manifest in both primitive and sophisticated cultures, as they are employed in both to serve many of the same ends. In the process, we have achieved some *degree of control* over the use of symbols in Western culture by the speculations associated with certain modern schools of psychology and philosophy. Many old and some ancient symbol systems, having found their way to us through the maze of history, retain their power, usefulness and relevance to contemporary society. Among them, one finds numerous forms of art and religion—both of which appear to employ profound and differential varieties of communication from men to men. That they have persisted into this era of symbol dissection indicates how indispensable the role of the analogue is to the process of human communication, even in a computer technology. The essence of symbolism is merely the deceptively simple ability to create the appropriate analogue (thence symbol) of the appropriate object at the appropriate time.

Chapter 5

SYMBOLISM AND SOCIETY

A N ANALOGUE, like its offspring the symbol, is a substitute for, or surrogate of, direct experience. It permits the capacity of the individual for experiences to be extended beyond his immediate environment. It allows him potential to experience vicariously something which might be too physically impossible, expensive, threatening, difficult or uncomfortable to endure directly.

Symbolism, as simple analogy or as complicated metaphor, mediates direct experience in such a manner that it may be handled acceptably and with facility as part of conscious experience as productively as possible, in most instances. Symbolic form may range from a simple emotional response to a complicated and multi-faceted poem or parable.[1]

The symbol itself is an idea that is transformed into a seemingly unrelated surrogate of that idea, the meaning of which stands for the original idea, either consciously or unconsciously. "Modernity" is an idea, for instance, that may be transformed into the unrelated surrogate of a "space capsule" by an advertising artist; the meaning of the original idea is now assimilated into the space capsule—*providing the latter is shown in the proper environment for the surrogate meaning to apply*: that is, in this instance, that the copy and context of the advertisement must allow the "modernity" aspect of the space capsule's possible meanings sufficient em-

---

1 Throughout history the books and literature which have had the deepest effect upon mankind have been almost invariably told in the form of parable, and usually in verse of some kind. The poetic parable, being a complex form of symbolism, does not demand from the reader a direct individual relationship to the world of experience. Rather, it deals with ambiguous material which the reader may relate to almost *any* environment, any time or any place. Most philosophical allegories and dramas utilize this sort of ambiguous communication, as do also the holy books of all known religions. Their timelessness is less a function of their wisdom than of their ambiguity as parables and their power as symbolism. See especially the *Psalms* and the *Song of Solomon* of the Old Testament for striking examples.

phasis to be noticed. The space capsule (the surrogate) functions as a *symbol*. The process by which the analogy between "modernism" and space capsules is made—by which the surrogate gains its new meaning—is the process of *symbolism*.

The Social Setting

Most of us prefer, usually, to talk about "facts" rather than "ideas" and "symbols." "Realistic" men prefer to think of their environment as made up of, or reflective of, facts. But what are facts? Their definition and identification alone are the source of a lively controversy, as one separates positive and negative, real and unreal, intellectual and concrete notions of facts, one from the other—to say nothing of differentiating *historical* fact, for instance from *scientific* fact, and assigning each a value of "factualness." [2]

J. L. Austin, the British philosopher, has observed that A. J. Ayer, one of the leaders of English linguistics, has unequivocally postulated that empirical facts are the only real "facts" we know, and the matter ends! "*The hard fact is that there are sense-data*," writes Austin, "these entities really exist and are what they are; what other entities we may care to *speak as if* there were is a pure matter of verbal convenience, but the facts to which these expressions are intended to refer will always be the same, facts about sense-data." [3] End of problem.

Ayer circumscribes our "fact environment" within specific limits, but he leaves us only with psycho-physical facts, eliminating the entire area of implied and semantic data, scientific and historical reports—except for the physical written *reports* themselves—that we usually assume as factual. Abstractions remain in his universe, however, because they are sense-data, just as the *number* or *idea* of "seven" is the *content* one finds between the preceding quote marks. (The same is true of "7.")

If we accept Ayer's proposition, we are left with a limited environment, but it is an environment in which symbols are still critical. Our age is an age of a plenitude of facts, such a plethora of sense and of non-sense, that the search for causes, meaning and truth is frequently impossible. To square facts away as just sense-data, following Ayer's suggestion, allows us to avoid some of the problems presented by Langer in making value judgments of facts.

Let us therefore assume that symbolism is largely the *obverse* of the

[2] See Langer, *Philosophy in a New Key*, pp. 217–227, for a discussion of the many philosophical interpretations of "fact" in our thinking today presented in the perspective of what the author calls "the realistic turn of mind which marks our civilization" (p. 223). This phrase is indicative that even a philosopher—an arbiter of "facts"—has a pretty clear notion of what is "realistic" (that is to say, "factually factual") in responsible discourse.

[3] J. L. Austin, *Sense and Sensibility* (Oxford, England: Oxford University Press, 1962), p. 60.

process of fact gathering. The individual tries to widen or deepen his empirical relationship to his environment in discovering what is really *there* despite appearances when he searches for facts. When he looks for *symbols*, however, he looks for what has *displaced* part of the environment—or notions and ideas concerning that environment. A world which consists merely of an environment (such as the one encountered by a Robinson Crusoe) without society, constitutes an unlimited gold mine of potential *facts* to be uncovered, limited by the intellectual capacities of the auditor rather than by the number of observations waiting to be made. The *symbols* with which he might deal, however, are mostly those symbols which he has brought from a previous social field into his new environment (his language, for instance) and the small spectrum of symbols he would be psychologically impelled to generate for his own purposes, *de novo*.

Symbolism is not only a result of the social process; it is a *condition* of social experience, which leads man on to communication, to art, to the record of history and to the great repository of symbolism involved in inductive reasoning and, finally, its resultant sciences.[4] It is naturally a condition of civilization.

One may examine first the complexity and second the sophistication of various societies and will probably find that both of these factors correlate with the importance of symbols to a specific culture at a specific time. The symbolizing feature of culture has been of major interest to many scientists, particularly anthropologists. Some of the latter have discovered that the *only way* of understanding behavior in certain cultures is through the study of symbolism.[5]

Occasionally we notice that symbol-making tendencies in societies begin to elude containment, particularly where social controls are not brought to limit their growth. A. N. Whitehead addresses the heart of the problem in this way:

> No account of the uses of symbolism is complete without this recognition that the symbolic elements in life have a tendency to run wild, like the vegetation in a tropical forest. The life of humanity can easily be overwhelmed by its symbolic accessories. The continuous process of pruning, and of adaptation to a future ever requiring new forms of expression, is a necessary function in every society. The successful adaptation of old symbols to changes of social structure is the final mark of wisdom in socio-

---

[4] While technology develops symbols, it is less dependent upon symbolism than upon sense data and facts. Highly symbolic devices are employed in *scientific reasoning* and *inductive thought*. Experimentalism also deals more with facts than symbols, except when the facts cannot be demonstrated empirically, as in certain phases of nuclear physics, mathematics, biology, and other sciences.

[5] Note Margaret Mead's explanation of her anthropological method of observation (and her dependence upon symbols as primary data) in *Coming of Age in Samoa* (New York: The New American Library, 1952), pp. 11–18, and *Growing Up in New Guinea* (New York: The New American Library, 1953), pp. 11–17. The former book was first published in 1928, the latter in 1930.

logical statesmanship. Also, an occasional revolution in symbolism is required.[6]

Does one bring *moral* criteria to this jungle growth of symbolism to
determine where and when the development of social symbols turns from
benign to malignant? Are morals relevant to the issue? Castro's revolution
of symbolism (which *always* follows a military or political revolution) en-
tailed necessary and drastic surgery, cutting away the accumulation of
countless years of symbolism relating to class, money, education and nationalism—and other matters that once amused tourists. These symbols are
gone now, and in their place there is a new lexicon of symbolism derived
from the Castro-Marx-Moscow triad, familiar to those who have heard (or
seen) Dr. Castro deliver his speeches on television, radio, or read them in
translation.

Was the "revolution in symbolism" good or bad; and for whom? History may provide clear answers to those questions. But, in the meantime,
our present political evaluations are little more than extemporizations of
our own moral convictions. One need not be a moralist, however, to observe that Mussolini's symbolic revision in Italy (attempting a futile neo-
Roman revival) served the Italian people less well than the older symbol
systems previously handed down by history.

In both these cases, note that Whitehead's prediction was vindicated:
a symbolic revolution occurred when the growth of extant symbols had
become too profuse and dense for intellectual containment for the "average
man." That we are living through—and/or on the brink of—a number of
such revolutions also in most English-speaking cultures today is, to many
observers, self-evident.[7]

Symbolism and Social Change

We have observed above that symbolism in the life of a culture is not
static; it tends to grow, change and require constant pruning. This is even
apparent in the most familiar symbol structure we employ: our language.
Words and manners of speech change both their form and content as soci-

---

[6] A. N. Whitehead, *Symbolism*, p. 61. Many of the ideas in this Chapter obviously depend upon Whitehead's lucid concept of the role of symbolism in a social field. His
lectures on symbolism were delivered at the University of Virginia in 1927.
[7] One of the most dramatic symbolic revolutions occurring in the United States today is
that of the American Negro, for whom the entire former panoply of social symbolism
prepared by a white society, and in which they have been forced to live since emanci-
pation, has become meaningless. Even the symbols that evolved from the Negro tradition itself—from Booker T. Washington to the idea of Negro middle class respectability
—are dying or dead. One result of the obsolescence of the old symbols is the Black
Power movement, a powerful social symbol structure and a force from which we will
hear a good deal in the future. See Claude Brown, *Manchild in the Promised Land*
(New York: The New American Library, 1966), pp. 342–349. A full examination of this
remarkable autobiography by a young Negro will demonstrate clearly *why* Whitehead's
description of how symbols (here in Negro urban life) have "run wild" and how a
reconstruction has simplified them into a few powerful constructs.

ety and culture change. There is a continual demand for new linguistic instruments that force old ones to be discarded and fall from the currency of communication.

A *social* revolution of some kind usually precedes revolutions in linguistic symbolisms. Social revolutions are rarely fought with guns; many are the result of seemingly slow cultural processes, for instance the revolution from Victorianism to the "roaring twenties" in the United States, which manifest a metamorphosis of symbolism that is now legendary.

Every revolt, no matter how small or subtle (or any kind of social change), leaves behind a certain amount of symbolic debris in the form of shattered ideals, altered values or, at its most acerbic, dead to bury and ruined lives requiring re-integration with society. Whitehead observes that the revolutions which have escaped a chaotic aftermath are those few which managed to leave intact the fundamental and efficient symbolisms in culture.[8] The American Revolution (or revolt), for example, did not destroy the essential symbolism of the British colonists, particularly their concepts of a capitalist agrarian aristocracy and the institution of slavery. They not only helped to maintain the *status quo* but to justify the eventual territorial expansion at the expense of the Indian people, who were perceived symbolically by the Americans as the same sort of "sub-humanity" as their slaves. Moral issues aside, the revolution created a minimum of disorder in the colonies; and the rapid and efficient consolidation of the new states into a Federation was less a testament to the cooperative spirit of our founding fathers than an affirmation of the fact that a common symbolism had survived the hostilities.

The Russian Revolutions of February and October, 1917, produced a different quality of symbolic metamorphosis. The symbol of the aristocracy, hegemony of French manners and education, refinements of court life under the Tsars, and the power of the Russian Orthodox Church upon millions, were *all* destroyed almost overnight. In their place was eventually generated the new and bewildering symbol of Lenin (first in life and then as a statue in his coffin), the apparent benign countenance of the Georgian autocrat Stalin, and the complex pseudo-scientific symbolism of German-born Marxism. The result—upon which even Soviet historians have finally agreed—was a socio-cultural debacle, an unbelievable period of symbolic disorder which, like the similar period following the French revolution, was redolent with inept social experiment, purges, assassinations, power struggles and chaos of values. One way that the Soviets handled the problem was to re-institute forcibly the old symbolisms wherever practical and whenever such tactics might be squared with a protean Stalinism. The civilities of the old aristocracy emerged here and there; French-style education was broadened at its base; the Russian Orthodox Church was permitted to operate within certain circumscriptions; and naïve Stakhanovite incentives

8 Whitehead, *op. cit.*, pp. 70–71.

were in time replaced by the once—hated symbolism of capitalist incentive.

Whitehead observes that the kind of upheavals experienced in the U.S.S.R. may be avoided if two conditions are met when symbolisms are threatened by social change. They are, oddly, the *desiderata* that many have been searching for in political life in the United States since World War II: a liberal conservativism and/or a conservative liberalism. Whether such an equilibrium can be achieved in symbolic usage is conjectural, but Whitehead steers us in this direction.

"Those societies," he says "which cannot combine reverence to their symbols with freedom of revision, must ultimately decay either from anarchy or from the slow atrophy of a life stifled by useless shadows." [9] The conservative, of course, emphasizes the need in culture for the reverence of symbols which recent changes in life-styles *appear* to have made obsolete; the liberal calls attention to obsolete obeisance paid to *outworn* symbolisms, particularly those of economic class and social caste.

No matter how much we desire that some of our present symbolisms survive (as conservatives hope), we do *not have at our command enough* reliable sense-data to maintain them on a national scale. Religion in its organized form today is unfortunately one of them. There are many more, but the attrition of none is as tragic. For the survival of other symbolisms (as liberals hope) we *have too much* sense-data to take them seriously. In this category one may find the symbolisms of emancipated womanhood, the aristocracy of the intelligentsia, the mystique of individual initiative, equality before the law, the wisdom of the majority, and so forth.

The result is a confusion of symbols in American life today. It has been described trenchantly by the psychologist Arnheim, as it relates to ornamental design:

> In our civilization the handling of ornament betrays the decay and confusion of values. Some things are assigned values they do not have. The inherent value of others is no longer understood, and therefore inappropriate values are attached to them. The dwelling of an insurance company is considered a temple or a palace; the bathtub, having lost the high symbolism of its function that Pilate's washing bowl still possessed, is equipped with the lion feet of a throne. And "functionalism" in its disconcerting honesty, reveals that to modern man a house is nothing but a container of bodies, and a chair a support of human anatomy. [10]

Social Utility of Symbolism

"It seems," says Whitehead "as though mankind must always be masquerading," [11] for the simple reason, of course, that societies are never

[9] *Ibid.*, p. 88.
[10] Rudolph Arnheim, *Art and Visual Perception*, (Berkeley and Los Angeles: The University of California Press, 1965), p. 138.
[11] Whitehead, *op. cit.*, p. 62.

"caught," by historians, archeologists or anthropologists, without an elaborate symbolism enveloping reality.

Perhaps the charm found in the ideas of a "natural" man—from Rousseau to *Tarzan of the Apes* and in the "back to nature" movements like nudism, so popular in Britain and in Western Europe—lies in a sentimental belief that man once lived in a world without symbolism. Clothes, cooked food or certain rituals (like marriage, for instance) become the target of small-time symbolic revolutionists and cultists. But, in turn, even they themselves must "masquerade" symbolically, pretending that a sunburn stands for a healthy body or that the cabals of their cult somehow unify man with nature. (Note the symbolic power of simple yoga breathing exercises.)

Symbols unfortunately abounded at man's right hand in the Garden of Eden, and the fallen sons of Adam have accomplished little more, since the expulsion, than find new places to hold their masks.[12] As one set of symbols was discarded—by revolution or evolution—a new one invariably managed to take its place.

In effect, the *object* of symbolism determines its social usage. Writes Whitehead, "The object of symbolism is the enhancement of the importance of *what is symbolized*." [13] Upon closer examination, the statement reveals a profound understanding not only of symbol, but of a social paradox that lies at the source of *all* our conventions:

> . . . man, proud man,
> Drest in a little brief authority,
> Most ignorant of what he's most assur'd,
> His glassy essence, like an angry age,
> Plays such fantastic tricks before high heaven
> To make the angels weep.

The Bard's pen was not the first to record the unimpressiveness, by men's criteria, of the human being when held beside the other works of nature, the transitory status of his civilizations, the frailty of his own body, the hypocrisy of premises upon which his laws and ethics are built. That man has been endowed with fancy enough to transform these limitations into "realistic fictions" of symbolism appears to be an ingenious psychological method he has devised to elevate to social importance the bulk of his essentially transitory and frequently futile endeavors. Armed with symbols of

---

[12] Many of us are delighted when a professional eccentric like Allen Ginsberg removes all his clothes at a poetry reading to demonstrate that he "sees through" the weary symbolism of costumes. Yet, Mr. Ginsberg himself needs to construct his own masquerade, especially since he himself is presently a symbol of various avant-garde movements. One may observe his stylized presence trudging along Manhattan's Bleeker Street in a bizarre costume of long hair, hunched shoulders, ragged clothes and ancient eyeglasses, "dressed up" for a symbolism he himself was instrumental in creating.
[13] Whitehead, *op. cit.*, p. 63. (Italics added.)

God, country, and "way of life," at least, culture is provided with value. Without symbols, such concepts would be reduced to psycho-physiological basics, like the search for pleasure versus pain, or mere conditioning and imitation.

Men have invariably employed their symbols in exceedingly clever ways. Of all of our magnificent inventions, none is as powerful, for instance, as the simple symbolic device of patriotism. We have also discovered innumerable ways and means of changing the meaning of symbols without changing the symbolism itself. An example is the Catholic mass, the cultural meaning of which has changed vastly over the centuries, but which as ceremony has remained more or less constant over the years, even considering recent modifications.

We have also discovered ways and means for the same symbol to gain different meanings and apply to different data for different people. The smaller the *ceremonial* aspect of a symbolism, the greater may be its general relevance within one society or to different cultures. Shaking hands, for instance, is a simple ceremony widely recognized; crossing one's self is a far more complicated, culture-laden symbol, and is less ubiquitously accepted *in American culture* than a handshake. In non-Christian cultures, it is meaningless. In a larger frame of reference, a phallic symbol is more universally understood everywhere in the world than a Japanese Noh drama even (or especially) in Japan today.

Once again we face the question of whether symbolism is primarily a manifestation of logical or psychological activity; and once again we are faced with equivocation. What symbolism appears to accomplish is the addition, as Whitehead has observed, of the elements of *instinct* (or appetency) and emotion *to* rationalization.[14] Symbolism is therefore *not* predominately a logical mode of apprehension. But neither is it mainly psychological, because it serves a larger cultural logic than the examination of the sense of any single symbol permits us to observe.

Most *psychological* observations do not lead one to a larger *logic*—or to conclusions independent of the physical and emotional process of the subject one is observing. *Symbolism does*; hence its tie with the universal force of instinct on one hand, and the continual tendency toward rationalization on the other. When the President of the United States takes his oath of office on a Bible, there is nothing essentially non-rational about the *symbolism* itself, whether performed on the steps of the Capitol or in the cabin of an Air Force jet plane. Neither is it an entirely rational act *per se*, because symbolism has added—as Whitehead explains—the mystique of significance to a dreary and minor enterprise—swearing on a book—that anyone may duplicate with ease. But the meaning of *one particular ceremony* is enhanced [15] and the symbolism therefore justified.

14 *Ibid.*, p. 70.
15 Presidential inaugurations are rare examples of this kind of ceremonial symbolism.

Whitehead's observation reverses the common notion that symbolism is useful because it allows man an unreasonable expression of the rational world: that is, a psychological by-product of logic. Instead, we consider symbolism as a device which allows man, thanks to certain psychological factors, to establish a firm foothold *on* reason or logic. Take the above-mentioned "swearing in" ceremonies of various kinds. These events—like most symbolized cultural manifestations—are highly rational conventions. Most sense-data articulated in symbolic form is considered logical, rational or "true" data in the society which constructs the symbols. Seemingly non-logical devices, like uniforms and oaths, are employed to give to what *is* already rational the additional psychological power inherent in symbolism.

In a complex mass society today, with its numerous sub-cultures, there run many currents of intricately expressed symbolisms of language and act that have been, at best, partially charted by behavior and social scientists, dramatists and novelists. To understand any one of these currents fully, it is probable that one must live in that sub-culture, partake of its symbol structure, and at the same time retain the role of auditor. This is difficult to accomplish.

A writer may *say*, "I am a camera," but his involvement in the activities around him usually demonstrates first, that cameras are poor instruments for making non-engaged observations, and, second, that objectivity is almost invariably sacrificed to participation in human affairs.

Symbolism itself, if we can accept Whitehead's interpretation, evokes from the members of a group continually fluctuating apprehensions of many mutual agreements of a predominately metaphorical nature. These apprehensions add color, flavor or importance to essentially dull and mundane acts, like earning a living, reproducing the race, protecting private property, exercising social control over our aggressive impulses, and other unexciting, and sometimes arbitrary chores, necessary to maintain society. Symbolism makes these behaviors seem not only *necessary* but rewarding because of the metaphorical benefits that symbolic behavior provides for its own sake.

To make them even more attractive, the artist may then arrive on the scene and capture the *essence* of this symbolism, modifying it to suit the needs of his medium, and re-expressing it with added clarity or conviction. He is a symbolic showmaster, a cultural interior decorator, a translator of a given symbolism into paradygms, either for a trained élite (as in fine art) or for the masses (in popular culture). In either case, his function is not only to render social symbolism more acceptable, but also to make it appear correct and desirable—or as in the case of an Alfred Jarry and other ma-

---

Marriage ceremonies are more common. The main symbolic difference between the two appears to be the rapidity with which the added importance is forgotten in the latter (or minimized in a *particular* ceremony) and the staying power of the symbolism in the former. There is no reason, intrinsic to the symbolisms themselves, however, why our Presidents should treat their vows of office any more seriously than men and women take their marriage vows. In America, at present, let us be thankful that they do!

cabre artists who have followed him—so repulsive that its symbolic "givens" are called for question.

Another function of symbolism is the evocation of relatively clear responses to vaguely conceived notions which have been clarified in the metaphor system of symbolism. For instance, in our society automobiles must stop and start in a regular pattern for traffic to flow properly. To meet this need directly in a conventional urban situation would require hoardes of skilled policemen making continual judgments to achieve an efficient flow of traffic. Since sufficient numbers of policemen are rarely available to achieve this control, the symbolic device of the traffic light—a partially satisfactory instrument of traffic control—clarifies with its two or three unmistakable color symbols, the necessity for certain automobiles to stop and start at certain intervals. What is unclear and difficult to understand in an entirely rational mode, is transmitted by symbolism into a series of stimulus and response systems that (while they are not perfect) *are* efficient and nonambiguous as communications: traffic lights.

Were we to describe in metaphor the function of symbolism in culture, we might relate it to a sort of glue which holds together the world of sense-data and symbols. These data, accordingly, become acceptable and facilitate communications and clarify meaning. Logical and rational matters are given emotional psychological value and related to the stream of psychological apprehensions distinctive of a given culture. In the process, facets of the environment which are unclear, disheartening or absurd are made acceptable by symbolism, given meaning, value and power which, taken objectively, they did not possess. In fact, they may make life itself bearable by revising sense-data around us to fit the dimensions of our illusions and the configuration of our dreams.[16]

Symbolism and Perception

The relationship between symbolism and perception remains in some degree a mystery. Many symbolic processes, such as the use of language, are largely unconsciously employed and constitute the very instruments of ideation by which we conceive of "symbols" themselves.

Whitehead suggests, however, two ways in which the perception of

---

[16] "It's not the thing but the principle of the thing," is a phrase that places this utility of symbolism into common parlance. Citing examples of the cultural role of symbolism is a difficult task, best suited to novelists and poets. But without symbols, might a gynecologist ever be able to fall in love? Would an actor ever "believe" another actor's performance? What would stop a General from shooting any subordinate who disagrees with him? (Occasionally, a General whose sensitivity to symbolism becomes distorted, does just this. The symbol of "the enemy" becomes any one who is against *him*.) We notice symbolism in our culture mostly when it *fails* to perform its necessary function. For instance, counterfeiters, it is believed, fail to understand the symbolism of the phrase "It is important to make money!" See Murray Teigh Bloom, *Money of Their Own* (New York: Ballantine Books, 1960), especially the Introduction, pp. 7–19, for a further exploration of the symbolism of money as it appears to the counterfeiter—a colorful type of criminal who is invariably a specialist!

sense-data plays a role in the operation of symbolism within an individual, and is therefore given social relevance.[17] Each is a polar point on a sliding scale, analogous to the compromises that always must be made between the logical and psychological aspect of symbol usage.

Symbolism may function, first, from the perspective of what Whitehead terms the "causal efficacy" of things. Symbolic application in this mode reveals the relationship of the past to the future, or the way in which some aspect of the environment got to be the way it *is*. Let us say a private in the Army (dressed in a proper uniform) salutes his Captain, also suitably dressed. The ritual, with its wealth of symbols, may be examined for a multitude of causes and effects in the sense-data of the history of warfare, nationalism, and an almost endless list of social behaviors germane to the act.

No symbol is free of causal efficacy, at least none that comes to mind, because *every* symbol has a history. Basing his discussion upon the burden of *time* through which all symbols grow, Whitehead accordingly challenges the importance of the immediate impact of sense-data upon individual consciousness. In his argument with classic philosophers like Hume and Kant, he stresses the significance of the interposition of causal efficacy between the individual and the sense-data with which he is dealing. This gap is filled by symbolism, the power of which *decreases*, notes Whitehead, the *greater* is the "vivid enjoyment of immediate sense-data." [18]

The second mode of perception is the ideational opposite of causal efficacy as described in the preceding paragraph, and termed by Whitehead "presentational immediacy," which is made up of the numerous immediate sense impressions to which we all react. Here, we perceive not only sense-data and discrete symbols. The emphasis in perception is *not* on time or cause and effect, "but at the moment we are absorbed in using this *immediate show as a symbol* for forces determining the immediate future." [19]

The *history* of any symbol is therefore irrelevant to our reaction, which is determined only by the immediate symbol and the social field to which it is wedded. After a day sightseeing in the city of Algiers, one probably reacts with presentational immediacy to the glitter of a knife perceived in the hand of a beggar whose photograph one tries to take in the legendary Casbah. One runs away. *Later*, the symbolism of the act might be explained in terms of causal efficacy: one frequently angers a Moslem by taking his picture without giving anything in return. But at the time one is running, one does not worry much about symbolic causes!

Apparently, differential perceptions, in the context of cause and effect and in the context of presentational immediacy, always yield *one* perception in the individual, with a dominant emphasis either in its historicity or

[17] Whitehead, *op. cit.*, 30–59.
[18] *Ibid.*, p. 42.
[19] *Ibid.*, p. 57. (Italics added.)

in immediate experience, but infused with some measure of each. So Whitehead expresses it, "The *how* of our present experience must conform with the *what* of the past in us." [20] He notes that the role of symbol in this process is to give man the benefit of linking the past, present and future into one, in order to "define with some accuracy those distant features in the immediate world by which (our) future lives are to be determined." [21] These definitions in social terms are symbols, series of analogues that, in effect, unite the *how* of the present with the *what* of the past—to yield the *may* of the future, continuing Whitehead's aphorism.

The main point that the consideration of the two modes teaches is that symbolic perception is not a single, special type of experience; it may be as varied as analogues vary and as differential as human experiences are one from the other. The apprehension of symbols is a *single mode of behavior*, which may occur in an unconscious manner just as easily as it is manifest in a most carefully rehearsed and self-conscious way.

Whitehead demonstrates such symbolic latitude in the perception of the symbol of the "once-man" Julius Caesar in our present symbolism.[22] There is the historical "Caesar," as a symbol of what he was as a man who was born and died; "Caesar" may stand as a symbol of Imperial Rome, the writer of diaries, the dictator, the conquerer or any single occasion *in* his historical life; or "Caesar" can be considered as a symbolic pattern, a constancy—a myth—repeated each time Caesar's life is written, or an actor plays the myth as written by Shakespeare or Shaw. Here then, without involving ourselves in any particular psychological peculiarities of perception, we are treated to three quiet distinct symbolic perspectives in which to view an historical object who presents us with little sense-data, except for a few memoirs and some things people have said about him.

In a pluralistic society—or world—there exists a mighty confusion of symbolisms and even, perhaps, a cultural incompatability of symbols of a universal nature that effects *every* aspect of human existence.[23] Whether or not this difference may be bridged, or common symbolisms found, or whether world-wide communication of symbols is, in fact, desirable are not questions for consideration here.

A relevant social danger that we face immediately in our own time is the trivialization of the symbolic process itself, by virtue of its exploitation by three major (and other minor) contemporary institutions, namely, the *propaganda* industries, including those employing radio, television and films; *education*, on all levels from grammar school to college, and *bureauc-*

---

[20] *Ibid.*, p. 58.
[21] *Ibid.*, p. 59.
[22] *Ibid.*, pp. 27–28.
[23] How discouraging that unanimity could *not* even be achieved by the United Nations (not representative of *all* of the cultures of the world, by any means) on so simple and basic a set of symbolic propositions as those in UNESCO'S *Declaration of Human Rights,* basic civilities inherent to most of the various symbolisms of the nations of the world.

racy, particularly as it is manifest in local, state and federal authorities.[24]

Briefly, the *propaganda* industries' major accomplishment in our culture is that they have "sold" the notion to their followers in industry, government and education[25]—that by means of the clever use of new technological instruments of communication, they have hypnotized the average American into behaving like an acquisitive, other-oriented consumer whose most significant personal symbols relate solely to materialism. *Nothing is further from the truth!* What they have accomplished is to palliate feebly certain old symbol structures and enhance somewhat the value of others already present in society.

Our institutions of *education* have not materially affected our symbol structures *except* to trivialize them, because they have followed rather than led intellectual life in the United States. They are therefore reflective rather than directive of our symbolisms. On the lower levels, they have been concerned with adapting children to symbols of society rather than developing in children the ability to influence their symbolic environments. Our colleges and universities, in large measure, have become diploma mills up to the Ph.D. level, producing the requisite number of engineers, doctors, and lawyers—and also the correct quotient of liberally educated "bright young men and women"—to keep the symbolic wheels of culture lubricated, while at the same time encouraging just enough symbolic loyal opposition to the academic party line to keep them from running too fast.

Lastly, *bureaucracy* has developed a complex symbolism of an authority which operates an instrument for the maintenance and self-perpetuation of big business, big government, big foundations, and big education, along with other impersonal arbiters of man's fate in a mass society. Most of us have had to learn to live with bureaucracy—to become, in fact, dependent one way or another upon it. Mercifully, we do not spend more than a fraction of our lives tangled in the symbols of bureaucracy; forty hours a week (out of a total of 168) is the most that many of us have to endure; others are whipped for shorter or longer periods. For others, there remains a good deal of time when we are reasonably free of impersonal and arbitrary authority inflicted on us by "the organization."

The quality of a culture is revealed in the quality of the symbols it

---

[24] Some observers would lump all of these institutions together, calling them "propaganda arms" of an industrial establishment in the U.S.A. Sociologists like the late C. Wright Mills and Jacques Ellul might stress their similarities and their mutual sources of power.

[25] Some years ago the writer collaborated on a book, with what he believed was a considered and moderate tone, on international propaganda. The one relatively consistent criticism of the volume from his colleagues on the campus is that his co-authors and he had underestimated the power of American commercial propaganda to "sell the American way of life" abroad. This, from his colleagues—while six other publishers subsequently entered the literary market with volumes recommending turning the United States Information Agency over to the artists of Madison Avenue!

respects or disdains. The inspection of *our* society and *our* symbols will be the function of the next Chapter.

Conclusion

Symbols are the means that men use to extend the sense-data they find in life. The process by which this occurs, which appears to be both logical (and necessary) and psychological (and efficient), is the process of symbolism. It is fair to assume that symbolism is the correlate, in many ways, of sheer fact-gathering. It makes possible the social experiences which, in turn, make it expedient for people to communicate one with the other for their common benefit. Communication on a social level would probably be impossible without symbolism.

Symbolism is so useful a force in helping society to function that the process—unless checked by countervailing forces—tends to run beyond the usual limits of social control. A revolution in symbolisms is therefore occasionally necessary, sometimes reducing extant symbols to older forms, or finding new meanings for old symbols. Social change itself—including the kind done with bullets and bayonets—also frequently creates rapid changes in symbolisms. Those revolutions, as Whitehead has noted, which have torn the social fabric least are those which have allowed major pre-revolutionary symbolisms to survive partially intact. At least, this is the lesson that history teaches.

Symbolism's main social function is to enhance in importance and significance the relatively and apparently inconsequential nature of many of the activities of man. Whitehead has observed that instinctive (and emotional) elements are added by symbolism to the rational content of life. There appears to be a "cultural logic" in symbolism, by which sacred objects, rites and ceremonies are created that we regard as worth living for, striving to maintain, and sometimes dying to uphold. These we understand to be mutual agreements of a metaphorical nature which clarify the ambiguities that individuals often perceive diversely in the social order.

Perceptively, symbolism is the means by which cause and effect in the behaviors of men are manifest, as well as the way, previously noted, that immediate impressions are sharpened, clarified and emphasized. Symbolism, therefore, permits individuals to enjoy numerous modes of individual or collective perceptions. This appears to be both a healthy and inevitable concomitant of the symbolic process. Our main contemporary problem regarding symbolism is possibly the trivialization of symbols by means of contemporary institutions of culture that are frequently (and incorrectly) blamed for their power to originate symbols, rather than for their ineffectiveness as mediators of symbolism.

Chapter 6

THE SYMBOLIC UMBRELLA

THE POINT of this chapter is to demonstrate that symbolism and the understanding of its metaphorical process is of prior importance to all other investigations in understanding communications, logically or psychologically, or of the processes by which they occur.[1] This process, many believe, is a swift and usually accurate key to a perception of certain values in a given culture (and/or subculture). While it cannot substitute for the detailed delineations of historians, sociologists, psychologists or aestheticians, it is prerequisite to most of their observations.

Were this page written little more than a generation ago, it would have been reduced to a single sentence and presented as an axiom. During the period directly before World War II, the intellectual and artistic community in the United States gave close attention to the symbolic umbrella that covered their culture, an umbrella woven of the cloth, largely, of symbols of technology, Freudianism and Marxism. In the arts[2] and in the sociopolitical arena, the power of symbolism was becoming increasingly apparent. In a self-conscious manner, it was believed that comprehension of the nature of the symbolic umbrella was necessary before it was possible to control the aesthetic and political life of a culture. In Nazi Germany, Dr.

[1] The nature of this understanding depends upon the culture studied and the distance the auditor must travel through time, space and language to interpret its symbolism. The objective of the interpretation is to make a direct connection between symbol and meaning, whether the meaning be a logical definition of the symbol or a description of its psychological potentialities, or both.

[2] See Ozenfant, *Foundations of Modern Art* (New York: Dover Publications, Inc., 1952). The original edition of this volume was published in the U.S.A. in 1931. It constitutes a comprehensive study of the nexus between modern symbolism and modern art in a well illustrated, non-systematic manner. Ozenfant's vision of art includes the universal acceptance of numerous symbolisms in many art forms of the post World War I generation.

Goebbels was apparently demonstrating the truth of this assumption. In America, phenomena like the rise of the Institute for Propaganda Analysis were our social scientists' immediate—and almost reflexive—answers to the potential dangers of malignant symbolisms abroad.[3] The dull dissection of the speeches of American neo-Nazis were the prices we had to pay, it appeared, for the control of totalitarian symbolisms in our culture.

Total war demands total allegiance, and the symbols of society are no less part of its military potential than its munitions factories. The artists and social scientists in the allied nations were therefore asked (or told) to suspend critical judgment of the symbol structures in society, support them and, where possible, use them for purposes immediately compatible with the war effort.

During this period, a class of symbol manipulators rose in the United States which, in the best faith, developed considerable skill in the *manipulation* of symbols. Their output is recorded in our social histories under the category of "War Propaganda", and we shall not pursue it in detail here. The *results*, however, of this "total propaganda" period (lasting roughly from 1940 to 1946) were many, and we *shall*, of necessity, examine these.

First, our attempt at total propaganda—including the abolition of the scholarly proclivity to examine critically the symbols with which we in the United States lived—was more or less successful. Political, social and economic symbols, ramifications of the concepts of businessmen, Democracy, Capitalism, Technology and Liberalism were integrated into propaganda for the war. Freudian symbolism seemed beyond the province of politics, but men like Erich Fromm,[4] exiles themselves from Nazism, ingeniously

---

[3] A record of the kinds of attention given to the power of symbolism can be found in Michael Choukas' *Propaganda Comes of Age* (Washington, D. C.: Public Affairs Press, 1965), pp. 13–18, pp. 257–292, where the author reiterates the approach the Propaganda Analysis Institute employed in this period and quotes from many of its documents. The Institute, like other symbolically sensitive movements of the period, did not survive World War II. Dr. Choukas' book is written, however, in the same behavioristic, socially oriented manner employed by the propaganda analysts of the nineteen-thirties and is useful as a reconstruction of the symbol-identifying assumptions of the period. He writes, for instance, "The modern propagandist is a social engineer attempting to construct behavior patterns as the physical engineer builds bridges. . . . Just as the latter has to depend on knowledge supplied to him by the physical sciences, so the propagandist must rely upon the knowledge and mental tools the psychological and social sciences can give him. . . . (Images), purely intellectual initially, have become charged with emotion; they have become *symbols*. These symbols serve as the link that connects the intellectual to the emotional functions of the human mind; a lever, that anyone interested in stirring up people emotionally may utilize for that purpose." (Pp. 93–94.) The book, like the late Propaganda Analysis Institute itself, continues in this mechanistic manner. For a further discussion of the fate of the Institute, see John Mulholland and George N. Gordon, *The Magical Mind* (New York: Hastings House, 1967), p. 124, and Aldous Huxley, *Brave New World Revisited* (New York: Harper and Brothers, 1957), pp. 131–133.
[4] Fromm's socio-political-psychological *magnum opus* is *Escape from Freedom* (New York: Rinehart and Company, Inc., 1942).

managed to bring Freud and analogues for anti-totalitarianism (like free-dom, justice and democracy) into one social-psychological-political conceptual mold.

War propaganda in the U.S.A. and England succeeded—in that our side won the war; just as we may record that Hitler's propaganda failed because his side lost. We had justified our "way of life" (or "way of symbolism") in the crucible of war, and warfare is without doubt the best symbolic test for "virtue" that men have yet devised!

Second, the symbolists (artists, writers, technicians and actors), had convinced *themselves* quite thoroughly that the symbols they had so readily and easily "sold" to the public were not symbols at all—that is not *analogues* of reality—but reality itself. In effect, the army of communicators at war—returned a generation ago to civilian life full in the belief that the symbols required in time of modern warfare, the fables of "good" and "bad" nations, the perfection of freedom, democratic man, free enterprise society, and military technology—were part of the real sense data of Western life. They were prepared to communicate with the public, therefore, predominantly in these terms during the post war period.[5]

Third, a wave of political opportunists from both the far left and right grasped, during the late forties and early fifties, at the naïveté of these communicators. For complex, self-seeking motives, they demonstrated by fair and foul means that the communications industries and their tributaries in the U.S.A. were guilty of incredible stupidity in overlooking the political realities of their time! The charge was true enough; they *were* living in an obsolete haze of antique symbolisms. On the one hand, the symbol manipulators were easily duped by communists and radicals on the left. On the other, they were exploited by self-seeking rabble-rousers who led them into the poison of "blacklisting", and badgered them into publicizing the paranoid tantrums of Senator Joe McCarthy.

Fourth, in the confusion (and partial enlightenment) which followed the "McCarthy era," the symbol makers discovered that the symbolic umbrella was still open, but the symbols of which it was constructed no longer sheltered society from reality, as in wartime. *Some* safe symbols were left: Freudian symbolism was returned to its former apolitical role in develop-

---

[5] A few novelists like Irwin Shaw, Norman Mailer and James Jones offered serious, immediate and powerful dissents from these assumptions. Invariably, their efforts were dissipated by the highly publicized release of romantic motion pictures "based" on their novels in the mode of the symbolism of the period, directed to that small segment of the public that might have been disturbed by their books. The writers themselves were urged on to affirm accepted prevailing symbols, such as those associated with liberal politics and/or Greenwich Village. They did. A later wave of humorists (*Tea House of the August Moon, Don't Go Near the Water, Catch 22,* etc.) tried another assault on the self-righteous veterans of war propaganda and were also ignored for reasons related to the declining state of humor in our culture discussed in Chapter 18.

mental psychology,[6] but the symbols themselves were disputed by neo-Freudians, particularly followers of the late Carl Jung. Psycho-symbolism, by the end of the nineteen-fifties, had become a Sunday Magazine Section cliché. With the release of a tidal wave of pornography into the over-the-counter marketplace and the wide dissemination of new birth control devices, the venerable Victorian sex symbols of psychoanalysis now attracted largely the sentimental or the aged.

Fifth, as the nineteen-fifties advanced, it became evident that a new repertoire of symbols was demanded to meet the needs of a new age. Fusing the symbols spontaneously generated by (mostly) middle-class leaders with certain necessary analogues needed to maintain the political and financial establishments, our instruments of *propaganda,* our *educators* and our *bureaucracies* designed the symbolic matrix of the nineteen-sixties.

They were—and are—aided by the force of a generally assenting young generation that has been raised to think that symbols are real and rarely question or challenge the symbolic lexicon employed by our mass communicators, professors and bureaucrats.[7] What, precisely, are these symbols, and to what facets of reality are they analogous?

Contemporary Symbology

In his major work on propaganda, Jacques Ellul [8] identifies the mythological structure of modern industrial culture: "Thus one can distinguish: the fundamental myths of our society are the myths of Work, Progress, Happiness. . . ." [9] He notes also that the fundamental ideologies of our time, Nationalism, Democracy and Socialism (including Communism) all partake variously of these basic myths.

Ellul's observation cuts close to the quick of our contemporary society, at least for middle-class (and much lower-class) culture in our country. Young people, of middle-class backgrounds particularly, seem peculiarly repelled at the suggestion that these are the *major* myths by which *they* live.

[6] The exceptions were a few analysts like the indefatigable Fromm who channeled his arguments into Freudian-style socialism and even pontificated on international politics. Others, like Hendrick M. Ruitenbeck in *The Individual and the Crowd* (New York: The New American Library, 1964), directed their Freudian probing into political and social corners of American life and emerged with dreary pictures of our culture.

[7] True, the young "protest" frequently these days. They are urged to such behavior in large part by an older generation of symbolic-idealists, many of them educators, who are in favor of this expenditure of energy as long as the protest is directed against symbols, not against reality. In other words, the protests are culturally permissible as long as the participants (as one can observe from examining reports of their actions) *do not comprehend the reality of that which they are protesting.* This is exactly the nature of most anti-war protests, the most frivolous and unrealistic of all the mass actions of the young at present, and various other simple-minded activities of the "New Left" whose "programs" correspond with available sense data even less adequately than those of the previous generation's *aucien* left.

[8] Jacques Ellul, *Propaganda, The Formation of Men's Attitudes* (New York: Alfred A. Knopf, 1965).

[9] *Ibid.,* p. 117.

They far prefer to think that the most important recent myths are conventions like "romantic love," "motherhood," "bravery," and other modern symbolic scratching posts. They argue that Ellul's symbols constitute, in fact, basic imperatives for them in our tradition which provide a meaning for life. To challenge the reality of these concepts, therefore, appears to challenge the validity of their world.

Precisely *because* young people appear to resist Ellul's ideas so competently, they are recommended to one's attention. Should the sanctity of the concept of *work* be destroyed—as recommended by economist John K. Galbraith[10]—should the idea of inevitable *progress* be questioned—as it was in the nineteen-twenties by José Ortega y Gasset [11]—and should the dream of *happiness* be shown to be a sham—as implied in the later works of a sick, but still realistic, Sigmund Freud [12]—might not our schools be emptied, our propagandists have to take their medicine shows elsewhere, and the merchants of joy and comfort be forced to dismantle their empires? If Ellul's myths and their attendant symbols were discarded and, as a nation, we were *forced* to accept the *realities* of Work, Progress and Happiness, we would —even at first glance—be forced to a period of generally agonizing symbol analysis.

In the first place, most *Work* in modern society is frequently dull, monotonous, apparently pointless and—worst of all—demeaning of the individual, in that it asks of him far less of his potential capacities than he is competent to give.

Progress is a strange symbol; it depends on one's viewpoint for a definition. Scientific and industrial Progress may well have already been bought at the price of the side effects of race degeneration and/or destruction. At any event, most Progress is psychologically ephemeral. Nobody *needed* air-conditioned bedrooms until it became possible to purchase instruments to cool bedrooms cheaply. A person with a full beard is indifferent to Progress in electric shavers. Progress usually means the construction of a social instrument which will create sufficient immediate discomfort in people so

---

[10] See John Kenneth Galbraith, *The Affluent Society* (Boston: Houghton Mifflin Company, 1958), pp. 336–348. While Galbraith and many of his social and economic notions have been taken seriously by the political establishment (particularly during the short Kennedy administration), his ideas about the non-sanctity of work have been largely ignored. They have been selected not because they are part of what Galbraith is fond of calling "conventional wisdom," but because they contravene a powerful mythology and question the value of cherished symbols.

[11] See José Ortega y Gasset, *The Revolt of the Masses* (New York: W. W. Norton and Company, 1957), pp. 35–37, 135–136, 181–182, 187–190. Ortega's pessimism has been derided by many who forget that he predicted quite clearly—and pessimistically—the barbarous depths to which Europe would sink under the Nazis and other fascists. This book was first published in English in 1930.

[12] See Freud's energetic destruction of the concept of spiritual happiness in *The Future of an Illusion* (Garden City, New York: Doubleday and Company, 1957), pp. 66–70, 86–102, and social happiness in practically all of *Civilization and Its Discontents* (Garden City, New York: Doubleday and Company, no date).

that they will choose to "benefit" from the invention or system to which we next progress, frequently an ameliorative for the previous advance in Progress. Examples are too numerous to mention.

And *Happiness?* This item may be dispensed in bottles, pills, dropped into sugar cubes or smoked in pipes or cigarettes. If the myth includes the symbols of peace of mind or soul, contentment and meaningful engagement, it means pursuing—realistically—the most difficult psychological objectives of which one can conceive today, and which few (if any) people experience for more than moments at a time.

The centrality, in our society, of the Work-Progress-Happiness myths —or verbal equivalents—offered by Ellul appear reasonable, as they are communicated to our people by the Bureaucratic, Propaganda and Educational institutions. They provide the major symbolic reservoirs that support these particular institutions and that sanction the symbols which they mediate to society at large. Also, they represent *serious business.* To trifle with them (as we have here been doing) is a form of heresy, certainly antisocial, unpatriotic and corruptive. These are precisely the reactions which *all* cultures show when serious symbolisms, woven into the symbolic umbrella, are attacked. To trifle with the sanctity of Work—which the beatniks did a decade ago—was tantamount to dismembering a prayer wheel in Tibet. No one is able, *for long,* to play with the myth-giving symbols of a society. The price is either death, exclusion from that society, or containment within a jail or asylum, depending upon the symbols of benevolence simultaneously accepted by the culture. These symbol reservoirs, incidentally, represent precisely the "benefits" of society from which our racial minorities claim they have been isolated in their ghettos.

Within these mythic structures, the symbol-givers in our culture have disseminated the modern metaphors of our time. In order to make short work of them, they are listed below under each of Ellul's major mythological categories. They are *not* intended to constitute a total picture of the symbolic umbrella over our society but what is probably the most dynamic —and the most obvious—part of it. Seventy-two symbols have been included in no particular hierarchy of importance, because symbolic values shift almost daily and are functions of geography, social, political and economic conditions, climate and numerous other factors. Certain important symbols are no doubt missing; for instance, the automobile is not listed, and instead subsumed under the general category "Available technology." Others may seem trivial or misplaced; for instance "Space conquest" is *not* implied under the heading "Available technology." Space technology seems to generate vastly different *symbols* in our culture from the symbols of machines which one may own, or use, or control himself. Each symbol, in a different way—from both logical and psychological perspectives—symbolizes a different kind of myth-metaphor current in our culture. (The list also, of course, reflects the personal biases and judgments of the author):

INSTITUTIONS: MYTHOLOGICAL SYMBOLS
(1969)

INSTITUTIONS

		Bureaucracy	Propaganda	Education
	Work:	Security Service Participation Law Taxes Respectability Conformist Be- havior Power	High Standard of Living Union Member- ship Corporate Alli- ance Leisure Time Productivity Individual Ad- vancement Success Push and Pull	Teaching The College Pro- fessor Liberal Arts Research Merit Grading Systems High I.Q. Universities Publication of Non-fiction
M Y T H S	Progress:	Efficiency Computerization Social Control Bigness Corporate Wis- dom Democracy Benevolence Accumulated Money	Consumer Abun- dance Product Perfec- tion Available Tech- nology Space Conquest Communications Atomic Age Travel Birth Control	Literacy Universal School- ing Scientific Method Mental Health Teaching Methods Human Relations Vocational Train- ing Scholarships
	Happiness:	Insurance Retirement Growing GNP National Virtue Competition Well-spent Life Money and Credit Expense Accounts	Ownership (Land and Things) Sex Domesticity Spirituality Physical Health Amusement Hobbies Adult Education Community In- volvement	Self-discovery Expertise Intellect Cultivated Tastes Museums and Art Centers Recorded Sounds Books Philanthropy

May one therefore indict the institutions of Propaganda, Education and Bureaucracy and the mythological elements of Work, Progress and Happiness for fraud, granting that this small symbolic lexicon even is, in part, adequate? Of course not. Bearing and raising children, for instance, is a highly propagandized part of the myth of Happiness (and mothers and babies are powerful symbols), but one cannot indict the institution of domesticity for fraud, nor call the joys and frustrations of parenthood unreal, merely because they are potent symbols.[13]

Unless one comprehends the inevitability and social utility of the symbolic umbrella, one is apt to think of a symbol as *false* because it is unreal, or because it does not serve as a literal description of some part of the environment. Quite the contrary. Symbols are *true*, both as logical data in life and as psychological phenomena affecting our lives, precisely because they are *not literal* descriptions of the environment, but metaphors for it instead!

In an age of science, symbolic truths are not easy for many of us to accept as sense data. A peculiar taint surrounds the entire symbolic concept, even when employed "scientifically" by men like Marx and Freud. The former utilized symbols implicitly and directly by associating them with an inevitable mysticism that served as a smoke-screen between the individual and socio-economic reality. The latter associated symbols with unconscious, primitive strivings, particularly sexual energy.

No instrument exists at present, unfortunately, by which we may make valid *scientific* observations of symbolic processes at work. Anthropologists have perhaps come closest to this mark in recent years by abandoning the discursive and arbitrary devices of symbol study used by the playwright and novelist. They have attempted to describe, as objectively as possible, exactly what symbols are employed by what people under what circumstances, and when. Their measure of success is open to debate. So are the attempts of linguists to apply their scientific scalpel to language, in various ways previously discussed;[14] and language is, after all, but *one* highly specialized part of the symbolic umbrella which covers a society.[15]

Symbolic Generation

The symbolic umbrella needs today, perhaps more than at any time in history, close and skeptical examination which questions the adequacy of our commonly accepted analogues, determining their congruence for our population in general to the realities of contemporary life.

We first might question the motives and techniques of the major

[13] An attempt was made to accomplish just this objective in the Soviet Union during the nineteen-twenties and thirties, not just because domesticity itself was merely a symbol, but because it was (correctly in the U.S.S.R.) a *capitalist, bourgoise* symbol. The attempt failed, and presently the concept of domesticity is a Soviet-communist symbol of national virtue. See Alex Ikeles and Raymond A. Bower, *The Soviet Citizen* (Cambridge, Mass.: Harvard University Press, 1959), pp. 189–230.

[14] See Chapter 3.

[15] Our languages may reveal less about us and our symbols than we think they do. In the modern world we are quite vain about our language and frequently put far more faith in it than it may merit. Martin Mayer, for instance, observes in *The Schools* that the prime fault he finds with American education is that nearly everyone connected with schooling *talks* far too much, and that language frequently gets in the way of learning as noted in another relevant context on page 242.

mediators of our symbols: namely, the institutions of Bureaucracy, Propaganda and Education. The answers may indicate which symbolic concepts
currently popular may continue into the future and which are moribund.

Bureaucracy's symbols seem clearly to function as rationalizations of
the penalties we pay for an enormous, complex society. They are formulated
into such thin fictions that some readers may not believe that many modern
men actually find them satisfying as symbols. Much evidence indicates that
they *do*.[16] A trip through the advertisements in the Sunday *New York
Times*, or *Time, Fortune* or *Business Week* magazines will tend to confirm
this judgment. In these periodicals, propagandists give these symbols form
and substance, relating them cleverly not only to the myths of Work, Progress and Happiness, but to the indispensability of propaganda itself and *its*
symbolic role in achieving the benefits of bureaucracy.

Neither the symbols of bureaucracy nor its functions are, *ipso facto*,
destructive to the welfare of a modern technological state or its citizens.
Max Lerner looks benignly,[17] for instance, upon government bureaucracy,
so frequently the whipping post of social critics. "It (bureaucracy) in itself," he writes, "is neither ogre nor Messiah, neither road to serfdom nor
way to salvation, but it can be used both destructively and creatively, depending on the inner social impulses and on the direction given them by
the policy makers at the top." [18] Probably true. What Lerner omits in his
discussion is the problem that bureaucracy, both politically and psychologically, reaches today beyond government to big industry, mass education,
and into the mechanisms of giant labor unions. Foundations, philanthro-
pies and community service agencies have also assumed bureaucratic man-
nerisms and contribute to the enforcement of bureaucratic symbols.

Bureaucratic symbols represent, to a degree that propaganda and educational symbols do *not*, reactions to and rationalizations of an ongoing
tension between the system itself and "the individual," both inside and
outside of it. Systems, statistics, carbon and Thermofax copies, forms, procedures and manuals of procedures, data processing devices, Centrex telephone systems, chains of command, rank and pay scales, and employee
benefits, carried usually *ad absurdum*, must be integrated somehow into the
functional personalities of those living with and by them. Symbolic analogies, as poorly drawn as they may seem to some outsiders, are the only
solution to the depersonalization, regimentation and demolition of individuality that participation in bureaucracy causes in culture.[19]

---

[16] See William H. Whyte, Jr.'s *The Organization Man* (New York: Simon and
Schuster, 1958), for a comprehensive analysis of the force of bureaucracy on the personality of the middle-class citizen, who must square the imperatives (and symbols) of
"the system" with his own needs as a human being.

[17] Max Lerner, *America As A Civilization* (New York: Simon and Schuster, 1957),
pp. 407–415.

[18] *Ibid.*, p. 410.

[19] It is also possible for *small* organizations to evolve bureaucratic procedures as complex and depersonalizing as *large* ones.

Our agencies of *Propaganda* derive their most trenchant power from their ubiquity. First, they employ skilfully all of the mediums of communication and are disseminated by every communications instrument available in our culture. Second, it is impossible to demonstrate that they are *not* (as is frequently claimed) inevitable by-products of a technological society in which access to masses of "information" and a government "establishment" are understood to be complements. As C. Wright Mills once noted, what we call propaganda consists "not only of opinions on a variety of topics and issues . . . (but also) of official definitions of reality." [20] And certainly an "official definition of reality" is required by our society and is closely linked to the psychological tonus of the nation.

On our chart, links between propaganda and technology, science, democracy, consumerism and fun are clearly shown. These symbolic notions constitute the main themes for propaganda in our culture. What are the relationships of these themes to reality?

Freed from their symbolic and mythological contexts, they seem indeed quite real—as *industrial complexes* upon which, in one way or another, life in our commonwealth depends. The heavy machine industries, the science industries, the "democracy" industries, the consumer industries and the fun industries may be called by more polite names,[21] but their corporate reality is indispensable to the status quo. A biting question one can ask of their hired propagandists is how satisfactory the *status quo* is in achieving for citizens of our society a good life, compared with other people in other cultures. We might also ask to what degree propaganda—so defensive of the cult of "progress"—prevents any revolution of symbols which, as we have already observed, society requires to permit new styles of living to evolve.

As far as *Education* is concerned, Lawrence Cremin has noted that America has displayed inordinate faith in the power of formal schooling to realize the idealism inherent in democracy. Writes Cremin: "Actually, those who launched our experiment with popular education were little troubled by the problems (of the proposition that culture can be democratized without being vulgarized). If anything, there is a wonderfully child-like optimism about their programs. 'The State which teaches one new truth to one of its citizens does something,' Horace Mann observed in 1842; 'but how much more, when, by teaching that truth to all, it multiplies its utilities and its pleasures by the number of all its citizens.' " [22] The United States devotes over 6% of its national income to education, far more than

---

[20] C. Wright Mills, *The Sociological Imagination* (New York. The Oxford Press, 1959), p. 191.
[21] For example, we may refer to them as branches (in order) of "the farm machinery industry, the research professions, state governmental organizations, the advertising professions and show business."
[22] Lawrence A. Cremin, *The Genius of American Education* (Pittsburgh, Pa.: University of Pittsburgh Press, 1965), p. 78.

most nations (including England), but somewhat less than some like Canada, Japan, Israel, Belgium and (recently) the U.S.S.R.[23] This enormous sum paid out for the mere *preparation* of citizens for citizenship indicates some measure of the elaborate images we hold of the symbols of education.

Most striking of the symbolic ideas on our chart pertaining to education is that nearly all of them bespeak "good things in life" *without* the hedonistic aspects of the propagandist's symbols. The myth of work applied to education yields symbolic connotations that intellectual development and activity are reserved for a special élite, symbolized by the college professor, shrouded in symbols of wisdom, productive research and publication. Note that material symbols—except insofar as books and museums are *vehicles* for education—are almost entirely absent from the list. This may appear unusual, considering the enormous amounts of money spent by the American educational establishment. One must consider also that the prime motive for the pursuit of an education is unquestionably materialistic.

It appears that the symbols relating to the myths of progress and happiness are suspect; that is, they do not appear to refer to the same *kind* of established cultural phenomena that concern the propagandist. Progress is partially measured, it seems, by the *absence* of breakdowns (mental and social). Happiness symbols seem, despite their viability, to be closely descriptive of the "good life," once associated with our leisure class in maintaining private museums and sporting contests, like billiards and "the sport of kings."

For all their respectability, therefore, the symbols generated by our educational institutions appear curiously out of phase with realities of the modern, technological, materialistic mass state. What are the sources from which they derive their power? The answers lie hidden in pages of cultural history, reflective, on the one hand, of our historical American idealism but, on the other, severely alienated, symbolically, from reality.[24]

Myths as Symbols

How well do Ellul's three particular myths relate to the *social* reality to which they refer?

How interesting, concerning the Work symbols, is the apparently odd fact that none of the symbols (read horizontally) is incompatible with generally accepted virtues of the Western world today! Similar compatability is *not* found unilaterally in those symbols attendant the myths of progress and happiness. At least, some of these analogues appear quite antagonistic, one to the other. Not so the symbols of work. All (even "Push and Pull," in proper degrees) sustain both our ethics and what, in our culture, we

23 UNESCO, *Statistical Yearbook* (Paris: The United Nations Educational, Cultural and Scientific Organization, 1966), p. 342–364.
24 Much the same charge has been directed lately at the symbolism of our churches that seems in no manner to reflect the realities of modern urban and suburban culture.

consider to be civilized. For the myth of work, therefore, propagandists, educators and bureaucrats seem to be generating mutually compatible and relatively similar types of analogues.

Their relationship to reality is another matter. It is possible that ideas like "Corporate Alliance," "Success," "the Liberal Arts," the "I.Q.," "Security," "Respectability" and "Power" are symbols without clear referents. For instance, what measure of "Security" is possible in an era when chances are high as they are for most of us that we shall expire in the next (and perhaps inevitable) World War? I.Q. measurement has been under such fire in recent years that this page might be filled with the names of reputable educational authorities who deny either the validity or the reliability of this concept. Merit grading systems are variantly spurious, as those of us who have been forced to use them for years are often the first to admit. And so it goes.

The reality to which the work symbols relate depend, it appears, on how naïve the symbol purveyor is. That work *itself* may be—under certain circumstances—boring, useless, asocial, degrading, foolish, unnecessary, unhealthy, stupid, unrespectable and immoral has been admitted by many economists and social critics.[25]

If any virtues attend the symbols of *Progress*, they are largely nineteenth-century images, the "tendency of our philosophy to present the workings and forces of history in an overly simplified manner," as Robert Heilbroner writes, ". . . a manner which has entirely failed to prepare us for the actual turnings which history has taken." But are such simplifications indeed virtuous today? *"The optimistic philosophy equates the movement of history's forces with the idea of progress."* [26] Heilbroner shows that this optimism is merely reflective of the self-image of certain societies. In these cultures, viewpoints of progress have been, first, psychologically possible and, second, current when "the human being has *wished* to believe in the rightness and fixity of the situation in which he has found himself." [27]

Progress invites to the symbolic umbrella not only a greater, grander and more glorious future for the individual, but also for industry, education and government, and the planet upon which he lives. The symbol of mother earth has been expanded to include space technology and earthly control of the universe! Science, of course, is integral to this perspective. Birth control, mental health and social controls are all symbolic evidence that progress includes prognostications about an integral change in *the nature of man himself*. Our "new Western Man" is just as commensurate with

---

[25] See, for instance, the essay published in book form by Daniel Bell, *Work and Its Discontents* (Boston: Beacon Press, 1956). Bell writes knowingly about the social and psychological origins and values of the work ethic and leaves the reader with the familiar question of what will happen to our myth (and symbols) if and when machines replace men in our labor force.

[26] Robert Heilbroner, *The Future As History* (New York: Harper and Brothers, 1960), pp. 190–191. (Italics are Heilbroner's.)

[27] *Ibid.*, p. 126.

our symbols in the democratic-capitalist tradition as the idea of "the new Soviet man" is vital to current symbols in the U.S.S.R.

How realistic are these optimistic symbols when held up to prospects for the future of the human race? Heilbroner reminds us[28] that our society has not been the only optimistic one in history. Neither has an historical faith in progress *per se* meant that progress followed. The predictions of Butler, Bellamy, Verne and other Utopians in our tradition are considered remarkable today because the prognosticators did not *entirely miss* the point of the history in the past. The future of every society has been and is, at any given moment, a total enigma. The record of history has given us at least as many correct pessimistic predictions of the future as optimistic ones. Nor do we suffer at the moment any shortage of highly vocal haruspices. Despite our current and fashionable general optimism, let us remember that the best symbol for the atomic age remains a mushroom cloud, not a cyclotron! [29]

The concept of *Happiness* introduces to the symbols of progress personal and quasi-spiritual or metaphysical considerations. A number of books have been written on this nexus.[30] Mental, physical and spiritual health are combined with sexuality, involvement, intelligence, access to "the better things in life," security, money. These are distinctive *human* traits, meaning that their pursuit is salted with selfishness, as the virtues of work, for instance, are not. What they demonstrate clearly is the all-encompassing, many-faceted symbolic complexion of happiness in our present myth structures.

How different from the picture frequently painted of our culture in which *happiness* is equated strictly with *materialism!* While such qualities as "physical health," "sexual enjoyment," and "access to books" have their materialistic sides, well over half the happiness symbols are oriented primarily to *non-materialistic considerations.* Even ideas like "insurance" and "retirement," as symbolized daily in the popular press, are often de-materialized. One insures one*self*, say the ads, to protect *others.* Retirement is seen

[28] *Ibid.,* pp. 13–40.
[29] The cloud may be employed symbolically in a malignant context, as at the end of the film *Dr. Strangelove,* to signify the destruction of the world. Or it may serve as a prelude to the story of how man has "harnessed the atom," an interesting metaphor but a feeble description of the peaceful utilization of atomic energy.
[30] For instance, Aldous Huxley's *Brave New World Revisited* tackles articulately discussion of chemically induced happiness that the author had begun in his futuristic novel *Brave New World.* Psychologist Abraham H. Maslow approaches the problem from another direction in *Toward A Psychology of Being* (Princeton, N. J.: D. Van Nostrand Company, Inc., 1962), by attempting to identify and to dissect experimentally "peak experiences" and "being awareness" of a population sample. This is a study which equates "happiness" (for want of a better word) cleverly with various symbols. Most of the self-help books on the market today have defined, by means of symbols (nearly all of them on our chart), "happiness" as a *desideratum.* The exception is, perhaps, magician John Mulholland's and this writer's *The Magical Mind,* simply because we could not agree on a proper hierarchy of symbols.

as a reward for a lifetime of *service* to society and family, rather than the pay-off on canny investment, or a result of capitalistic know-how. Divine qualities may even be ascribed to our expanding Gross National Product! Young people seem to regard this growth as God-given and frequently consider talk about the depression of the nineteen-thirties as heresy.

Is happiness real? Or, put another way, is it possible to find realistic referents for the concept of happiness? One is reminded of the man who was not happy at all; he merely *thought* he was happy. Should we wish to find authorities of many kinds of the opinion that ours is neither a happy time or happy society, we would have little difficulty. Our Almanac is also filled with tiresome statistics concerning increasing suicides, mental aberrations, narcotics addiction, alcoholism, divorce and/or other symptoms, usually cited as indices of cultural misery.

None of these statistics is meaningful, wanting further qualifying evidence, and authority is useless in determining the happiness quotient of a given culture. From his perspective, an anthropologist may claim with justice that South American natives, addicted to narcotic beans, are happier, by and large, than the average residents of garden apartments. Mental patients, having undergone mutilation of the frontal lobes of their brains, generally *appear* happier than most book publishers and some editors.

Our American tradition indeed guarantees for us the "pursuit of happiness." It is therefore not surprising that many symbols still enhance and embellish this bitter cultural myth, best considered right now a promise made long ago and in another country.

Conclusion

No contemporary instrument of communication (or any medium utilizing that instrument) lies beyond the cover of a symbolic umbrella. Today, our symbols are (in the main) related to cultural myths, three of which we have examined closely. There are, of course, many more—some correlates or sub-categories of those discussed, some embroideries upon them, and some of a different nature entirely.

The myth of *Private Property*, for instance, is a correlate of the myth of *Work*. Soviet Marxists have seen fit to derogate the former but not the latter, while we in the United States accept both.

The myth of *Self-fulfillment by Sexuality*, as another example, is a subcategory of other major myths and a correlate of the various sexual and sex-related symbols. In various manifestations, it appears to be a highly agreeable symbol in our society. Sex gratification symbolism colors an enormous part of what is communicated between persons and groups informally. It also accounts for much of the serious and trivial content of our instruments of commercial mass communication. The symbolism of sex is now common in the discourse of fields as disparate as industry, religion, science, literature, and many others.

Our *Tradition of Schooling* has spawned other symbols, distinguished less by caps and gowns than by degrees, transcripts, pipe-smoking professors, text books, grinning college presidents, seedy high school teachers, and hosts of other travesties, tragedies or necessary evils, depending upon how one views them.

We have, in this chapter, just begun to examine the endless combinations that the juxtaposition of these symbols, one with another, creates. They constitute the foundations for human discourse, without which our present languages of communication would not possibly function. If, therefore, there is one universal language of communications, it is the language of symbols, not because certain symbols are common to all cultures but because man *is*.

Part Three

MEDIUMS OF
COMMUNICATION

Chapter 7

INVENTION, MECHANICS
AND TECHNOLOGY

I N THE PREVIOUS Parts of this book we have been concerned with some of
the main reasons why the many languages of communication work or
fail to work. We have noted the tendency to mix logical and psychological
statements, employing what are adequate criteria for one category against
the other, despite the latter's irrelevancies. We have observed the social
power of the symbolic umbrella and the social need for symbols that invest
both logical and psychological meanings in almost every aspect of culture.

These concepts have been discussed to provide a background against
which to begin to explore less familiar aspects of communication. Unfortunately, many—if not *most*—of the principles upon which we base our
common sense evaluations of the day-to-day communications around us are
assumptions. Many of them are framed in the logical mode without sufficient regard for the psychological one. Others take as given the influence of
symbols on human behavior and culture and are thereby, in effect, statements of fantasy, built not on reality but upon metaphors.

Certainly, there has been no shortage of novel theories of communications mediums, differentially defined.

The French physician, Gustave Le Bon, was probably the first communications theorist in the modern mode, noting, in the final years of the
nineteenth century, that certain types of addresses to certain people, under
certain conditions, modified in a regular pattern their collective responses,
making them appear more primitive and atavistic.[1] Le Bon is known as the

---

[1] See Gustave Le Bon, *The Crowd* (New York: Compass Books Edition, 1960). It is
believed that Lenin kept this book on his night table. Hitler referred to it in a number
of his written works and "secret conversations." It served both men well. *The Crowd*
remains a fascinating, if cynical, textbook on mass manipulation, and Robert Merton
in the introduction to the edition above indicates that it remains to this day one of
the most influential books in social psychology, in spite (or because of) its Machia-
vellian tone. A short reprise of the book appears in George N. Gordon, Irving Falk and

father of "audience psychology," and his work is still immediately relevant
to the concerns of communications scholars. In his own time, Le Bon impelled Sigmund Freud to write an impassioned—and equally provocative—
response to his essay,[2] reinterpreting Le Bon's observations in terms of psychoanalytical symbology, but generally accepting Le Bon's central thesis of
a regression reaction in mobs or masses responding to highly emotionally
charged communications.

Another landmark in the field of audience psychology, following Le
Bon, was the publication of the theories of the Russian film maker, Sergei
Eisenstein, which were not gathered into organized and edited form until
after World War II.[3] For some time, however, they had been topics of
argument among the artistic community in Europe and America because,
largely, of their novel integration of aesthetics with social theory. Other
philosophers of communication have also more recently spoken about what
they assumed were differential mediums of communication: language
(written and spoken) radio (or sound), film, television, comic strips, projected still pictures, plastic models, photographs and other esoteric "media." Within the past decade, of course, the notions of Dr. Marshall Mc-
Luhan (which he claims are less theories than "sparkplugs") have received considerable attention in the United States and his native Canada.

Because of this plethora of what is often loosely called "theory," warn-
ings are here posted that the considerations of the nature of the *mediums*
of communication, while modestly offered in the present chapter, will differ
considerably with both the current "common sense" evaluations of the
so-called "media"[4] and commonly held theoretical formulations of them.

William Hodapp, *The Idea Invaders* (New York: Hastings House, Publishers, Inc.,
1963), pp. 25–28, where it is related cursorily to international propaganda.
[2] See Sigmund Freud, *Group Psychology and the Analysis of the Ego* (New York:
Bantam Books, 1965), pp. 6–18. This work was published in 1920, a quarter of a
century after Le Bon's essay. The latter had already become, in its French editions, a
"revolutionists handbook," hence Freud's response, discussing Le Bon in a "modern"
frame of reference.
[3] See Sergei Eisenstein, *Film Form and Film Sense* (New York: The World Publishing
Company, 1963). Eisenstein's contribution to pictorial aesthetics will be discussed
briefly below and in Chapter 18.
[4] "Common sense" evaluations of the mediums of communications refer largely to the
judgments, rules and principles which professional craftsmen and artists at any given
time *using* the technologies of communication generally employ. Therefore, common
sense judgments of modern narratives are heard from writers, publishers and editors;
common sense judgments about films come from various film makers. The term
"common sense" does *not* refer to ideas of the so-called "common-man," simply because he usually does not profess *any* theories of how or why communications mediums
work. He is generally satisfied with their roles in his life and can think of few ways to
improve them, except to make them more "educational." Beyond this, he does not
appear to think much about them. Genuine theoretical ideas are those of craftsmen,
artists, critics or philosophers, whether or not they happen to be involved in producing
the material about which they theorize. To be a competent theorist of certain aspects
of the mediums of communication, one does not need to have been exposed widely to
them. Maxim Gorki, for instance, noticed the similarity between the hypnotic trance

They will differ in their ideas as to the nature of what a mediums are and how and what they communicate, both in their logical and psychological phases.

Invention as History

The story of the development of devices for communication has been treated often in literature.[5] As a history of invention, this is a fascinating tale usually told with *post hoc* logic. Each discovery of a new device for communication, so it is said, appears to have sprung from the previous one—if not from the one before it, at least its invention was influenced crucially by the technological climate preceeding it. Eventually, the story takes us to the present era, a virtual apotheosis of invention and discovery, where, it appears, the sum of our inventiveness yields a magnificent new world, transformed in all respects and logically built by a nebulous "communications revolution." Much history, told with wisdom of hindsight from effect to cause, may be told in such a manner as to be the envy of a museum keeper! [6]

As the developments of communications are described in this historical adventure, spoken language constitutes an anthropological gift. Somehow, (it is written) man cleaves from other higher mammals, and, in a hundred thousand years or two, appears in full (and complex) social groups with rites, rituals and mores, speaking a full blown language displaying a vocabulary, syntax and grammar.

Man speaks for a while (how many, many thousands of years, we are not sure) until somehow, and almost invariably, wherever he speaks he feels an urge to preserve what he says in a manner less uncertain than the primitive method of verbal messages. He invents written language: one of two types. He either finds a pictorial equivalent for each of the sounds he makes, as in most Western languages, or he develops pictograms which

---

and the kind of attention induced by the motion picture, for instance, the *first time* he had seen a cinema presentation. His idea is still of psychological interest more than fifty years later.
[5] Some of these books contain technical histories of the advance of invention, like Robert C. O'Hara, *Media for Millions* (New York: Random House, 1961), or Theodore Peterson, Jay V. Jenson and William L. Rivers, *The Mass Media and Modern Society* (New York: Holt, Rinehart and Winston, Inc., 1965). Others trace the history of particular devices like S. H. Steinberg, *Five Hundred Years of Printing* (Harmondsworth, Middlesex, England: Penguin Books, Inc., 1955), Ivor Montagu, *Film World* (Baltimore Md.: Penguin Books, 1964), or E. S. Turner, *The Shocking History of Advertising* (New York: Ballantine Books, 1953), all excellent, specialized studies. Other works deal with the general development of communications with an anthropological bias, like Lancelot Hogben, *From Cave Painting to Comic Strip* (New York: Chanticleer Press, 1949), and David K. Berlo, *The Process of Communication*, previously cited. The books above are typical of many easily obtained in paper back or hard cover.
[6] Authors of histories of communications are not the only parties culpable of this *a posterori* reasoning in this field. Professors in the field, including the author, are particularly prone to this neat and incorrect interpretation of the natural evolution of the instruments of communication because it is easy to *teach*.

have nothing to do with what he *says* but describe the object of his speech.

At this point "man" becomes (in the story) Western man, and in the fifteenth century he re-invents (following the orientals) the printing press. The reason for inventing the press, it appears, is at first to print Bibles and, second, to spread abroad the heresy of the Reformation. Printing sparks a multiple number of neat social and cultural changes, mostly in the eighteenth and nineteenth centuries, for reasons that this history does not clarify. Results of printing, of course, include the rise of popular education, the awakening of the common man to democratic government, the spread of scientific information, the industrial revolution, a widespread distrust of clergymen and the invention of the novel—among other things.

Then, with the rise of technology in the nineteenth century, the steam engine is harnessed to the printing press, and the result is the miracle of modern printing methods, a belt line of startling inventions from the Linotype to the Xerox. Results: modern education *en masse* becomes possible. A great semi-literate population emerges, consuming, in the United States alone, about fifty million newspapers a day, ten million news magazines a week and twenty million *Reader's Digests* a month. "Public opinion," in the modern sense, is born. Each individual citizen joins the community of sentient, well informed men around him to create, for the first time since Periclean Athens, an "enlightened electorate."

Meanwhile, back on the historical front—as a direct result of the spread of scientific information due to printing—advances in knowledge are moving in two directions, one in the studies of vision, the other of sound. The former lead to the work of Daguerre, Muybridge, Marey, Goodwin, Eastman and Edison, and the invention of motion pictures. This non-print novelty (naturally) proved to be immensely popular with illiterate immigrants.

Progress in sound passes through the inventions of Morse, Bell, Edison and Marconi and produces the telephone, the phonograph and radio (in that order). When finally inventions involving sight and sound are commercially fused in the nineteen-twenties, talking pictures result. Sight is added to radio broadcasting at the hands of Zworkyn, and the era of television is upon us.

Our capsule history above is, of course, mostly nonsense. But longer histories of communications, more "scholarly" and detailed, filling out this framework, are likewise nonsense. It is probably true, for instance, that the scientific environment of the nineteenth century had a good deal to do with the invention of the movies, but no one can tell exactly to what degree or in what manner. *Many* things probably influenced the development of the movies, including the ideas, centuries old, of Leonardo da Vinci, trends in oil painting, the development of children's toys, the nature of show business, Newton's experiments with light, the art of lens grinding, the development of the motor, the invention of the sprocket, and random historical matters which cannot possibly be determined definitively today.

The same may be observed of the inventions relating to sound and recording technology, with one added factor, namely, the existence of waves in the ether through which small charges of energy could be sent great distances and be modulated to recreate changes in frequency and amplitude. The discovery of these waves and their use in radio transmission was probably largely accidental.[7]

The history of the logical growth of communications mediums makes consistent *moral* (if not historical) sense when told as outlined above. The point is that man's progress in communication has been due largely to his native inventiveness, an inventiveness which started in mystery and grew at first slowly. Then, suddenly, with the invention of technology, it miraculously freed man from the fetters of his environment by virtue of the sequential and rapid inventions of the modern "wonders" of mass communication. No longer were individuals "private" or "public" selves. Mass communication had broken down barriers of old relationships, reorganized irrevocably man's environment, preparing him to live in the Age of Technology. Invention's moral purpose, in other words, was deduced by reading history backwards to vindicate its role in our contemporary culture.

"Sometimes the historian is consciously a painter of morals"; writes Louis Gottschalk, "sometimes he is consciously so. It is when he is unaware that he has a philosophy, or more particularly when he thinks he has a philosophy which in fact he does not have, that he is dangerous." [8] Gottschalk's observation applies directly to nearly every attempt so far made to tell the story of the development of communications, including previous efforts by the present writer.[9]

The inventions of mediums of communication was, as we shall see, but *one* component of the fabric of our race's experience, and in some ways an unimpressive one. Although it cannot yet be proved, man's development of speech was probably *neither* mysterious nor rapid. His written language resulted from social need. Printing was *one* part—quite a minor part, many believe—of the many more or less accidental (or providential) convergence of extraordinary factors that changed the course of European life (or were

[7] One wonders, in regard to the advances of wireless telegraphy, radio and television, what the twentieth century might have been like had hertzian waves not existed in the earth's atmosphere, or if some natural phenomenon had stood guard over them, preventing man from ever developing instruments for discovering them.

Virologists and other organic chemists seem to face such protective mechanisms which prevent them—and perhaps *will* forever prevent them—from fully understanding the nature of certain substances, be they viruses or the mysterious life directing nucleic acids. So the possibility above is not as far fetched a revision of history as it may seem.
[8] Louis Gottschalk, *Understanding History* (New York: Alfred A. Knopf, 1964), p. 9.
[9] These books were written for children as "adventure tales," but their yearning after false morals is nonetheless egregious.

the result of change) during the latter part of the fifteenth and beginning of the sixteenth centuries.

Philosophic, religious and economic forces were probably of primary importance behind the scientific and technical developments of the remarkable instruments of communication during the nineteenth century. At any event, if one examines the record carefully to find *one* or *two* major factors impelling the invention of devices for *mass* communication, one discovers certain and specific pressures built into the progress of the century.

First, the economic power of the new *man of the masses*, who was given conceptual birth in the era of Jacksonian democracy in the United States (an era which has not yet ended) was one such force. Second, an industrial "establishment" arose in America, demanding instruments for manipulating the populace into clearing a path for capitalistic expansion, hegemony of a new élite of political power and money, and innumerable tyrannies of technology or "by-products of progress."

What one misses, of course, when isolating single forces in this manner, is the crazy-quilt pattern of expansion of American industry and economy during the past century. Few contemporary books do justice to this metamorphosis in our national life as related to the development of ways and means of communication. Memoirs of actors, novelists, playwrights, and adventurers provide best insight into this incredible period of great inventiveness in the arts of mass exploitation which was the nineteenth century. It is especially difficult to understand the role that newspapers played in such a culture, or to track down the sources of myths concerning "the power of the press" which persist to this day. One faces a similar problem in plotting the progress, during the twentieth century, of the movies, radio and television, so various were the facets of American life which they influenced or which influenced them.[10] The latter three institutions are still so inchoate that one wonders if they have indeed a "history" in the sense that the press has.[11]

10 Some flavor of this period may be tasted in such histories as Edwin Emery and Henry Ladd Smith, *The Press and America* (New York: Prentice Hall, Inc., 1954), for newspapers. Kenneth MacGowan, *Behind the Screen* (New York: Delacorte Press, 1965), for the motion pictures, and Erik Barnouw, *A Tower in Babel* (New York: Oxford University Press, 1966), for radio. Nothing comparable to these three books has yet been written about television, although Harold Mehling, *The Great Time Killer* (New York: The World Publishing Company, 1962), and the autobiographical," Merle Miller and Evan Rhodes, *Only You, Dick Daring!* (New York: Bantam Books, 1965), add up to a profitable and (taken together) realistic appraisal of the relationships of business, government and the consumer public that are involved in the American TV industry.

11 C. W. Ceram has wisely entitled his picture book on the inventions involved in the development of the motion picture, *Archaeology of the Cinema* (New York: Harcourt, Brace and World, Inc., 1965).

Technology as Psychologic

The history of technology is also a provocative and frequently neglected story. To disregard or underestimate the psychological force of technology's heritage in the modern state is to close one's eyes to a matter of
prime significance for understanding communications.

First, man invented inventions. The event was probably accidental—so
accidental that he could not help ascribing it to divine intervention. Invention yielded the art of mechanics, because it was mostly artisans who prac-
ticed it. Men were excellent mechanics long before they *knew*, analytically,
what they were doing, or why. The Egyptians, of course, frequently used
their mechanical genius, not only for building tombs and statues, but also
as inventors of an elaborate pharmacopeia and in devising techniques of
public health and plague control.[12]

Over a great period, mechanics led eventually, in an unexpected manner, to the beginnings of science. The mechanics of hurling projectiles
through air made necessary clever scientific investigation of the force of
gravity; the mechanics of herbology, primitive pharmacology and alchemy
led inevitably to the development of chemistry; the mechanics of geometry,
along with the development of suitable telescopes, were prerequisite for the
birth of astronomy. The first experimental scientists were, in fact, a hybrid
strain of old-style mechanics and new-style philosophers.

Science and mechanics yielded a powerful offspring, technology, which
may be defined as the art of the utilization of mechanics or a mechanical
system. Machines and mechanisms became increasingly sophisticated. Motion, which in nineteenth century technology had been considered mechanical (kinetic), became, with the twentieth century, the province also of a
submolecular universe. Its sources were magnetic, electronic or nuclear. We
are moving now towards a period when another technology of non-
mechanics will appear as a separate lineal descendant of our present techniques. It will probably be called "cybernology." [13] This development will
no more spell out the death of former technologies than the growth of
technology eliminated science, or the birth of science made obsolete the
need for the art of mechanics, or mechanics vitiated the need for invention.[14]

12 The mechanical device for controlling the virulence of the plague was to develop
the cult of Egyptian cat worship. Since cats were sacred in ancient Egypt, they flour-
ished, killed plague-bearing rodents and prevented much illness. Again, this mechanical
device was probably the result of the "accidental" discovery that houses with many
cats produced less plague than those without cats. The feline, therefore, had "magical"
powers. Accordingly, he became an object of worship and, eventually, a god. See Carl
Van Vechten, *The Tiger in the House* (New York: Alfred A. Knopf, 1960).
13 Unlike "cybernetics," "cybernology" as a discrete technology remains a subject for
science fiction writers and has by no means been developed beyond its infant stage
yet.
14 These observations are predicated upon the assumption that Western culture will

"Technology" has other possible meanings, however, as one may notice from the above outline history of the phenomenon. Jacques Ellul, the French sociologist, uses the term "technology" to describe what Americans call "know how." In fact, he indicates that what we know as "technique" and "technology" are in many ways similar and that even mechanical inventions which are derived *independently of science are technologies*.[15] In addition to physical, mechanical devices, Ellul would include in the consideration of technology *all* machine-like functions in modern society where technique (or means) dictates the operation of an object or group of objects, including human beings. Ellul, therefore, adds to our lexicon of technology the following crucial items: *economic technique* or the organization of labor and fiscal matters; *the technique of organization or administration;* police power, warfare and other *methods of control of the masses;* and *human technique* "ranging all the way" as he says "from medicine and genetics to propaganda." [16]

Ellul bases these postulates concerning technology on historical evidence. They appear also to be statements relevant to the psychological *impact* of technology in our culture. They represent instruments which we have devised to mechanize a technological society in the interest of efficiency. Ellul does not take pains to defend their logic. He argues only for their historical accuracy and empirical truth. Their value as descriptive statements, he regards as self-evident psychologically.

In summation, Ellul's points are:

1. *In a given civilization, technical progress is irreversible.*
2. *Technical progress tends to move, not according to an arithmetic, but according to a geometric progression.*[17]

Ellul sees, with pessimism, *all* factors in society subordinated eventually to the demands of technology with the rapidity noted above. In the end, most humanistic values are subsumed to this "know how," and both art and science in all their phases are doomed to the dominance of technique. All institutions of education and communications are turned into instruments of propaganda or persuasion. This is necessary to convince the masses to accept the brutal side effects of technology and to disregard the ends it achieves at the expense of the perfection of means.

Ellul's conclusions are projections of present psychological trends in

---

develop in a consistent linear historical fashion, doubts about which the author shares with observers as different as Aldous Huxley, Arnold Toynbee and the Jehovah's Witnesses!

[15] Jacques Ellul, *The Technological Society* (New York: Alfred A. Knopf, 1965), pp. 1–60.

[16] *Ibid.,* p. 22.

[17] *Ibid.,* p. 89.

the role played by technique in the lives of twentieth-century men, judging by what he can see of mass society's effects on culture, as instrumentalized by the educational force of mass communications.[18]

A toll for technology, one imagines, will be paid somehow—if not in the model of Ellul's gloomy predictions, then in some other manner. The result of the overuse of technique, it seems, is frequently psychological pressure of some sort upon society and its institutions. If technology does *no more* than confuse the ends to which social institutions are directed with their means, Ellul's gloom is justified. The picture of a university, a government, a community of artists, or a social sub-group without clearly articulated and achievable goals is frightening to contemplate.

Should an obsession with technology rob us of our power to formulate simply and to our satisfaction *reasons* for beautiful cars, modern houses, and color television sets, are these examples of "twentieth century ingenuity" worth their room and board even to the most penurious of us? It is the irreversible element in Ellul's postulates that is naturally most unsettling in calculating the psychological price of modernity. One may hardly recommend a return to the horse drawn buggy after once riding in a new automobile, any more than one would prefer a hand copied edition of this book to a printed one!

In those nations (and the United States is one) which have been deeply affected by technology (or Ellul's "technique") *every phase* of life has been in some degree transformed by it.[19] It was inevitable therefore that the mediums of communications were intimately influenced by technology. One does not need to accept Ellul's hypotheses to comprehend how completely and irrefutably man's methods of communication were transformed along with the rest of his life. Communications changed from relatively stable patterns of relationships in such classic forms of expression as conversation, painting, theatre and songs to mass made and distributed materials of many kinds. This output was made up of psychologically baffling profusions of printed, spoken and photographed ideas produced according

[18] Reference here is *not* made to the "survey" kind of evidence which is supposed to tell us what the "effects of mass communications" are, and almost always indicate that mass communications (or other techniques in mass societies) have "no effects" on people—in the terms in which the concept of "effects" is framed. Please note here that the evidence referred to above is the evidence that most of us notice in our experiences with the mass instruments of communication, the effects that these devices have had upon *us in our own subjective lives*, evidence which it is possible to evaluate for ourselves without either social scientists, surveys, or statistics.

[19] Note that even the most personal aspects of our private lives, those having to do with elimination and cleanliness, for instance, have been as prone to the incursion "techniques" as any others. We depend upon plumbing devices of various degrees of elaboration, electric toothbrushes, mass produced and distributed shaving instruments, hair sprays, deodorants and a phalanx of physicians, dentists, veterinarians, medical technicians and trained nurses whose special "techniques" include the diagnosis and care of ailments in our alimentary canals (top and bottom), our urinary-genital systems, bloodstreams and so forth, each utilizing a discrete technical specialty in medicine.

to the patterns of invention. Their evolution was dictated by the development of technology alone, not to meet the psychological *needs* of the various segments of the population, or because of any logical historical
necessity.

The pattern of technological progress has been capricious, driven by
economic forces, military needs and moments of genius. The same sorts of
random technological treasure hunt that gave the West photography a half
century before sound recording impels us today to travel to the moon before we have even explored the bottom of our own ocean. Technological
change bursts unpredictably upon society, transforms it, and waits for psychological reactions to set in. When they do (in their frequently surprising
and diverse ways) *new* technology is then introduced to "contain" the liberated force of these reactions. Hence the geometric pattern of growth,
contributed to, partially of course, by the spread of transportation and communications which make *all* technological changes matters of national or
worldwide significance.[20] There are literally *no technological secrets*, except
from corporation to corporation within capitalist societies, which utilize pro-
visional patent laws to give the inventive (or wily) a brief economic advantage in the competitive market place.

Nor can psychological reactions to new technology be contained in simplistic sub-categories like the "Age of the Automobile," the "Space Age," or
the "Age of Television"! These categories are fictions, because old technologies do not die as new ones are developed. *Our time* is the age of print,
sound, pictures, automobiles, airplanes, rockets, nuclear warheads, mass-
produced tranquilizers, computers, credit cards *and* all the other know how
which has been piled into the curiosity shop of our mass society.

The ubiquity of technology does not seem, however, noticeably to
have discouraged the progressive thrust of culture, Ellul notwithstanding. It
has killed—and is killing—many people in many ways, but population control is a central humanistic problem in a technological society, and technology appears to be solving it, one way or another. If confusion and alienation
from nature are conditions of life today, they may be the price that modern
man must pay for the rapid changes in life-style that technology brings.
(Men in highly stable societies were rarely confused or alienated; neither,
frequently, were they well fed or housed.)

Technology has produced considerable psychological revolt: in literature and letters, from muck-raking to pop-op art; in cultural patterns, from
ascending alcoholic rates and drug addiction (of many sorts) to new social
sanctions for homosexuality and other eccentricities.

These revolts, however, mean little or nothing, except that the power
of technology is growing, and that reactive psychological forces are keeping

---

[20] This was written in first draft shortly after the announcement of the first nuclear
bomb explosions by the Red Chinese. By the time this is published it is possible that a
greater number of "backward" Asian and African nations also "will have the bomb."

up with its apparent depersonalization of individuals. Newer technological devices will also keep up with the feeble efforts of artists to resist the uniformity that technological communications demands of them. New techniques will "handle" alcoholism, drug addiction and homosexuality, which themselves will produce psychological by-products, probably increases in the conditions they were supposed to alleviate, but impossible to anticipate in the long run. The religious will also be "cured" of their religion by technology. There are techniques for dealing with religiosity, if only by confining it to the church and campus, and encouraging its proponents to write books and articles which are read only within their own circles.

The most remarkable psychological result of technology is that most of us enjoy most of it! We revel in it either through participation, like gawkers at a never ending Worlds Fair, or in imitating it, or by joining a rebellion against it. Eloquent critics bemoan the depravities of modernity, hardly mindful that, were they born in another time or place, they could not savor the pleasure of such elaborate discontents—or cosset the chance to publish them widely.

The Force of Interaction

What is being proposed, therefore, are a relatively simple number of propositions that fly directly in the face of most current accepted assumptions concerning communications, and are induced from the previous discussion.

Invention has a history; it does not appear (except in its most rudimentary forms) to yield a logic which investigators can profitably follow. Most logical histories of the inventions which trace the growth of the modern communications are, in fact, "stories," derived *post hoc* from some moral or ethical principle *imposed* upon history by their authors. Tiny fragments of logic—like the economic incentives, for instance, which encouraged (or sped up) the invention of the television tape recorder—may be gleaned from the cause and effect relationships of some sub-components of the total story. But these are side plots to the main theme of invention.

The history of what are fruitlessly called the "mediums" of communication at present is quite like most other histories of technology. Events are usually forced into a determined theoretical mold. To note that one can discern no clear pattern of development in the inventions of the devices for communication, from cave man's grunts to satellite television, is no more innacurate or disheartening than for an ethical historian to say that the history of morals also yields no discernible logical pattern, only a fascinating story.

What both provide is a remarkably interesting study of *experiences* from which, hopefully, we may glean guidelines for future behavior.

Technology, the by-product of science and invention, has a history in this sense, too. It is clarified less by our shiny technological consumer products in the West than by its psychological by-products that pervade, as we have noted, all aspects of our environment. Western man today suffers from a rare disease, an *embarass de choix* of technologically oriented "truths."

The disease is exacerbated because technology has had built into it no value system, no morality, no ethics, no guarantee that it will relieve our miseries any more than it will compound them. We have discovered in technology (and the nuclear bomb is the ultimate symbol of this) what Faust found in nature (according to Morse Peckham): that he was trapped by the complete indifference of the natural world towards him, that man has not adapted to the holocaust of pressures around him, and that there is "no natural power which has but to be learned in order to make us perfectly happy." [21] We live, as children of the technological age, with this same disillusioning truth.

Precisely, then, technology's effect upon us has been clearly random, irrelevant to good or evil or to the welfare or detriment of the human organism. Techniques that lowered the death rate of our infants by immunizing them against diphtheria and other childhood diseases have condemned millions to starvation when they survive to adulthood. Automobiles and airplanes that speed us to new places also kill and maim us by the thousands every year.

Is there a psychological pattern to all of this? Of course not; the psychologics of technology are as random as Faust's natural forces. The irony one finds in the psychology of modernity is no less sharp than arbitrary cycles of life and death and the capriciousness of floods, fires and famines.

The technology of communications is no different, therefore, from any other technology. Why should it be? It possesses neither value, ethics, morality, purpose or reason, other than that which man chooses to give it. Its by-products (or results) are unpredictable psychologically, except insofar as conditions of past experience are repeated in the future.

Most of the instruments of this technology are accordingly analogous to an automobile, except that an automobile is more elaborate artistically than many of them.[22] A car does not have programmed into it the

[21] Morse Peckham, *Beyond the Tragic Vision* (New York: George Braziller, 1962), p. 172. Peckham equates Faust's predicament with modern man's impotence in the face of the threat of total destruction by atomic warfare. "Wouldn't it be terrible, we cry today," he writes, "if atomic warfare wiped out the human race? There is no reason, Faust would now tell us, to think so. If nature has purposes, we cannot know them; certainly there is no reason to think these purposes are directed to our benefit." The analogy above between the impersonal workings of nature and those of technology is quite fair. Mankind has yet to assume directive control of either.

[22] The exception would perhaps be some instruments like the modern phonographs and television sets that are constructed to look like decent pieces of furniture. Pens, pencils, papers, films, cameras, tape decks and the other impediments of communications technology (including the human larynx) are not distinguished by their aesthetic charm.

direction in which it will go, the places at which it will stop, or the speed at which it will be driven. All of these factors depend upon the driver, and upon forces within both the reasoning part of his make-up (the logical component) and his psychological dispositions. Without a skilled driver, an automobile is nothing more than a technological heap.

The only characteristics it manifests must be considered *potentials*, potentials that must be activated by the driver. And these potentials take the form of limits. The automobile will only travel within certain speeds; it will steer only in a specific way under specific conditions; its brakes will only operate with certain stopping power at certain speeds on certain surfaces, and so forth.

Generally speaking then, without a driver to operate it, an automobile demonstrates to one no logical place in the history of invention, nor does it serve any psychological function as an instrument of technology.

Under these circumstances, an automobile *per se* can hardly be said to "exist" at all! Without a driver to provide it with control, it has no reality—above and beyond its sheer bulk—merely potentials and limits.

Conclusion

There exists, therefore, no such entity as an automobile which is an "instrument of transportation." There are only cars driven by drivers *within the limits* that the technology of automobile manufacture creates for these instruments. True, one automobile will run in a manner remarkably like another (especially if the drivers agree to obey the same rules of the road), but any one automobile's logical and psychological role in the history of transportation is a unique function of one peculiar adventure with one particular car.

Every technique of communication yet devised by man responds to the same logical, psychological, historical force, and displays the same psychological recreative power as an automobile does.

One cannot escape the conclusion, therefore, that the instruments of communication considered as *techniques*—that is, as written or spoken languages, the print medium, the film, radio, television and the rest—are equally logically devoid of anything but the stories of their invention as history. They also operate at the mercy of the same confusion-inducing psychological tendencies as *all other technology.*

The remaining chapters of this section will bear out this contention by an analysis of what *does indeed* exist: the basic *arts or mediums* of communication, in both their logical and psychological modes, as they are utilized as content for various kinds of technological instruments, just as a car is utilized as a vehicle for transportation.

What we refer to today as "media" of communications are usually technological devices for supply. They limit what may be carried in the conduits,[23] but they have neither value nor form by themselves—except, again, as analogues of sheer bulk.

Granting that differences exist between *instruments* of communication, like the press, radio and film, and genuine *mediums*, what are these mediums and what role do they play in communication? How relevant are they to the content of a given communication? Of course, they are important—even crucial, but let us pause here, before we move to this problem, to consider an observation made by Rudolph Arnheim: "Why do some landscapes, anecdotes or gestures 'ring the bell'? Because they suggest, *in some particular medium*, significant form for relevant truth." [24]

[23] This limitation may be likened to the way a pipe limits the kind of fluid that it permits to run through it as to both amount and viscosity.
[24] Rudolph Arnheim, *Art and Visual Perception*, p. 163. "Significant form" is, as the reader is probably aware, the catch phrase of Susanne K. Langer's often quoted description of art. "Relevant truth" is Arnheim's contribution, as well as the observation about the medium, to which italics were added by the author.

Chapter 8

IN THE BEGINNING: NARRATIVE

NARRATIVE OR "telling" was the most pervasive of the pre-technological inventions for intellectual and emotive communication that appears *not* to have been an immediate function of man's biological nature.[1]

One easily uncovers a narrative aspect in all of the arts of communication developed before the era of technology. That is, drawing, painting, dancing, playing musical instruments or composing music are attempts to tell or communicate usually discursive thoughts or dispositions to others. The technological instruments of communication are generally hospitable to narrative. When these devices are considered according to their technological status as "radio, cinema, television" and so forth,[2] *all* of them may be employed to communicate narratives.

On FM radio, for instance, one may hear songs which attempt to communicate certain ideas of the composer. These ideas may be *narrated* or *told* much more efficiently than in song—but with less psychological pleasure for the listener. The songs are interrupted by announcers who *tell* things concerning consumer goods and services, and what we are *told* is "news." None of the sounds we hear have anything essentially to do with the technical nature of the instrument (a radio set) or the modulated impulses carried in the ether that transmit sound. But the sounds we hear, in one degree or another, attempt to communicate narratives. Hence the sepa-

[1] Fighting and copulating of course preceded telling in the anthropological history of communication. They are the outstanding—and sometimes only—observable means of communication between certain animals.

[2] These categories as instruments of communication are satisfactory for descriptive purposes here. For instance, when we talk about "radio," we usually have a common concept in mind. "Radio," however (and "cinema," "press" etc.), are poor terms for either logical or psychological discussion of these devices of communications. From a logical or psychological perspective, we are talking about technological *devices*, not *mediums* either of art or communication.

111

ration necessary between the *medium* of narrative and the *instrument* or *device* of radio transmission.

The current ubiquity of narrative gives us a clue to its antiquity. So does the observation that every individual seems to re-live the entire experience of the race in the development of his narrative abilities, just as a foetus' evolutionary background is repeated from single cell to human individual in nine months of uterine development.[3] Narrative is verbal before it is written, historically and organically, and it travels the distance from meaningless baby noises in the infant to compound circumlocutions in the adult entirely within its first or most primitive form, that of the spoken word.

What was the pre-verbal form of narrative? Logic tells us that it probably existed, and psychologic permits a measure of speculation as to what pre-verbal narrative may have been like. Writes I. A. Richards:

> Originally language may have been almost purely *emotive*; that is to say, a means of expressing feelings about situations (the danger cry), a means of expressing interpersonal attitudes (cooing, growling, etc.), and a means of bringing about concerted action (compare the rhythmical grunts that a number of individuals will utter while pulling at some heavy object). Its use for statement, as a more or less neutral means of representing states of affairs, is probably a later development. But this later development is more familiar to us now than the earlier forms, and we tend, when we reflect upon language, to take this use as the fundamental use.[4]

Other theorists, says LaBarre, particularly anthropologists, have more closely associated the origins of speech with the development and use of gesture. He cautiously suggests that:

> . . . speech may have originated from the *vocal* gestures of higher primate phatic communication, i.e., those vocalizations involved with danger-warning, territorialism, fighting, courtship and the like—vocalizations "international" from ape group to ape group. . . . The notion is one owed to Edward Sapir; but before him the chain of theorists in this vein include Rousseau, Vico, Lucretius, Epicurus and Democritus. It is important to note, however, that in the later theorists at least the notion always implies primate and hominoid *vocalization* or "vocal gesture," that is, the change from "phatic" cries to semantic speech.[5]

[3] One may infer, therefore, that narrative also has an evolutionary background as well as a history. Perhaps it *did* evolve, but the evidence of this evolution has, unfortunately, left no fossil record. When first we meet the most primitive men on earth—say the aborigines of Australia—they have already developed their skills of narration into complex arts. By the period of the beginning of recorded history, man had had hundreds of thousands of years of social experience on earth, and was already an expert narrator.
[4] I. A. Richards, *Practical Criticism*, p. 353.
[5] Weston LaBarre, "Paralinguistics and Kinesics" in Matson and Montagu, *The Human Dialogue*, p. 470.

LaBarre does not specify how he or other anthropologists imagine the change was accomplished.

Whatever else his skills, mature man is almost ideally physically suited to indulge in verbal narrative.[6] His cortical potential, his stance, the anatomy of his mouth, lips and tongue (to say nothing of his larynx) are obviously designed for operations vastly more elaborate than biting, chewing, kissing, swallowing and sucking. No known cultures have used in their language the full measure of man's verbal potential. "Of the sum total of possible human speech sounds," says Julian Whatmough, "and their permutations and combinations, only *a small submultiple appear in a given language*, and even this does not exploit fully its potential range." [7]

No specific organic directives, however, seem to have impelled man to write down what he said, however, unless one considers the mobile thumb a prerequisite for written language, which is doubtful. Written language is largely a configuration of human *intelligence* which began at many different cultural and historical starting points. One discovers cross-cultural "imitative" uses in writing of natural geometric shapes like the circle, the cross, the triangle and the square—a few of the designs noticeable in most written alphabets and pictographic writings. They probably represent little more than common, near universal responses to stimuli in nature, which are and were everywhere identical.

We are not primarily concerned here with theories of the generation of language *per se* but rather with its narrative or the *telling function*. The difference between the two is articulated with awesome clarity in Hannah Green's remarkable novel, *I Never Promised You a Rose Garden*.[8] The schizophrenic protagonist, Deborah, retreats into an imaginary and psychotic world of Yri, where the creatures with whom she dwells speak to her only in the language of Yri, her private means of communication with them. We are given to understand that this private language breaks most of the linguistic laws of English (Deborah's native tongue), but its ability to carry the narrative quality of speech appears entirely unimpaired by the

---

[6] See Whatmough, *Language, A Modern Synthesis*, pp. 151–153.

[7] *Ibid.*, p. 154. To the question of *why* man has been so satisfied with such a small percentage of potential power of speech, one can speculate that he employs merely that portion of his natural gifts that he *needs* to meet his immediate circumstances. One might as well inquire why, in the course of our life times, no matter how long, the most intelligent of us use only a fraction of our potential cortical brain power. Obviously, we use what we need—or *think* or *feel* or *intuit* we need—which may be man's most tragic organic shortcoming.

[8] Hannah Green, *I Never Promised You a Rose Garden* (New York: Signet Books, 1965). Insights which may be gleaned from this provocative novel for the student of communications are many. One may also come to some understanding from the travails of the central character into how the qualities of what we call "sanity" (or freedom from psychosis) relate to the communication processes within an individual psyche, and why schizophrenia is so frequently described as a malfunction of communication systems within the organism, taking on various forms in its various symptomologies.

fictional (?) character's illness. *Word meaning* is damaged by her psychosis
—*but not the need for her illusory friends to "tell" her things.* Narrative
(or telling) and language itself are thus vividly illustrated, in the context of
a deranged fantasy, as they accomplish psychologically separate functions.
In normal persons, language and telling are complements of the *same*
process. For Deborah, they are *discrete*, in much the same manner that
they are for some semanticists and linguists.

The Logical Bias

Its origins notwithstanding, language has survived throughout history
largely *in its narrative mode* with a distinct bias towards logic rather than
psychologic. However one *tells* anything—using words or pictures or
dramas—and however one disseminates what he tells—by letter, by snap-
shots or by impersonation—there is usually a logical formulation possible
for what he communicates. This formulation constitutes a narrative.

Should one recount, for instance, a highly charged *emotional* story—
say *Oedipus Rex*—the burden of the telling is still upon the *logic* of the
narration. This is true whether *Oedipus* is mediated to an audience as a
play, as a film performed by marionettes, as an opera, or a dance-drama. If
it fails to narrate the logical (or sense) component of the story, it fails
absolutely to communicate *Oedipus.*[9]

The source of narrative's power is in its simplicity; it is the most spare
medium of communication that man has devised. Arnheim has noticed [10] a
tendency towards simplicity in most of man's spontaneous affairs as the
state towards which we continually strive psychologically, particularly in art.
Our general impulse is towards the direction of harmonious logic. Says Arnheim, "In an absolute sense, a thing is simple when it consists in a small
number of structural features. In a relative sense, a thing has simplicity
when it organizes complex material with the smallest possible number of
structural features." [11] Arnheim notes that it is not accidental that scientists
and philosophers (as well as artists) seek simplicity in most of their propositions. Simplicity means satisfactory logic, and it usually means satisfactory
psychologic as well.

The *logical* content of narrative is therefore the simplest medium of
meaningful communication possible. The simplest form of *non-meaningful*
communication may be a picture, say, with *one* element like the line
"_____." But a line, standing alone, is not meaningful logically. The sen-

[9] One may *enjoy* an abstract dance version of *Oedipus*, but unless he can follow it
rationally as a story, it is not *Oedipus* any longer but simply *Dance* #1, or whatever
one may choose to call it. Perhaps it has become so abstruse that it only becomes
Oedipus by reading program notes, but the chances are that the notes will be almost
an entirely logical narrative of the story of *Oedipus Rex.*
[10] Arnheim, *Art and Visual Perception*, pp. 44–61.
[11] *Ibid.*, p. 49.

tence "It is raining," however, narrates its meaningful story simply, logically and (Arnheim might say) beautifully.

All narrative, no matter where it is found, or no matter what its function, is more closely related to logical than psychological types of meaning. Even for modern abstract art, atonal music, and "happenings," narrative statements may be presented about the events at hand. These statements invariably rely heavily upon narrative *in its logical mode*. For example: "The canvas was entirely blue, with three white circles in the center," or "The symphony sounded like a Chopin sonata played on garbage can lids."

The logical aspect of communications is, accordingly, the sum total of *meanings* evoked from thought when freed—for purposes of analysis— from feeling. Ogden and Richards[12] list about twenty-five non-equivalent and frequently incompatible specific meanings often observed in the English language. Their observations boil down specifically to two logical genera: 1) *objective* factors in the outside world; that is, what something *is* or *what is done with it,* and 2) *subjective* factors, depending upon what people *perceive* (or report they perceive) of how, where and when words are used. While the second category includes psychological interpretations of phenomena, note the words in parentheses. *Reports* given of psychological processes are logical data, and to qualify the nature of the meaning of anything, reported evidence (verbally mediated or signified any other way) is all that is necessary to infer logical meaning.

How glib to ask for a "sum total" of intangibles like meanings, when, obviously, no total in a cumulative mathematical sense may conceivably be formulated without resort to the hokum of quantifying qualities by means of arbitrary measuring sticks! Yet what we are referring to is indeed a total of qualities, possibly understood in the manner of the *Gestalt* psychologists. Their effort is to perceive "only as much as will enable us to identify what we see, that is to say, to allocate it to a particular class of objects or shapes with which we are familiar." [13]

Should the Gestaltist's "objects and shapes" be regarded, for our purposes as "themes and ideas," it is possible that his model provides a notion of how we perceive narrative: rather as a rabbit hops. With every cognitive jump, we bring together the inherent logic of each sub-segment of the nar-

---

[12] C. K. Ogden and I. A. Richards, *The Meaning of Meaning* (New York: Harcourt, Brace and Company, Inc., 1953), pp. 186–187. The author's three kinds of meanings are 1) *labels* (logical), 2) *usages* (both logical and psychological) and 3) *reactions* (psychological) which all satisfy one or another criterion for the word "meaning" as it is used in English. This book is, of course, a classic, but the impression of obscurity that it gives many readers is due less to the discursive writing of the authors than their reluctance or inability, at the time it was written (between 1910 and 1920) to distinguish between the logics and psychologics of human communication—particularly in terms of the central concept of meaning.

[13] M. D. Vernon, *The Psychology of Perception* (Baltimore Md.: Penguin Books, 1962), pp. 52–53.

rative element in a communication. Drawing our logical "sum total" is then less difficult than if we were forced to add up all the logical discrete elements of even simple narratives.

While this integrating function is apparently an individual psychological process, it satisfies the universal demand of the sender of a message to be understood. The basic unit of narrative is undoubtedly "the word" (or some sorts of impulses in the form of short phrases), mediated either in spoken or written form, which, in a series of logical propositions, has the power to encapsulate ideas of a extremely complex nature.

Plots and Logic

When narrative is forced into the modern literary form of the novel or enters the dramatic-artistic mediums (by way of live theatre, cinema, television, radio or printed play), the medium may be equated logically with the familiar concept of *plot*. The plot is the story of the narrative.

For the ancient masters of theatrical tragedies like Aeschylus, Sophocles and Euripides, this task of plotting was not a major creative problem, nor was it for later generations of authors of what today we call "folk dramas." The plots of these stories were already legends or myths; creativity was demonstrated non-logically by finding a new framework for the creation of a story in a psychologically satisfying way. Skilled playwrights and performers might then emphasize *their* own special (and socially relevant) constructions of the particular legend.[14]

Greek comic writers like Aristophanes and Menander could not, however, use traditional narratives. Few comic writers,[15] for that matter, of any generation have had any measure of choice but to create their own narratives. While a comic narrative may stay fresh logically, psychologically it uses up its point or potential for humor as soon as it is told once.[16] Comic plots are therefore given less serious consideration by students of literature

[14] Notation should be made here of the one contemporary playwright who has attempted to re-tell biblical stories in modern settings with a high degree of faithfulness to the logic of the original story and with much psychological justification for his liberties. That playwright is Tennessee Williams. See, for instance, his *Cat on a Hot Tin Roof* (New York: New Directions, 1955), for the manner in which he has re-told the old testament story of Isaac, Jacob and Esau.

[15] An exception would be the forty or so writers who have retold the Amphitryon story, which is a funny narrative on its face. Note, however, that it is described by Plautus, one of its early interpreters, as a "tragi-comedy," the first, I believe, known in the Western theatre.

[16] Burlesque skits have been handed down through time by generations of comics. But 1) the main *theme* of the narrative is the only element preserved; the rest is improvisation, and 2) the playlets come and go, falling in disuse on a certain burlesque "circuit" until a new audience matures, or an old one has forgotten the basic material. The variations in the well known circus act where twenty or more clowns step from a small automobile is a case in point. There are always enough "newcomers" or forgetful "oldsters" in the audience to guarantee the humorous effect of this simple logical narrative concept, providing that it is not repeated *too* often. It is dropped, accordingly, from most circus repertoires every now and then, and revived a few seasons later.

and drama than tragedies, the latter well dignified by the prestige of antiquity.[17] The difference between the two kinds of plots relates to the *illusion
of logical relevance*, which is usually greater in serious than in comic narrative, printed or spoken.

Few masters of rhetoric understood this particular cleavage in narrative
forms more clearly than Aristotle, although he could not recognize (utilizing the conceptual instruments of his time) the logical bias of *all* narrative.[18] In the *Poetics*, he recognizes that complications (logic) and development (psychologic) are the two essentials of both poetic narrative and
drama. He points out in his discussion that "many poets complicate well
and develop badly," [19] that is, they lean heavily towards the logical bias of
narrative.

Logical statements concerning the aesthetics of narrative are not difficult to formulate. If one has ever had the task of writing literary or theatrical reviews and becomes suspicious of his own psychological reactions (due
to special prejudices or an overdose of tranquilizers) he can usually retreat
behind statements of a logical aesthetic nature. "The first act ran too long";
"The book lacks a clear central theme"; "The characters are not motivated
sufficiently"; "No mention was made of the contributions of Erik Satie to
modern music," are familiar samples.

The logical bias of narrative must be old indeed, because it appears
nearly indispensable to human communication. Even today, most students
of communications center upon it when they wish to create scientific or
verifiable postulates about the communications process. The familiar statement "Who says what to whom with what effect and how," may (if desired) be answered in purely logical narrative terms; hence its appeal to so
many academic communications scholars. Analyses in this mode[20] are, in all
probability, conducted at present at the cave-man level of this discipline,

[17] Shakespeare uses this device in *Pericles*. Gower, as the chorus, begins:

> To sing a song that old was sung,
> From ashes ancient Gower is come;
> Assuming man's infirmities
> To glad your ears and your eyes . . .
> It hath been sung at festivals,
> On Ember-eyes and holy-ales;
> And lords and ladies in their lives
> Have read it for restoratives . . .

[18] Aristotle unfortunately makes his case for the logical bias of the *drama*, as opposed
to narrative—an issue that scholars of theatre still debate. Aristotle is, however, scrupu-
lously fair in his argument of the "question whether epic or tragic imitation is more
excellent," and his observations are still relevant to contemporary communications
problems.
[19] Aristotle, "The Poetics," in Barret H. Clark, *European Theories of the Drama*, p.
20.
[20] "Content analysis" is one example of such a popular methodology. See, for instance,
the outstanding handbook in this area: Bernard Berleson, *Content Analysis in Communications Research* (Glencoe, Ill.: The Free Press, 1952).

whether the messages involved are relayed by smoke signals, color television, or mediated by sophisticated computers.[21]

The Psychological Mode

The logical phrase of narrative is not, by any means, its most interesting or colorful mode or manifestation.[22] Mindful of this truism, within the past decade millions of dollars have been spent attempting to force the main thrust of primary and secondary education *out* of the *logical narrative* mode into which it was cast centuries ago by church scholars. The attempt has been justified by the claim that non-logical narrative schooling "works better" because students "enjoy" it more, and the subject matter is clearer.

The apparent failure of logical narrative in education justified the introduction into schooling of various mediums of communications[23] which have undoubtedly left their mark on thousands of classrooms. Many teachers have been encouraged to change their means of classroom operations as a result. Psychologically oriented narrative, pictures and dramatic recreation are at present employed widely in our schools in many ways. What we cannot calculate is the overall effect of this shift, and whether *the right parts of subject matter disciplines* have been transferred to these "new" mediums. Most research in this area has been designed merely to measure the influence of technology (not mediums) upon academic grades, rather than determine the real differences between the mediums themselves. That these experiments have shown that the *same kind of teaching* operates more or less the same way with and without technological aids (like television, films or tape recordings) might have been anticipated before experimentation began.[24]

Few teachers or public speakers do not desire to develop skill at mastering the art of utilizing the psychological mode of narrative communication. Yet most of them are powerless to improve markedly this aspect of their "performances." This is because the psychologics of narrative—like the psychologics of all mediums—relate more to *reaction* than to *action*, and

[21] Clear explanations of the present state of inquiry by modern scientists, most of whom have followed the mathematical path cut for them in the late nineteen-forties by Claude E. Shannon, can be found in J. R. Pierce's *Symbols, Signals and Noise*, in which the mathematical aspect of this field is kept to a minimum. Pierce's book is intended for the non-mathematically oriented layman, and, in general, makes good its intention. It is recommended once again as a clear description of progress being made in the study of the logical aspects of certain selected kinds of communications.

[22] We shall see that the logical modes of all the mediums we discuss in Part Three are not as generally pedestrian as the logic of narrative.

[23] We are discussing here solely the introduction of *mediums* into school work, not the introductions of *gadgets* which may by themselves make the logical narrative itself easier for students to swallow.

[24] See, for instance, John M. Kitross, "The Failures of ETV Research" in *Educational Broadcasting Review*, October 1967, pp. 41–48, one of many sensible articles on the waste of time and money that this "research" has engendered.

causal factors involved in the simplest of reactions, while often fairly simple to analyze, are usually difficult to control.

To note that they are "usually difficult" does not mean to say that they are *impossible* to modify. Quite the contrary; but far too little systematic study has been done yet (except by a handful of social psychologists) into the more subtle reactive aspects of communications. One exception is the Semantic Differential device which purports to measure "connotative meanings of concepts" (psychological meanings with a logical bias) on scales representing factors like *Activity, Potency* and *Evaluation,* although other elements such as *Understandability* have been employed as well in the construction of Semantic Differential instruments.[25] The Semantic Differential, however, is more effective at describing how meanings of words are being construed by certain individuals than in predicting what psychological effects of communications will (or may) result in given situations.

As a method of studying specific attitudes (providing the notion "attitude" is defined within a small enough compass), *post hoc* devices like the Semantic Differential have their special and limited uses. Their limitations become most apparent when their results are held up to the tremendous number of variables in the *psychological* study of one medium—narrative—alone! If such tests meet the needs of psychologists, sociologists and educators in helping them to "define their terms," they are serving the behavior sciences well. If, however, they are of service because behavior scientists have chosen their terms (like *Activity,* for instance) for their *logical* simplicity and their *psychological* shallowness, they are not likely to increase much our understanding of reactions to communications. When Kerlinger speaks, for example, about finally achieving definitive consensus by means of the Semantic Differential in the connotative definition of "discipline" or "progressive education," [26] he is not encouraging the study of the human communication of meaning at a high level of significance.

Of the systematic devices for studies of components of narrative that have been attempted, the Semantic Differential is one of the best known and most widely used today—particularly in dissertations for Ph.D. degrees. A mountain of labor has (so far) brought forth a mouse: a genuine, well constructed and active mouse, but a mouse, nevertheless. Hardly any of this output is of practical value yet to communications students of any stripe.

A broader approach to the analysis of the psychological mode of the medium of narrative is found in certain concepts drawn from the literature of psychoanalysis. It relates to the theory of the non-conscious as a

[25] See Fred N. Kerlinger, *Foundations of Behavioral Research* (New York: Holt, Rinehart and Winston, Inc., 1966), pp. 569–580. Dr. Kerlinger outlines here some of the main methods, results and applications of the work of Osgood and others in the development of this instrument for which he sees many possibilities in the further studies of the logics of verbal communications.
[26] *Ibid.*, p. 579.

source of stimuli for human thought and feeling. Both the non-conscious and the conscious are, of course, dimensions of *mind*, not protoplasm. If they exist in any manner as physical entities capable of measurement, they possibly take the forms of *energy* rather than matter. They probably have their physical locus, also, in our brains, along with our centers of consciousness.

Reactive Aspects of Narrative

We may consider most reactions to communications as *communalities of experience*, either *cognitive* (that is, sense reactions) or *emotional* (that is, felt reactions).[27] While reactions are mostly subjective matters, they are fundamentally related to the social orientation of the individual, except perhaps in cases of psychological abnormality.

Our reactions to narrative, therefore, may exist on two levels of apprehension: first, they may be *conscious*, perceptible and controlled responses, or second, they may be *non-conscious* dispositions, which are generally charged more with emotional power than the former. Proponents of nearly all psychoanalytical theories, however, find intense, apparently logically ordered patterns (and priorities of *value* between certain emotions) in the non-conscious.

The psychologics of our reactions on the conscious level are not difficult to isolate and categorize. If we weep at Anne Frank's diary, most of the conscious, and some of the non-conscious factors causing our tears probably are not enigmas after a few attempts at self-searching—for most of us. On the other hand, our conscious and non-conscious reactions to a book like *Lolita* (for numerous reasons) will probably both tend to be more complex. We may find, without perceptible cause, that they will vary from hearty humor to unexplained rage. And reactions to *Lolita* vacillate more in most contemporary populations than to the Anne Frank diary.[28]

Communication—in this case narrative—elicits from us, however, different degrees of conscious and non-conscious response which depend both upon the nature of the narrative *and* the nature of the perceiver. Non-conscious responses are mediated to consciousness through various "censoring" mechanisms as "acceptable" reactions, either by diminishing their power or metamorphosizing them into ideas that we are able to entertain consciously. These censoring forces are probably alike, one to one, for most of us who play similar roles in one culture. Here we discover one explanation of why certain distinctive narrative communications "take," or "catch on" at a given time for a certain population, and why certain others do not.[29]

---

[27] Chapters 14 and 15 will be concerned entirely with these two aspects of communication and demonstrate how and why cognitions and emotions modify the many aspects of all three mediums of communications.
[28] The assumption is made here that the auditors of whom we are speaking are all relatively homogeneous in regard to environmental and cultural factors.
[29] The surprising success of Dr. Eric Berne's *Games People Play* (New York: The

Differences in reactions which appear entirely capricious will always make psychological sense—if the psychological origins of the reactions can be discovered. So will the seemingly irrational reactions of numerous people to narratives like a long-winded speech by a pet candidate or the special delight a young man may take in his intended's near-illiterate correspondence.

At its most profound level, narrative (like other mediums of communication) acts upon basic human drives and repressed material which, psychoanalytic theory tells us, is maintained individually as potential psychic energy within the unconscious. It is not necessary to comment here upon the nature of this material.[30] Whether repressed material is predominantly sexual or power-assertive, whether guilt is repressed more intently than "forgotten" material, is not at issue here. It is sufficient to note that the bulk of psychologics in the reactive aspect of the narrative medium seems to depend upon non-conscious material, by its nature emotional, and quite similar from individual to individual who has each acculturated similarly.

This unconscious material appears to be handled through the non-conscious in a manner somewhat similar to the process shown in the diagram below, although the implication of a geographical dimension for metaphorical "space" is unfortunate. The following design, however, represents an analogous guess as to how this non-conscious material finally reaches the conscious state:

Grove Press, 1964), may be explained in this manner. Published to sell (at best) less than 10,000 copies, the volume became a national best seller within a few months. Why? To say that the stratagems of human behavior described by the clever Dr. Berne "struck a responsive chord" for millions of Americans means little. To note, however, that non-conscious emotional material shared by millions of Americans yielded the same response consciously (that is, that Dr. Berne was "explaining" various bewildering facets of contemporary middle-class behavior) sheds some considerable light. Berne's book is especially interesting in this regard because it has little to recommend it as logical narrative: it is arbitrarily arranged, poorly written, disorganized, artless, etc. But, in a sense, these defects are virtues because they force the reader to concentrate upon the relevance of Berne's delightful categories to his *own* spectrum of non-conscious emotional dispositions. The book is a fine exercise, ironically, in self-exploration, rather than the volume of "do it yourself" psychoanalysis it was designed to be.

30 Kenneth Burke has articulated eight varieties of unconscious, from the non-conscious processes by which wounds heal and our (his) endocrine glands work, to "Error, Ignorance and Uncertainty" in human affairs. Whether these eight categories are genuine unconscious aspects of existence or just "manners of speaking" is not relevant here. Nor is the observation that about half of them are loosely Freudian (that is, concerned with repressed or forgotten material or related to manifestations of the "id") significant to the psychologics of narrative. Their value may be found in the way in which they add both sophistication and maneuverability to the original Freudian notion of a gross unconscious. They demonstrate that we may speak of unconscious processes with a good deal of cognitive latitude, without connoting that the discussion is revolving solely about "sex" or "instinct" or even a more generalized "libido." Briefly stated, Burke's eight categories concern 1) bodily processes, 2) historical processes, 3) usable but forgotten memories, 4) submerged personality characteristics, 5) a sense of futurity, 6) non-conscious backlash or dialectic, 7) intuition, and 8) mistakes and ignorances. While we have no *specific* need for them in this chapter, their mention here will hopefully broaden the popular idea of unconscious as a reservoir of repressions and instinctual strivings. See Kenneth Burke, *Language As Symbolic Action*, pp. 67–72.

PROCESS OF MEDIATION

———————→   ———————→   ———————→

DEEP UNCONSCIOUS
drives and highly threat-
ening material, only
aroused by violent stimuli
and capable of being used
consciously only in modi-
fied form. By the time
this material becomes
conscious, it has been
"handled" and changed
by intervening processes.
Much of this material re-
lates to what are loosely
called "instincts."

PRE-CONSCIOUS or
more lightly held modi-
fied basic drives—those
which may be accepted
into consciousness. Also
other slightly repressed
material—both cognitive
and emotive once han-
dled by consciousness
but now "forgotten," or
material which was ap-
parently threatening and
therefore "misunder-
stood."

CONSCIOUSLY held
materials which we can
"know" and "feel" and
which give perceptible
meaning to stimuli, in-
cluding narrative.

———————→   ———————→

(Between these states, various censoring forces, previously mentioned, operate continually. Energy remains in a constant state of
activity, slowing down as it moves against the drift (←) and towards
pre-conscious and more subjective deep unconscious material.)

The model above may naturally relate to our reactions to all communications. Why, therefore, raise the issue in the context of the psychological
mode of narrative?

The question can be answered by examination of the narrative medium. Of the three major mediums of communication discussed in this and
the ensuing chapters, *the cleavage between the logical and psychological
mode is most apparent in the case of narrative.* This contrast is also intimately related to the difference between conscious and non-conscious
processes themselves. It is generally appropriate to associate narrative's logical bias with the conscious use of the material narrated, just as we may
roughly (but accurately) note that the psychologics of narrative are closely
related to non-conscious reactions to narrative material.[31]

We do not perceive *meaning* in narrative entirely in our conscious
states of perception. As the diagram above shows, we *may* find meaning
perceptible in the conscious state which may be either logical or psychological. Because of the peculiar nature of the narrative medium, *most* of this
perceptible meaning is logical, but some of it (like e. e. cummings' unusual

[31] These associations are less relevant in regard to the mediums of pictures and re-
enactments than to narrative. Aesthetic considerations of the mediums make it difficult,
in fact, frequently to decide in what degree pictures and reenactments incline to logic
or psychologic (much less consciousness or non-consciousness) since, in matters of art,
"feeling" is so consistently objectified, and these mediums show so little of narrative's
innate logical bias.

poetic narratives, Stephen Crane's startling word use, T. S. Eliot's intentional obscurities or Henry Miller's vulgarities) is both easily amenable to consciousness and at the same time predominantly psychological in its reactive aspects. *The fact that one is conscious of meaning, therefore, does not mean that that meaning must be logical.* Quite the contrary, frequently.

Nor is meaning elicited from narrative entirely because of conscious reactions to it. Meaning may be evoked from narrative in the deep unconscious or in the pre-consciousness. These meanings, however, will be manifest psychologically and will probably be associated with certain specific *kinds* of stimuli, for instance, material of an intensely emotional nature (perhaps religious narratives, poetry, myths and stories), associated with repressed or basic impulses. Symbols, common emotional stimulants (in the form of clichés and fairy tales for children or adults), arresting and bold language use, and humorous material may stimulate our less deeply held pre-conscious processes and yield psychologically significant meanings.

Such psychological reactions will be mediated to consciousness as feeling states, not necessarily deep or pungent emotions, but as dispositions, outlooks, senses of discontent or satisfaction, minor pleasures or pains, comforts or discomforts. Ghost stories that we may remember from childhood were perceived largely in this way. They were built on slim logical threads, but were replete with trappings and embellishments designed to activate non-conscious fears of "things that go bump in the night." [32] As we pass these stories on to our own children, we pass on not only the psychological continuation of our childhoods to theirs, but we also play upon commonly understood cultural values and sensitivities. All of us in a given culture—or in one social class, geographical region or religious or racial subgroup—live in the same household of psychologics, and therefore share some measure of common material available for non-conscious activation with countless other individuals.

[32] All children's literature, from *Peter Rabbit* to *Batman*, is blessed by a shortage of logic and a plethora of psychologic. In my opinion, while certain forms and stories appear more satisfying than others (and much of it *is* unimaginative), the fuller the range of stops that any individual opus plays upon in the non-consciousness of children, the more enjoyable it is likely to be for them. Thus *cruel* and *violent* stories, like *Alice in Wonderland* or the Grimm Stories (unabridged), or even war stories, or horror tales are unlikely to "seduce the innocent" who are, psychologically speaking, dying to be seduced and far from innocent. Thus, also, was David Riesman correct in *The Lonely Crowd* (Garden City, New York: Doubleday and Company, Inc., 1953), in using modern children's literature as an index of the kind of value structure a culture attempts to induce its young to ingest on a non-conscious level, if we remember that most respectable children's books are written today for adults who buy them. They are geared to *their* psychological reactions rather than those of children. (See Riesman, *op. cit.*, pp. 120–132.) The kids, however, remain true to their basic natures, and almost invariably prefer ghost stories, their gruesome comic books, war and horror movies on television to "approved literature."

Narrative's Psychological Determinants

Both the emotional and cognitive determinants for psychological reactions to the medium of narration may be discovered in the on-going experience of the recipient of a communication. To *locate* a source for a stimulus, however, does not mean that one is able to *qualify* the nature of that source so as to hazard precise judgments about it. As with the psychologics of all the major mediums of communications, the locations of sources provides for us merely a set of limits within which to explain—usually *post hoc*— why certain people react as they do to certain types of narratives. More accurately, they usually illuminate some of the reasons why *we* behave or feel as *we* do when exposed to a certain kind of communication in the narrative medium.

The list which follows does not exhaust the possibilities of determinants, nor may each category be mutually exclusive, but their relevance to our perceptions of narrative is significant.

Culture has already been mentioned and discussed. Narrative is highly sensitive to cultural orientation, both in terms of *what* is said and *how* it is said. In both Western and Eastern societies, parables, allegories and metaphorical narratives appear to have had, historically, a deeper influence on the collective behaviors of man than any other form of the narrative medium.[33] Parables, allegories and metaphors are logically culture bound; psychologically, they frequently may be transferred from culture to culture, varying slightly in meaning but constant in impact. All myths, says Theodore Reik "present reactions to events and situations within the early family of mankind. The comparison helps us to understand that there is a 'family resemblance' between them since they reflect the common adventures of mankind of the Old Stone Age. They reveal, to quote Josef Campbell, 'such constant features that innumerable mythologies of the world resemble each other as dialects of a single language.' The oneness of mankind is better manifested in myths than in other productions." [34] Culture places its unmistakable variable stamp on these narratives, however.

Indicating the psychological power of narrative in this regard, Malinowski writes, "Mythology . . . or the sacred tradition of society, is a body of narratives woven into their culture, dictating their belief, defining their ritual, acting as a chart of their social order and the pattern of their moral behavior. Every myth has naturally a literary content, since it is always a narrative, but this narrative is not merely a piece of entertaining fiction or explanatory statement to the believer. It is a true account of sensational events which have determined the constitution of the world, the essence of

---

[33] From the *Bible* to Orwell's *1984*, from the sayings of Lao-tsu to ancient Chinese fables dressed up in Marxian morality, the fundamental narratives in most written traditions are parables, and their method of instruction has been by precept and insinuation rather than by logical, didactic discourse.

[34] Theodore Reik, *Myth and Guilt* (New York: George Braziller, Inc. 1957), p. 56.

moral conduct, and determines the ritual contact between man and his maker, or other powers that be." [35]

Language is of course a facet of culture of primary importance in determining the nature and direction of narrative's psychological impact. All narrative, no matter how it is eventually expressed, is containable in the language of the cultures where we find it. The narrative element of a silent film like *The Last Laugh* (which is devoid of titles) can be competently articulated in two or three paragraphs of prose.

The essential powers of language (whatever they are), as mediators of meaning, will influence the nuances of narrative. Certain jokes, for instance, *cannot* be translated from Yiddish, German or French into English and remain funny! Conversely, many American "wisecracks" are insipid in any language but English. English, though, does not have a "familiar" form of address like the French *tu*, and it is difficult, accordingly, to get the point of certain French narratives across in it. We have observed that most languages can be used to illuminate most *logical* points,[36] but *psychological* distortion from language to language is quite severe, and it is particularly important when political, social or religious narratives are translated.

Individual dispositions, both immediate and permanent, must be considered as factors influencing psychological reactions to narratives. Aside from the force of culture, there are immediate and long range influences working on people—from hunger and fatigue to glandular abnormalities; malfunctioning organs of perceptions to drug induced conditions—that are vitally related to the psychologics of narrative. What popular literature calls "brainwashing" is frequently the induction within an individual (by means of severe and often brutal forms of conditioning) of a psychological state wherein the individual is receptive to certain narratives, the content of which would be repellent to him were he in a "normal" condition.[37]

Rhetorical skill is another factor in determining the psychological outcome of narrative. The manner of telling has something to do with the nature of reaction. Telling refers, of course, to any sort of device, be it language or filmed ballet, by which narrated ideas are mediated to the perceiver. Neither clarity, nor brevity, nor simplicity are the only issues at stake here, although clear, brief, simple narratives are usually more logically satisfying than muddied, long complicated ones.

Rhetorical ease in the use of the medium of narration through any devices (*including* written or spoken language) is a *skill*. It is often believed to be an art. Perhaps it is, when a master orator like Churchill or Hitler

---

[35] Bronislaw Malinowski, *Sex, Culture and Myth* (New York: Harcourt, Brace and World, Inc., 1962), pp. 249–250.
[36] See Chapter 3.
[37] See William Sargent, *Battle for the Mind* (Garden City, New York: Doubleday and Company, Inc., 1957), for the mechanics of this process, according to the principles of Pavlovian psychology, as well as much interesting material on how individual dispositions have been modified to accept religious and political ideologies.

makes a speech, or a Nabakov writes a story. At any rate, the psychological end product may be quite different when the same narration is told by individuals employing similar devices but possessing different degrees of rhetorical skill. The logical aspect of the narrative is also disturbed by the acuity of these skills, but to a lesser degree than its psychologics.

The Prestige of the Communicator has been demonstrated experimentally[38] to constitute a powerful psychological factor in modifying the attitudes of an individual or group towards any type of narrative. The prestige factor relates not only to the actual presence of a personality narrating, but to such matters as the authorship of a book or magazine article, the aegis under which a communication is offered or the nature of the device employed to deliver it. Despite the fact that they use the identical medium of narrative, identical comments by similar politicians produce different psychological effects on certain people when they are printed in the newspaper or read by the politician himself on radio or television. Logically, they are identical and employ the same basic medium of communication: narrative. What has changed (among other things) is the way in which the image of the politician has influenced various readers or viewers psychologically due to the cultural prestige of the instruments employed.

Conclusion

We have traced the languages of communication to their historical roots and even speculated concerning their anthropological beginnings. As spoken language evolved, the medium of narrative became the first means of communication to employ any number of artistic forms, and its influence has been felt in the development of all other mediums (and the arts and sciences) over the years.

In its earliest forms, narrative was probably employed to exchange crude cognitive ideas of men to one another. Whatever the reasons, narrative usually displayed (and still displays) a distinct bias towards logical communication. We tell each other sensible things. Narratives found in paintings, sculpture, music, drama, dance, and those distributed by modern instruments of communication concern mostly the logical phase of communication experiences. If narrative does not travel primarily in a channel of logical discourse, it is not narrative; it is nonsense.

The psychological mode of the medium of narrative is also visible in the emotional reactions of people. When we examine these reactions from the psychoanalytical perspective, we discover that they may be both conscious and non-conscious, and in no way different from other sorts of conscious and non-conscious reactions to the mediums of picture and re-

[38] See Helen Black Lewis, "An Experiment on the Operation of Prestige Suggestion" in Guy E. Swanson, Theodore M. Newcomb and Eugene Hartley (eds.), Readings in Social Psychology, Revised Edition (New York: Henry Holt and Company, 1952), pp. 18–29, and Carl I. Hovland and Walter Weiss "The Influence of Source Credibility on Communication Effectiveness" in Daniel Katz et al. (eds.) Public Opinion and Propaganda (New York: The Dryden Press, 1954), pp. 337–347.

enactment. They fall into certain categories of covert or overt experience, functioning as part of the perceptual processes of the individual. Certain sorts of narrative are almost sure to evoke various strong non-conscious feeling states in people from a given cultural background. Also, a number of specialized conditions for communicating narrative (like culture, language, character, rhetorical skill and prestige) seem to influence this psychological mode quite extensively, but have less effect upon the logics of perception.

This latter psychological peculiarity is misunderstood frequently and identified as the "distinctive aesthetic nature" of so-called "media" (really *instruments*) of print, film, radio, television and so forth. Because the psychologics of narrative have little to do with the "distinctiveness" of print, film, etc., attempts at articulating these non-existent aesthetics have *all* been failures. They have yielded neither theories nor principles which are even perfunctorily relevant either to the history or current utilization of the instruments (radio, television and film particularly) to which they are supposed to refer.

Chapter 9

PICTURES

Pictures of all sorts have become so commonplace in our environment that we cannot appreciate them for what pre-photographic man knew they were: basic tools for men to use to communicate over periods of time with one another. And the pictures he appreciated (and sometimes worshipped) utilized most of the same visual forms we consider "pictorial" today, not only in the graphic arts, but in sculpture, fountain construction, cathedral architecture, carriage building, and costume. Pre-photographic man's communication by picture was both socially important and emotionally intense, as images were captured or created by skilled and gifted artists.[1]

---

[1] Self-evident but curious is the observation that pictorial art has apparently moved *away from* the main stream of life in the technological societies of the modern world. Note that Sir Herbert Read in *To Hell With Culture* (New York: Schocken Books, 1963), locates the beginning of modern "Culture" (and the end of a world in which art was a part of life) in 1510, more than three hundred years before the invention of photography, but immediately after the development of printing technology. Read also associates it with the rise of democratic capitalism in the following way:

> Culture, we are told, went underground in the Dark Ages, and it was a long time before it came to the surface again. The next epoch, known as the Middle Ages, is rivaled only by the Greek age; but, oddly, it was not conscious of its culture. Its architects, its illuminators, its painters were clerks. They had no word for art in the sense of our "fine arts": art was all that was pleasing to the *sight*: a candlestick, a chessman, a cheese-press.
>
> But the Middle Ages came to an end, and with them the guild system and the making of things for use. Certain clever people began to grab things—church property, common land, minerals, especially gold. . . . And thus the capitalist system came into existence, and with it the things we call "culture." (P. 11.)

Read might well consider that among the destroyers of art as culture were modern printing and photographic industries and the surfeit of *sights* man is now fed via instruments for reproducing pictures of all kinds, still and moving. Although this phenomenon occurred late, it was—and is—a lucrative adjunct of capitalism, from East-

Two dates stand out in the history of pictures as a modern language of communication. The first in 1430, which marks the invention of central perspective in painting in Europe; the other is 1837, the date usually given for the invention of photography by Louis J. M. Daguerre in France. Both inventions are similar in that they were logical moves towards perfecting the literal representation of reality on a two-dimensional plane, thereby integrating more closely than previously the work of the artist with what appeared to be "real life." On the other hand, the first date represents a significant change in the way individuals *perceived* the world around them psychologically and *what* in nature they considered *worth* seeing. It thus marks a major *modification* of a fundamental medium of communication. The second date signifies the moment when invention led to a technology which was to spread abroad this still relatively new method of perceiving to the masses. It allowed them to see nature with "accuracy" (meaning an adherence to the psychological novelty of central perspective) by freezing the motion of the ever-moving world and their usually-shifting eyes, and stamping it onto a two dimensional plane. Eventually, of course, this technology permitted pictures to extend through time as well as space by means of motion pictures and television. A third plane (or depth perspective) was added to photography in the last century, although methods for the recreation of a depth illusion had been discovered by painters centuries before.[2]

The logical history of the medium of picture may therefore be divided into three periods, descriptive of how pictures were employed by the cultures in which they were created. They are, 1) the pre-central perspective period, 2) the post-central perspective period, and 3) the post-photographic period. Certain primitive societies exist today which are still in period 1) because they have not yet (and will probably never) pass through the cultural experiences leading up to the discovery of central perspective. Other

man Kodak to *Life Magazine* to Hollywood, U.S.A. to the swarming free-lance news photographers of Rome.
[2] The ability to add the perception of the third plane to photography has stirred surprisingly little enthusiasm in the general public, from the era of the stereoptican photographs to today's 3-D movies. It is possible that the recently developed technique of holography, using laser beams, will generate more sustained interest, but this is doubtful. The illusion of depth which technological devices add to photography merely makes the end product of this medium—the still or moving picture—more *real*. This carries the instrument to its near-logical aesthetic finite end. Since the medium of picture is most satisfactory logically *as a picture* (as opposed to reality), what is the *psychological* use of making it look so real that it might be real and not a picture? An objection may well be raised that high fidelity recordings of music are similarly unnecessary. Not true. Hi-fi, stereo music gives us a more faithful reproduction of *art* than former phonograph systems; color, 3-D films merely give us more faithful reproductions of *visual reality*. The art of the photographer—a formidable one—is as likely to be expressed by a picture taken in a box camera as by means of the most sophisticated photographic equipment! This is simply because *picture* is the medium of communication, not the technology of the photographic device, which is merely one way of *making pictures* according to the skill, imagination and artistic ability of the photographer.

cultures, like the Japanese, have been influenced by Western invention, both pre- and post-photographic, and the role of the medium of picture in such cultures cannot be explained as neatly as in the West.

We are mainly interested first in the *logical* reasons that pictorial art existed—and succeeded in whatever its cultural mission was—*without* the comparatively simple invention of central perspective, what *logical* changes occurred to picture as a communications medium with the invention of central perspective, and how the technology of photography modified further the role of pictures in communication.

We will not be able to understand the profound psychological connotations of these changes until these logical matters have to some degree been resolved.

Pictures and Logic

The reason that men probably resorted to pictures for communication —from the historical and/or logical viewpoint—remains a relatively elemental matter. Colin Cherry has noted succinctly that there are "simply not enough words to express the subtlety of every shade of thought. If we had words for everything, their numbers would be astronomically large and beyond our powers of memory or our skill to use them." [3] Man therefore resorts to non-verbal behavior, communications involving either sight and sound or both, but not words. Some of them are described by Jurgen Ruesch in this manner:

> Verbal signals . . . are accompanied by an enormous variety of non-verbal signals that depend upon the activities of the muscles, glands, skin or mucosa. Some of these involve involuntary structures—the autonomic nervous systems, the smooth muscles, and the endocrine glands; some are mediated through voluntary structures—the central nervous system and the striped muscles affecting tonus, posture, and voluntary movement. Since emotional expression is under both voluntary and involuntary control, it is difficult to hide, particularly when it is intense. Changes in skin and muscles inform the observer by visual means, whereas changes in voice patterns impinge upon his ears.[4]

Our non-verbal vocabulary is probably tremendous, as large or larger than our verbal vocabulary, but it must reach a logical limit in terms of what it can accomplish pragmatically. There are two major communications functions which neither verbal nor non-verbal communications may accomplish.

First, and logically most important, there was (and is) nothing permanent about the most elaborate statements made with the multitude of

[3] Colin Cherry, *On Human Communication* (New York: John Wiley and Sons, Inc., 1961), p. 69.
[4] Jurgen Ruesch, *Nonverbal Communication* (Los Angeles: University of California Press, 1959), pp. 45–46.

units combined and recombined in both the verbal and non-verbal mediums of communication.[5] Man himself, though individually vulnerable, seemed to the pre-scientific mind always to *have* inhabited an earth he *will* always inhabit. Nature, despite her curious cycles, appeared permanent. Environments changed but slowly, and most men remembered worlds that had changed little since their birth, despite occasional devastations of fire or flood.

Communications, however, were different from the rest of culture because they vanished immediately. The one exception to this difference (in addition eventually to written language) was the art of picture making. It is difficult *not* to conclude that the earliest prehistoric pictures were crude and childlike, but we have no evidence that they were either. They were created with simple implements, but so is a contemporary charcoal sketch. They did not adhere to our modern psychological concepts of "seeing," but neither does modern sculpture. Some of them were remarkably permanent, because we have lately discovered well-preserved samples. In their manner, it is agreed, even to modern tastes, they are quite beautiful. Most art historians concur that they were drawn or molded to communicate *something* (exactly what, we cannot be sure), and that, as instruments of communication, they were probably successful.[6]

Second, picture provided man with a logical spectrum of *meaning* closed to him as long as he depended upon verbal and non-verbal vocabularies. Picture (and sculpture) literally gave him some measure of control over the entire natural world that he could communicate to others. Now, he could reactivate at will the power of animals, or of other men, or of hunts, or rituals by virtue of his own artistic talents.

In other words, the *symbolic aspect* of picture was opened up to him, and along with it the power of picture to conjure up both supernatural

---

[5] The logical appeal of permanence *alone* is still a power in "selling" the medium of pictures. The comparatively recent idea of a *museum* for pictures was a socialized answer to the problems of permanence in industrial societies which had discarded both their élite leisure class and notions of a total *public* culture *per se* for rich and poor alike. (Relics of such latter civilizations may still be found in Italy and France where cities and towns are virtual museums.) The success of photography as a hobby relates to the concept of preserving, in black and white or in color, the flavor of an experience for the future. The proclivity, however, of all dyes employed in color photographic processes (still and filmed) to change in time is not publicized by film or camera manufacturers. Amateur photographers seem to remain curiously unaware of this fact, leading one to believe that few of them keep their pictures long enough for them to notice the defect. It is therefore probably fair to assume that they are searching for the psychological *illusion* of permanency—not permanency itself.
[6] We must not base our ideas of primitive Western art on a handful of surviving relics of caves in Altamira, Spain; Font de Gaume, France; Ariege and similar places, simply because these are the only relics that have survived to our time, or because they look like primitive drawings in other cultures. Historically, primitive art may have been far more aesthetically elaborate and may have performed functions different from those we commonly ascribe to it. See Lancelot Hogben, *From Cave Painting to Comic Strip*, pp. 11–69, for an interesting review of what we *do* know.

forces and the magic powers of ritual invented to contain these forces. Susanne Langer describes the process in general terms:

> A subject which has emotional meaning for the artist may thereby rivet his attention and cause him to see its form with a discerning, active eye, and to keep that form present in his excited imagination until its highest reaches of significance are evident to him; then he will have, and will paint, a deep and original conception of it. That is why men long in love or in religious fervor are inspired to produce great, convincing works of art. Not the importance of these theme, nor the accuracy of its depiction, nor the fantasies stirred in the beholder, make a work of art significant, but the articulation of visual forms which Hoeslin would call its "melody." [7]

The original pictures man made in his many primitive cultures may or may not have been fine art in a modern observer's terms, but one cannot gainsay the significance that these images must have had for him. Nor can one belittle the probable degree of success achieved from this clever method of communicating with the future and into the consciousness of others the structure of nature as it appeared to primitive man's eye.

Central to the understanding of the logic of picture is an appreciation of the way *all* pictures relate to life and the fact that *it is impossible for pictures to function as abstractions as long as they are perceived in the logical mode.* (Psychologically, abstraction is not only possible, it is—and has been since primitive times—ubiquitous.) *Every* picture, logically, represents man's experience, even if it is the design on wallpaper or painted by a machine, by an ape, or by someone with defective vision. Modern abstract art may show us circles, blank canvases, blobs, streaks and blurs. Circles, blank canvases, blobs, streaks and blurs are as much a part of the world of our perceptions and experience, however, as nudes, violins, flowers or college presidents. And the pictures which contain them are therefore logically meaningful structures, although they look like a child's scribbles and may (from the psychological perspective of the artist) be an actual or symbolic *denial* of logic, form, or sense—or of the very existence of nature itself! In the clothing trades, so called "abstract" patterns have been created and reproduced as logical forms of picture for many years. Necktie design is perhaps one of the most abstract of all art forms in the world today, and yet (in its logical mode) one is able to describe the color, texture, and design of most neckties easily.

All ornament, all design—and all *revolts* against ornament and design —therefore relate to man's sensual experiences and yield to the descriptive powers of logic. As long as they serve a pictorial function which *one* man may describe, they cannot logically be abstract. On the other hand, should one replace a broken pane of glass in his window with plywood, the piece of wood would not be a picture—unless one decided it was. Then the configu-

[7] Langer, *Philosophy in a New Key*, pp. 203–204.

ration in the wood and the brown loops and swirls would be part of the aesthetic structure of a new picture! Were one given to taking photographs, he might even photograph the plywood, using color film with various filters, and come up with both startling and satisfying results. Then others might join him in the belief that the configurations in the wood were indeed a true picture!

Any part of nature, or anything in the world that can be arranged in a manner desired by an artist—including the substances we call "paints"—may become, one way or another, part of the structure we recognize as a picture. A picture requires merely that there be made a (more or less) permanent rendition, within certain territorial limits, of some part of nature, and that the rendition have the potential power to display one or more generalizations about the natural world. The latter may be as simple as "a line" (a generalization of a primitive sort) or a statue of George Washington (a generalization of a complex sort). Picture making in its logical mode is therefore as simple or as complex as logic itself, and the criticism of pictures in this mode requires knowledge of the aesthetic realities of line, form, color and the rest of the components of visual nature as we have learned to see it.

Perspective and Logic

One of the most difficult logical problems connected with pictorial communication is the comprehension of how culture and history relate to the phases of invention through which the medium of picture has passed. We have previously noted the three main periods: pre-central perspective, post-central perspective, and post-photography. These phases were marked by socio-cultural changes—whether causes or results is not at issue here—which modified considerably the logical function of picture in culture at large, excluding the universal elements discussed above. The logical history of picture, in other words, has moved from one major frame of cultural reference to another *twice* in the period from 1400 A.D. to the present. It is necessary to consider these shifts, not as changes in style or schools of art, but as significant upheaval in the history of our society which involved numerous institutions other than the arts.

In the first place, the invention of central perspective in the fifteenth century is described clearly *as a cultural event* by Rudolph Arnheim:

> On the one hand it (central perspective) is the culmination of the centuries-old effort to reintegrate pictorial space. In this sense it is simply a new solution of a problem that had been solved in different ways by other cultures. It is no better or worse than the (illusion of) two-dimensional space of the Egyptians or the system of parallels in an oblique cube employed by the Japanese. Each of these solutions is equally complete and perfect, different from the others only in the particular concept of the world it conveys.

Considered in this way, central perspective is a strictly intropictorial matter. It is a product of visual imagination, a method of organizing the shapes available in the medium. It reflects reality, but it is no more connected with the conception of it than the systems developed by other cultures. . . .

But at the same time central perspective is also the result of a completely different procedure. It is what we get when we set up between our eyes and the physical world a vertical plate of glass, on which we trace the exact contours of the objects as we see them through the glass. In this sense central perspective is the product of a mechanical copy of reality. In principle, neither knowledge of the geometrical formula nor effort of pictorial organization is needed to obtain the results. . . .

It is no mere accident that central perspective was discovered only a few years after the first woodcuts had been printed in Europe. The woodcut establishes for the European mind the almost completely new principle of mechanical reproduction. But the print is a mechanical replica of the wooden matrix. The tracing on the pane of glass is just such a replica. It is a mechanical print made from the matrix of nature. It creates a new, scientific criterion of correctness. All human arbitrariness is excluded. The tracing is an objectively exact copy of reality.

It was a dangerous moment in the history of Western thought. The discovery suggested that the product of successful human creation was identical with mechanical reproduction and, in consequence, that the truth about reality was to be obtained by transforming the mind into a recording device. The new principle did away with the creative freedom of both perception and representation.[8]

Central perspective was therefore an invention yielding an ambiguous result. It liberated artists (and the public) to deal with a form of picturization satisfying the demands of a mechanical-scientific culture for a medium of communication which would, in a visual manner, record reality with an accuracy, precision and permanence similar to that obtained by the printed word. At the same time, it also necessitated that the imprimatur of mechanical and scientific precision be placed upon pictures as the result of the rules which laws of perspective were forced to follow. This limited to what the eye saw in reality conceptions about the nature of reality which *might* be expressed in a picture. The individual perceptions, of course, varied somewhat according to the psychological and physiological natures of individual artists. The main effect, nevertheless, of the invention of central perspective was the objectification of the pictures that were now produced.[9] Artists, however, remained psychologically free to draw or paint

[8] Arnheim, *op. cit.*, p. 279. (Italics added.)
[9] The rapidity with which the new discovery was accepted by European painters is interesting. By the last half of the fifteenth century, one finds it used everywhere in Europe. By the sixteenth and seventeenth century it became a critical standard that encouraged painters to invent techniques to outdo one another in employing optical stunts to heighten perspective. The most extreme example of the ambivalent power of

more or less what they chose in the manner they chose—*providing that the laws of central perspective were obeyed.*

The artistic photographers of the past and present century have also maintained a large measure of this psychological freedom. In fact, logical near-perfection was reached with the invention of the camera that would record reality as accurately as the most gifted graphic artist. When Brady and his assistants' cameras went into the battlefields of the American Civil War, not only graphic art but the popular concept of war itself was transformed by his pictures. Neither the symbolism of a Goya nor the satire of Hogarth or Daumier could simulate the power of the camera's cold, logical eye. It recorded impassively on its wet glass plates the sight of dead warriors, spread out on a quiet battlefield and the unheroic pathos of the tired and wounded soldiers in the front lines.

So enormous a pressure was photography upon the creative spirit of picture-makers that graphic artists in France and elsewhere launched a rebellion against it which stimulated eventually the various non-realistic art forms which lasted from the period of early Impressionism to the present time. What the photograph could *not* do in picture was, of course, "clown around" in the form of caricature or cartoon. It could not capriciously distort, not only central perspective, but the very aesthetics of graphic art themselves and reflect the peculiar psychological visions in the mind's eye of the artist. The new pictures could now *mean* little or nothing whatsoever, objectively. A multitude of abstractions, that once might have been considered a form of decoration, were objectified as pictures and given status as "mediums of communication," even when neither the artist nor the viewer was quite sure what, if anything, was being communicated.[10]

Photography provided a wider logical dimension for communication than painting and sculpture, because it was no less an ambiguous invention than had been the invention of central perspective. Erich Kahler writes:

> While photography has accustomed us to its unfeeling perception, it has simultaneously trained us to observe a host of details, minutiae, shades of reality which we were unable to detect before. Through the sharpness and magnification of photographic techniques, we have learned to see the textures of natural tissues and substances in their infinite design, the intricate network of living cells, the veins of leaves, and so forth; a butterfly wing unveils landscapes and a snow crystal the ultimate

---

central perspective vis-à-vis reality was a time during the eighteenth century when numerous painters achieved the *tours de force* of canvases showing painters' private studios and collections of paintings, each specimen of which would contain numerous other miniature paintings, old and new, as well as artists and spectators viewing them. "Reality" in these paintings included the world of paintings, and paintings were even painted of people looking at people painting paintings of paintings. Mechanical, scientific and logical perfection had reached a point near psychological absurdity.

[10] We have noted above, and repeat here, that such abstract paintings *always* communicate the *logical* nature of their intrinsic being.

perfection of geometric architecture. Correspondences of structure have been revealed between the most different forms of existence and new spheres opened to our vision and to artistic endeavor. By uncovering all these, photography has often changed the whole aspect of a phenomenon. In the same way, photography has also effected a fragmentation of phenomena and has taught us the charm, the infinite imaginary vistas of the fragment.[11]

Technologically, photography offered the artist the ability to make pictures of a kind literally inconceivable before the modern era. Magnification, infra-red photography, color processes and (in moving pictures) time-stop photography and animation techniques have provided for us pictures of reorganized space and time sequences of microcosmic and macrocosmic universes of which we have only recently become aware. Communication, in other words, has come to us by pictures from loci previously closed to our senses. The camera has been employed to make pictures of various "new" facets of reality, including "heat" reality, "color" reality, "slow motion" reality, "microscopic" reality and other previously invisible "realities" in the environment. That they are realities as fantastic as the dreams of the most imaginative artists of the past is an irony essential to their full appreciation.

To consider photography analogous logically to the recording of sound (as some critics do) is an error relating to the technological merger of two inventions in the development of talking motion pictures and the use of sound broadcasting production methods in contemporary television. They are quite different logically, although they share certain surface psychological characteristics.

There exists no event in all of technological invention comparable to the cultural impact of the photograph on Western art and life. This is the direct result of the perfection of the medium of picture as an instrument for objectifying the realities of the environment. The invention of photography became a vehicle for the expression of an *unlimited* number of *brand new* visions of reality. No significant logical, cultural advances in the development of the languages of communications comparable to the invention of central perspective and of photography occurred with later developments, like those of radio broadcasting or sound recording. Neither technique may however be considered mediums of communication in the logical sense that narrative, picture and (as we shall discover in Chapter 10) reenactment may.

The Psychologic of Pictures

We discover the meaning of a picture mainly from the communality of responses to it, hence the considerable value of pictures and their interpretation to students of the mind-life of individuals. This value may be dem-

---

[11] Erich Kahler, *The Tower and the Abyss* (New York: George Braziller, 1957), p. 96.

onstrated in three ways, all of which are directly relevant to the role of this medium in the psychologics of communications.

In the first place, the pictures we *draw*—whether we have been trained as artists or not—are highly indicative of both our conscious or unconscious feelings. Psychologists have demonstrated by means of a number of techniques[12] that when individuals are asked to draw pictures of certain kinds— a human figure is frequently employed—they can, if they have been trained to understand the communal aspects of perception, determine how various people sharing certain psychological traits will respond to this challenge. What they discover may have little value taken alone, but when combined with other data like interviews and responses to various testing devices, it may accurately uncover certain aspects of feeling and personality that are not readily displayed in overt behavior. This procedure appears, for many reasons, to work best on children, but in principle it applies to any type of picture drawn by anyone (even a skilled artist or copyist) or taken by a photographer. All picture-makers choose certain viewpoints of subjects, emphasize certain factors in their perceptive field differentially, and so forth. Relevance to personality will, of course, be contingent upon the measure of *choice* the subject feels in creating his picture.

In the second place, the way we interpret the pictures we observe is a function of our personalities, interests, unconscious dispositions, values and every other aspect of our psychological lives. Hence, many psychologists employ pictures to elicit from a subject descriptions of what "he sees," in a (psychological) abstraction like an ink-blot in the famous Rorschach procedure or ambiguous photographs in the Thematic Apperception Test.[13] What the subject actually describes, of course, is largely how *he* interprets a highly ambiguous pictorial communication. While auditory versions of projective tests have also been constructed, pictures are a peculiarly and distinctly productive medium for eliciting these psychological data, mixed, of course, with various logical responses. Once again, the tester must be trained to comprehend how communalities or configurations of interpretation occur in the population at large in order to relate the meanings of specific responses to both normal and abnormal populations.

The utility of this process need not necessarily be confined to the psychologist's clinic. The dimension of understanding, or confusion, in the responses that all of us have to all pictures is contingent upon our psychological disposition at the time of the viewing. The less ambiguous the pic-

---

[12] See Florence Z. Goodenough, *Measurement of Intelligence by Drawings* (New York: World Book Company, 1926), one of the earliest and clearest explanations of how considerable precision is achieved using this simple technique.

[13] See H. J. Eysenck, *Sense and Nonsense in Psychology* (Middlesex, England: Penguin Books, 1957), pp. 218–230, and also consult Joseph Zubin, Leonard D. Eron and Florence Schumer, *An Experimental Approach to Projective Techniques* (New York: John Wiley and Sons, 1965), pp. 1–49, for the background and history of projective techniques in psychology.

ture, in all probability, the less free play given our interpretive faculties. But even so rigorously defined a picture as James Montgomery Flagg's "Uncle Sam Wants *You*" poster allows for considerable latitude in the way different individuals may respond to it, which is to say, in terms of each one's individual constructions of matters considered relevant to it.

Third, pictures are doubtless important vehicles for the expression and reception of artistic ideas. By artistic ideas, it is meant that certain levels of skills and insights were combined in their creation, so that in addition to satisfying certain logical criteria for meaning, a consistent level of meaningful personal insights emerges frequently enough from experienced auditors to predict such responses in the future. This definition therefore transcends the limits of the so-called "fine" arts and also includes the possibility of a photograph being a vehicle for artistic ideas.[14] Included here may be any kind of pictures, even abstractions, comic-strips, motion picture images (as images rather than as attempted re-creations of life), pop art, op art, primitive art—in fact, all kinds of picture from pornographic photographs to the illustrations in children's books. (One finds few artistic ideas in either of the latter two, but the possibility is always present.)

The process of artistic communication is described expertly by Arnheim:

> The artistic concept of an object or event is much more like the invention of a musical theme than like the activity of a photographic camera. It consists of the creation of a visual pattern that can be described as the final result of a whole series of embodiments. The abstract core of Michelangelo's *Creation of Adam* is, let us say, the interplay of an active and receptive principle. The theme is embodied in the shape of a life-giving power that animates matter. On the next level of concretization is the story of the book of Genesis. The story must be made visual, which means making images of God, Adam, the setting, the action. For example, the Biblical motif of the breath of life is transplanted into a pictorially more concrete one: Adam raises his arm to meet the outstretched arm of God, through which enlivening energy seems to be conveyed. Finally, the scene must be adapted to pictorial representation in a plane of given proportions. At each of these levels, imagination is needed in order to invent a translation of one stage into the next.[15]

Arnheim enters the caveat that he is not attempting to read the artist's mind in describing the steps involved, but that some such processes as he discusses *must have* occurred in the creation of this masterpiece. One reason is that they *re-occurred* for Arnheim and for countless other intelligent,

---

[14] A definition of this sort is not limited to artistic ideas in pictures alone. To relate it to the narrative or representational mediums, however, would necessitate its extension to the idea of collective response (including many individual responses) over a period of time and dealing with the *one total reflective response*. Arnheim moves in the direction of this kind of integration concerning a single picture in the quote below.

[15] Arnheim, *op. cit.*, p. 143.

sensitive individuals who have looked up at the ceiling of the Sistine Chapel from 1513 to the present. That the cumulative popularity of the work is vastly greater than the popularity of our most successful television show (or other technological fancy) is an indication of the power or artistic ideas in their full elaboration when held beside ideas of lesser cultural impact. We must not forget, as well, that the medium of picture was here used in its most elegant and powerful symbolic form to portray one of the most crucial moments in religion, and therefore one of the most psychologically potent.

The Psychological Problem of Picture

The previous section centers upon the observation that the medium of pictures is biased in the direction of the psychological mode of apprehension. From a developmental point of view, as children grow, we observe their grasp of the psychological aspects of pictures long before they make any logical demands upon them.[16] That artists have attempted throughout history to throw logic to the winds and use picture for sheer ornament or decoration, or at present for rebellion or shock, and that these attempts have succeeded in stimulating psychological reactions, should give us a clue as to the extent of this bias.

In our present society, where much active interest is displayed in the trappings of Freudian symbology, and where psychological patois is heard from saloon to salon, some modern painting appears purposely designed to make obscure "psychological statements" which exclude logic but definitely elicit strong feeling reactions. Such paintings may deal in artistic ideas, but they appear self-conscious and manipulative, and therefore relatively easy to separate from more spontaneous artistic attempts which communicate more than psychological responses which exploit pseudo-psychological symbol systems. Critical judgments, however, that they are a less legitimate use of the picture medium than an alternative kind of graphic art are transient value judgments which may be modified by the demands of a changing world which asks different things from its mediums of communication at different times—and under different circumstances.

An issue is therefore raised concerning the comparative ease with which psychological reactions may be elicited by the picture medium. One notes also the curiosity that no obligation (moral or artistic) exists on the part of the creator of a picture (or the perceiver) to match this psychologic, in kind or degree, with logic. Thus one may enjoy on a psychological level what is generally agreed to be a great work of art without *any* logical under-

16 Children are frequently first exposed to television pictures for instance, before they are a year old. The moving image quiets them, and they are often content to sit or lie and watch what they obviously cannot understand for substantial periods of time. Television is used by many mothers in this manner as a pacifier, and it does not seem to do their children noticeable harm. And why should it—any more than looking at any other kind of pictures?

standing of it; or one may, as we have noted above, achieve enormous psychological gratification as the result of the manipulation of crude pictorial symbols—or sheer design. This situation is neither "good" nor "bad." It merely accounts for many of the peculiar reactions one observes to much pictorial communication—reactions that will be discussed further in Chapters 14, 15 and 16, as they relate to the communication of cognitions and emotions and to the apprehension of style in art.

Quantitative reports, accordingly, that we are a "nation of picture lovers" are cold consolation for those who may be awaiting a cultural renaissance in the visual arts in the United States. True, we are fast becoming a nation of museum-goers and amateur painters. Some observers see this obsession with museums and paint as signs that we are achieving the maturity that some older cultures display in their reverence for the fine arts.[17]

Of course, we are a nation of picture lovers! Do we not circulate millions of copies of *Life* magazine weekly? Did not Americans develop the basically pictorial instrument of modern motion picture production? Are not picture books of many types our most popular forms of literature? Was not the instantaneous national success of television broadcasting an indication of our proclivity for pictures? Is not the United States the nation of the picture newspaper, the Kodak Brownie, the pin-up girl and the picture calendar? Do we not flock by the thousands to gawk at masterpieces like the Rembrandt which was reputed to be the most expensive picture (sold for $2,300,000) in the world? Are not countless adults taking art appreciation and painting courses by mail?

The point at issue is not quantitative but qualitative. If we examine closely this contemporary obsession with the medium of picture, we may begin to explain it in terms of the logical and psychological qualities of picture as a medium of communication.

If pictures have become merely a *device* for the mediation of psychological communications between people for the gratification of psychological drives, they serve us almost entirely in *one* major capacity, that of therapy. If, on the other hand, they communicate logical insights germane to the aesthetic of picture and evoke psychological reactions relevant to the needs of mature people in our culture, then they are serving as forces which integrate the thinking and feeling aspects of life. In other words, in Lan-

---

[17] See Alvin Toffler, *The Culture Consumers* (New York: St. Martin's Press, 1964), pp. 19–20, where the author enthusiastically reports that the number of art galleries across America is increasing vigorously in such places as Quincy, Illinois; Phoenix, Arizona; Rochester, New York; and Detroit, Michigan. He also notes that forty million Americans are "Sunday painters" and that the sale of art materials and enrollment in courses in picture-making have reached enormous proportions. The question, of course, is what so much activity *means*; whether it is a symptom of a desire to enrich our logical and psychological sensibilities or merely diversion, directed at calming and satisfying psychological needs created by the pressures of competition, technology, capitalism, fear of war, etc. Toffler's optimism flies in the face of much expert observation to the contrary.

ger's terms, are our pictures mediators of "significant form" for the masses
or are they tranquilizing pills?

Jacques Barzun has become extremely disturbed [18] about the well-
known picture book, *The Family of Man*,[19] issued in 1955 by the Museum
of Modern Art in New York City. It has been a great popular (and critical)
success and has been printed in many editions. Here is a galaxy of unbeliev-
ably moving photographs of men and women—young and old, rich and
poor—drawn from all over the earth, working, making love, eating, praying,
laughing and crying.

Barzun's objection to the collection is precisely that photographs of a
highly potent emotional nature are unexplained and, lacking any but puerile commentary, employed to "sell" to the reader (or viewer) an enormous number of highly complicated *logical* assumptions about man and his
society at the price of exalting and exploiting only the psychologics of life.

"Whatever is formed and constituted (the work seems to say),'" writes
Barzun, "whatever is adult, whatever exerts power, whatever is characteristically Western, whatever is unique or has a name, or embodies a complexity of thought, is of less interest and thought than what is native, common,
and sensual; what is weak and confused; what is unhappy, anonymous and
elemental," [20] these are the ideas (?) which the set of photographs communicates so effectively.

Barzun puts his finger exactly on the basic psychological problem of
pictorial communication—the psychological power of the medium of picture itself. Barzun continues, "It is easy to believe that *The Family of Man*
has been 'created in a passionate spirit of devoted love and faith in man,'
but one may be permitted to ask whether that love was not blind—blind to
a whole range of man's life, blind to the effects of certain iterations, blind
to the requirements of sense and manly pride, blind to the discretion which
judgment owes to even the sincerest faith." [21]

So speaks the logic of pictures to its own psychologic.

Conclusion

The problem above is relevant to the study of all the languages of
communication, as important as the logical bias of the narrative medium.
The tendency of pictures to accent the psychologics of existence may not be
referred to as a "bias," however, as in the instance of narrative. Narrative's
proclivity seems to relate *to a quality inherent in the medium itself*. Pic-

[18] Jacques Barzun, *The House of Intellect*, pp. 27–30. Here is an excellent study of the
duality of logic and psychologic in our culture, although Barzun uses "intellect" on the
one hand, and a concept of optimism *cum* voluntarism on the other, to explain the
duality.
[19] Edward Steichen (ed.), *The Family of Man* (New York: The Museum of Modern
Art, 1955).
[20] Barzun, *op. cit.*, p. 29.
[21] *Ibid.*, p. 30.

ture's proclivity appears not to be involved with the *nature* of the pictorial medium *but rather depends upon the character and disposition of the recipient of the communication and the values he learns from his culture.*

Societies have existed—and probably still do—where the enormous psychological power of picture as a medium did not—and does not—exist. In fact, in *all* societies where pictures are used for social or ceremonial purposes—or when they are used this way in our *own* culture[22]—they are saved from the apparent pointlessness of serving as mediums of psychological communication without an accompanying function of logical communication, no matter how trivial this latter use may appear.

It is quite simple to explain why pictures *qua pictures* are not considered at present, in the conventional literature of communications, *mediums* of communication. We concentrate on the *techniques of* or *instruments for* spreading pictures abroad to the public, like museums, magazines, newspapers, movies, television, etc., and call these *instruments* "media," when in fact they mediate little or nothing. We are simply not accustomed to dealing with pictures as operative in the logical mode of communication as readily as we are in the psychological mode. While pictures may communicate much, we frequently do not allow them to communicate a wide spectrum of *sense.*[23] They therefore seem not to communicate at *all*, but merely to facilitate psychological processes that they so adeptly stimulate.

This concept of picture would indeed be difficult to explain to a Florentine at the time of Lorenzo, or to a Greek or Roman in the golden ages of their respective cultures, or to an artisan at work on a cathedral during the Dark Ages of Europe. The logic and psychologic of the medium of picture were, for them, one and the same!

---

[22] The employment of photographs for purpose of clarifying (rather than sensationalizing) a news story in the newspapers or on television is an example, as well as numerous religious uses of paintings and statues.

[23] How neatly we turn our back on sense! The proud father who shows off a picture of his children is displaying a talisman of what, sensibly, might well be near tragedy to him: pictorial affirmation that he knows his children will grow up and never again look as his camera saw them! *All* photographs of those we love turn to personal tragedies in time—if we live long enough and keep photographs. As the ghost of the heroine Emily discovers in Wilder's *Our Town*, even the most mundane moment of our past is bitter in the light of what we discover about the future. *All* photographs show us a time that has passed, even those we make with Polaroid cameras and tear up.

Chapter 10

IMPERSONATION

F ROM THE naturalist's perspective, all somatic activity, from the beginnings of life in the pre-Cambrian era, is imitative by virtue of the system of reproduction necessary to the continuation of even the most uncomplicated species of protozoa. Nature, in the macrocosmic world, goes through visible, continual processes of imitation, countering season with season, flora with new and more or less identical flora, and by the continual repetition of cycles the growth, reproduction, death and decay, processes in which all life is involved.

Among the vertebrates, all surviving species are well fitted by nature to imitate at least the basic survival behaviors of their own kind by means of specialized organs of perception and response,[1] and through the existence of certain appetencies (sometimes regarded as instincts) which appear to *impel* organisms to various imitative behaviors. *What* they may imitate is either (and most frequently) behaviors of their own kind or of some other species, including human beings.[2]

In man, the process of imitation appears to be fundamental to most of the learning that permits him to assume a role in society. In an anthropological sense, then, imitation is a definite means of communication of the components, not only of the somatic nature of mankind, but of the conditions of culture themselves: the folkways, mores, traditions, and customs that must be passed from generation to generation, if civilization is to survive.

---

[1] See Loris J. and Margery Milne, *The Senses of Animals and Men* (New York: Atheneum, 1952), for a well-told and beautifully produced account of animal perception, including numerous amusing analogies to human sensory behavior.
[2] Many mammals and some birds may be encouraged to imitate behaviors of other species—*particularly* humans—and can therefore be trained to perform remarkable acts. Strangely, however, some animals will spontaneously imitate other species. Certain

How are they "passed"? We have already noted some of the ways in the preceding chapters. But imitation is, of course, an extremely direct and effective method of accomplishment, simply because it utilizes no specific vocabulary or aesthetic, nor is imitation limited to the surfaces upon which man may draw, or to the places where his technological recording devices will work. A modern Australian aboriginal who teaches his son to throw a boomerang in the patient manner of these gentle natives is repeating, in our time, the fundamental process of imitative communication found in culture since the dawn of civilization.

Mimicry's most primitive form is probably that of pantomime and simple gesture. Susanne Langer notes this,[3] challenging philosopher John Dewey's notion that imitations occur only when such events provide "enjoyment of the drama of life without the latter's liabilities,"[4] on the grounds that many imitations obviously involve pain as well as pleasure. The source of such basic imitations, however, is the "demand for a world-picture that fills all experience and gives each individual a definite *orientation* amid the terrifying forces of nature and society."[5] In other words, their function is to communicate from the past the logical aspects of behavior which are rewarding psychologically (involving pleasure *or* pain) to others in the present. They may subsequently continue to communicate them into the future. In this manner, imitation is generalized to perform functions which may be regarded as "educational," in the word's broadest sense, providing for the individual prototypes of social skills he must know to survive. At the same time, the individual becomes the object of further imitation by the coming generation.

Imitation as Drama

For these reasons, Aristotle regarded drama as an educational force, but not in the manner of today's schoolhouses and teachers. For Aristotle, imitation was a manifestation of *art*, which was in itself the force (discussed above) for both acculturation and education. He differentiated between the various arts according to the degree and quality of imitation involved in their pursuits.[6] By Aristotle's time, 400 years before Christ, the understood value of an experience had already been located in both the intensity and balance between the psychological and logical attributes of that experience.[7]

---

individual parrots and apes may be considered abnormally stupid if they cannot (or do not wish to) imitate certain facets of the behaviors of other kinds of animals.
[3] Langer, *Philosophy in a New Key*, pp. 126–128.
[4] *Ibid.*, p. 128.
[5] *Loc. cit.*
[6] See Clark, *European Theories of the Drama*, p. 6.
[7] This is a criterion for the measurement of the value of art that has been given decreasing emphasis by aestheticians since the age of Pericles, and it is almost irrelevant in most artistic criticism today. When critics now ask for better balance in art in

We have reason to believe that imitation as communication may have been manifest early in primitive man's behavior through what we today call "dancing." It was probably, at first, a fairly informal part of inchoate forms of rites and rituals, later elaborated into complicated rituals of polytheistic, anthropomorphic religions, which are, almost everywhere, quite similar among primitive people. In describing the birth of these rituals, Langer writes: "First, the actions of the 'dance' would tend to become panto-mimic, reminiscent of what had caused the great excitement. They would become ritualized, and hold the mind to the celebrated event. In other words, there would be conventional modes of dancing appropriate to certain occasions, so intimately associated with *that kind of occasion* that they would presently uphold and embody the concept of it—in other words, there would emerge *symbolic gestures*." [8]

These dances were precursors of the sorts of dramas that Aristotle knew, and which remain to this day prototypical elaborations of imitation as a basic medium of human communication. Imitation is a medium capable of unfolding narratives, of using still or moving pictures, and of being conveyed to an audience by most mechanical and electronic instruments, from hand-printed pages of dialogue read by amateur actors to televised images in color projected on a wide screen.

Ivor Smith describes the beginnings of drama in this way:

> The first paintings of primitive man . . . (were) a form of sympathetic magic: the hunter thus depicted in the act of killing his prey would be assisted in the chase by the limning of his victory. . . . Miming had the same origin. Instead of painting what he wanted, the huntsman or the farmer might perform or copy in action what he wanted. . . . So the first acting, like the earliest mural decoration, had really been a form of prayer.
>
> It was an activity with a social and utilitarian purpose. The hunter drew, or obtained a drawing man, to help win his trophy: he mimed, or obtained a mummer, in order to ensure a better harvest, or, more ambitiously, to overcome the monster Death himself. Drama, after all, is scarcely a natural occupation. The cave man would not have wasted so much effort and skill on imitation unless there was, in his opinion, great gains to be won thereby. . . .
>
> The earliest acting, the start of the whole business, was a serious purposive activity, like prayer and the prayer-painting of the caves. Man was mimic of his own desires. Did he want the king-god of the community to be eternally beside him, strong to save? Then he copies in action the legend or narrative of a king's death and a supposed resurrection, since that would give Heaven the hint. To act the renewal of life would win that renewal. . . .

these terms—as do some drama and film critics—they are accused of "not understanding the medium" about which they are writing!
[8] Langer, *op. cit.*, p. 106.

All this performance was arranged for times of holy festival, done to get the king-god on one's side, done to procure, as far as might be, security for the State and to ensure immortality for the national leader and then, through him, for all. (The destruction between kings and gods is shadowy in primitive times: kings rise to god-head after death and are assisted by the prayers of their people to immortality.) Of course, there was no gain sought in such solemn ceremonial nor any thought of professional entertainment.[9]

What is most remarkable about imitation—or re-enactment—or impersonation—or drama[10]—is its sheer *efficiency* as communication. Since it is, indeed, the "imitation of life," in Aristotle's terms, it is capable of communicating apparent volumes of logical and psychological material with little effort on the part of the receiver. The great onus is placed on the talent of the communicator. Whether he is a creator (like a playwright) or an interpreter (like an actor), the clarity of communication will depend largely on his ability at "phrasing" what is said. True, the receivers (or audience) must be in some measure prepared to understand the discourse, but, since the days of the origins of the drama, the central responsibility for the efficacy of re-enactment has fallen to the performer. If he is not artful enough to communicate, it is his *audience* which abandons *him*. The art of impersonation, accordingly, has been important to nearly every known society—Eastern and Western—of which we have records. And re-enactment itself is a medium of communication for which every possible mechanical and technological instrument available is utilized, almost immediately it is invented.[11]

Popularity in the face of numerous obstacles to communicating clearly with an audience engendered a need for "specialists" in this medium of communication: dancers and witch doctors in primitive cultures, and play-

[9] Ivor Brown, *Shakespeare* (New York: Time Incorporated, 1962), pp. 122–124.
[10] Naturally, there is both a substantive as well as a semantic difference between these various manifestations of the same medium of communication. Since "re-enactment" and "impersonation" are the most inclusive terms available to describe them, one or the other will be used in this chapter, unless an highly specific aesthetic form of the medium is being described, such as "dance."
[11] The bulk of material on view in the world's movie theatres and on its television sets is impersonation of one or another type. Re-enactments fill the comic pages of its newspapers, the comments of its columnists and provide the stylistic mold for the picture stories in illustrated magazines. This tendency is *not* an indication of the debasement of culture by American technology, as claimed by some social critics. To believe that these instruments might give less attention to re-enactment and more to discursive and didactic kinds of communication than they do, indicates how little such critics know of the history of mankind. More realistic have been the attempts of many artists—most notably the late Bertolt Brecht—to cross impersonation with didacticism by creating a new type of "problem drama." See Eric Bentley, *The Playwright As Thinker* (New York: Meridian Books, 1955), pp. 209–231, for a description of what Brecht was attempting to accomplish with the medium of impersonation in his Epic Theatre, using impersonation as a device for the communication of didactic political and social ideas.

wrights, actors, producers and directors in modern society, from all of whom special skills of different sorts were (and are) expected.

The Logic of Re-enactment

The conditions for effective communication by re-enactment were recognized by Aristotle in the *Poetics*. There is little that can be added to the spirit—if not the letter—of his observations. They are valid today despite the increase in means for the dissemination of re-enactments and the elaboration of imitations as they passed from religious to secular discourse and utilized the inventions of both mechanics and technology, when and where they were developed.[12]

Throughout their history, and including the forms of dance and drama we know today, re-enactments have been more noticeably social occasions than are communications accomplished solely by narrative or picture. The latter two are frequently involved in "person to person" communication, even when a museum guide explains the background of a painting to a group of tourists. Impersonation usually happens in front of an *audience*, which is understood (logically) to manifest a "collective" or "group" psychology. At any rate, an audience is usually regarded as the molecular unit of respondents to re-enacted communications.

Re-enactment also appears more closely to relate to real life than either of the other two mediums.[13] Artists have explained this phenomenon by resorting to the psychological mystique of "aesthetic distance." This is a proposition that it is possible for a person to partake of a re-enacted situation (by means of "empathy") and, at the same time, know that he is witnessing an imitation of life. Because it is a necessary condition for all impersonation, and because re-enactment could not communicate without it, "aesthetic distance" appears to be a *logical* quality of impersonation.[14]

[12] By the time of the Greek theatre, simple mechanical devices were already in use, particularly instruments for "flying" actors on to and off the stage. The Romans with their considerable technical inventiveness, added more mechanical ingenuity to their plays, some of which is still in use in the modern theatre. See Sheldon Cheney, *The Theatre* (New York: Longmans, Green and Co., 1952), pp. 30–303, for details.
[13] By way of example, *Lady Chatterley's Lover* (third edition), is presently permitted publication in our country. It is doubtful that living (or photographed) literal impersonation of the sexual scenes in the book would be permitted on the marketplace. Certainly *exact* dramatizations would be taboo. They would be too "life-like." Nor might living reproductions of many of the nude figures in classical painting and sculpture (including religious works) be allowed a showing were they re-enacted live on the stage or shown in films. We have seen the values society holds of decorum change in the recent past, but notice that inter-medium differences of what is "proper" remain relatively in the same ratio despite these variations. We are permitted to *print in words* or *draw* many, many things that we do *not* allow to be re-enacted and subsequently viewed directly (on the stage) or indirectly (by photographic or electronic means).
[14] Brecht, as noted above, and other playwrights, including Arthur Arent in the United States, have attempted to produce didactic dramas where impersonation was employed without demanding the quality of aesthetic distance from the audience. In

Concepts of *action* and *character* also apply (in different degrees) to the various sorts of re-enactments or impersonations. *Action* in narrative tends to be discursive, running often into apparently random streams and tributaries. Action in re-enactment is usually unitary—a series of related events which add up to a total experience. Events that are re-enacted are, of course, always abstracted from the non-unitary source of *life*, even if only the mind-life of the impersonator. But the demand is present for unity—a beginning, a middle and an end—whether the re-enactment be in the form of ritual, dance, pantomime or drama. Occasionally, by way of novelty, a "first act" drama may be attempted (as in the case of Sir James Barrie's "one act" play *Shall We Join the Ladies?*), but such impersonations are more diversions than completed communications.

The concept of *character* relates to the content of action, because the main currency of re-enactment is invariably the human being. Humans may depict animals, gods, inanimate objects or simply ideas, but they are human, nevertheless. Even if puppets or marionettes substitute for real actors, they are invested with human characteristics. One would have a difficult argument were he to claim that Disney's Donald Duck was any less a human impersonation for being a figure painted on celluloid than Marilyn Monroe was because she was "real".

For most impersonations, we are interested primarily in *what* character is mediated to us by a performance, and, second, in how that character *changes* by virtue of what he or she discovers about the world or about the self. Few re-enacted statements merely communicate static human existence. This may be too easily accomplished by means of narrative or picture.

What re-enactment accomplishes most effectively, however, is to display the results of the passage of *time* upon *character*. By means of impersonation, the oscillations of growth and decay, defeat and discovery, elation and despair, may be portrayed at various points in their motion, and accordingly communicate statements about the human condition which are as pungent as they are parsimonious.

In all impersonation, however, the external world is always present. Every re-enactment requires a *mise-en-scene*, whether it be the immediate environment of the impersonation itself (as in a war dance), or a background wrought of imagination (like heaven or hell). The environment then acts upon character in the form of *fate*, which allows the drama to occur in the first place. Fate brings together the Babbitt and the Bromide, Oedipus and Jocasta, and Clayton, Jackson and Durante, just as it brings

---

other words, the audience was asked not to believe in the reality of the impersonation they were viewing, and to bear continually in mind that a re-enactment is not the genuine event. While some of these plays succeeded in production, it is generally conceded that no performances of such Epic Theatre plays achieved their dramatic communication without the pretense to reality that appears fundamental for an audience involved in this mode of communication.

players to Elsinore, Box and Cox to the same rooming house, and Willy Loman to Brooklyn. Whenever fate unties a crucial enough situational knot in drama, we employ the term used by the Greeks: *deus ex machina*, the god sent down in a machine who straightens everything out by (as often as not) rewarding the virtuous and punishing the wicked.

When events are dynamically re-enacted, one usually looks less carefully for reality in the *mise-en-scene* than in the behavior of the characters.[15] If communication occurs by means of re-enactment, we are therefore ready to accept fate as the ultimate and inevitable arbiter of events in life with which characters must deal.[16]

Impersonation communicates by means of exposure. It does not necessarily expose an individual or an event, but produces an *equivalent* of them, distorted in some manner so as to make their essential qualities clear to the audience. Life itself has never been—and probably never will be—successfully dramatized by exact duplications of social situations, either live or by means of technological devices. This does not mean that certain facets of life may not be *momentarily* captured in photographs, on films, or tape recordings. These communications are not, however, usually dramatic. That is to say, they lack the essential qualities of the logics of re-enactment. They will tend to be similar to narrative and/or pictorial communications unless somehow (perhaps by accident) they emulate familiar re-enactments, or someone edits them in such a way to confuse them successfully with re-enactments.[17]

Forces and counter forces are forever at work in re-enactment, with character at the source of the counterforce. These forces constitute the *complications* of drama, the point of dramatic ritual, the *functions* of dance and the *script* itself of solo pantomime.

[15] Directors like David Belasco and certain film makers have provided a remarkable degree of surface reality in the *look* of their settings. Such attempts to make the drama "realistic" frequently fail. They provide only an illusion of a real environment which is then manipulated according to the needs of the dramatist or director, as in the case of the documentary film. The most apparently realistic setting is therefore no closer to "life" than suggested scenery, an expressionistic set, or (as in *Our Town*) no setting at all. The true role of scenery in relation to drama (and films) is periodically rediscovered in our theatre, but designers have a tendency continually to search out environmental "realism" in the mistaken belief that impersonation carried out in front of the life-like setting will also be "real." Such vain efforts were rarely made in the theatres which existed before the age of photography.

[16] The literary equivalent of fate is the "plot" of a poem, novel or play.

[17] The most frequent way this is accomplished, I think, is by editing material transcribed on a sound tape recorder. Tony Schwartz, whose work in recording the sounds of life is distinctive, is capable of turning reality into drama, using his subtle ear and by careful tape editing. Schwartz is essentially a painter *cum* dramatist, probably each at different times. As a painter, he uses a palatte of sounds; as a dramatist, he employs the alphabet of speech and the noises he hears in life.

Impersonation as Convention

The process of impersonation has accumulated certain and explicit conventions, results of the experiences of artists and craftsmen in vanished cultures. Conventions of re-enactment, like the conventions of narrative, language or picture, are fundamentally pragmatic matters. They are, in effect, a record of techniques that have made impersonation *work* during the past two thousand years. They represent the accumulation of devices by means of which individuals who have re-enacted events have accomplished effective communication. They constitute the conventions which appear to work still in our own time when transmitted by the various modern instruments of communications. If one medium of communication is today a favorite of the general public, it is the medium of re-enactment.[18]

Among the earliest of these conventions (of which we know) was the tragedy, the particular *form* of re-enactment which Aristotle defended against narrative in *The Poetics*. Critics and professors never appear to tire of the argument of whether this form of representation can be re-enacted properly by modern actors and appreciated fully by contemporary audiences. They also dispute whether dramatic forms analogous to classic tragedy may even be written by today's playwrights.

On the positive side of the ledger, works like Miller's *Death of a Salesman* or O'Neil's *The Iceman Cometh,* or *Emperor Jones* or Sartre's *Red Gloves* are entered as evidence that tragedy (of a sort) is compatible with contemporary life. Perhaps it only occurs when the original flavor of Greek barbarousness is somehow duplicated in the re-enactment, as in the film *High Noon,* or in American Indian dance-dramas, or in psychological stripteases by the Tennessee Williams' female characters.

On the other side of the page, Joseph Wood Krutch has argued:

> . . . too sophisticated society . . . one which, like ours, has outgrown not merely the simple optimism of the child but also that vigorous, one might say almost adolescent, faith in the nobility of man which marks a Sophocles or Shakespeare—has neither fairy tales to assure it that all is always right in the end nor tragedies to make it believe that it rises superior in soul to the outward calamaties which befall it. . . . Instead, mean misery piles on mean misery, petty misfortune follows petty misfortune, and despair becomes intolerable because it is no longer even significant or important.[19]

18 While the masses have their television and ubiquitous movies, the classes have their highbrow theatre and opera. So let it be understood that a penchant for re-enactment is by no means a middle or lowbrow phenomenon. Its popularity is almost universal, except for certain intellectuals (Freud was among them) or poorly educated individuals who find little stimulation in impersonation.

19 Joseph Wood Krutch, *The Modern Temper* (New York: Harcourt, Brace and Company, 1929), p. 88. Note that these observations—repeated in one way or another in all of Krutch's books on drama—were written well before the period of the recent existentialist drama and literature of *desespoir*. Krutch addresses himself here to the total thrust of the realistic drama in America and Europe beginning with Ibsen.

This discussion is neither unimportant nor academic, because a vital issue concerning modern life is here at stake: whether or not a people as receptive as we are of the determinisms of science in *its* many manifestations may reproduce experiential qualities in former societies which were at the mercy of the gods in *their* many manifestations. We may unquestionably partake of some facets of these latter experiences when so skilled a performer as Laurence Olivier re-creates *Oedipus* in our theatres. But the question remains as to whether we are experiencing the psychological qualities of experience that Aristotle discovered in the same play. There is, of course, no logical way to tell.

The problem appears less significant in regard to comedy, although the function of ancient satyr comedies may be loosely likened to the sort of stimulation experienced at such a slick burlesque show as A *Funny Thing Happened On the Way to the Forum* (play or film), or much of today's nonsense on television. Despite the enormous differences between Aristophanes and Groucho Marx, the pulse beat of comedy has continued at much the same rate throughout history. The anatomically grotesque performer in a phallic comedy two thousand years ago has his symbolic counterpart today in the great "Schnozzola" himself. While notation of this brotherhood of comics over the centuries is a logical observation, it demonstrates a common response pattern which most audiences seem to share: that of laughter, a phenomenon that is examined most productively in its psychological mode.[20]

The other outstanding conventions of re-enactment in its contemporary forms appear to relate mostly to the modern drama. They are, however, extremely old devices, used by impersonators of many kinds to achieve the immediate recognition which facilitates communication. They represent prototypical ratios of three elements: *plot, character* and *dominant mood*, that yield certain, easily recognizable contexts of re-enactment that audiences have been schooled (by repeated exposure) to identify. They are points on a continuum from comic absurdity to serious absurdity, and are frequently identified as *farce, comedy, drama* and *melodrama*. The myriad definitions of these terms usually tell us primarily about the degree of *probability* of the plot (the "thing done" in the impersonation), the degree of emphasis on personality and character exposed in the writing (or acting), and whether or not the audience is meant to take the impersonation seriously.

These definitions may refer to written drama played in the theatre of the mind, impersonations caried out in amphitheatres, or over the airwaves. Because each form stands for a stopping point on a continuum, one rarely, if ever, comes upon an impersonation which can be exclusively pigeonholed as one particular type of experience, that is, as a farce, comedy, drama or melodrama. Broadly speaking, Chaplin was farce; Martha

[20] See Chapter 18 for a detailed discussion of the communication of humor.

Graham was dramatic; Katherine Hepburn was comic; and Boris Karloff was melodramatic, but such thumbnail characterizations alone tell us little. Each performer (and, of course, every impersonation) has a place on the continuum, a place which does not remain constant even through one single re-enactment but which strikes a mean for each individual's performances.

To note, for instance, that most humorous programs on television tend to be *farces* and most serious plays are *melodramas*—most of the time—is a *useful* observation. So is the impression shared by many that more American motion pictures from 1960 to 1969 tended toward *drama* than during the nineteen fifties, when *melodrama* was the dominant serious convention for filmed re-enactments.[21]

Impersonation as Replica

If re-enactment is a predominantly social form of communication, and if it invariably deals with complications of action, it must display at least one other logical characteristic. Impersonation must always deal with human "types" who function at a given time in a specific society.[22] Since a wide degree of latitude exists in their interpretation, one cannot call them *stereotypes* in the modern sense, as originally coined by Walter Lippmann.[23] Rigidity and shallowness characterized Lippmann's use of the term. Since impersonations displayed in many re-enactments need be neither rigid in concept nor shallow in complexity of ideation, they serve as general *replicas* of currently accepted characterological manifestations which have been sanctioned by society at large.

Performers in the theatre, in films and on television complain that they are "typed." Monologists, impersonators and caricaturists (who either draw or act out their comedies), playwrights, novelists and others bemoan, on the one hand, the prevalence of "typing" in dramatic and literary discourse. But, on the other hand, they are the first to take advantage of the proclivity of the medium of impersonation to make swift and clear logical statements by means of replica or "typed" characterization.

[21] Possibly these categories tend to be more useful for impersonators than for students or critics. Certain latitudes of behaviors are appropriate for performances in farces, certain in comedies, etc. They therefore constitute a manual of decorum for players.
[22] These types—insofar as the theatre of a culture is concerned—are never independent of the styles of performance that are currently popular. The smiling, tanned William Gaxton musical comedy hero of the 'twenties and 'thirties is one such example. The highly stylized male products of the Actors' Studio in New York—like Marlon Brando and Paul Newman—are another. Since schools of acting are highly responsive to social currents in society, they become arbiters of various familiar characterizations which appear as versions of "reality" on stage and screen. They are, thereafter, undoubtedly directive or re-enforcing agents in society as well, because members of the audience so frequently imitate outstanding imitators.
[23] Walter Lippmann, *Public Opinion* (New York: Penguin Books, 1946), pp. 59–97. A stereotype is, in fact, a cast metal plate used in the printing process.

Actors talk about themselves as "juveniles," "leading men," "heavies," and in other specialized theatrical terms. Nearly every character we see on stage or in the films is a type, even when we think of some of the most original statements made by these dramatic instruments in recent years: for instance, Steiner, the Jewish Roman intellectual, in *La Dolce Vita*, is a replica of a type, just as Fellini (as he sees himself) is a type in 8½. The Marquis de Sade, Marat, Charlotte Corday and the assorted lunatics and keepers in the Peter Weiss *Marat-Sade* entertainment are replicas, and so are the weird characters of Beckett, Genet and Harold Pinter. George and Martha in *Virginia Woolf* are walking-talking generalizations of weak, dipsomaniac, Ivy league-type intellectuals[24] on stage or screen. Their essential qualities did not vary from life to motion picture theatre; the interpretations of the different impersonators did vary, however, within limits of the replicas drawn by the playwright.

John O'Hara is our best quick sketch artist of fiction. In a few words, he has drawn a character without describing him—merely by telling us what he wears, signaling to us a physical idiosyncrasy or pattern of speech. Immediate and sharp replicas are drawn. Communication occurs because the reader is able to make logical associations from the picture O'Hara limns swiftly to certain general characteristics he has learned (sometimes from earlier O'Hara writings) that are relevant to many contemporary types.

Does the inevitable dependence upon replication or typing debase or injure re-enactment as a medium for the communication of logic? Decidedly not, no more than the stylistic framework within which a painter works must diminish the logical power of his communication, or the limits upon the vocabulary of a narrator necessarily diminishes his.

Re-enactment is fundamentally a function of culture which communicates ideas and feelings from individual to individual. The currency for this communication is dependent upon current cultural norms and values. Because the fundamental unit of communication by re-enactment is the individual human being (either impersonated or drawn by word or pen), each unit, to achieve its logical effect, *must stand for some instantly recognizable social characteristic*, because all humans play social roles in life. Without replication or typing, therefore, communication by means of impersonation becomes meaningless—a logical nonentity.

Where the artist—be he writer, actor or painter—exercises his skill is in the ingenuity he calls forth to articulate *exactly* the replication he wants in order to elicit a precise reaction. The main question, therefore, that typ-

---

[24] On a number of college campuses this play (and film) has been criticized because it is "too much like an evening at home," or "just like a visit to Professor X's house." The expertness of the replicas on Albee's part was probably an uncomfortable statement of truth for many members of his audience.

ing poses to the problem of communications is *not* whether replication is *desirable* in re-enactment, but whether the replica portrayed in a given impersonation is first, *the right one,* and second, whether it is *being communicated efficiently.* Here evaluations of the relationship of the various conventions employed in re-enactment (like the relationship of plot to character and the clarity of the communicator's objective) are relevant to the ideational success or failure of a particular impersonation.

The accomplished analyst of the logical phase of the medium of re-enactment has clear (but difficult) guide lines by which to operate. He is more or less in the position of Clifton Fadiman's literary critic: a whole man exercising his wholeness in the incidental medium of re-enactment. His main troubles begin when he attempts to judge the *reactive* power of re-enactment[25]—in other words, to examine it from a psychological perspective.

The Psychologics of Re-enactment

Re-enactment has attracted the attention of psychologists since their discipline cleaved from philosophy and neurology in the nineteenth century. The James-Lange theory of emotions[26] and William James' own ideas about emotional states,[27] which exerted considerable influence upon psychologists for many years, was based largely upon observations of impersonators. James himself was one of the few important psychologists who was keenly interested in the theatre and the psychology of performing and impersonation.

The actors James studied at the end of the last century were trained, as previously noted, by methods drawn from the well-known *Delsarte System.*[28] They were coached to strike stylized poses depicting emotions such as "love," "hate," or "grief," and informed James that *the feeling of a particular emotion followed the physical action of imitating it.* The James-Lange theory accordingly postulated that "particular perceptions certainly do produce widespread bodily effects by a sort of immediate physical influence, antecedant to the arousal of an emotion or an emotional idea." [29] While the observation of the primacy of physical action over feelings or emotion has

---

25 Note that the process *sounds* redundant, and, of course, it *is,* as the following section demonstrates. Redundancy, however, is just one of the critical problems inherent in the psychologics of re-enactment.

26 See Robert Plutchik, *The Emotions* (New York: Random House, 1962), pp. 20, 25–26, for a clear description of the James-Lange theory.

27 See William James, *Psychology,* pp. 240–257.

28 See Genevieve Stebbins, *The Delsarte System of Expression* (New York: Edgar S. Werner Publishing and Supply Co., 1902). This unique book is a complete summary of Delsarte exercises with photographs of statues, diagrams and drawings and instructions on how to "pose" for almost all emotions in the vocabulary of the period. Various charts and metaphysical speculations clearly indicate a religious as well as physical basis for these postural ideas which are still employed by ballet dancers and pantomimists, if one may judge from their behavior during rehearsals and performances.

29 James, *op. cit.,* p. 243.

been challenged by many psychologists since James,[30] the principle still obtains for the context in which it was derived.

As far as one can observe, impersonation appears to function as a stimulus to re-experiencing the emotional content of some initial experience that is being imitated. Certainly, the feeling has usually been experienced somehow (if only at rehearsal) by the imitator; it also *may*, when communication occurs, stimulate a similar experience in an audience. The experiences of many observers, including critics, bears this out.

Freud's concepts of emotion are, of course, more familiar to us than those of James. Although Freud employed figures from classical dramas (and mythology) to label various behavioral curiosities, according to Brigid Brophy,[31] he had little interest either in the music or theatre of his times. Deriving *his* observations from the clinic, Freud minimized the power of impersonation on the mental states. His theory of motivation clearly pointed to unconscious conflicts as antecedent to the feelings of emotions which themselves produce a physiological change in the individual.[32] Here was a concept directly opposed to the theories of the psychology of imitation, like Delsarte's or James', which related more directly to the medium of re-enactment.

Freudian theory indirectly found its way into the psychologics of re-enactment via one of Freud's contemporaries, Constantin Stanislavsky.[33] Like Freud, the great Russian theatrical impresario was vitally interested in the wellsprings of human motivation. He had, also like Freud, been exposed to the French psychologists of the nineteenth century—the original inventors of the concept of the unconscious. In place of Freud's Teutonic training in neurology, Stanislavsky brought to this psychology a Russian (and French) aristocratic interest in art as an apogean manifestation of human experience. The result was his theory of impersonation which remains to this day fundamentally compatible in many ways with psychoanalytic theory. It has also influenced the drama and arts of impersonation and the teaching and analysis of these arts, particularly in the United States.

Stanislavsky's problem was similar to Freud's. The latter wanted to know exactly why individuals behaved as they did in spite of their conscious wishes to the contrary. Stanislavsky was concerned with why a *real* beggar on a stage appeared to an audience *less* real than a skilled actor *impersonating* a beggar. In other words, both men were concerned with the genuine source of characterological reality, but the least likely of the two to succeed in capturing that reality accomplished it best.

To claim that either succeed absolutely in solving their problem would

[30] See Chapter 15.
[31] Brigid Brophy, *Black Ship to Hell* (New York: Harcourt, Brace and World, 1962), pp. 135–136.
[32] Plutchik, *op. cit.*, pp. 32–34.
[33] The observations about Stanislavsky which follow are taken from his autobiographical volume, *My Life in Art* (New York: Theatre Arts Books, 1948).

give both psychoanalytic psychology and the Stanislavsky system authority that many of their advocates do not even claim for them. We are generally familiar with Freud's solutions in terms of psychoanalysis' relationship to communications.[34]

Stanislavsky's solution is immediately relevant to impersonation. The imitator, he noted, must somehow *activate non-conscious basic drives* to re-experience certain kinds of feelings which will in turn stimulate both his conscious reactions and their physical accompanyments. Wrote Stanislavsky quite specifically, "as you progress, you will learn more and more ways to stimulate your subconscious selves, and to draw them into your creative process, but it must be admitted that we cannot reduce the inner life of other human beings to a scientific technique." [35]

Both men were apparently aware, in the context of the process of re-enactment, of precisely the same mind-body continuum from which the field of psychosomatics eventually emerged. Stanislavsky's challenge to psychoanalytic psychology was to explain the relationship of thought and feeling to the subsequent re-enactments which result from them. Psychoanalysis has answered only in therapeutic terms: should an imitator (be he actor, dancer, writer or painter) submit himself to the probings of a competent analyst, the dynamics of the impersonation process will, in theory at least, be clarified.[36]

The Stanislavsky-Freudian problem of communication by impersonation appears to force one into postulating an unseen and unheard mystical flow of energy between actor and audience—not unlike the fraudulent rationale for extra-sensory perception—by means of which *communication* is effected. If unconscious *internal* processes exist, might not a social equivalent of these processes also exist between an impersonator and his audience? Certainly, lecturers, actors, animal trainers and even "exotic dancers" tell us about the feelings they have when an audience is "with them" and "getting the message," or when the audience is unreceptive and the house is "cold." Those of us who have experienced this phenomenon—and almost every professional performer and teacher has—are aware that we often depend more upon feeling or hunch to judge an audience or class reaction than we do to overt objective clues.[37]

34 See Chapter 2.
35 Constantin Stanislavsky, *An Actor Preposes* (New York: Theatre Arts, Inc., 1945), pp. 88–89.
36 This is one reason why creative people are frequently afraid of psychoanalysis. They fear that the unconscious sources of their creative energy will, upon close inspection, dissolve along with their anxieties and neuroses. They would best be counseled not to worry—*not* because psychoanalysts generally exercise judgment in sparing neurotic sources of creativity while re-channeling neurotic sources of dysfunction. Unfortunately, they are likely to discover that even long term psychoanalysis is likely to affect—for good or evil—*neither* very much, although, as therapy, it may prove a valuable experience for them in other ways.
37 There *are* many objective audience reactions, however, to which we *can* respond, like throwing vegetables at performers, or students who read newspapers in class. Perhaps we

The existence of such an unseen wireless system is, of course, highly unlikely. Far more probable is the process of sympathetically evoked states that *appear* to communicate information below the threshold of consciousness, but which merely excite within each individual his own unique reaction. This notion depends upon the concept associated with the James-Lange theory, that members of an audience repeat in small measure the *physical* aspect of the impersonation they watch. Each member, therefore, feels the attendant emotions. This is also probably the reason that communication by re-enactment works, even when the instrument of communication is sound broadcasting or recording, and no visual physical model is available.

Conclusion

We may now explain with some precision a number of phenomena concerning communication by means of re-enactment.

First, the accuracy of any re-enactment is less important than its immediate identifiability, explaining why replication works even when cliché's and caricatures are employed.

Second, the energy level of the impersonation is crucial to its communication; it is necessary therefore for a man imitating a beggar to *project* (a term used in the theatre) the vital qualities of the impersonation to an audience. A real beggar would not know how to utilize proper and sufficient energy to perform in a manner which activates properly the sensibilities of the audience. Stanislavsky's puzzle is therefore explained.[38]

Third, variability and similarities of audience response which seem unexplainable may result from both conscious and unconscious differences and/or similarities in the audience. What is the reason for frequent *disagreements* among similarly trained, intelligent people concerning the theatre of the absurd, or the films of Alain Resnais, or the personality of some perfectly harmless performer like Jack Paar or Dave Garroway? What explains the *communality* of response to such dim nonsense as the late Walt Disney's live films, or the circus, or the perennial Tarzan (and why is he perennial?), or Batman? No evidence exists that the patrons of the mass arts in America are morons, or that they do not have intellectual equipment to appreciate the programs that our Educational Television stations offer. Yet

---

frequently disregard these overt stimuli when they are negative in an attempt to save face. It is easier to blame a "cold house" for our poor reception than to blame our own shoddy performances.

[38] The problem of projection in communication is handled by different instruments in different ways, one of the reasons that these instruments seem to be mediums when in fact they are not. Motion pictures, for instance, increase energy by using close-ups, amplifying or re-dubbing speech, and adding music to the sound track, as well as by forceful editing, and other techniques. A competent performer on radio or in the live theatre achieves similar effects in different—and frequently less subtle—manners. The problem of controling projection is a constant factor relating to *all* instruments employing the medium of re-enactment.

virtually *no one* watches our many ETV stations unless forced to. Why? Answers to all these questions probably lie in response mechanisms of an audience which have not as yet been explained, either by measuring conscious behavior or by socio-psychological theory.

Fourth, our examination underscores the potency and value of reenactment as a *medium of communication,* rather than merely a mode of behavior.

We have, for at least half a century, fallen into the habit of regarding our attractive technology—movie projectors, television receivers, revolving stages, etc.—not only as mediums but as messages. In the first place, they are not mediums, and, in the second place, they are not messages. They *are,* of course, extremely effective devices which serve as instruments by which mediums of communication of three sorts (narrative, picture and impersonation) may be distributed to wide audiences.

QUALITIES OF
COMMUNICATION

Part Four

QUESTIONS FOR
COMMUNICATION

Chapter 11

COGNITION AND COMMUNICATION

WE HAVE examined some of the countless ways "sense" or cognition acts as a significant function of communication, and other ways in which it does *not*. Our symbol-making prowess, for instance, for all the assistance it provides in articulating communications of permanence and giving them importance, is not necessarily a "sensible" process—one reason that some eminently "sensible" men experience difficulty in understanding symbols and are therefore insensible to their subtleties.

Many art forms contain great amounts of material which affect communications of various types with a minimum of cognitive content. Critics and interpreters may, of course, *read in* as much sense as they wish to a painting, a play, a poem, or a piece of music. It is accordingly impossible to find any communication which lacks sense content entirely for all possible auditors. Miss Stein's famous "rose is a rose is a rose" probably has had *more* sense constructions applied to it than her equally famous (but more sensible) "Pigeons on the grass, alas!" Ambiguity and/or nonsense do not exclude the possibility that cognition may not be found somehow, by someone, in the most apparently senseless communication.[1] Neither may we be sure precisely how sense communication has occurred in extremely simple communications. The misunderstandings involved in day-to-day human relationships gives us some notion concerning enormous possibility for breakdowns in cognitive intercourse between people who may even have been *trained* to understand one another.

---

[1] Even the nonsense word "grumzil" (which was made up for this sentence) is open to, at least, a psychological interpretation (or search) for sense. Here is a factor that is rarely considered in the construction of "meaningless" terms for devices like the semantic differential or the "unknown X or Y" in mathematical equations. Teachers sometimes report reactions on the part of students to the psychological sense (or feelings of repulsion and attraction, usually) associated with such symbols.

Sense Analysis

The basic analytic concept of a quantifiable "semantic space" is derived from the older field of semantics itself and interpreted finally in the early nineteen-fifties by Charles E. Osgood and his co-workers.[2] As we have noted,[3] mathematical models created by Osgood are utilized in accepted techniques for certain kinds of behavioral research today. They differ considerably in letter—if not in spirit—from the looser, less precise analysis given language by "General Semanticists" who follow Count Korzybski.

Sense analysis is also the aim of the descriptive linguists like Noam Chomsky[4] who have devised communication "models" (some even called "machines") by which to test the various products of human linguistic communication. In order for these tests to take place, the logic of language —and only the logic, usually—must be coded for translation in a lexicon of quantification, usually a numerical language (like arithmetic, or algebra or, sometimes, for pictorial purposes, trigonometry). The coding process is arbitrarily chosen albeit, in every case, highly consistent.[5] In coding, what is understood to be the vital or rational elements of language (*invariably* cognitive) are changed into other more precise symbols. This was largely what Norbert Weiner had in mind when he asked, some time ago, for precise methods for "the acquisition, use, retention and transmission of information," [6] prerequisite to self-understanding of our present society, a notion then at odds with the best techniques of American social science.

While it is far too early to evaluate the linguists, semanticists and others who have followed Wiener,[7] it is fair to note that should their analytic attempts succeed, they will, at best, have discovered only a small portion of how cognition itself is communicated by the mediums discussed in the previous chapters. At present these limits result from their strongest methods: the devices used for quantification. These symbols almost invariably take the form of statistics, translated so that they can be most adequately programmed into high-quantity, low-quality computing instruments.

[2] See Charles E. Osgood, George E. Suci and Percy H. Tannenbaum, *The Measurement of Meaning* (Urbana, Ill.: University of Illinois Press, 1957).
[3] See Chapter 8.
[4] See Noam Chomsky, "Three Models for the Description of Language" in Alfred G. Smith (ed.) *Communication and Culture*, pp. 140–152. See also a clear explanation of some of Chomsky's work in J. R. Pierce, *Symbols, Signals and Noise*, pp. 112–115.
[5] See Gregory Bateson, "Information, Codification and Metacommunication" in *ibid.*, pp. 412–426.
[6] Wiener, *Cybernetics*, p. 161.
[7] Unlike many modern myths, the hero worship which is currently given the ghost of the eccentric and one-time child prodigy does not seem either excessive or ill spent. Wiener's facility for finding statistical equivalents for human processes—in fact, his literary talent for colorful analogies—was sharp and clever. While little of the cybernetic notion is original with Weiner, his ability to express its possibilities with vigor was outstanding. So was his sense of humanistic despair concerning the social tragedies that becloud so much of our apparent intellectual progress.

In other words, these scholars have discovered regularities in the communication of sense which lend themselves to relatively simple propositions occurring a vast number of times. Statistical instruments and electronic computations may therefore show variance (or lack of it) in these observations—as well as eccentricities in them—with excellent reliability. The main problem of these sorting procedures is usually how to employ the data received.

What will eventually be given us by these studies is a highly accurate picture of how a *portion* of a *tiny regular segment* of *one part* of a *single* communication process (the narrative medium) seems to be working within the limits of a *certain* language. Let us hope the result is worth the effort.

Should these scholars, impressed with the precision of their results rather than their relevance, then be impelled to redefine "communication" as "that process about which statistical computations may yield meaningful data," and proceed to explain, therefore, how we transmit and receive messages, their efforts will yield little of interest to anyone but themselves.

We would be wise here to repeat Bertrand Russell's well-known commentary on the British linguistic philosophers, whose work in many ways resembles their American counterparts:

> When I was a boy, I had a clock with a pendulum which could be lifted off. I found that the clock went very much faster without the pendulum. If the main purpose of the clock is to go, the clock was better for losing its pendulum. True, it could no longer tell the time, but that did not matter if one could teach oneself to be indifferent to the passage of time. The linguistic philosophy, which cares only about language, and not about the world, is like a boy who preferred the clock without the pendulum because, although it no longer told the time, it went more easily than before and at a more exhilarating pace.[8]

Our present discussion of cognition in communications must therefore neither exclude the interplay of sense with other qualities of communication, nor define "sense" so restrictively as to change the processes of cognition into Russell's clock without a pendulum, unrelated to the functions which cognitions play in the *mediation of both thoughts and feelings* from man to man. We cannot so construe our study of sense to fit models satisfactory to the methods of statisticians, scientists, semanticists and/or grammarians, simply because the models are available and work.

The Essence of Sense

The conscious attempt to create a seemingly "sensible" field around ourselves is probably one of the strongest of our drives, a development which must have occurred quite early in man's socio-intellectual growth.

[8] Quoted in Crane Brinton, *The Fate of Man* (New York: George Braziller, 1961), p. 321.

His capacity for cognitive reorganization has been studied in detail by psychologists of various schools. It has been demonstrated, both theoretically and experimentally, to constitute a remarkable, near universal, adaptive talent.[9] Show him an ink-blot, and he will see a panther in a forest; he will explain footprints on his ceiling in numerous ways, until he satisfies himself that his cognitions are "real." In the case of optical and auditory illusions, he will let himself accept the most preposterous "explanations" for the chaos he sometimes observes, so long as that chaos yields a "sense" which it is possible for him to accept—even if he must accept it with *caveat* that it *is* indeed an "illusion" and therefore not to be trusted. Whether this function of mind is explained as part of the ego theory of the Freudians or as a specific instance of how conditioning effects an organism, cognitive reorganization of stimuli remains a central stabilizing force in the mind-life of man—and perhaps for other animals also.[10]

The concept that sense is a factor of virtue or excellence in human perception—and therefore in communications—has been handed down to us through the rational philosophers of society from the eighteenth century followers of John Locke.[11] A skeptic in his own times, Locke disassociated sense from being, which is exactly where Descartes had left it, and recognized that all efforts at sensibly quantifying or qualifying our environments were, at best, risks. "We must," he wrote, ". . . appeal to trial in particular subjects, which can reach but a little way. We must content ourselves to probability in the rest." [12] Nor did he affirm that learning or formal education, no matter how well intentioned or expert, would raise men above "the service of their bellies," as he put it. While recognizing the power and force of training to transmute the inclinations of men into vehicles for sense, he understood that this process had natural limits. Locke's total vision of society was contingent upon how adequately men mastered the communication of sense: hence, the vital role of education for the citizens of a democracy, of freedom for the discourse of ideas, and of a common language for the perception of political arguments. In essence, Locke was putting all man's

[9] See, for instance, such a standard social psychology text as David Krech and Richard S. Crutchfield, *Social Psychology* (New York: McGraw-Hill Book Company, Inc., 1948), pp. 110–145. Various schools of psychology offer theories as to why and how we fabricate certain cognitions out of certain specific perceptions, but most observers agree that re-organization of our cognitions moves in the direction of higher and more satisfactory logical or psychological sense orders—or what we imagine to be sense orders—than experienced previously. This apparent re-organization in the direction of the most sensible possible definition of stimuli around us even appears in the case of mental patients who strive, despite apparent distortion of their sense-making mechanisms, to re-organize their perceptions according to the limits of their unique viewpoints of realistic environments!

[10] See Leon Festinger, "Cognitive Dissonance" in Stanley Coopersmith, (ed.) *Frontiers of Psychological Research* (San Francisco and London: W. H. Freeman, 1966), pp. 207–213.

[11] See Alfred Corban, *In Search of Humanity* (New York: George Braziller, 1960), pp. 68–74, for an adequate review of Locke's philosophical realism.

[12] Quoted in *ibid.*, p. 72.

apples of destiny in the basket of rationality, full in the recognition that the basket might at any moment rip at the seams without care, delicate handling and constant repair. Sense and virtue were thus united.

In the West, sense communication has become *the apparently* fundamental communication: that is, all other types of communications are understood either to be reductions of rational communications—as in the case of a kiss between lovers—or modifications of sense—as in the instance of a high-school English teacher's contention that the "beauty of language" *enhances the meaning* of poetry. Cognitive qualities in both of these instances are understood to be of prior importance to the emotional, stylistic or intentional qualities they exploit.[13]

Locke—and subsequent exponents of man's virtue via rationality—were affirming nothing new. Pericles had asked for much the same acceptance of sensible priorities from the people of Athens centuries before Christ.

The only classical enemies of cognition in communication have subsequently been the great religions in their historical "humanitarian" phases, and behaviors that have been differentially called "madness" in their anti-humanistic phases. (Paradoxically, warfare, mass murder, torture and genocide have often been cognitively understood as sensible, and subsequently humanitarian; while love, compassion, charity, selflessness and humility have been taken for anti-humanitarian madness many times in our tradition, up to the moment of the present writing.)

The priority of sense in communication appears to have been a universal tendency from pre-history onwards. It was accelerated and emphasized by the introduction of science to the West and an apparent subsequent dependence of scientific methods upon what Europeans and Americans understood to be sensible and virtuous ideas.[14] The yardstick for the evaluation of most communications has been, and still is, a question of *cognition*. The first and best query one can make about most communications boils down to the idea: "What did he say?", a bald admission, logical and psychological, of cognitive bewilderment.

One may conclude that we are accordingly living in a rational era, a time where the highest value is placed upon *cognitive contents* of communication. The irony of this conclusion, however, is that one cannot conceive of a time or place which did *not* understand itself to be rational, and where sense communication did *not* dominate the social exchange. Countless cultures in history have objectified emotions, capricious intentions and mystical phenomena of all sorts, reducing them ultimately to cognitive communications, rather than to spread them (correctly) as nonsense. Let us not forget that the wildest behaviors and strangest eccentricities visible in psy-

[13] See Chapters 12, 13 and 14.

[14] The remarks in the paragraph above need for verification only the reminder that the nuclear bomb was understood to be both "sensible" and "humanitarian" in the early 1940's by such eminent men of reason as Einstein, Fermi and Oppenheimer, among others.

chiatric wards usually have their cognitive explanations, satisfactory, at least, in their own contexts, just as the nonsenses of history and contemporary culture have been (and are currently) defended as the highest manifestations of sense.

Sensible People

Sense and nonsense are as dependent one upon the other as good and evil, light and darkness or any other set of opposites. This is true not only in the philosopher's world, but in the psychologist's as well. Such cognitions are frequently the objectification of emotions or reductions of numerous varieties of nonsense to a discourse acceptable by the individual and his society. A *purely* cognitive phase of communication is difficult to conceive. (Exceptions would include individuals who *must* communicate in the limited cognitive vocabulary, like elemental but rapid communications from machine to machine.)

For most of us, the idea of cognition unrelated to emotion, style and/or motive is unthinkable: namely, the de-humanized thought, the removal of the word "life" from our intellectualism, and the trivialization of an intellectual heritage, which is, in fact, the major content of the discipline of history. One may abstract—as Arthur Koestler has done brilliantly[15] —scientific "types" of human beings and the "inhuman"—in fact *anti-humanistic*—trend pervading the climate in which science is taught in our classrooms and by means of our textbooks.[16]

We may even know university pedants who appear to be walking reference books: bundles of cognitions. Perhaps the abstract physicist or mathematician, at the moment that he is dealing with his specialty, is indeed handling purely cognitive material, but one is inclined to doubt it. As Koestler notes, Copernicus, Galileo, Franklin, Faraday, Maxwell, Darwin and Pasteur, as well as the scientists of our present century like Eddington, Jeans and Schrödinger, have provided ample evidence that effective cognitive reports of scientific speculation *may be* similar to works of art, in that they *must* at least be emotively and stylistically clear and consistent.

Judging by the content of their professional journals, one would accuse our present *behavioral* scientists of graver infractions of aesthetic clarity than our natural scientists. The crudest practitioners, though, are those nonscientists who assay the respectability of science without sufficient regard for its disciplines; for example, professional educationists whose publications are largely travesties of *both* communication of cognition and proper

[15] See Arthur Koestler, *The Act of Creation* (New York: The Macmillan Company, 1964), pp. 255–267. Koestler's grasp of the relationship between thought styles and character is one of his most remarkable attributes—in addition to his encyclopedic grasp on the history of science and culture. Unlike many former ideologists, he appears to have fortified his illusions with a sense of irony and humor. One is led to wonder how, even as a young man, he could have fallen under the deadpan spell of dialectical materialism.

[16] *Ibid.*, p. 261.

language. Koestler observes correctly that our great tradition of the communication of scientific cognitions is also a great tradition of literary *art*, despite the arguments of critics of our current cultural pluralism like C. P. Snow.[17]

When people appear to be dealing in cognitions *and only cognitions*, the student of communications had best beware. It is difficult, for instance, to level direct criticisms at most of the new pedagogical devices that strive for greater efficiency and speed in schooling, unless one sincerely questions the present *need* for greater efficiency and speed in schooling.[18] Where these devices fail most critically is in the same function that the worst textbooks of the past generations also failed; they are communications in only one key, that of cognition. The older textbooks, it was understood, would be accompanied by the motivation, drive and example of a skilled teacher, thus augmenting the cognitive bias of the desiccated volumes we ourselves were handed as youngsters. When such teachers did *not* accompany the book, the volume was usually worse than useless: that is, frustrating.

The new teaching devices, no matter how cleverly they are constructed, are not only equally biased towards cognitive communication, but are also designed (or at least touted) to effect economies in teaching talent by *minimizing* the role of the instructor. Films, TV or tape recordings may, in some manner, rectify this situation by offering students a counterfeit teacher (certainly better than *no* teacher), but their effectiveness depends upon the talents of the artists and technicians who use these instruments to

[17] Snow's observations about the "two cultures" in our society has been discussed enough and requires no comment here except to note, as Professor Leavis has, that Snow's division appears arbitrary. Specialism has neither excluded—not does it need to exclude—realms of discourse beyond an individual's specialty. The whole point of this chapter centers on the argument that *one* of Snow's cultures—the technological world—*could* not exist as a unique entity. If it did, it would lack the power to communicate successfully enough with the rest of society for other antithetical cultures to rise beside it. See C. P. Snow, *The Two Cultures: and a Second Look* (New York: The New American Library, 1964).

[18] Speeding up the process of education is, for many, a notion of little significance. Jerome Bruner's dictum that "any subject can be taught effectively in some intellectually honest form to any child at any stage of development" in *The Process of Education*, (Cambridge: Harvard University Press, 1961), p. 33, has created a stir in the world of professional education that has resulted in considerable shuffling of curricula and pedagogical manipulation. The proposition appears to miss the point that education is first, best judged in *sum total*, and second, *necessarily* attenuated for many reasons in technological societies, and third, *non-cognitive* to a great degree. There also appears to be very little wrong with efficiency-oriented concepts like "Programmed Instruction," except to inquire exactly why so many educators appear to be upset when exposed to the inefficiencies of conventional education! See Jerome P. Lysaught and Clarence M. Williams, *A Guide to Programmed Instruction* (New York: John Wiley and Sons, Inc., 1963), pp. vii–69, for a well reasoned case *for* this kind of teaching. Then ask yourself just what the big hurry *is* towards efficiency in the schooling of our youngsters that justifies so crude an assumption that learning is the mere matter of collecting cognitions and passing examinations with high grades as early in life as possible. *Perhaps if we slowed down* some of our educational processes, we would find that they would produce more *worthy* results more *effectively* than they do now.

record the teaching. So far, most of them have concentrated on the communication of cognition rather than the character and style of the instructor. They have therefore developed educational instruments much like our ancient textbooks, demanding anew the presence of a vibrant teacher who may communicate with her students more broadly than cognition alone permits.

The man (or his message) of pure intellect is almost invariably a fraud, unless his message (or presence) is unusually short and simple. Whitehead called the merely well informed man "the most useless bore on God's earth," but Whitehead was describing (charitably) the well informed man as more than a mere bundle of cognitions—or the kind of ignoramus who can and will only talk and think "sense." Such a man is worse than a bore; he is a menace, even if his context of discourse is plane geometry, sewage disposal or the technique of open-heart operations. He dehumanizes communication and renders what should be intensively redolent with meaning, the vocabulary of human ideation, sterile and inconsequent. This notion is difficult to bear in mind in an era such as ours, with its deep and misleading rationalizations for the pursuit of science and the utilization of technology. These fantasies are so commonly accepted by many of us, because they are necessary for fooling ourselves and others into believing that the communication of cognition *is* somehow synonymous with virtue.

Making Sense of Cognition

While there is little proof, except that derived from analogous observations of perception,[19] it is doubtful that human cognition represents one entire class or homogeneous form of response. We know that stimulation of, or damage to, certain portions of the human nervous system influences how and when certain cognitions are available to an individual's sensing powers. Such knowledge is confusing, however, because physiological manipulation of our brains and allied organs seem almost always to involve other processes, usually of a neuro-muscular nature, as well as cognition.

Where cognitions are a function of memory, for instance, drugs like the so-called "truth serums" may seemingly improve memories of certain classes of events, but only at the expense of letting loose floodgates of emotion which may distort memory beyond the limits of "truth." More recently, experiments (both scientific and performed for "kicks") with consciousness-expanding drugs like LSD appear to demonstrate that different classes or interpretations of cognitions occur quite differently in different people, depending upon their psycho-physiological makeup. The effects of these drugs also have such intense and immediate *emotional* consequences that their influence (if any) upon sense-making faculties appears most noticeably *after* an LSD "trip" rather than during it.[20]

[19] See Gregory, *Eye and Brain*, pp. 189–219.
[20] The reader is advised to consult one of the first books on the subject, written at a

At best, experiments with drugs have provided only a number of clues indicating vaguely how and what our cognitive processes may operate and how they may someday be classified.[21] It is highly probable, however, that the sense of a communication is first perceived by the individual *contextually* or in general relationship to other usually *expected* cognitions. Much has been made of the selective factors in perception—on the basis of some near-classical experiments demonstrating that individuals tend to choose, expose themselves to, and retain those stimuli which previous experience leads them to believe will enhance their expectations.[22] Whatever else these experiments may indicate, they seem to show that nearly every communication relates (or fails to relate) to a significant context of cognitions in the recipient made up of the results of past experiences.

Our first cognitive efforts in discovering meaning in an environment is to recognize and identify the new, the unfamiliar, or, perhaps, the unrecognizable. To carry the point almost to absurdity: the sudden appearance of a green object six feet tall with four heads and seven arms might lead us instantly to "recognize" it as a "man" (from Mars, possibly), just as the mountain bears or some other beasts in the Himalayas have been "recognized" by Sherpas as "abominable snowmen." When a stimulus has *no* cognitive contextual setting into which it can be placed, our usual reaction is to cease the attempt to make sense of it and generate emotions: fear, laughter, nausea, or some other non-cognitive reaction.

The process of contextual cognition is therefore capricious, which accounts for the large number and various types of "abominable snowmen" of one sort or another in our annals. The operation of contextual cognition is most noticeable in the human being during the years of childhood and adolescence when, for great periods of time, things *are seldom* what they seem, and the child learns to face the probability that a considerable proportion of his cognitive assumptions may be subsequently proven inadequate. Is it any wonder, therefore, that our modern attempts to *reason* with children so frequently fail? Sense (or reason) proves to them to be as poor a guide as nonsense or emotion. Adults are also victims of mistaken or widely disoriented contextual cognitions, but they cannot excuse to themselves their often considerable confusions as facilely as a child can.

---

time before the development of the present psychedelic "cults" and the treatment given them in the periodical press. See David Solomon (ed.), *LSD, The Consciousness Expanding Drug* (New York: G. P. Putnam's Sons, 1964).

[21] The following discussion relies heavily upon the speculation in I. A. Richards (*Practical Criticism*, pp. 205–224.

[22] Two such early efforts are recorded in Leo Postman, Jerome S. Bruner and Elliott McGinnes, "Personal Values as Selective Factors in Perception" in Swanson, etc. (eds.) *Readings in Social Psychology* (New York: Henry Holt and Company, 1952) pp. 375–383, and Eunice Cooper and Marie Johoda, "The Evasion of Propaganda," in Daniel Katz, etc. (eds.), *Public Opinion and Propaganda* (New York: The Dryden Press, 1954), pp. 313–319. There are a number of other such experiments, and most of them have been synthesized in the standard texts of Social Psychology.

Some of the most baffling misinterpretations of communications may result from the confusion of cognitive contexts. These are invariably psychological disorientations which *appear* logical but are not solved by the application of logical corrections. Why, for instance, are Fellini's films—or Bergman's—considered by many obscure? Nothing they *contain* is difficult to understand. But to explain logically that the context of the former's films nearly always deal with moral decadence, the trivialization of religion and the magic of art; or to identify the latter as a showman who applies the perspective of showmanship to a variety of life's problems, does *nothing* to clear up the contextual cognitive confusion of those who misunderstand them in the first place.

To claim that the *context* of nearly *all* our modern art schools and fads is misunderstood in a basic cognitive manner may seem excessive. But rephrasing the notion to aver that *most sense aspects* of our external environments in general are not fully understood by the average man, makes the proposition seem more reasonable.

Individual cognitions present different problems entirely. It is quite possible to misinterpret completely the contextual sense of a communication and "understand what it is all about"—that is, "understand" its individual elements without comprehension of a totality. Some modern "prophets" like Professor McLuhan or Timothy Leary may be easily understandable from an atomic perspective but impossible to comprehend contextually.

In like manner (on the other side of the coin), one's individual cognitions may run amok, while the context of what is being said remains clear, as in many people's reactions to the *Marat-Sade* play and film, or Genet's *The Balcony* or *The Blacks*. At any one moment, you may not be aware of what is going on in these dramas, but their contextual meaning is so insistently stated that they are difficult to misinterpret totally. Much the same observation may be made of Joyce's *Ulysses*, or *Remembrance of Things Past*, or the recently republished brilliant novel by Malcolm Lowrey, *Under the Volcano*.

Modern instruments of communication are excellent devices for the transmission of atomized cognitions, probably superior to the older ones like the live drama, dance and written or printed words. We, therefore, tend to be confused most often by the contexts of these instruments rather than their individual parts. We disregard the clear point, for instance, that the comic strip is an excellent instrument for narrative, a device for pictorial comment of major importance, and a dramatic form potentially as powerful as the film. Most of us do not understand why political cartoons are (and have been) of great significance in American life, or what the comic strip *Blondie* tells us about American middle-class life. Yet most of us understand clearly any *one single* political cartoon or any *single Blondie* strip in the funny papers.

Various mediums of communication treat differently contextual and atomic cognitions. Most modern narrative seems to make its sense statement first in contextual, and subsequently in atomic form. For instance, first we tell someone that we saw an article in a newspaper or magazine; then, and second, we describe its contents. Or we announce that the type of narrative we are about to unfold is (hopefully) a joke, and then we tell it.

Pictures, on the other hand, usually impress us first with salient significant details which leads us into the immediate assimilation of context. This appears true for photographs, drawings, pictures in monochrome or color, and motion pictures. Cognitively, a picture is *of* a new-born baby; secondly, it is an etching, photograph, or what have you, surrounded by various details. When thumbing one's way through a photograph album, one is assaulted by the cognitions of individual items: people, animals, houses, trees, etc., in quite a different manner from the way words appear when we swiftly scan a book.

What is true of pictures seems also to apply to re-creation, although contextual meaning is also all-important. When the curtain rises, the film begins, or the chorus enters, it is a general *mood* or overall *theme* that assaults us first and probably stays with us through the entire performance, unless a switch in cognitive environment is planned by the playwright or director.[23] On the other hand, certain individual cognitions have extraordinary effects upon audiences, usually because they are explanations of emotional involvements displayed in the re-enactment. The eternal problem of Ophelia's madness—whether it is real or feigned—is a clear example of such an atomized cognition that appears almost as a diversion from the main intellectual current of *Hamlet*. If properly performed, the problem may leave the audience with a deeper cognitive impression than the more flamboyant and dramatic action in the play, even, perhaps at the expense of the contextual sense of the entire production.[24]

Cognition and Confusion

The major logical and psychological difficulty presented by the communication of cognitions is *not* the difficulty (as the semanticists and lin-

---

[23] Scenic and lighting designers are extremely aware of the dominance of contextual sense in the recreation of an event. No matter how stereotyped the setting, the skilled theatre critic will be able to tell the type of play to follow by means of a well designed and lit setting alone. For instance, the farce, *Room Service*, and the drama, *Sweet Bird of Youth*, both take place in hotel rooms. The locale and needs of the action notwithstanding, the setting and lighting for one would not be satisfactory for the other.

[24] The example would necessitate an extremely skilled actress as Ophelia and a lesser performer as Hamlet. This was the case in a recent professional performance of the play. While the audience was left with mixed emotions about the production, our good *sense* told us that the question of Ophelia's madness—and her fate—was far more logically important than anything that we *saw* happen on stage either to Hamlet or his unfortunate family.

guists would have us believe) of obtaining correspondence of ideas between different individuals, but rather the apparent *ease* with which such correspondence is usually obtained. So forceful is the desire of the human organism to make sense of his environment, that he will usually rush to the first ostensibly meaningful construction of his perceptions. The construction may be incorrect, or require qualification and modification, in spite of its logical adequacy and psychological satisfactions. This is one of the main causes of confusion in cognitive communication.

The current output of dramatic material on television and in film is one example. It is most easily "understood" sensibly as entertainment, commercially oriented, escapist, pitched to a low common denominator of tastes and interests, in other words, cultural *kitsch*. But this simplistic cognition is as incorrect as it is facile! It takes into account neither the educational environment into which these programs and films obtrude, the history of our drama in relation to our cultural development, the economics of the culture (and the needs of that economic system for propaganda support), nor various critical behavioral factors about the relatively small portion of our total population affected by them. The *real* issues are avoided because bogus cognitive issues are too satisfying. Both the entrepreneurs of these industries and observers studying them have been duped by their own reactions to stop inquiring into them somewhere short of genuine "sense." The same may be said of much of our modern cultural and educational phenomena including children's stories[25] and adult fiction, to architectural styles and legal practices, with the possible exception of techniques of warfare and a few other selected manifestations of technology.

Sense analysis of almost *any* portion of culture is, in fact, difficult, if the cognitions involved are employed by society as more than objects vaguely noticed while passing over the terrain of life. The virtuosity of much of our contemporary cultural criticism (or, in some cases, its *only* virtuosity) results in some measure from simple identification of certain dissatisfactions with apparently generally satisfying cognitions of the environment. A not-too-bright drama, movie or music critic may, accordingly, seem extremely wise, not because of the depth of his insights or the correctness of his views, but merely because of their cognitive novelty.

The *impression* of emotional responses upon the human organism in most communication is possibly far greater, in most instances, than the *impression* of sense. Most of us, most of the time, tend to trust, in our private lives, our emotional responses more fully than our cognitive reactions. We thus reserve our feelings for most of the significant choices we are forced to

---

[25] The result of what happens with the discovery of the sense beyond the sense of common phenomena in an environment is often startling. For example, David Riesman's analysis of children's literature in *The Lonely Crowd*, pp. 125–132, is a most impressively sensible grasp of the communication of extremely subtle cultural cognitions. They *must* miss the eye of most observers of children's fiction who are not attuned to the same sorts of perceptions as a sensible observer like Reisman.

make in life and trust cognition only when it is rigidly structured for us and emotionally "safe."

In addition, elements of "art"—or the satisfying aesthetic qualities we perceive in our environment—seemingly tend to force us to distrust sense and lead us into accepting what satisfies emotion. Art confuses many of us by limning certain guidelines of what is *appropriate* or *proper* for us to believe at certain times. Artistic ideas are subject to rites of passage, cabals and pronunciamentoes of critics to the degree that many of us are confused as to the nature of precisely what communications we are *supposed* to appreciate, or respond to, or enjoy or abjure, and why. Ideas (when they are labeled "artistic") tend to become discursive. Society does not allow us to use our logical razors upon them, and so we stare dumbfounded at "pop" and "op" paintings or underground movies. Ideas that might be crisp and clear are now confused.

Reactions of multitudes, also, to as obvious a painter as Gainsborough have been diffused through schools of painting and critical obfuscations that militate against the understanding of his work as cognitive, pictorial communication. Sensibly, Gainsborough's portraits were realistic, elaborate and quite clear as communications via a colorful pictorial value system.

These ideas may easily be put into cultural references, played upon emotionally and used as stimuli for the mind's eye of imagination. They gain immeasurably from such handling in subtlety and fullness of insight, but they also lose cognitive power apace. Sense becomes but *one* part—perhaps an unimportant one—of the subsequent elaboration of the role of a man and his art in social, aesthetic, and psychological frameworks. The sense of an artist's pictures is often lost among many perceptions of his works and life. Searching for sense within so complex a scheme of elaboration is difficult even for the trained individual, and impossible for most of us.

Conclusion

One major order, or qualifying factor, of all communications is cognition. It relates primarily to what man regards as the sensible or logical aspects of his environment. That any *single* form of communications or perception is cognitive is doubtful. More likely, many classes of perceptions may be termed cognitive. Schools of communication analysis, accordingly, built primarily around the idea of quantifying or qualifying cognitions, may be dealing with such highly specialized types of phenomena that they come to conclusions of questionable value.

Nor does cognition seem to occur unmodified by other qualities of perception, particularly those of feeling or emotion. We know of no time in history when "thinking men" have not considered themselves rational and propelled primarily by cognition of the environment. But neither do we known of a period or society in which this conceit has been reasonably justified, except by accident.

Our conclusion is that people, neither collectively nor individually, tend to trust their cognitive powers for long or for much. The spread of education to masses in the West, advances of science, and the ubiquity of mass communications appear to have had little or no effect on two vital aspects of cognition in communication. First, the immediate impulse of most people, when faced with a communication of any degree of ambiguity, is to make sense or discover a psychologically satisfying cognitive value for it. Second, having discovered this assumed cognitive aspect (which is often likely to be incorrect), they frequently either misinterpret or disregard *it* in favor of their feelings about the stylistic, artistic or persuasive qualities of the message.

Chapter 12

COMMUNICATING
EMOTION

EMOTIONS are individually perceived as feelings, states, impossible to describe exactly and usually ambiguously experienced. They all seem to share certain characteristics.

First, they are special classes or types of generalized feelings, different and distinguishable from *specific* feelings, like pains of various sorts, or even simple tactile and/or cognitive pleasures, although they may accompany, or appear to result from, specific pleasures and pains. Second, they are feelings over which we have certain degrees of sensible control, or which are often mediated to us or changed in quality by cognitions. Third, they display a seemingly profound inner generated power that impels them—in normal people at least—to the primacy of attention for differential lengths of time, depending upon the psychological setting in which they occur. Fourth, while they are largely internal, subjective kinds of feelings, most—if not all—emotional activity produces one or more physical manifestations of long or short duration.[1] In their dramatic manifestations, tears flow from eyes, blood supplies to various parts of the body are altered, ductless glands operate involuntarily and knees shake. One may also be propelled to the *voluntary* action of flight or involuntary paralysis. In this last respect, emotion is most noticeably different from cognition, which appears much more remotely related to our immediate somatic condition—except as cognitions directly excite emotions.

[1] Poets from antiquity have noticed the physical concomitants of emotion which occur in the *short* run. More recent studies and theories of psychomatic relationships concentrate upon physical dysfunctions caused in the *long* run by emotions, including such physical phenomena as allergies and tendencies to the high incidence of multiple accidents. Psychosomatic assumptions, of course, have been for centuries made in all types of "faith healing," including Christian Science, but only in recent times have efforts been made to classify such observations scientifically. See Flanders Dunbar, *Mind and Body* (New York: Random House, 1948).

The Nature of Emotion

Psychologist Robert Plutchik offers twenty-one definitions of emotion in his short book on the subject,[2] including his own which states that ". . . an emotion may be defined as a patterned bodily reaction of either destruction, reproduction, deprivation, rejection or exploration or some combination of these, which is brought about by a stimulus." [3] The combination or "pattern" to which Plutchik refers bears a rough analogy to mixtures on a color wheel. Basic feeling reactions combine subjectively within the individual in enough different ways to cover definitively the entire vocabulary of *words* by which we usually identify emotion.[4] By centering his essentially behavioral descriptions upon the apparent physical aspects of emotion, Plutchik therefore (and cleverly) avoids most of the semantic and symbolic problem into which his twenty colleagues run. In his review of the literature on emotion,[5] as well as in the definitions, he demonstrates that the attention of emotion theorists seem also to have been primarily directed to its physical aspects. They discuss emotion largely as muscular, postural, glandular or neurological phenomena. Characteristically, the Freudians disregard somatic primacy in their offhand rejection of "clear-cut relations between emotion felt and bodily processes" [6] because of the lack of demonstrable (to them) correspondence between unconscious processes and perceptions of one's physical state.

On the basis of a number of experiments involving college students (and the psychologist's faith in language to describe feelings), Plutchik works out various emotional combinations and interactions with near mathematical precision.[7] He is, of course, not the first observer to have developed such a lexicon, but his particular ideas, although tested against extremely small and (perhaps) atypical populations of the kind usually available to experimental psychologists, are probably a good deal more elegantly developed than any other yet attempted. Their application is another matter. Developing functions for such elaborate psychological vocabularies as Plutchik proposes (aside from their semantic utility) had perhaps best be left to posterity.[8]

No definition of emotion more inclusive than Plutchik's appears avail-

---

[2] Robert Plutchik, *The Emotions*, pp. 173–176.
[3] *Ibid.*, p. 176.
[4] *Ibid.*, pp. 40–53.
[5] *Ibid.*, pp. 24–34.
[6] *Ibid.*, p. 33.
[7] See *ibid.*, pp. 108–125. Says Plutchik, for instance, ". . . the assumption of the mixing of eight primaries will permit the synthesis of the manifold emotions which our language describes (sic). Eight primaries lead to 24 dyads and 32 triads, a total of 56 different emotions at one intensity level. If we assume even four discernable levels of intensity, this would produce over 224 combinations of emotions, and if we assume further interactions between intensity levels, thousands of combinations are possible." (p. 124.)
[8] See his section of "Implications and New Directions," *ibid.*, pp. 150–172.

able, however, in current literature.[9] It is difficult to deny that individuals' feelings vary, and that their general quality seems to relate to certain specific and basic interactions of the human organism with his environment, perhaps adequately described as "destruction, reproduction, incorporation, orientation, protection, deprivation, rejection or exploration," as Plutchik understands them. But one must not underestimate somatic aspects of emotion and the general agreement that "feeling" involves considerable physical "doing." Emotions, probably, are usually "mixed," and mixtures of terms usually occur even as we try to verbalize our experiences. "Pure" feelings of fear, love, hate or rejection are, one imagines, rare experiences in the lives of most of us, so much so that they are usually worthy of special notice or comment when they occur.

Most definitions of emotion—wisely—avoid the problem of temporal and/or causal relationships in their adumbrations. One exception is the early James-Lange theory, which seems to indicate that feeling is *caused* by physical action, while most later theories implied or stated a reverse of this causal relationship. Physical and psychological characteristics of emotions are today usually understood to occur simultaneously. It is, however, granted that most emotional reactions are the result of a neurological stimulus of some kind, usually related to a perceived environmental "cause," although many of us have experienced spontaneous "cold sweats" or unexplainable bursts of feeling that Freudians generally associate with the unconscious.[10]

Emotions and Intelligence

Observation, literature and folklore have led us frequently to think of intelligence and emotion as antithetical, as if the presence of one in a person's behavior, life-style or character precluded the other. The pervasiveness of such continual and abundant "common wisdom" indicates that there may well be some degree of reliability to the observation. Ancient astrological character divisions were based upon whether people were guided by intellect or emotion, as were the categories of "body humors." Even such modern concepts of psycho-physical characterological divisions as those of

[9] Certain familiar works on emotion may be helpful to the student of communications. See the various editions, short and long, paperback and hard cover of the *Psychologies* of William James; Nina Bull, "The Attitude Theory of Emotion" in *Nervous and Mental Diseases Monographs*, No. 81, 1951; W. B. Cannon, *The Wisdom of the Body* (New York: W. W. Norton & Co., Inc. 1939); D. Rapaport, *Emotions and Memory* (New York: International University Press, 1950); J. B. Watson, *Psychology from the Standpoint of a Behaviorist* (Philadelphia: Lippincott Co., 1924); B. F. Skinner, *Science and Human Behavior* (New York: The Macmillan Company, 1953); D. O. Hebb, *The Organization of Behavior* (New York: John Wiley and Sons, Inc., 1949).

[10] In his first speech delivered in the U.S.A. at Clark University in 1910, Freud made direct reference to this relationship of the unconscious to emotion *unperceived by the person experiencing it*. See J. S. Von Teslaar (ed.), *An Outline of Psychoanalysis* (New York: The Modern Library, 1925), pp. 30–31.

W. H. Sheldon roughly equate ectomorphy, for instance, with cranial dominance in behavior and endomorphy with feelings, appetites and emotions.[11]
Most of us have also dealt with people we might describe cursorily as
"highly emotional but not too bright" or "cooly and coldly intelligent,"
rough judgments but serviceable ones.

Whether, in fact, intelligence and emotion (however counterposed)
are antithetical to one another, or whether easily observable behavioral and
character traits like those mentioned above are merely culturally oriented
stereotypes—and fulfillment of certain "role playing" dispositions—is another matter. On the basis of a number of experiments in communicating
emotion, J. R. Davitz has presented [12] considerable evidence that emotional
sensitivity and intelligence (as shown by tests and limited to certain populations) were, in the sample groups, in fact, closely *related*, and that people
of extreme emotional awareness also tended to be on the upper intelligence
levels of his samples.

Writes Davitz about these experiments, ". . . I believe that most of
us were looking for some mysterious dimension of being that would account for emotional sensitivity. We were searching for a 'third ear' that
could be investigated empirically. Therefore, our discovery of rather simple,
common-sense, perceptual and cognitive correlates of sensitivity come as
something of a surprise, though upon further reflection it seems obvious
that perceptual and cognitive processes must be involved in responding to
complex stimuli." [13] He concludes that "probably no one can be highly sensitive to emotional meanings without a good deal of general intellectual
ability, but certainly a high I.Q. is no *guarantee* of emotional sensitivity.
Our emphasis, perhaps, should *be on different kinds of intelligence, all
sharing some common ability to deal with symbolic stimuli,*" [14] including
responses, incidentally, *both* to verbal and non-verbal stimuli in experimental situations. Davitz is in favor of a conception of emotional sensitivity,
therefore, as an ". . . intellectual factor involving, without doubt, non-
intellectual variables in the total response . . . ," [15] a conclusion with which
it is difficult to quarrel.

The problem faced by the common observer over centuries is his near
inevitable confusion of emotionality with sheer volubility, on one hand, or
with an arrest of inhibitions brought on by fatigue or the use of a drug like
alcohol, on the other. Fast, intensive and dramatic reactions often appear to
be displays of intensive emotional activity, when, in fact, they may indicate

[11] See Anne Anastasi and John P. Foley, Jr., *Differential Psychology* (New York: The
Macmillan Company, 1954), pp. 446–452.
[12] Joel R. Davitz (ed.), *The Communication of Emotional Meeting* (New York:
McGraw–Hill Book Company, 1964), pp. 197–200.
[13] *Ibid.*, p. 197.
[14] *Ibid.*, p. 200. (Italics added.)
[15] *Ibid.*, p. 199.

an *absence* of genuine feeling. That is, they may serve as attention-attracting devices that amplify shallow feelings in a crude but effective manipulative manner. A genuinely emotionally sensitive individual—granting that this sensitivity is also a function of cognitive awareness—may often of necessity *inhibit displays* of emotion beyond their rational utility as uneconomical and essentially destructive or degrading excessive behaviors.

If we spare our concept of intelligence to *awareness* of the environment and our relationship to it, then feeling or emotion most unquestionably constitutes one aspect of this awareness, and is in itself a *measure* of intelligence. Obviously, the individual who has developed his cognitions will also have available for emotional reaction a wider range of possible stimuli than one who is more limited cognitively. There is the question as to whether (and how) he will *use* what he has developed, but, since emotions are essentially techniques of adaptation to environments, the individual experienced in handling his cognitions is likely to know how to handle his immediate world better than one who is inexperienced.

Konrad Lorenz, from his perspective as a naturalist has, for instance, written, "In reality, even the fullest rational insight into the consequences of an action and into the logical consistency of its premise would not result in an imperative or a prohibition were it not for some emotional, in other words instinctive, source of energy supplying motivation. . . . Man as a purely rational being, divested of his animal heritage of instincts, would certainly not be an angel—quite the opposite." [16] Once more—and here in a non-experimental context—we are offered a view of cognition and emotion as interdependent. Certainly, they do not signify the *same* or necessarily similar manifestations of awareness, but each is modified by the other. Acting together, they yield the kind of human behaviors which the thoughtless are quick to characterize as either "rational" or "emotional" (the result *either* of cognition *or* of feeling), but rarely of *both* in indeterminate proportions.

A belief has long existed that men who are dominated largely by cognitions—that is, "intelligent" men—are in some measure emotionally invulnerable and accordingly best fitted to lead mankind. The notion has been current in the West since Plato, and has been given particular impetus since the development of the scientific method, which appears (when unexamined historically or appreciated mainly for its resultant technology) to exclude emotion almost entirely from its *modi operandorum*. This is a paradox; the scientific age has seen developed multiple intellectual devices for the study of our species which have returned near invariable conclusions that both man and his society require optimum universal and individual cultivation of cognition *and* emotion, particularly the latter, if civilization is to survive. Whitehead's characterization of culture as "activity of thought,

[16] Konrad Lorenz, *On Aggression*, p. 247.

receptiveness to beauty and humane feeling," [17] enunciates the simple truth that "intelligence" cannot be judged solely by cognitive ability, but rather by the relationship of that ability to dimensions of emotion which are simultaneously manifest by an individual alone or in the company of other people.

Emotions and Metaphors

Langer writes, "In creating an emotive symbol, or work of art, the creator does articulate a vital import which he could not imagine apart from its expression, and consequently cannot know before he expresses it." [18] In the act of communication by any medium, through any instrument, cognition appears to be a function of the desire to communicate, and emotion is therefore related closely to the activity of communicating itself. This viewpoint is not incommensurate with theories that credit the origins of language with the fundamental desire to communicate primarily emotions rather than cognitions.[19] Certainly the *active* aspects of communication often appear closely akin to the transference of emotion between individuals. Cognitive content gives the impression of greater passivity, and accordingly is less difficult to quantify and qualify than forms of feeling that flow between people with apparent mystery.

Despite the amount of psychological theory developed to explain their manifestations—and despite some recent and revealing experimental efforts described above at qualifying them—the exact nature of our emotions remains an enigma, unless they are described by means of analogy. Bio-chemical explanations do not tell much, nor, as we have seen, do manipulations of the vocabulary by which we describe them. If we relate emotions to mankind's feral evolutionary heritage[20] we may clarify some of the colorful frustrations that "civilization" has caused our species to employ in controlling certain atavistic impulses (usually emotions) in the interests either of society or of our individual watchdog cortical impulses. But analogies of man's behavior to that of the animal kingdom are more satisfying romantically than intellectually—that is, emotionally than cognitively.[21] While we may glean from these analogies outlines of the *sources* of our emotions and reasons for the *range* of them, we learn little else.

For these reasons (and in the shortage of utilitarian truth), such bizarre notions as "brainwashing" and "menticide" have peculiar appeal in

[17] A. N. Whitehead, *The Aims of Education* (New York: The New American Library, 1953), p. 13.
[18] Langer, *Feeling and Form*, p. 389.
[19] See Chapter 8.
[20] See Albert T. W. Simeons, *Man's Presumptuous Brain* (New York: E. P. Dutton & Co., 1961).
[21] This same criticism may be applied to some of the observations made in Chapter 15. Their defense in this latter context (humor) is based on the paucity of alternatives to such analogies.

our time and have developed their own mystiques.[22] Nor are we entirely willing to give up the previously discussed ancient notion that people are characterologically "emotional" or "intellectual." While certain individuals at certain times *do indeed* seem propelled more by thought than feeling, and vice-versa, they are not inflexible determinants of "human nature," or built-in properties of character.[23] In fact, their dependence upon one another is so vital that to cleave one from the other is more a literary or semantic achievement than a realistic description of actual components of human behavior.[24] We know emotions exist more because we *feel* them than because we can observe them with certainty in others!

What does, accordingly, clarify the role of emotions in communication is the close examination of them as subjective phenomena. From this perspective, it appears that *three* subjective sets of emotions are involved somehow in *every single communication of emotion* rather than *one* individual emotion so favored by empiricists and playwrights. They are, first, the *intended* emotion to be communicated, real or simulated;[25] second, the emotion as *perceived* by the individual who receives the message (that is, what it is taken to mean); and, third, the resultant emotion which is *felt* by

[22] See Joost A. Meerloo, *The Rape of the Mind* (New York: The World Publishing Company, 1956). Meerloo is a psychiatrist who discusses realistically the many forces in modern life which attempt to control individual emotional life by means of coercive methods. While the total picture Meerloo paints may be somewhat alarmist in the light of events during the decade since his book was written, his insights into the emotional vulnerability of modern man are interestingly set forth, particularly his ideas of mass psychology, pp. 196–207. The success of the novel and film, *The Manchurian Candidate*, is evidence, however, of the absurd extremes to which popularization of the supposed methodologies of "brainwashing" have been taken—and probably accepted—by the public. Neither Richard Condon's style in the book nor the realistic film production gave the reader or viewer a clear idea of how fanciful the science-fiction premise of the plot actually was.

[23] Included here is the idea that women are more "emotional" than men or, conversely, that men tend to be more "intellectual" than women. The observations of Margaret Mead and Ashley Montagu in this regard are too familiar and numerous to cite, but their works should convince the skeptics that neither human males nor females have a right to claim intellect or emotion as sex-determined. Rather, *sex* in variant cultures appear to determine in large measure which of the two will *apparently* dominate.

[24] Writers of fiction will hardly stop using phrases like "He was an emotional man," or "Contrary to many of her sex, Fern had a sharp, masculine intellect," in the light of psychological evidence, because such figures of speech *do* serve a literary purpose. But they are merely figures of speech and relate to reality as adequately as many literary and dramatic conventions: there is *something* to them, but not enough to permit accurate, productive generalizations.

[25] The question of whether the emotion communicated by an actor, for instance, is "genuine" or not is irrelevant here, because the *result* in communication of either a *felt* or *shown* emotion is likely to be the same, that is, if an actor has the skill to project the "genuine" emotion or feign convincingly the false one. Also, the only foolproof way of determining whether an emotion is "genuine" involves asking the individual involved (who might dissemble) or by employing a lie-detector apparatus which would tell whether *an* emotion had been felt without classifying it. The question is likely to be a thorn in the experimental psychologist's side for some time to come, but does not concern this discussion.

the latter. For example, a student tries to communicate the emotion of enthusiasm to his teacher; he succeeds merely in getting him to perceive that he is frightened of failure; as a result the teacher feels discouraged. Three *different* emotions are herein involved. In another instance, a student tries to communicate the emotion of enthusiasm; the teacher perceives it as enthusiasm; accordingly, he also feels enthusiastic. Three emotions are involved here, but they are similar emotions,[26] separated by their differential loci.

Emotions, when viewed as subjective qualities of communications, appear to function much like symbols, in that the basic currency of exchange is not the emotion itself—in the sense that words, a picture, or re-enactments are—but is, in all probability, a metaphor.[27] We have seen that the basic means by which individuals symbolize is also metaphorical.[28] There is little doubt that the symbolic quality of much emotional exchange relates to the simultaneous closeness of *both* phenomena (emotions and symbols) to metaphor. Or is it the other way around? It *is* possible that the emotional quality of most symbols is explained by their metaphorical nature. Or both propositions may be true in some measure: a symbol and emotion may interact in one setting whenever they are communicated by the mediums of narrative, picture or re-enactment.

Must emotions be formulated as metaphors when they are communicated? The answer is not simple, nor does an affirmative one refer to *all* emotional communications, particularly those mainly involving tactile or kinesthetic elements.[29] But much recognizable communication of emotions by people is probably translated into metaphor *before it happens*. That is, a message similar or analogous to "something else" (in words, pictures, or combinations of both) produces within us (in the phases previously described) the reaction *we might have had were we actually involved in the initial emotion-creating process we are experiencing artificially*. In most instances, as recipients of a communication, we are not *actually* involved in the emotion generation described above. We are exposed *only to a meta-*

[26] Some people appear more competent at communicating emotions according to the latter mode than the former, particularly those who have been trained to do so. Moreover, certain simple emotions, like mutual sexual attraction, seem easily to communicate the same way in all three phases, although occasionally this sort of communication is also muddled with resultant misunderstandings too complex for discussion here.
[27] Richards, *Practical Criticism*, pp. 221–224.
[28] See Chapters 4, 5 and 6.
[29] This may be one reason why the late Aldous Huxley's concept of the "feelies" (actually involving the spectator in the tactile aspect of cinematic communication) is so amusing. Huxley conjured up the idea of mechanical communication which would permit the transfer of various emotions *without metaphor*. Periodically, the press reports that an instrument for producing "feelies" is about to be unveiled for public use. It is doubtful that such direct, non-metaphorical transfer of emotion would be very attractive to the masses—despite its obvious sensual potentialities. Films that stimulated the sense of smell, for instance, have been attempted. Despite the fact that the movies *did* indeed *smell*, the appeal to the audience's emotions directly via their sense organs in this manner failed.

JUNE 5

BICYCLE   2 MINUTES
LEG CURLS   3 X 6   50 lbs
HIP ADDUCTION 3 X 6   50 lbs
ABDOMINAL   3 X 6   40 lbs
LEG EXTENSION 3 X 6   60 lbs

phor of that emotion: the *picture* of a face contorted in pain, a *printed* section of dialogue, or the *sound* of a scream. First of all, we must handle this metaphor cognitively, indicating the importance of cognition in the communication of emotion. Then, it must be related to our own individual past emotional experiences. When the metaphor is thereby clarified, and only then, do we *feel* the last and resultant emotion that has been communicated.

Like symbolism, we are faced here with an elaborate and involved psychological process, but nevertheless its logics are quite clear, clarifying a number of curiosities in the communications of emotions. For instance, some time ago, one of the James Bond mystery movies was exhibited in the same neighborhood at the same time as Roman Polanski's *Repulsion*. The former was a Technicolor action-thriller, highly stylized, expertly produced. The latter was a black-and-white study of the deterioration of a schizophrenic girl, propelled to multiple murder by her delusions, shown to the spectator through her eyes. The suburban audiences attending both films were probably similar in social class and educational background, at least.[30]

The Bond film was by far the "bloodier" of the two; great gobs of brightly colored red Hollywood gore were used in profusion during its many scenes of violence. Particularly clever was one sequence of undersea combat featuring a good deal of carnage, wherein blood floated, cloud-like, into greenish tropical water. The audience was neither noticeably delighted nor repulsed. They viewed the Technicolor violence quietly and with the same general display of excitement (and probably enjoyment) as the rest of the film.

Polanski's *Repulsion* was another matter. Very *little* blood was *shown* in the black-and-white film, but when it *was* visible (as in one instance where a man with a smashed skull lies dead on the floor) it is unmistakably thick, oozing, blood. In this film, too, a corpse is shown underwater in a bathtub, and blood colors (or blackens) the bathwater in hideous spurts. The reaction of this audience was grotesque; groans and sounds of nausea were audible. A few men and women headed queasily to the sanitary facilities. Others manifest various symptoms of tension; many were visibly perspiring despite the comfortable temperature of the theatre. Hardly a member of the audience appeared to be unmoved by these scenes.

Why the difference in the emotional reaction of similar groups of people to these two films, especially since the one in color showed blood more frequently, utilized its "effect" more cleverly, and probably was more realistic (superficially) than the black and white film?

[30] Film audiences at expensive movie houses in Forest Hills, New York, tend generally to be homogeneous, according to local theatre managers, except for differences between weekends and weekdays, and afternoons and evenings. Both of the audiences discussed here were evening weekend groups, observed during the same weekend. No claims are made, however, for more than impressionistic reliability or validity of these observations.

The answer centers on the probability that the spectators of the Bond opus were not permitting the *metaphor* of photographed blood (or death or violence) to turn into its equivalent emotion or feeling for them. They were instead probably more intent upon sexual (and other mischievous) metaphors in the film, and reacted to *them* with considerable vocal evidence of emotion: most frequently laughter. The audience at *Repulsion* understood and accepted the blood metaphors exactly and immediately as Polanski had intended, and the resultant emotions were exact and immediate.

The *amount* of metaphorical material was irrelevant; more violence was visible in the Bond film than in *Repulsion*. So-called "realism" meant nothing; the colored blood looked far more like the real thing than the chocolate syrup that, it appeared, was used for *Repulsion*. What *was* of significance was the *settings* in which the blood appeared. In the first instance, this background was so artificial, so obviously satirical of reality that the metaphors were accepted for what, in fact, they were: production artifacts, stylized reproductions of Hollywood's universe. In the second, the audience was slowly conditioned by the director and the film editor to accept the metaphors as equivalent to situations in real life. The case study of the girl was developed artfully and realistically. The context of the film was charged so as to provide realistic metaphors for an audience which had been, literally, educated to translate them into emotions and subsequently *feel* them. One had little choice but to refer these metaphors to past experience and respond to them emotionally.[31]

The Sources of Emotion

In considering the origins of emotion, one is brought back to the James-Lange theory, despite its fate at the hands of recent theoretical psychologists.[32] James had posited that—whatever *else* emotions signified—they resulted from cognitions and/or subsequent neuro-muscular states associated with them. His concept was, as noted, in direct causal opposition to the later psychoanalytic idea of the non-cognitive unconscious.

From the perspective of communication, it is possible to accept the concept that cognitions serve as prior factors in the engendering of emotions. Unless cognition precedes emotion, one is led to believe that mind reading (or some form of extra-sensory perception) must occur to mediate unconscious manifestations between individuals through interpersonal, mechanical and electronic instruments of communication. That such an occult cognitive bridge exists seems unlikely. It is, however, a possibility which may one day vindicate a fully developed psychoanalytic approach to communications.

---

[31] Of course, policemen, butchers and operating-room nurses were probably less emotionally aroused by these metaphors than most other members of the audience.
[32] See Roback, A *History of American Psychology*, pp. 162–164.

Granting that cognitions communicated via various mediums may be quite subtle and difficult to observe, we lack evidence to demonstrate that they are *in any phase* unconscious. For an explanation, therefore, of the source of emotion *in communications* of any kind,[33] one or another kind of sense communication must precede the transfer of emotion from one person to another.

Cognitions, in these instances, may be atomistic or contextual, concrete or abstract, culturally "sensible" or "nonsensical," "classical" or "pop," lowbrow or highbrow, clear or obscure, sacred or profane, stated or implied, or they may take any number of forms. The emotional *result* of these communications is more or less instantaneous. But the *vehicle for emotional transfer is not the emotion itself*. It is—as we have seen—a metaphor for that emotion. It is, in effect, *a cognitive symbol of an emotional state*, formulated in such a way as to be capable of communication.

We arrive, then, at the simple explanation of why experiments have shown that the communication of emotion is a function of intelligence. It *is* intelligence, or the segment of the cognitive part of it that relates to our abilities to speak and interpret feelings by means of a powerful metaphorical language.[34] William James was indeed correct in identifying a cognitive "reaction" as the prime motive force in the generation of human emotion in the context of communications of re-enactment, the results of his studies of actors and actresses.

The student of communications is less concerned, however, with *sources* of emotions than the *control* of them. If there is an overriding art to emotional communication, it may be found in the control of various metaphors by which emotional reactions are elicited from others. This is a matter of wisdom and talent, as well as sensitivity to cues in the environment that lead to the prudent selection and juxtaposition of metaphors.

From the communicator's viewpoint, it is unfortunate that sensitivity to metaphor and degree of emotional receptivity of any given audience for any communication is not stable, even for short periods of time. Some of the most mercurial aspects of living are frequently centered on the workings of emotions, and they are also often the most unpredictable. Our measure of emotional control over our *own* feelings is limited and variable from person to person. It depends so critically upon time and circumstance that many fundamental neurotic behaviors appear to stem from the intensity

[33] Such an explanation need not apply logically to the development of emotion—spontaneously or otherwise—*within* one individual. Freudian theory appears applicable here. There is no theoretical reason why, in such instances, emotions may not arise *before* cognitive manifestations, or in their complete absence.

[34] Experiments have been performed on the communication of emotion by metaphor, but unfortunately emphasis has been placed upon the development of tests which reliably identify subjects' ability to recognize emotional meanings expressed in severely limited constructions of metaphors. See Joel R. Davitz and Stephen Mattis, "The Communication of Emotional Meaning by Metaphor," in J. Davitz, *The Communication of Emotional Meaning*, pp. 157–176.

and amount of emotion we succeed in displacing at a given time with cognition or thought.[35] For many of us, various facets of our emotional lives appear to exert a will of their own—to operate at variance with our intellectual dispositions—thereby giving us "common sense" confirmation of the notion that they originate in the unconscious. Common sense is neither, however, a substitute for rational theory nor experimental evidence.

When communication occurs for a group, emotional responses may vary from individual to individual, or they may reflect apparent consensus. Individuals, like audiences, may be unpredictably emotionally vulnerable: that is, any number of metaphors (some only vaguely connected cognitively with the stimulus) may set off certain emotional responses. Most of us have experienced, for instance, "crazy spells" when we laughed at almost anything said or done around us. Begging etiological questions, we had progressed to an emotional state of "trigger happiness" in which we were almost non-selective in the cognitions setting off our responses. Much the same sort of reaction occurs *en masse* when a group of individuals, large or small, responds (seemingly unthinkingly) to the "magic" of a leader like Castro or Hitler. Similar behaviors are visible in audiences of powerful religious leaders, although the interpersonal factors in these situations are quite complicated to explain.[36] In the theatre, a great clown like the late Ed Wynn was able to break down an audience's cognitive resistance until they accepted as hilarious almost every move he made. The late Boris Karloff, in his early films, accomplished much the same end within the context of fear.

Most of us, most of the time, respond emotionally in a most selective manner, however, to the stimuli around us. Sometimes our responses seem too elaborate for the specific occasion, for example, in the cliché's situation when a husband's mild criticism of her cooking stimulates his bride to an outburst of tears. At other times, severe stimuli evoke little noticeable emotional reaction; this accounted for much of the charm of the light plays of Noël Coward, like *Private Lives* and *Design for Living*. Emotionally charged situations (or metaphors for these situations) left his characters unruffled in their evening clothes as they played the game of life as if it were bridge.[37]

Emotions may also be categorized as *developed* or educated in various

[35] See Fenichel, *The Psychoanalytic Theory of Neurosis*, pp. 288–290.
[36] See Kurt and Gladys E. Lang, *Collective Dynamics*, (New York: Thomas Y. Crowell Company, 1961), pp. 111–148, 265–289, for further discussions of the social and personal factors that activate crowds to these relatively non-selective behaviors and for a consideration of the personality attributes of the members of such crowds. The formation of such groups themselves are highly selective processes.
[37] Whether these plays would succeed *today* in the United States is questionable. One must take into account the shallowness of emotional response that one witnesses in everyday life from individuals who regularly use large doses of tranquilizing agents which allow them to "control" their emotions. How would Coward's tranquil sophisticates fare before a present-day audience made up in good part of similarly tranquil drug users?

degrees. Individual experience (as well as studies in developmental psychology) show that our emotional lives usually tend to become increasingly refined and selective with growth and learning. This refinement is inevitable if emotions are, as suggested, part of our cognitive life. Roughly speaking, immature or crude emotions may be set off by a wide range of stimuli, and one accordingly responds in an undifferentiated manner to numerous metaphors. Educated or refined emotions require highly specific, clearly articulated stimuli within a narrow range of situational possibilities.

In normal individuals, age, wisdom, experience, and intellectual growth all tend to narrow our responses to stimuli. To illustrate, imagine an audience of six-year-old children watching a puppet show. Almost every stimulus evokes a wild and gleeful response from them. Now consider an audience of film-makers at a festival judging the best motion pictures of the year. Their emotional responses (while quite likely charitable) will be highly specialized, sophisticated and, usually, relatively uniform.

One may take this observation to mean that a cultural or educational hierarchy of value exists in the priority of emotional responses we give the various stimuli in life. From the *individual's own perspective*, such a priority does *not* seem to exist. An enormous range of developmental differences have probably generated emotional spectrums for each of us as different, one from the other, as our fingerprints. While one of us may be emotionally vulnerable in a specific and loving manner to alley cats, his neighbor may not respond to them at all, or be repelled by them. It is impossible to assign either reaction a value in terms of culture or education.

From the *communications perspective*, however, such a hierarchy may indeed exist, extrapolated from the relationship of the logics and psychologics of communication in a given society. For example, in our present culture, the emotional reactions of a male college professor of literature to a football game will probably differ vastly from, let us say, his discovery of a "lost" poem written by an obscure sixteenth century bard. The professor's emotional life may be involved in both experiences, and his reactions to both are probably "true" or "honest." The difference in their quality results largely, one suspects, in the degree of refinement each manifests as a function of special cognitions. One might almost spell out, therefore, an axiom that, *as the cognitive quality of an emotion increases in complexity, its refinement increases apace.* Put another way, the simpler or more common emotion the individual experiences, the more likely it is *not* to depend upon his cognitive powers but to be disassociated from it.

Last, in communications we are almost invariably concerned with a quality we label "sincerity." We are frequently aware of the likelihood that "insincere" communications may not call forth certain desired emotional responses. Such concerns can be dealt with by referring them to our observation that the more life-like the metaphor involved *appears to be,* the more likely it will be to stimulate the intended emotion. We are left with Pope's advice, "Honor and shame from no condition rise/Act well your part, there all the honor lies."

Conclusion

Emotions have been observed and described in many different ways. Most of us tend to cosset a special and subjective construction of the nature of our own personal feelings. There are probably, however, a distinct and limited number of basic emotions which any one person may feel that are, in one degree or another, similar from person to person. Subtle emotions described in literature are likely to be blends drawn from a conventional spectrum. Our emotional lives are also closely related to our somatic lives, even in regard to such elementary matters as the order in which various emotional and/or physical activities occur.

Considerable evidence (as well as theory) leads us to believe that folklore concerning the difference between emotions and cognitions is a bald simplification of a sophisticated process. Emotional behavior, in fact, necessitates cognitive perception of many factors. It is even possible that a profitable perspective of emotions considers them as one class of cognition itself. The concept of "emotional men" as opposed to "thinking men" probably has logical and historical validity but is useless psychologically. Sex differences based on assumptions regarding emotions are also false.

The close relationship between the communication of emotions and the employment of symbols in communication underscores our use of metaphor as the main currency of communication by which emotions are mediated between individuals. (Excluded are tactile and kinesthetic emotional communication of specialized natures.) Metaphors are mainly cognitive data, and therefore their communication is basically a cognitive act involving three apparent emotional states: the emotion *intended* to be communicated, the emotion *perceived* as communicated, and, lastly, the emotion (if any) *felt* as the result of the communication. Logical statements concerning the cognitive aspects of this process explain the way that these three steps in emotional mediation occur.

Sources of communication have been associated with cognitive reactions to a changing environment at the rejection of theories in which emotions are regarded as products of the unconscious. Regardless of the role of the unconscious in the mediation of emotion, a stimulus in a given instance, and an individual's response to it, are of major significance to the student of communications. Responses vary in different individuals in enormous degrees, and, for various reasons discussed, certain people react at times unselectively to *many* types of stimuli. On the other hand, when emotions are communicated from individual to individual, it is often possible to determine the degree of special learning or cultural inclination in the selection of *particular* metaphors which influence feeling states.

Learning and maturity appear to constitute the two basic factors that, for most of us, modify our apprehensions of emotion and our feelings about the numerous communications we receive. One may speak, therefore, of a hierarchy of emotions, not as they are felt by individuals, but rather as they are communicated by different mediums using various instruments to individuals whose cognitive abilities have been tuned to respond with differential sensitivity to certain kinds of metaphors.

Chapter 13

STYLES IN
COMMUNICATION

Style," said Whitehead, "is the ultimate morality of mind." [1]
Why morality?

Because the quality of style connotes to Whitehead the essential "right" and "wrong" (meaning the morality, the unmorality or immorality) of communications. Little is self-evidently and intentionally *bad* in much of the mass communications we see and hear today as the result of its uniform standardized technical development. The main critical issue involving most of it is therefore purely moral, because its values relate so intimately to whether it is "right" or "wrong."

To question whether the bulk of our science fiction, films and books, for instance, are "good" or "bad" is irrelevant either to literary or cultural criticism today. Obviously, it is *both* good *and* bad, depending on what it is compared to. But the question of whether these fantasies are *right* or *wrong* introduces a clear problem of morality, far less arbitrary. The elements of style of most science fiction are a reflection, in the opinion of many, of their specifically *childish immorality*, the jejune *wrong* sets of value judgments most writers in the genre express towards technology. This immorality helps to explain not only the reasons for the pleasure-producing aspects of many science fiction characters and plots, but their popularity also. For a public that demands style allowing and/or encouraging *wrong* (and therefore unmoral) fantastic regression to childhood, such stories and films, if exploited fully, must be popular. Stylistically, they may be excellent (that is, *right* and moral) children's entertainments. [2]

Whitehead called the sense for style "the most austere of all mental qualities. It is an aesthetic sense," said he, "based for admiration for the

[1] Whitehead, *The Aims of Education*, p. 24.
[2] That they have also been favorite readings for Presidents of the United States of America is cause for wonder, if not concern.

direct attainment of a foreseen and, simply and without waste. Style in art, style in literature, style in science, style in logic, style in practical execution have fundamentally the same aesthetic qualities, namely, attainment and restraint. The love of a subject in itself and for itself, where it is not the sleepy pleasure of pacing a mental quarter-deck, is the love of style as manifested in that study." [3]

The Meaning of Style

Our dictionaries throw much logical but little psychological heat or light on style as a qualifying factor in communications. Lexicographers emphasize the *accent* or *inflection* of a message as a quality of mind of the creator of a communication. They also speak about "manner of approach," again a facet of creation. Reference is made as well to the "general effect" of the object at hand, emphasizing the reactions of a receptor and the prevailing *character* of a work of art. This latter definition brings together both the communicator and the audience in terms of a result that is presumably either or both logically correct and psychologically sensible. Thus do the priests of words recognize that stylistic matters are both subjective and objective, functions of aesthetic consistency on the one hand, but also of reactive states of the beholder on the other.

If we take their definitions literally, there can, of course, be no profitable debates concerning the quality of style, because the term must necessarily be objectified and concerned entirely with aesthetics. To them, style is largely a *philosophical* problem of classification. The much admired book called, appropriately, *The Elements of Style*,[4] may be useful to the would-be writer for its generalizations about the psychologics of how people react to language use, but it is least successful as a list of obsolescent "do's" and "don'ts," to which there are exceptions. When it advises simplicity opposed to complexity, it is providing solid stylistic advice which might apply to Chaucer or Churchill. When it characterizes the word "personalize" as pretentious, it is making an aesthetic judgment which may be meaningless in a generation. Unfortunately, such a book is of little utility in helping students to develop a literary style. Style in writing (or the lack of it) relates to the mental qualities to which Whitehead refers and resists the sort of "handbook guidance" or teaching methods that seems to work for other

---

[3] *Loc. Cit.*
[4] See William Strunk, Jr. and E. B. White, *The Elements of Style* (New York: The Macmillan Company, 1959). University book stores across the nation invariably show signs of brisk sales of this volume. It is required reading in many English and Journalism courses. How its ubiquity relates (if it does) to the miserable prose most college students hand their professors to read and grade is a mystery. The volume may have nothing to do with the generally poor style of college newspapers, literary magazines and doctoral dissertations, but it certainly has not helped the students who produce these documents. The worst style, however, that one frequently finds on a university campus, is used by professors in their communications with each other, particularly among "English" and "Communications" faculties.

skills. This observation applies to other instruments of communication (particularly to their non-technical aspects) beside written and spoken language, and certainly to a fundamental mastery to the three major mediums, narrative, pictures and re-enactment.

Books like *The Elements of Style* do not convey to the reader what *right* and *wrong* style (of any sort) *are* and precisely *why* these moral judgments are made. Because it fails at this task, it fails absolutely. A volume, however, which tells one how to *write* in the style of *The New York Times*[5] or according to the cannons of Prentice-Hall's publishing pundits[6] may be helpful to a writer, providing that he is willing to accept the stylistic judgments of his betters—and all editors are, by nature of the peculiar tactical tyranny of communications, superiors to the communicator himself.

Such concerns as these center on style in written prose. But style is an all-pervading characteristic of all the mediums and the instruments of communication, including architecture, clothes, household utensils, and even the sense of design manifest in the common-man's life-style. Middle-class suburban life, for instance, in the United States is characterized today by a certain style, just as urban upper class life was at the turn of the century. The so-called Negro ghetto displays a style different from most white ghettos, where they exist, in America. Styles of living change even in an homogeneous technological society, and vary according to tradition, financial and social climates, as well as geography.

A synonym for style is the "tone" which may be considered a manifestation of style. Richards associates the word "tone" with the attitude that a communicator takes toward his intended audiences "in automatic or deliberate relation to them. The tone of his utterance reflects his awareness of this relation, his sense of *how* he stands towards those he is addressing." [7]

Style and/or tone are then displays of attitude; hence Whitehead's ingenious notation (at the outset of this chapter) that the "morality of mind" of a communicator is intimate with all manifestations of the languages he uses. Because style is attitudinal, one also comprehends why style in writing or style in drawing are not discrete or singular characteristics of *communications* alone. Numerous attitudinal factors and inter-related dispositions are functions of the psychological make-up of the communicator in action. This is not to say that one may not dissemble a style, just as one may dissemble an attitude. Nor must one's attitudes towards different aspects of life be necessarily consistent with each other. Style and attitude, for

5 See Theodore M. Bernstein, *Watch Your Language* (Great Neck, N.Y.: Channel Press, 1958), for an introduction to the linguistic view from the *Times'* editorial offices.
6 See Anonymous, *Author's Guide* (Englewood Cliffs, N.J.: Prentice-Hall, Inc., 1964). Most large publishers print and distribute "style books" similar to this one, usually designed for their non-fiction writers. Authors of fiction, presumably deserving of less help, are left to their own devices. Using the McGraw-Hill stylebook, incidentally, one may locate numerous errors in the Prentice-Hall volume, and vice versa.
7 Richards, *Practical Criticism*, p. 182. (Italics added.)

example, manifest by Cellini in his artist-artisan role appears to be in many ways opposite to the man we meet in his autobiography.

"Attitude" is, however, a concept that has undergone considerable revision in the past generation, particularly when it is isolated as a factor measured on *opinion* tests that are misnamed "Attitude Inventories." The value of these tests is moot, but the current availability of statistical references to indicate the "attitudes" of people to certain issues has apparently caused a shift in many interpretations of the term itself. We are wise to remain with the generally accepted psychological definition of an attitude as "an enduring organization of motivational, emotional, perceptual and cognitive processes with respect to some aspect of the individual's world." [8]

Wide ranges of attitudinal dispositions lie open to a communicator using any medium or instrument. His power lies in his ability to manipulate his own attitudes regarding the communication itself and those of the intended audience. He may, therefore, modify the tonal or stylistic quality of his effort through a usually large spectrum of stylistic possibilities when concerned with the communication of art, or through quite a small one in scientific and technological communications. In the latter instance, the way in which a mathematician solves a problem is exemplimatic of his style—that is to say his attitude—towards both his discipline and his fellow mathematicians. But his stylistic choices are, of course, far fewer than those which are open to a novelist who faces a blank piece of paper in his typewriter—unless the novelist's attitudes towards both his work and his public have been frozen, as is frequently the case.[9] Faults in style are then indeed characterological problems, as Arnold Bennett claimed.

Whatever his limitations, the communicator, in effect, chooses to arrange words, sounds or pictures so that they exemplify—either unconsciously or deliberately—his relationship to them, and through them to his audience. This relationship, a function of attitude, is what we understand finally as style.

That styles of communication differ in various societies is indicative of the fact that attitudes towards communication and audiences are different everywhere. That this relationship is a variable function of culture is fre-

[8] David Krech and Richard S. Crutchfield, *Theory and Problems of Social Psychology*, p. 173. The difference between their definition of "beliefs" and "attitudes" is that a "belief" is defined as "an enduring organization of perceptions and cognitions about some aspect of the individual's world" (*Loc. cit.*). An "opinion," we understand, is much like an attitude, except that it is usually more cognitive than emotional and far less stable.
[9] Many writers are "typed" just as actors are; hence the frequent use of pseudonyms by authors who wish to vary their styles and break a lock-step in a set of attitudes over which they no longer have control. Is the problem of the "first novelist," who never writes a second book worth reading, primarily an attitudinal difficulty in communication? Does the writer feel trapped by his former style and therefore freezes his attitudes? This is also a serious sickness among non-fiction writers whose stylistic rigidities make all their books and articles appear identical.

quently the subject of critical dispute. No better example may be found than the late sociologist, C. Wright Mills' attack on the "Grand Theory" style of Harvard sociologist Talcott Parsons. His critique reduces much discussion about style to its attitudinal bones.[10] Parson's *attitude* towards sociology reflects an outlook as abstruse as quantum mechanics; his attitude towards his readers (or audience) is that, roughly speaking, they have all obtained their doctorates at his feet. Mills takes delight in boiling down complicated pages of Parsons' "irrelevant ponderosity" and "splendid lack of intelligibility," to simple statements like "People often share standards and expect one another to stick to them. Insofar as they do, their society may be orderly." [11]

Mills' barbs at Parsons illustrate—aside from a delightful proclivity for mischief—one fundamental point about the function of style in *all* communication. While style is a qualifying factor of most human endeavor, it is also related intimately to *content* or *what* is communicated. An attitude displayed by a communicator will not only effect the quality of what he says, but appears to influence the nature of his statement. To some, this will seem a truism, particularly those familiar with the fine arts. For instance, the styles of impressionism or cubism in painting are often largely responsible for the determination of the content of certain paintings. To some degree, style exerts this influence on the content of most communications. Vary style and you will vary content slightly or greatly, inconsequentially or seriously. As much misunderstanding has occurred in the analysis of communication due to oversight of this principle as because of any other factor.[12]

A serviceable understanding of style must include the consideration of other psychological factors. Audiences respond to attitudes in two dimensions: indirectly to the communicator's own attitude towards his message and directly to his attitude towards *them*. The latter response is mercurial. Most readers today are still responding to the poems of Homer in ways that have little to do with the original style of his Attic verse, but rather with how his style is perceived *today*.[13]

10 Mills, *The Sociological Imagination*, pp. 25–39.
11 *Ibid.*, p. 26.
12 Consider, for instance, the puzzle of why novels so frequently are so poorly dramatized by competent playwrights. Usually this failure is blamed upon the "difference between the media," which is rarely explained and almost invariably incorrect. The problem usually is that the novelist's *style* is not replicated in the transition. The content is therefore modified, and the main points of the original are missed. Filmed versions, for example, of Hemingway's novels and stories have—with a few exceptions—been stylistic travesties of the originals. The result has been distortion of plot, character, dialogue, and so forth, all problems of *content*. In the end, these changes are blamed on "the demands of the cinema," which at times may be only slightly different from certain dramatic-narrative "demands of the printed page." The excuse provided an alibi for screenwriters and directors, who rarely seemed to comprehend Hemingway's *attitude* towards both his work and his readers.
13 The perception of a particular member of Homer's audience, his translator, is vital

What concerns the communications analyst deeply is, of course, *how the communicator perceives his audience's response to him.* This is a complicated matter and facilely obfuscated by many artists who claim naively that they merely try to "say what they have to say as clearly as possible" to someone like themselves. Such statements yield little of psychological or logical value in the understanding of style as a qualifying force in communications.

The Functions of Style

Lucid and simple illustrations of style in operation are numerous. Advertisements for a mail order art appreciation course test prospective students' "sense of style" by displaying two poorly reproduced paintings of, roughly, the same subject and asking them to make comparative value judgments. These simple expressions of attitude are presumably illustrative of an individual's ability to appreciate art. The famous Graduate Record Examination contains, in its *Humanities* section, a large color reproduction of a painting about which numerous multiple-choice attitude statements are made. The victim of the test is supposed to check the "correct" statement —that is, the one most compatible with the attitudes of certain selected art critics and teachers.

Orwell provides this example of the power of style:

> I returned and saw under the sun, that the race is not to the swift, nor the battle to the strong, neither yet bread to the wise, nor yet riches to men of understanding, nor yet favour to men of skill; but time and chance happeneth to them all.
> Here it is in modern English:
> Objective consideration of contemporary phenomena compels the conclusion that success or failure in competitive activities exhibits no tendency to be commensurate with innate capacity, but that a considerable element of the unpredictable must invariably be taken into account.[14]

Of the practical function of style, Herbert Spencer wrote:

> To ask whether the composition of a picture is good, is really to ask *how the perceptions and feelings of observers will be affected by it.* To ask whether a drama is well constructed, is to ask whether its situations are so arranged as duly to *consult the power of attention of an audience,* and duly to avoid over-taxing any one class of feelings. Equally in arranging the leading divisions of a poem or fiction, and in combining the words of a single sentence, the goodness of the effect depends upon the skill with which *the mental energies and susceptibilities of the reader* are economized. Every artist, in the course of his education and after-life,

---

here because *his* peculiar impression of the original manuscript will be stylistically mediated to the new audience.

[14] George Orwell, "Politics in the English Language" in Maurice R. Stein, etc. (eds.,) *Identity and Anxiety* (Glencoe, Illinois: The Free Press, 1960), p. 313.

accumulates a stock of maxims by which his practice is regulated. Trace these maxims to their roots, and you find they inevitably lead you down to psychological principles. And only when the artist rationally understands these psychological principles and their various corollaries, can he work in harmony with them.[15]

A recent edition of the *New York Times Book Review* notes the following familiar propositions:

Style is the manner of a sentence, not its matter. Yet the distinction between manner and matter is a slippery one; manner affects matter. When *Time* used to tell us that President Truman slouched into one room, while General Eisenhower strode into another, their manner was attempting to prejudice our feelings. The hotel which invites me to enjoy my favorite beverage at the Crown Room is trying not to sound crass ("Have a drink at the bar"). One linguist, in discussing this problem, took Caesar's "I came —I saw—I conquered," and revised it into "I arrived on the scene of battle, I observed the situation, I won the victory." Here the matter is the same, but the tone of arrogant dignity in Caesar disappears into the pallid pedantry of the longer version. It is impossible to say that the matter is unaffected. Still, let us say that this kind of difference in the two versions of Caesar, is what we mean by style.[16]

Attitudes and psychological astuteness are woven into every communicator's style. (But does our knowledge of the *components* of style infer that we understand its *function?* Yes, but analytically—not creatively—and solely in terms of *end product* rather than in terms of *process.*) This statement satisfies critics, it appears, to a far higher degree than it satisfies communicators themselves. When one associates style with human character (as the statement does) most of the unanswered questions concerning the actual functions of style may be subsumed into the lacuna of what we *do not know* about human character and proverbial "dark places in the human soul." When Voltaire said that the style was the man, he clarified little, simply because men are more difficult to comprehend functionally than styles.

Certain stylistic qualities, far from the apparently least sophisticated, are recognizable in non-human communications. False tones or insincerities of voice can be discerned by various varieties of domestic mammals. Call "nice doggie" in the tone in which "bad doggie" is usually spoken, and you fool a canine pet not one bit. Most dogs seem to listen for the tone of what is said or the style of saying it rather than word sounds, although some word sounds do at times seem to impress them. This communication phenomenon occurs also for infants who, during one stage in their development, ap-

---

[15] Herbert Spencer, *Education* (New York: D. Appleton and Company, 1900), pp. 68–69. (Italics added.)
[16] Donald Hall, "Speaking of Books" in *The New York Times Book Review*, May 7, 1967, p. 2.

pear disinterested in any quality of verbal communication *other than style.* Later in their lives, words, tones and styles appear to be separated from the totality of language. Then the assignment of specific meaning to various words take on primary importance to the developing youngster. A lingering concern with the discrete power of style, however, probably remains with us throughout life.

Communication in a "false" style—or a tone that others perceive as false[17]—is apparent evidence of an *attitude* that was not intended to be expressed. Communications via any medium may *ring false.* Narratives told in many ways may be construed (intentionally or unintentionally) as poppycock. Pictures may be indicted as "mere craftsmanship." In the novel, *The Hucksters,* there is discussion about "sincere" and "insincere" neckties. When an audience does not "suspend disbelief," re-creation fails stylistically to create the illusion of quasi-reality demanded by drama.

When style, therefore, militates against "truth" in any form of communication, it becomes the critical factor in the distortion of *that particular* communication. We discover, accordingly, that a specific stylistic adequacy appears to exist for all forms of communication—and consequently for all modes of art as well—without which *intended* communication cannot occur. Style may be considered the gyro-compass of much communication, responsible for its directive power.

Different mediums and combinations of mediums, as well as different instruments of communication, make constantly changing impressions upon the stylistic quality of their content. Style as a singular identifiable element may be, at times, the *one* peculiar quality upon which the success or failure of a particular communication depends. It is possible to discover a number of examples of communication of an artistic sort that are distinguished neither by cleverness nor profundity nor emotional depth, but which nevertheless make striking impressions by virtue of their stylistic qualities.

Might the drawings of Aubrey V. Beardsley fall into this category? The plays of Clyde Fitch or, more recently, Moss Hart? The short stories of John O'Hara? The acting of George Sanders? The theatrical designs of Donald Oenslager? The singing of Frank Sinatra? The social criticism of Marya Mannes? The *content* of many communications of all of these (and other) figures may be difficult to remember. What we probably recall most vividly is their style; and further examination of our reactions may lead us to discover that we are really and naturally discussing our perceived atti-

---

[17] Some unfortunates are unable to communicate in a tone *not* perceived as false by many of their listeners. An administrator of a certain university gained a reputation as a "manipulator" simply because the tonal quality of his verbal communications had for most people a false ring. Nothing he proposed was given serious consideration because of his reputation as a "good politician." The "good politicians" on the same university's staff, on the other hand, knew how to make their numerous fabrications ring true, like "good politicians" in the world of politics.

tudes. Contrast the acerbic attitude, for instance, of Miss Mannes' essays with the gentler comic outlook of Moss Hart in most of his comedies and in his autobiography. Think of the elegance of Oenslager's settings next to the eccentric Victorian blacks and whites of Beardsley's drawings. These attitudinal differences, of course, are just stylistic. But, in these instances, attitudinal qualities are probably as important, or *more* important, than the actual content of the communications of these particular artists.

No claim is made here that "the medium is the message." Such a statement is absurd on its face. For *certain* communications, however, at the hands of *certain* communicators, style (or attitude) tends to be of greater importance to content—in that it provides distinction for the communication.[18]

The less sanguine aspect of this situation centers on an observation that there is *little* wrong with much (or most) popular culture—so-called *kitsch*—be it Hollywood films, TV broadcasts or stories in womens' magazines—*except* style.[19] This is, ironically, the particular quality in which its producers take their greatest pride, either by discovering or giving their own "touch" to raw creative efforts which arrive at their desks in "crude form." They are re-written and blue-penciled into the puerile attitudes of the "publication"—be it a film factory or magazine editorial desk—towards first, appropriate content (meaning content agreeable to the biases of the producers), and second, the prospective audience (considered as jejune as the production staff itself). *The Reader's Digest* is an example of the distinctive power of style in the hands of expert "stylists" whose attitudes are, if nothing else, consistent.[20]

While style most usually centers on matters of art, stylistic manifestations are seen in almost every aspect of culture. Certain surgeons in the operating room are known as great stylists. So are the stylistic accomplish-

[18] The artist who depends mostly upon style for effective communication is probably not one whose work will endure. Longevity operates at the mercy of cultural fashion. When the fashion for a certain style disappears, so usually does the content phrased in that style, no matter how accomplished its execution. But pendulums swing, and Beardsley's work, for instance, is not incompatible with accepted art styles of the moment. Some-day we may revive successfully the plays of Clyde Fitch, if styles change enough to make them acceptable. We will probably, by then, be amazed to discover how "modern" they are!

[19] The stylistic problem is implied by Dwight Macdonald in his essay "A Theory of Mass Culture" in Bernard Rosenberg and David M. White (eds.), *Mass Culture* (Glencoe, Ill.: 1957), pp. 59–73, one of the most perceptive essays yet written on *kitsch* in our culture. Further attention will be devoted to this problem of mass culture in Part V of this volume.

[20] It is difficult to believe that the producers of our mass culture underestimate the intelligence of their audiences, as is commonly charged. This illusion obtains, because, in their attitudinal stance, *they attempt to please their own tastes* that have been severely abused by expensive educations and subsequently eroded by professional experiences. For a fair but slightly dated essay on the *Digest* see John Bainbridge, *Little Wonder* (New York: Reynal and Hitchcock, 1946). The sorriest aspect of our mass culture is that the "cultivated" writers, artists, musicians and creative talents are doing their *best* to produce mediocre products.

ments of master butchers. A fine cook manifests his uniqueness through style, visual and gustatory.

In America, it is charged that we are increasingly interested in the style of our political candidates, rather than the substance of their platforms. *Was* John F. Kennedy's style indeed part and parcel of his substance as a political figure? Have stylistic problems in culture at large been spread wider today than in previous generations before radio and television? Was Lincoln's "victory" over Douglas as much a matter of style as Nixon's supposed defeat by Kennedy in the "Great Debates" of 1960? None of these questions may be answered definitively at present. Public evaluation of politicians as stylists is not a new manifestation. Nor do we face an age of the "image candidate" whose main attribute is style without content.[21]

The Generalization of Style

It is possible to locate numerous immediate, relevant and clear manifestations of the relationships of style to all manner of communications. Style as a *specific* quality of a given communicator is in any case less important than style as a *general* all-pervading quality that determines in some degree the logical and psychological quality of the relationship involved between audience and communicator, although neither may be aware of it. Artistic biographies and critical essays are written about the specific styles of certain communicators. It is difficult to capture in words the stylistic qualities of first, the *medium* through which he is operating or, second, the *stylistic biases* of the instruments or devices of communication used.[22] Various writers have attempted stylistic-cultural histories. Few have succeeded in capturing the style of mediums and instruments which have over the years changed their social roles. The medium of re-enactment and the instrument of the printed word have, for instance, gone through a number of cultural metamorphoses in the past century, and even competent historians have difficulty in translating their stylistic impressions on past events into terms comprehensible to the modern reader.

General styles in a given period must naturally be unnoticeable or else they are not general. Style boils down to the current *best* way of accom-

---

[21] See David J. Boorstein, *The Image*, pp. 41–44, 249. Others have echoed Boorstein's concern that the real (content) environment in which we live has been overshadowed by a pseudo (stylistic) environment, manipulated largely by the newer instruments of mass communication. That his argument has relevance to our cultural life at present seems beyond dispute. Social and psychological degrees and the effects of the spread of these pseudo-events are more complex than Boorstein, in his one-note argument, appears to realize. For further political discussion, see Gene Wyckoff, *The Image Candidates*, (New York: The Macmillan Company, 1968).

[22] The late Edward R. Murrow's style, for instance, as a television personality is less significant as datum for comprehending television as an instrument of communication than the ways in which his specific attitudinal qualities differed from most other performers' styles on television during the nineteen forties. See Gilbert Seldes' remarks concerning this difference in *The Public Arts* (New York: Simon and Schuster, 1956), pp. 212–228.

plishing ends under the best of current attitudinal circumstances. We are not concerned with the fastest, most economical, most elegant, prettiest, cleverest or most sophisticated ways of reaching an end—merely the *best*. And the determination of what is best (or right or wrong) in such attainment is obviously a moral judgment. Hence, the already stated necessity for moral considerations in the meaningful discussion of style.

Style in communication may probably be considered *best* when, by means of cognitive processes and/or feelings the audiences of that communication arrive at an *appropriate* and reasonably *correct* understanding of the attitude of the individual (be he artist, artisan or scribe), who addresses them in his particular context. To conceive of architecture, for example, as a means of communication in this manner may be difficult, but the appropriateness of a building's style is a function of coordinations of attitudes between those who live, work, play or pray in a structure and the man who designed it.[23] Such a relationship is manifest by the chef who prepares a *haute cuisine* dinner and the gourmet who consumes it, the poet and the lover of his poetry, and so forth, through endless facets of culture. The mediums used are all variations of the three we have discussed in this volume, although the devices and instruments employed in their dissemination are endless, limited only by circumscriptions upon the inventiveness of our technologists.

No wonder, therefore, the centrality of style (and its moral imperatives) in every type of communication imaginable, from immediate and tactile impressions to the outside chance of extra-sensory perceptions. Style is apparent in cognitive emotive aspects of all communications, conditions of perception, the way words are spoken, printed or bound, and in the manner pictures or people are lighted, directed to perform, or encouraged to act spontaneously. Style is as significantly related to a Greenwich Village "happening" as to the design of a new airplane or political campaign strategy. We manifest style in the way we bury our dead or receive our newborn. (There exist familiar styles of regimen for prospective mothers, just as there are styles of delivery, like "painless childbirth" or "induced labor.") As difficult as it is for some to believe, there are styles of illness—including so-called "mental illnesses"—just as there are countless styles of therapy, a good number of which frequently "work" for the same disorder!

The reason for this centrality is clear. The factor of *attitude* is basic to all human endeavors in which individuals control their own behavior. All

[23] One faces few problems in understanding the attitudes of the countless artisans and architects who built the Cathedral at Chartres—or designed the dismal Albert Hall. The attitudes that impelled the late Eero Saarinen to design the New York headquarters of the Columbia Broadcasting System, however, evade numerous individuals who work in the structure. No doubt he shared a vision common with the officers of the organization, but what of the rank and file of the company—or an outside observer? On the other hand, the late Frank Lloyd Wright communicates to any tourist to New York City his attitudes towards museums and cities, in all their playful irreverencies, in his design for the Guggenheim museum.

discrete communication styles are fundamentally manifestations of an individual life style which is the unique possession of each individual on earth, no matter how faceless he may appear among the masses. How different (or similar) these life styles are, one from the other, no man can say. That they are, and have been, different enough at any time and place in history to provide a wide range of response to various environments is axiomatic. Conformity of attitudes is therefore immediately apparent in any culture, insofar as they are viewed from a stylistic perspective.

In communications, for instance, is there a moral insight we can discern in the generalized style of the flow of messages to the masses in our culture? Can one find, in our piles of printed literature, bulging film libraries, and tape repositories a stylistic "given" adequate to uncover common attitudes in the languages of communication in our time?

If so, it is probably both ancient, elementary, and manifest in the most simple kind of communication, and a function of consistency. The simpler the communication, the greater the likelihood that style will indeed be consistent. The more sophisticated or complex the attitude of the communicator, the more difficult it is to remain consistent, that is, to remain stylistically integral. Comic strip cartoonists develop a relatively simple style and maintain it evenly for years. Wide and apparently uncontrolled stylistic variations, on the contrary, are common among even the most skillful playwrights in history.[24] The number of aesthetic elements in any communication as well as its length (under certain circumstances) are also involved. Consistent use, for instance, of line and color may at times be more demanding upon a visual communicator than consistency in the employment of line alone.

There exists, however, the peculiar challenge of *parsimony* leveled at the composer of sonnets (or limericks) to produce the most *modest* meaningful communication *under the limitations imposed* which permits simultaneously the widest and fullest display of style. Here is a formidable art: to confront instantaneously an audience with a brief and restricted communication that must make its stylistic statement with both profundity and speed. That few artists have accomplished so testing an attitudinal sophistication combined with skill is to be expected. That some have used these talents for diabolical purposes is probably also inevitable.[25] "Morality of

[24] Could the Shakespeare who wrote *Twelfth Night* have written *Titus Andronicus*? Of course he could, just as Maxwell Anderson wrote *Winterset* and also *Trunkline Cafe*; or G.B.S. *The Applecart* and *St. Joan*; or Tennessee Williams *A Streetcar Named Desire* and *Camino Real*. People who tackle complex communications are rarely consistent. This is the predicament of many artists who are always searching for that investiture of novelty which we call "creativity" and which necessarily causes some modifications of style.

[25] Adolph Hitler's uncanny ability to make profound and immediate stylistic impressions upon his audience comes to mind. Others, less heinous than Hitler, have used the same sort of talent for less malignant ends. The devil himself probably manifests "style" (as the word is used in this chapter) by turning conventional moral imperatives quickly and effectively upside down.

mind," in Whitehead's terms, as opposed to personal immorality of total orientation to life is a matter of value judgment. Most of us have personally discovered, for instance, from experience that truth is not *necessarily* beauty, and that beautiful things may be malevolent, depending upon the values we assign to "truth" or "malevolence."

An artistic stance, like that common in the Soviet Union, which equates social realism with truth, and truth with aesthetic "correctness," and correctness with beauty, does not appear to provide a culturally adequate value system in the modern Western world. Soviet artists, sometimes at the risk of banishment, often refuse to accept imposed value judgments. They demand the right to search for their own personal moral values and hence turn their backs on officially prescribed artistic and cultural styles.

Similar rebels also exist in non-communist countries, but their acts of defiance against cultural moral norms may appear less vigorous and healthy (from *our* peculiar value orientation) than their opposite numbers in Communist nations. We are too close to them to render final judgments of the influence on styles that their moral rebellions exert. Without question, however, their presence in all cultures, and their effects on the artistic and intellectual community, are healthy. In totalitarian nations, they keep alive the concept of man as a non-materialist. In the democracies, they shout their outrages at our middlebrow culture with its "better things in life," and our tastemaking establishments in museums, libraries, theatres and universities. Their artistic and critical output may be considered of secondary importance to their influence on the generalization of style by mass communications in technological cultures of various political persuasions.

Conclusion

Communications of every type are qualified as much by their styles as by any other factors discussed in this volume. Some of our present instruments of art-photography or abstract painting, for example, may even support in some measure the contention that style may abound in communication where content is *almost* of no significance. No aspect of human existence is possible to qualify without consideration of its stylistic context. The thoughtful historian, when asked for the major difference between our culture and that of the ancient Greeks, might answer simply "style."

This chapter has not attempted an etiology of style—nor is one possible to develop. Certain writers like Harold A. Innis[26] appear to find the causes of style in "oral" or "literary" traditions or in inventions, discoveries or economics. The imputation of such causal relationships takes for granted a priority of events in history for which no reasonable proof can be demonstrated. That the Nile culture influenced the life styles of the Egyptians is beyond doubt. But it is impossible to show that the early settlers along the

---

[26] Harold A. Innis, *The Bias of Communication* (Toronto: The University of Toronto Press, 1951). This fascinating book will be discussed further in Chapter 16.

great river did not choose to live there because the environment permitted them to indulge in certain formerly determined styles of life. Early American colonists, for instance, imposed a European style of life upon a virgin territory that would seem to demand a more barbarous structure than they actually built. Why? Problems of etiology of style may best be left for academicians to argue.

The tonal aspect of communication has been associated with three forces, each of which relates directly, determines, and is in turn also determined by the other: style, morality and content. They are interrelated in every possible combination. Style depends upon morality and content. Morality (or any code of morals) depends upon style and content. Content—or lack of it—is determined by the influence of morality upon style. In its simplest construction, consider this diagram as a crude but satisfactory representation of this relationship:

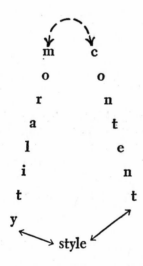

Note that arrows connecting style with morality and content are straight and black, while those connecting morality to content are curved and dotted. Let the dots symbolize the mysterious connection of value judgments of "right" and "wrong" to the flow of communications in each culture which are somehow intertwined with public morality. Let the straight black lines represent the timeless manifestations of style as an inevitable function of the same two forces in every culture our earth has known.

Chapter 14

OBJECTIVES OF
COMMUNICATION

A COMMUNICATION without an objective is possible to conceive of but difficult to find. When one justifies "art for art's sake," he is stating an objective as clearly as a political polemicist. The seemingly meaningless verbal outpourings of small children contain distinctive psychological intentions. Even the purpose of Tarzan's cry is to attract attention of apes or audiences.

While experiment redundantly enhances what common sense avers, impressive evidence exists that the intention of a communicator, as perceived by the members of his audience, will modify (at least) their cognitive and emotional reactions to *what* he says.[1] Moreover, their perceptions themselves are altered according to the way in which they interpret his objectives. As Krech and Crutchfield note,[2] the true intent of a communicator may be of little or no significance to an audience, while the *perceived* intention is, or may be, critical.

Experience with advertising provides rule of thumb confirmation of this principle. If our neighbor recommends a consumer product, and we perceive his intentions as similar to our own interests, we are likely to act on his suggestion. Should we be approached by someone we perceive as involved in the exploitation of the same product, we are likely to discount his advice as mercantile rather than altruistic.

The *objective* of the stranger at our front door is of first concern, and our interpretation of *it* will modify our response to *him*.[3] If he is a re-

---

[1] Two of many such experiments described in one volume are found in Irving A. Janis and Seymour Fesbach, "Effects of Fear Arousing Communications" in Daniel Katz (ed.), *Public Opinion and Propaganda*, pp. 320–335 and Carl I. Hovland and Walter Weiss, "The Influence of Source Credibility on Communication Effectiveness," *ibid.*, pp. 337–347.
[2] David Krech and Richard S. Crutchfield, *Theory and Problems of Social Psychology*, pp. 330–332.
[3] The "secret" of salesmanship is to act so as to *be perceived* as interested more in the

searcher taking a poll, we understand his presence in *one* way; if he is a detective in search of information, we interpret it in *another*; if he remains unidentified and refuses to tell us his objective, we will respond yet in *another* way (theoretically, at least) to identical statements.

We are able probably to predict *cognitive* reactions of individuals to objectives of communicators with greater reliability than we can plot their *emotional* reactions. Certain factors like the *identification* of individuals with a communicator may, however, produce foreseeable emotional reactions. On the contrary, perceptions of intentions or objectives may result from "hunches" or "feelings" rather than cognitions and are therefore impossible to predict.

The perception of an objective in communications is also closely related to our reaction to its style. Because the attitude of a communicator is so intimately related to style, it follows that the perception of that style must also be affected by his apparent objective. One's attitude towards one's audience, or what one tells one's audience, will necessarily be a function of *why* an audience is addressed. As an example, traffic signs in most of the world are stylistically different from roadside advertising billboards, even when the latter attempt (as in the case of the defunct *Burma Shave* advertisements) to confuse perceptions of objectives to attract attention.

Communicators' objectives may be conscious or unconscious, important or trivial, clear or vague, funny or serious. They represent, however, the psychological *starting point of all communications*, and for this reason the nature of all messages between men may be referred back to their intentions. The choice of and use of mediums and instruments of communications will inevitably be a direct function of the objective of communication. This is a useful principle, except that for a relatively small, but incalculable, percentage of communications for which it is impossible to divine externally the objective or intentions, either logically, psychologically, or both, on the basis of the instruments used. This occurs when mediums and/or instruments are forced upon the communicator by circumstances he cannot control.

Conscious Intention

The objectives of any communication—or a class of communications—may be said to be *conscious* when the communicator is able to articulate clearly his reasons for the dissemination of his message, and there exists sufficient *reactive* evidence to believe him. Note that the latter qualification eliminates intended objectives of all kinds *that are not perceptible*. While we, perforce, must disregard some interesting psychological phenomena, a

---

customer's welfare than in selling a product. Since this is a matter of *perception* rather than presentation, salesmanship may in great measure be a talent that cannot be reduced to a formula, although many attempts have been made to isolate the factors that makes people perceive other people as interested in *them*.

clear behavioral test is brought to bear upon the concept of "consciousness," and thereby the range of communications confined to this category is limited to those which, within reasonable degrees of certainty, *must* be consciously generated.[4]

Most conscious intentions yield objectives which can be articulated in precise behavioral terms. They are *not* merely functions of the psychological state of the communicator, as in the case of an individual who sings in the shower simply because it makes bathing pleasant.

Conscious intention may usually be subsumed under the general categories either of "persuasion" or "education."[5] Both of these genera of communication, meeting our standards of consciousness, will usually indicate clearly either by content, context or both, the general direction their intent takes, reasons for their objectives, and, frequently, the likelihood of success in achieving their ends. Their content may be analyzed by numerous devices with considerable precision, including a study of the vocabulary of symbols used, quantitative measures of key cognitions, and careful analysis of emotional tonality.[6]

Skill or sophistication in the introduction of intent to communications is a function of style, and frequently a function which appears to be a matter of art, primarily because it defies mechanical regularities and requires talent. For this reason, both propaganda and education (or at least schoolteaching), while they may utilize both the findings of science and the developments of technology, are fundamentally artistic enterprises. A science of *propaganda analysis* may be (and has been) constructed,[7] and schooling

[4] Just because a specific intention is in some manner perceived by the receiver of a message, one cannot accordingly assume that the message has been "successfully" communicated. The "boomerang" syndrome, or what the British psychologist J. A. C. Brown calls the "Law of Reversed Effect," may indicate that an intention was received and *accordingly* the message was ignored, denied or misunderstood—*as a result* of the perception of an objective repellent to the receiver. See Brown's *Techniques of Persuasion* (Baltimore, Md.: Penguin Books, 1963), pp. 80–81.

[5] Precise definition of these categories are difficult to formulate. "Persuasion" is frequently associated with the concept of "propaganda," and justly so. "Education" is usually related to the idea of helping an individual student to achieve his potential as a citizen. Jacques Ellul has brutally included both notions in one definition: "Propaganda is a set of methods employed by an organized group that wants to bring about the active or passive participation in its actions of a mass of individuals, psychologically unified through pyschological manipulations and incorporated in an organization." From *Propaganda* (New York: Alfred A. Knopf, 1965), p. 61. Both "persuasion" and "education" have been socialized in Ellul's thinking. He appears to believe that the objectives of *all* conscious intensions of communication in a modern state are generated by carefully nurtured fictions of specific interest groups in society.

[6] Many factors must be considered in such analyses. The sentence, "I love you" means nothing, except insofar as we really understand its logical and psychological context. The clearer this framework, the more insight we gain into the communicator's objective in using it. This particular phrase is often employed in highly ambiguous contexts, or so it may appear to the receiver at the particular time it is used. The context is often clarified with the passage of time.

[7] See Alexander L. George, *Propaganda Analysis* (Evanston, Ill. Row, Peterson and Company, 1959), for as scientific a study of propaganda—in this case that of Ger-

may sometimes depend upon techniques which have been more or less scientifically developed.[8] But the basic discourse for both types of communication, meaning effective mediations of intent between individuals, is primarily artistic.

The nebulous quality we call "artlessness" is frequently or inevitably a symptom of the instrusion of intention to an inappropriate degree into some aspect of a communication. Appropriateness is, of course, determined by *who* the communicator is, *what* he has to say, the *medium* he chooses, the *instrument* he employs, the *social setting* of the communication, and the *expectations* and *abilities* of the audience he hopes to reach.

Inappropriate intrusion of objectives usually leads to a conclusion that a certain communication is unnecessarily or overly didactic. Didacticism, however, may not always be an intrusion. It may signify a proper intent for certain propaganda and much education. But it is almost invariably the enemy of style and the assassin of art. Efforts have been made in the drama, for instance, to create a socially sensitive, didactic theatre.[9] In the United States, during the nineteen-thirties, a number of playwrights, most particularly Arthur Arent and Clifford Odets, attempted to fuse didacticism with re-enactment on the stage.[10]

In the history of the theatre, *much bad* drama has been written with specific objectives that were artlessly articulated to re-enactment. We laugh at many of these plays, like *The Drunkard* for instance, precisely *because* of the bold intrusions of intentions at inappropriate places. Many motion picture films are (and have been) primarily didactic. Presently, most "educational films" certainly are (which may explain the artlessness of most of them). They demonstrate misuses of the medium of re-enactment rather than examples of cinematic incompetence. Their intentions are mediated

---

many during World War II—as has yet been attempted. Intended as a "study of inferences" of this propaganda, and kept to rigorous techniques (many of which are capable of being manipulated statistically), the study fails in that it considers neither the art nor artlessness of the Germans' persuasion, nor its non-cognitive objectives, or possible results of them. The findings, so objectively reported, are remarkably inconsequential to the fundamental research problem: the *nature* of German propaganda by radio during the war.

[8] See Arthur A. Lumsdaine and Robert Glaser (eds.), *Teaching Machines and Programmed Learning: A Source Book* (Washington, D.C.: National Education Association Department of Audio-Visual Instruction, 1960), for a clear example of how scientific investigation may lead to a technological methodology in the development of devices which talented teachers may, or may not, one day utilize extensively. The devices depend to a high degree upon adequate and precise articulation of conscious objectives, a difficult, and sometimes impossible, educational task.

[9] The *Living Newspaper* plays of the W.P.A. theatre during the nineteen-thirties are usually associated with the concept of a didactic theatre. Objectives of the playwright were communicated in much the same way as the objectives of lessons in school, and the audience was considered a group of students.

[10] See John Gassner, *Masters of the Drama* (New York: Random House, 1940), pp. 687–693, for a brief but accurate description of this period in American theatre history emphasizing the dramatists who made up the core of the movement.

to the audience in inappropriate ways. They are frequently examples of near-ubiquitous poor attempts at isolating so-called "objectives" in education, that makes the pursuit of art in both teaching and film making nearly impossible.[11]

Conscious intention in much persuasion, particularly as manifest in "propaganda" and much of what passes for education today, is inept art. One might also claim that most of it is poor persuasion *and* education to the degree that objectives or intentions of the communicators intrude into the integrity of their messages. This occurs not because intentions force the communicators to *include* inappropriate material in their messages, but rather because the communicator must *exclude* pertinent material which might confuse his "objectives" while increasing the audience's interest in the communication. At the other extreme, it is the intention of most television writers to *entertain* us. They often fail, less because of the banality of their material than the overzealous pursuit of their intention. Television's entrepreneurs have, accordingly, amply demonstrated their inability to interest a large number of people *for long* in *most* of their games, plays and romps. Their producers and writers have failed at the subtle objective of entertainment simply because of the boorish exclusion of material that is entertaining to anyone but themselves.[12]

Well articulated and cleverly stated objectives in communication *need not*, however, militate against achievements of art. In fact, clear objectives, appropriately stated, may well be one fundamental criterion for most artfully communicated words, pictures and re-enactments. No matter how well the artist's objective may be consciously and explicitly stated, however, he almost invariably faces the possibility that his intentions will in the end be misread by his audience, or part of it.

Previously cited was Fellini's film, *La Dolce Vita,* an enormous popular success, but hardly, one suspects, because of the creative artists' original intentions—which were admittedly somewhat difficult to glean after a single exposure to the film. Viewed as an attempt to satire "high-life" in modern Rome, it unquestionably succeeds in its mission, but only as technical filmic exercise in sensationalism. Another film, popular at the same time, *Mondo Cane,* achieved much the same objective with far more artistic

[11] See, for instance, Robert F. Mager, *Preparing Instructional Objectives* (Palo Alto, California: Fearon Publishers, 1962), currently popular in schools of education largely because of its pseudo-programmed format. This childish volume purports to teach the neophyte teacher how to "develop meaningful objectives," "identify terminal behavior," and "create criteria for recognizing success" in teaching. It is an excellent example, first, of inappropriate mediation of intention in a narrative and second, a good book on how to eliminate art in all types of teaching.

[12] Those American television programs which have entertained people for a long period of time are either non-didactically stimulating to their audience, because they are addressed to children like *Captain Kangaroo,* or because their objectives are not artlessly presented, as in the case of *The Ed Sullivan Show.* The latter program's success may be credited almost entirely to the manner in which Sullivan speaks to the viewer and artfully and unpretentiously mediates the program's simple objectives to them.

economy. Intended to show how strangely numerous people and some animals in the world act, the latter exposed this behavior clearly in documentary style, and made good its intention.

Multiple viewings, and a reading of the *La Dolce Vita* script,[13] may cause one to revise his facile, original and generally agreed upon estimate of the film's basic objectives. The intent is obviously to show the failure of one man, the central character, to achieve a "good life" in the city of Rome (chosen apparently because of its role as the geographical center of modern Catholicism) without accepting his heritage of spiritual values. We discover, for instance, that it is not only sophisticated "high-life" that disillusions the hero, but domestic life, small-town life, and, as powerfully demonstrated in the suicide and infanticide of the gloomy intellectual Steiner, life of the intelligentsia. The film ends with a portrait of a brainwashed, intoxicated, beaten protagonist, literally unable to hear the frantic calls of a symbolic child-angel he once encountered during his adventures.

Given *this* intention—far from simple in its justification but conceptually not extraordinarily complex—the film, as a work of art, has new meaning, when compared to the more obvious, prior objective. But how general was this latter understanding of intention among its audiences—or even among professional critics? The director, Fellini, at first glance, did not apparently care whether his audience understood him, particularly in view of the enormous box-office success of his work.[14]

Whose fault is the misreading of conscious intention: the artist's or the audience's? The point has been argued for centuries. A skilled artist, it is claimed, should know how to make clear his objective, despite the collective ignorance, biases or miseducation of his audience. His objectives, by virtue of the enormity of his talent, must be, at least, intuited by his audience sufficiently to be, first, understood and, second, appreciated.

Modern writers, particularly, continually express dissatisfaction with their critics, readers, editors and audiences with the claim that they are misinterpreted. It is argued that an artist is a figure in advance of his time. This applies particularly to the "fine" artist, whose output, it is understood, requires refinement of perception for appreciation, and whose objectives *cannot* be understood by any except those initiated into the cabals of his particular art. (This notion is most frequently heard today in painting and musical circles; less often among theatrical and cinema enthusiasts.) The understanding of the conscious intention of the communicator, according to this construction, is therefore mainly a social and/or educational problem. Its solution rests upon the enlightenment of the public. This unresolved dispute in modern artistic life is one of the main causes for the

---

[13] Federico Fellini, *La Dolce Vita* (New York: Ballantine Books, Inc., 1961).
[14] There is considerable evidence in Fellini's next film, *8½*, that he did indeed chafe at the misinterpretation his previous work suffered. The central character of this later movie, intended to be Fellini himself, is continually assaulted by boors who misconstrue his motives as an artist and as a man, and his annoyance at them is apparent.

confusion that we behold today in delineating common understandings of objectives and intentions for the mediums of mass communication, in both their serious and humorous aspects.

Unconscious Intention

Experience indicates that it is by no means necessary for a communicator to be able to articulate exactly (or even approximately) what the objectives of his communications are. Nor, for that matter, need he even be aware that he *has* specific objectives. What the communicator—particularly if he is an artist—must be aware of is whether or not a certain course of action, or choice of symbols, or manner of execution, is *right* or *wrong*. In other words, he *feels* competent to make moral judgments regarding his style, but need not be ostensibly concerned with the outcome of his production. Like many moral judgments, his are self-justifying. They are value statements that need not refer to social utility, although the judgment itself is frequently opened to criticism by that segment of society which is supposedly sophisticated in a relevant aesthetic. The degree of consonance between the artist and his auditors is the main factor determining the comprehension and "success" of any particular communication at any given time.

Many non-conscious factors, obviously, impel individuals to attempt to express themselves through the mediums of communication. These are functions of personal character traits such as gregariousness, vanity, isolation, and so forth, all necessarily functions of culture. Certain people with special aptitudes develop these talents to a degree that impels them to "say something" by means of a given medium. This need is often difficult for the artist to justify to himself, but quite simple to rationalize for others.

Most artists defend their activities on financial or materialistic bases, or even by resorting to the cliché that art must be pursued for its own sake. Many remain unaware of their own true objectives, and deny adequate statements of their intentions, simply because they seem irrelevant to their conscious impulses towards self expression. They are over-reacting to the pressures placed upon the creative force of many communicators (whose intention is usually the examination, for better or worse, of the status quo) by society.

To some degree, therefore, all art and much communication is a threat to the stability of society. Its pursuit is accordingly justified by a wide range of culturally viable rationalizations. To brand artists as "eccentrics" and consign them to poverty is one way of tolerating them. At the same time, they are thereby permitted to disturb least the tranquility of the social order. Hanging their paintings in museums and making them respectable achieves much the same result.[15]

15 There is no need here for an extended discussion of the psychology of the creative experience, which is the most extreme manifestation of the communicator's impulse to

questions and reservations concerning the reliability of projective instruments.

Whatever the difficulties involved in interpreting responses of subjects
to questions put to them by pollsters, psychologists, census-takers and
others, they are compounded when one wishes to determine both the validity *and* the reliability of *any* statement of *objectives* on the part of a re-
spondent. In the first place, as we have noted, many intentions are not
capable of individual recall, because they have not been (or cannot be)
articulated consciously. Secondly, the individual questioned may be ration-
alizing or dissembling his objectives: that is to say, he may be lying for one
reason or another.

Richards has noted that our general, day-to-day criticisms of literature arise from social motives.[20] We have reason to believe that stated
objectives for much of the random communication in which we indulge
has been truthfully motivated by ego-serving objectives, rationalized to be
acceptable to consciousness. In the case of a salesman or teacher or writer
or painter, stated intentions in regard to nearly *all* communications are
suspect. One reads in his morning newspaper, for instance, an advertisement about a Scotch Whiskey "that makes history," that "pours more
pleasure," and he knows generally what the copywriter was attempting.
That is, one knows his professional motives for the lies, but not, of course,
his personal ones.[21]

Since we cannot reliably depend upon a communicator's statement of
intention in determining his objectives, how may we discover them? In
fact, we frequently *cannot*, particularly when works of art are involved. As
subtle as both our neurological and psychological sciences have grown, they
preclude any method of either empathizing reliably with another person's
feelings or, in any manner or form, reading his mind. This state of affairs
obtains, no matter how many clues to the function of that mind we discover in a painting, the score of a symphony or in a philippic. The measure
of social motivation (or other covert intentions) is impossible to determine,
even if they are communicated with tears and/or gnashing of teeth.

Fundamental qualities of the objectives communications are, however,
certain aesthetic characteristics which are likely, in most cases, to be more
reliable as informal guides to understanding intentions than psychological
signposts. The *stress* placed upon a particular point of a communication, or
the *number* of times it is repeated, or the *way* in which it appears when

[20] I. A. Richards, *Practical Criticism*, pp. 310–321.
[21] That most readers *know* that much advertising is fraudulent does not seem to influence the objectives of advertisers. The latter may not intend that readers *believe* what
is written, but rather get them to purchase a product for reasons having less to do with
the real nature of the item than the psychological gratification that the product yields.
Thus, in Martin Mayer's terms, advertising of a certain type adds a plus value to com-
modities which is not only worthwhile to the manufacturer but which is his actual
objective in advertising. See Martin Mayer, *Madison Avenue, U.S.A.* (New York:
Harper and Brothers, 1958), pp. 309–324.

communicated by different instruments, may be indicative of intention. Examples are countless, but certainly the stress upon Gothic, macabre symbolism more indicative of objectives in Poe's *Raven* than the number of lines chosen for the poem. Likewise, the repetition of classical allusions in T. S. Eliot's *The Wasteland* is more closely related to intention than the author's explanatory "footnotes," which explain little, if anything, about the work. In science fiction films and novels, the sheer degree of emphasis upon destructive potentials of technology indicates quite clearly the evocative mindset of both the authors of the novels and their screen treatments. *Planet of the Apes* (book and film) is a fine example.

Intention is also demonstrated in how arrangements *within* a given communication are shaped. Concerned here are the matters of *order* and *design* rather than stress. Sequence is extremely significant: in the opening and closing of almost any serious drama, from *Antigone* to *The Iceman Cometh*, something of the author's intention is revealed in the juxtaposition of these two sequences alone.

While novels tend to be more discursive than dramas (because of their greater reliance upon the narrative medium), fiction editors know that objectives, at least, will probably be clarified for them by reading the beginning and end of a manuscript. Attitudes or style will be indicated by scanning the rest of the piece. Modern sequential devices like the "flashback" were originally utilized by early novelists writing in the first person, and subsequently employed first by film makers and later by stage dramatists. They are made up almost entirely of statements of objectives, frequently offered in the person of the author himself, as in plays such as *I Am A Camera* and the *Glass Menagerie*.

A skilled communicator (or artist) may not, under various circumstances, wish to show his intentional hand for reasons that are almost always obvious. An old novelty play called *The Spider* began as a vaudeville show but ended as a murder mystery. Intention may be obscurely hidden within the fabric of a communication, as in the films of Michaelangelo Antonioni, but eventually they somehow surface. In his early works like *L'Aventura*, Antonioni's objectives were nearly lost in the emphasis upon magnificent photography. In his later works, particularly *Blow-Up*, his intentions are also carefully hidden within the context of the work, but, like the solution to a clever riddle, they are revealed in the final sequences. In all of Antonioni's films, intention is purposely (or seemingly) withheld from the audience as a device to stimulate curiosity, or to encourage one to examine the evidence within the communication as closely as possible.

The mystery novel (and to a lesser degree the mystery drama and film) is likewise a form of communication stylized in such a way that the author's intentional hand is hidden. It is discernible only to the initiated or gifted, until precisely the right place for the correct objective of the communication to be revealed. That true objective is the *modus operandi* which deceives the reader or audience: for example, the skill of the actress who plays the central role in *Witness for the Prosecution*. It is also the *deus ex machina* in the plot by which justice is done or undone. The intention of deception is thereby justified by the author, and herein lies the pleasure that addicts of mystery stories, films and plays receive from them.

For many forms of communication, including those involving the graphic arts, effectiveness depends more upon the manner in which objectives are *purposely concealed* than the manner in which they are revealed. Certainly, most overt propaganda, including advertising, deals to some extent with purposely concealed intentions in a manner not unlike that employed in the mystery story.[22]

Misread Objectives

If intentions are basic to communication, why are they so severely and often misunderstood? Of course, the answer to this question relies in some measure on the qualities of perceptions of the receiver, the effectiveness of his formal and informal education, and the way in which he is accustomed to the spread of persuasion in his society. The study of misread objectives is a field of rich promise for experimental psychologists.

On the other hand, certain overt factors contribute directly to these misunderstandings. First, most (or many) non-didactic, non-propagandistic, reasonably spontaneous communications are so formulated as to leave objectives *implied but unspoken*, and with much justification. The speaker, writer, or artist leaves intention and its perception to the listener, reader, or viewer, and may—by accident frequently—leave behind an unintentional false trail of intentions. He may unwittingly stress elements irrelevant to his conscious objectives. He may emphasize cognitive aspects of a communication which is fundamentally emotional or vice versa. He may emphasize unduly stylistic qualities of the message at the expense of content, or content may receive such prominence that its all-important style may be hardly noticed.[23]

He may, in effect, modify the inappropriate aspect of his communication in the wrong way because of ignorance or inexperience or both, and therefore his intentions will be thoroughly misread, or—worse—the audience will merely be confused. As a result of this confusion, its members

[22] A problem here arises when the perceiver resents being fooled by a communicator. The feeling that one frequently gets from such deceptions is that "there is less here than meets the eye," probably because sufficient credit is not given the communicator for having fooled us. On the other hand, artful deception may be perceived as enjoyable, judging from the popularity of propaganda, advertising, magicians and mystery stories.
[23] Professional actors often emphasize style at the expense of content. Teachers, speakers and panelists at academic conferences tend to emphasize content and sacrifice style. The result in either case is frequently misunderstanding—moreso in the former instance than the latter, because content-biased communications tend to be directed to audiences primarily interested in that content, not in style. The stylist communicates mostly with other stylists.

will, according to the tenets of accepted psychological theory and observation, selectively *read* an objective *into* the communication which best accords with their previous dispositions, opinions, and prejudices.[24] In other words, they are thrust back upon their own sensory mechanisms and, for all practical purposes, may not have noticed the intention of the communication in the first place. The communication was simply a general stimulus which precipitated highly *specific* apperceptions on the part of the perceiver.

There appear to be, curiously, definite patterns to the misinterpretation of the messages likely to reach an individual in a given environment. Some of them are logical, like mistaking an "o" for a "o" or the word "size" for "seize." Children especially, tend to read words they *know* into words that are unfamiliar.

Other misunderstandings are psychologically based upon (as yet) only slightly understood selective proclivities in the processes of gaining *attention*, using our *perception*, and *retaining* or *remembering* items after exposure.[25] Mistakes of this sort do not only occur in the interpretation of objectives. But if the objectives of any communication are misunderstood, it is likely that other perceptions will also be distorted according to the expectations of the perceiver.[26]

Put another way, unless one understands the objectives or intentions of a communication, he is highly likely to misinterpret other aspects of the same communication as well. Hence, the vital nature of intention to all types of communication—most especially those which are educational or persuasive—and the degree of misunderstanding visible in so much discourse in society today. For instance, experts in the field claim that most Americans do not understand Soviet propaganda basically because they misinterpret the essential objective of it: to frighten, and, at the same time, to reassure a population already neurotically oriented to warfare, and thereby ultimately to *confuse* the recipient. Hence, say they, the continual and glaring contradictions in the U.S.S.R.'s foreign propaganda "line." These contradictions can be easily misinterpreted, either as signs of weakness or as indications of internal discord in the U.S.S.R.

One of the severest problems facing the modern educator at all levels

[24] See Bernard Berelson and Gary A. Steiner, *Human Behavior* (New York: Harcourt, Brace and World, Inc., 1964), pp. 183–187, 530–532, for a review of the pertinent experimental evidence of this phenomenon of apperception.
[25] See Leo Postman, Jerome S. Bruner and Elliot McGiunies, "Personal Values as Selective Factors in Perception" in G. Swanson, T. Newcomb and E. Hartley (eds.), *Readings in Social Psychology*, pp. 375–383, for an early study of this phenomenon and brief reports of other findings.
[26] See the reports of the "Mr. Biggott" experiments in Eunice Cooper and Marie Jahodas' "The Evasion of Propaganda: How Prejudiced People Respond to Anti-Prejudice Propaganda" in Daniel Katz (ed.), *Public Opinion and Propaganda*, pp. 313–319. These subjects, because of their anti-semitism, contrived to "miss the point" or objective of anti-anti-semitic cartoons and distorted the contents of these drawings according to their own attitudes.

of education is to communicate precisely to students, not as much the discrete facts of various disciplines, but *objectives* for understanding and learning them. We are faced here with the need to communicate a sense of purpose more relevant to life than passing an exam or a course of study, or attaining a license, or accumulating near meaningless academic and professional degrees. This failure, from kindergarten to graduate school, is no longer a well-kept professional secret among the teachers and the taught. It is now legend.

Conclusion

Communicators are usually concerned less with how objectives are perceived than with the psychological nuances of their conception, that is, with the concept of "creativity." An interest in objectives or intentions necessarily centers upon the didactic or persuasive aspects of messages and how these aspects are likely to effect the person receiving them or the audiences attending them.

Most intentions are clear if the recipient pays attention to what is said and/or they are pointed out to him. The more clearly a communicator articulates a conscious intention, the more likely it is to be perceived correctly by his audience. The less likely, however, is that particular communication to be distinguished either by its style or may it be justified as a work of art.

Didacticism and propaganda tend to militate against the achievement of art. While many fine artists are consciously aware of their intentions, they leave the joy of discovering them to their audiences as a form of participation in the communication itself. No one is necessarily at fault if an artistically ingenious intention is misread. If blame may be placed anywhere, it probably centers on the the public's perception of an artist's function.

Psychological waters are muddier when unconscious objectives are considered. At present, a cultural-artistic game is frequently played in critical efforts at pseudo-scientific artistic mind reading. Perceptions of unconscious objectives of communications have produced, nevertheless, an interesting critical literature, less as a result of the way in which the unconscious of various artists has been excavated than in the stimulus that these exercises have given the critical community to muse seriously, and to their profit, on the vital matter of intention *per se.*

Objectives are manifest in various ways. Matters like stress, order, or arrangements of the sub-components of certain communications clearly demonstrate what the authors intend. At other times, it is virtually impossible to understand a communicator's objectives by means of a study of the communication itself, because he covers his tracks purposely, or is unclear about his own objectives to the degree that his audience is therefore confused—intentionally or otherwise.

Finally, the major result of misunderstanding intentions is that the perceiver usually resolves his confusion by searching into his *own* predispositions to find hidden meanings. He thus introduces his own opinions, prejudices, attitudes and beliefs into an ambiguous field, with the result that he *believes* that he has cleared up his confusion. He has not. He has simply succeeded in eliminating the psychological tension that invariably results when an individual faces chaos in his perceptions. How commonly such pseudo-resolutions of misunderstood communications occur is open to conjecture, but it is highly likely that many of the understandings we have of the "ideas" of others, in both formal and informal discourse, misconstrue profoundly their true objectives. We never discover, furthermore, the nature of these chronic, and sometimes serious, errors.

Chapter 15

COMMUNICATING

HUMOR

I N THE DREARY literature of comedy, a certain few works stand out, both as individual pieces and in anthology.[1] Sigmund Freud was possibly the bravest analyst of this complex subject, because he insisted—and may have been the first to insist—that there *was* indeed a *totally logical* phase to humor. Freud explained wit in a most meticulous way,[2] by associating laughter with repression, with the unconscious and the libidinal pleasure received from dealing with forbidden linguistic or ideational matter contained in a joke or "gag." Illustrating his point with a remarkably complete lexicon of "sick jokes," [3] the thrust of the psychoanalytic argument superceded the essentially sophistic explanations of his predecessors and demonstrated that humor was a logical response to certain kinds of stimuli—pro-

[1] A recent anthology of writings about humor is Robert W. Corrigan's *Comedy: Meaning and Form* (San Francisco, Calif.: Chandler Publishing Company, 1965). While the works of the minor writers reprinted in this volume are well represented, Freud's unfortunate *Jokes and the Comic* (in James Strachey's translation) rather than his better known *Wit and Its Relation to the Unconscious* is included. Also, both Bergson's and Meredith's essays on comedy have been excerpted (at the expense of breadth) and presented in the final pages. As an anthology of pieces relevant to comedy on stage, however, the collection is extremely useful. Individually, Freud's piece in *The Basic Writings of Sigmund Freud*, pp. 633–803, is printed in full in A. A. Brill's excellent translation. Wylie Sypher (ed.), *Comedy* (Garden City, N. Y.: Doubleday Anchor Books, 1956), contains complete and clear versions of the Meredith and Bergson essays. Other citations of useful material on comedy are given below.

[2] S. Freud, *op. cit.*, pp. 688–703.

[3] Freud's proclivity for humor about poverty, physical malformations, stupidity and human misery is interesting. A typical example of one of his illustrative "jokes" follows: "The agent (marriage broker) brought along an assistant to a conference about a bride. The assistant was to confirm his assertions. 'She is as well built as a pine tree,' said the agent. 'Like a pine tree,' repeated the echo. 'She has eyes which one must appreciate,' 'Wonderful eyes,' confirmed the echo. 'She is cultured beyond words. She possesses extraordinary culture.' 'Wonderfully cultured,' repeated the assistant. 'However, one thing is true,' confessed the agent. 'She has a slight hunch on her back.' 'And what a hunch!' confirmed the echo." *Ibid.*, p. 669.

viding one accepted as logical the psychoanalytic postulates upon which the explanation was based.

Essayists since Freud have either accepted this position or avoided it, first, by creating their own psychologically valid mystique of humor. Second, many have completely ignored the etiology of laughter by diverting their arguments to why we laugh at certain events or what role laughter plays in social processes.

A critic like Elmer Blistein[4] falls into the second category. In his Introduction, he writes with justification, "I soon discovered that there was no universal theory of laughter. Aristotle would help in one place, Hobbes in another, Freud in still another, but no theorist or theory was universally applicable." [5] Accordingly, in his analyses of comedy and comics, a mystical orientation prevails; comedians and comedy are either good or bad, better or worse, funny or more or less funny, *ad hoc*, as determined by the author-as-critic.

Constance Rourke,[6] for instance, may state without apparent concern for how or why laughter is generated, "Humor has been a fashioning instrument in America, cleaving its way through national life, holding tenaciously to the spread elements of that life. Its mode has often been swift and coarse and ruthless, beyond art and beyond established civilization. It has engaged in warfare against the established civilization, against the established heritage, against the bonds of pioneer existence. Its objective—the unconscious objective of a disunited people—has seemed to be that of creating fresh bonds, a new unity, the semblance of a society and the rounded completion of an American type." [7] These judgments have, of course, emerged from the narrative fabric of Rourke's cultural history.

Theorists who have followed Freud most usually apply his original thinking to specific instances. Noting that many of Freud's jokes (in his first essays on humor) concerned Judaism, and recalling that Freud himself had expressed to him the desire to study further Jewish humor, the prolific writer and psychoanalyst, Theodor Reik, refined an ingenious theory of comedy, applicable particularly to semitic comedy, based on Freud's postulates:

> (The) masochistic element in Jewish jokes, is founded on an unconscious guilt feeling. Psychoanalytic exploration of that unconscious guilt-feeling, manifested in the self-degradation and expressed in the jokes, would trace its origins to crimes committed in thoughts, especially to a rebellious attitude towards God and His laws. If I previously stated that the masochistic, self-humiliating side of Jewish jokes corresponds to a confession,

[4] Elmer Blistein, *Comedy in Action* (Durham, N.C.: Duke University Press, 1964).
[5] *Ibid.*, p. 15.
[6] Constance Rourke, *American Humor* (Garden City, N.Y.: Doubleday Anchor Books, 1953).
[7] *Ibid.*, pp. 231–232.

it might now be added that it has the character of a substitute confession, since the true nature of that thought-crime remains unconscious, and the confession concerns only descendants of that primal atrocious rebellion against God.[8]

In a more developmental vein, Martin Grotjohn[9] traces the etiology of laughter to the smile of a baby a few days old. Writes he, "The human mother is more a mother than any other animal mother, and the human infant is more and longer an infant than any animal baby. . . . With the mother smiling at the child in her arms and the child looking up into the mother's face and smiling back, human communication was born and facial expression originated." [10] Depending upon how one construes "origination," perhaps this statement is true of the developmental experience of all human beings. It also helps to explain why babies deprived of the tender, loving care of a mother (or mother substitute) display symptoms of physical and mental retardation, including a stunted ability to communicate with their environment.

The Humanity of Laughter

In the nineteenth century thinking of George Meredith,[11] comedy followed the lead of Molière who stood at the time for the highest form of satire—apparently an emphatically cognitive aspect of behavior. Man, the only animal who appeared to laugh, obviously used his *intelligence* to create and communicate that which was "funny." To laugh crudely at a wide range of stimuli meant that powers of differentiation were not employed intelligently in order to discriminate less cognitive humor from its highly cognitive variety.

"*C'est n'estimer rien qu'estimer tout le monde*," wrote Meredith, "and to laugh at everything is to have no appreciation of the comic of comedy." [12] Meredith took great pains to associate the origin of laughter with culture and *kinds of humor* with the *quality* of laughter evoked. "The laughter of satire," he writes, for instance, "is a blow in the back or face. The laughter of comedy is impersonal and of unrivaled politeness, nearer a smile. . . . It (satire) laughs through the mind for the mind directs it; and it might be called the humor of the mind."

"One excellent test" he notes, "of the civilization of a country, as I

[8] Theodor Reik, *Jewish Wit* (New York: Gamut Press, 1962), p. 221. To readers unfamiliar with Reik's ingenious applications of Freud's ideas of mythology and collective cultural experience, his hypothesis may seem quite far-fetched. Reik's arguments, however, in his special terms of discourse, are built upon a keen and perceptive knowledge of both Jewish history and Jewish humor.
[9] Martin Grotjohn, "Beyond Laughter: A Summing Up," in Corrigan, *op. cit.*, pp. 270–275.
[10] *Ibid.*, p. 272.
[11] Sypher, *Comedy*, pp. 3–57.
[12] *Ibid.*, p. 4.

have said, I take to be the flourishing of the comic idea and comedy; and the test of true comedy is that it shall waken *thoughtful* laughter." [13]

With the possible exception of Bernard Shaw, the comic spirit was never again to attract another so cognitively oriented—or logically biased—defender.

In 1900, Henri Bergson's essay, *Laughter*,[14] was published. It proved to be the single most influential document yet written on why men laugh. Discursive and ill-organized as an essay, Bergson's argument rests on three observations: that laughter is *human*, that it is *devoid of feeling* (or empathetic emotion) and that *laughter is social* in its orientation.[15] Humor itself derives, either logically or psychologically, therefore, from the juxtaposition of human, non-mechanical qualities with rigid "mechanical inelasticity" of some sort. Natural or disorganized processes are held against rigid or highly organized activities: for instance, man's essential nature opposed to social convention. The result is the incongruity we call humor.

In one construction, his contentions rest on the concept that ". . . *the attitudes, gestures and movements of the human body are* laughable in exact proportion as that body remind us of a mere machine." [16] This dichotomy is carried out in most human affairs: when our attention is called to *physical* problems of an individual; while he is in a *moral* crisis; when a person resembles a mechanical object; when life is mistaken for a mechanical arrangement; when forbidden or repressed words are repeated like a Jack-in-the-box; when events are compounded mechanistically; or when the progressions of a situation are so arranged that they can be interpreted in different ways. The principle relates to verbal statements, plots or characters. Perhaps it is best summed up in Bergson's phrase, "A *comic effect is always obtainable by transposing the natural expression of an idea into* another key." [17]

Lest this principle be mistaken for the operation of mere psychological abberation, he writes, "Laughter is, above all, a *corrective*. Being intended to humiliate, it must make a painful impression on the person against whom it is directed. By laughter, society avenges itself for the liberties taken with it. It would fail in its object if it bore the stamp of sympathy or kindness." [18]

---

[13] *Ibid.*, p. 47. (Italics added.)

[14] *Ibid.*, pp. 61–190.

[15] After Freud, of course, the second assumption fell into general disrepute. The father of psychoanalysis implied that the wellsprings of humor depended upon repressed feeling as well as thought. Bergson's ideas were not discarded with Freud's hypothesis, however, since it was understood that the former was talking about *one* more or less intellectual type of social humor or satire.

[16] Sypher, *op. cit.*, p. 79. (Italics are Bergson's.)

[17] *Ibid.*, p. 140.

[18] *Ibid.*, p. 187. (Italics added.) Freud, of course, postulated a short time later that "the person against whom it is directed" was the individual laughing himself—or, at least, that component of self dominated by his repressed feelings. Thus, to Freud,

Charles Chaplin, many believe, has been the most "Bergsonian" of the modern comics. He is, unfortunately, far from the funniest of them, even compared to other clowns of the silent cinema. The Bergsonian Chaplin has passed through two periods of extreme over-estimation, first by the masses who originally attended his movies, and second (and later) by the critics who wrote about them.[19] The Bergsonian quality of his work acts as a double-edged blade, cutting into both his comedy and his much-esteemed pathos.

Of all Chaplin's works, *Modern Times* is the one which falls closest to Bergson's principle, and it is also the one Chaplin film which fails most noticeably to live up to its humorous premise. When Chaplin shows us humanity devoured by the impersonal mechanistic forces of contemporary life, we are amused. When gas pains embarrass the pathetic worker-tramp, we smile (as Bergson predicts, in both cases). But the social truth of the little protagonist's plight is so overwhelming, that *nothing* that happens to him is comically absurd or absurdly comic—even his mechanical repetitions of his belt-line motions after he has stopped working! (Doesn't the same terrifying phenomenon occur at times to *most* of us?)

Nor is the movie redeemed by the sentimental love affair—repeated in various versions *ad nauseam* in *all* Chaplin's films—with the beautiful girl who can feel no more than pity for the asexual tramp. These aspects of the film probably fare better as theatre than the comic parts, because at least Chaplin succeeds (as he does most satisfactorily in *City Lights*) in evoking momentary feelings of pity from the situation on the screen. But do we— *can* we—as the critics' clichés state, "ever laugh through our tears" at this sort of Bergsonian comedy? Probably not, because we simply cannot laugh hard enough to *overcome*, in the first place, tears, and in the second place, truth.

Bergson's concepts, which have been so influential in the analysis (and possibly creation) of comedy during the past half century, have unfortunately also limited the possibilities for varieties of comic attitudes. The thesis demands that humanity be tempered by mechanics. It has thus thrust the comedian intensively into the contemporary social matrix. His individual humanity, so often an analogy for the fundamental absurdity of the human condition (which is the simplistic but actual basis of laughter, as we shall see) is circumscribed by nineteenth century sociology.

Granted that, when Laurel and Hardy move a grand piano over a yawning crevass on a jerry-built, swaying suspension bridge, the premise of

---

laughter appeared to be less a social than an individual corrective (or therapeutic manifestation) than to Bergson.

[19] Chaplin's films in revival often elicit less gusty laughter, from apparently well-meaning audiences, than some of Valentino's. The discovery that, while Chaplin was an inventive scenarist and remarkable acrobat, he was not nearly as funny as many of his contemporaries (like Buster Keaton or Laurel and Hardy) is disheartening but inevitable for persistent followers of "Chaplin revivals."

the situation is wonderfully comic—and in Bergson's sense—just as Chaplin's feast on a boiled shoe is in *The Gold Rush*. But these situations, like all humorous situations, are funny more because they are exaggerations primarily of the *kind* of absurd things *people in fact attempt*, than by virtue of their less significant juxtaposition of humanity to mechanics.[20]

As Bergson and others since his time have known, little about mechanics is, by and of itself, funny. A machine of whirring gears and springs is not an object of humor, unless those gears and springs become somehow analogous to comprehensible human behaviors. A spring mechanism may power an elaborate nineteenth-century music box in which a doll conductor leads a doll orchestra. But even this mechanical analogy—unless extremely cleverly devised, and then only instantaneously—is usually not comic. It is "cute" or diverting, because almost *all* comparisons of mechanics to humanity are *at least* interesting.

There appears to be nothing *essentially* humorous about a machine attempting to be human, or a human held to an obviously mechanical behavior pattern. Bergson seems today to have been speaking for a value structure of humor relevant only to the early part of the twentieth century in Europe.

At present, a machine which is human (or super-human) is, in most respects, neither comic nor tragic. The mechanistic aspects of life are simply as dull or as interesting as we personally perceive them to be. Nor is there anything shocking—humorously or seriously—about man regarded *as* a machine. Generations of youngsters, raised on newsreels of Hitler's goose-stepping storm troopers, growing up in suburban traffic jams, educated to the conformities and regimentations of a modern industrial society, accept the mechanization of human beings as natural. It is recognized as an unfortunate, but certainly inevitable, by-product of industrialization. If social critics protest, with Bergson, that man has become a pawn of mechanized mass society,[21] the man-in-the-street has answered these critics with neither rage nor laughter—merely with a yawn.

The Bergsonian model has therefore lost its relevance to modern life and humor. The mechanical-human concept remains just *one* of *numerous* formulae which may evoke various degrees of comic response from different audiences. Our nation is so heterogeneous, and intellectual, social

[20] Donald Duck (who unfortunately no longer seems comic to many) has often been cited as a Bergsonian character. Anthropomorphic (but nearly human) Donald flies into a mechanistic, uncontrollable rage, reminiscent of a windmill in action, at the slightest human provocation. If Donald is indeed humorous, he is funny in the degree that his extravagant, non-productive, inarticulate, vaguely duck-like quacking rage is absurdly similar to the rages that all of us experience—and/or repress.

[21] For a collection of these and counter viewpoints, see the anthology of contemporary cultural criticism by Philip Olson (ed.), *America As A Mass Society* (New York: The Free Press of Glencoe, 1963). Much of interesting contemporary thinking about the pressures of mass society by the sociological community is represented in this volume. Most of it owes a debt to Bergson's speculations on the subject.

and cultural levels of substantial portions of our population vary so vastly, that *any one* type of humor is rarely appreciated in similar degrees by different members of plural groups.

Probably the more *naïve* or *childlike* comedy is, the larger its prospective audience in a nation like ours, explaining, perhaps, the success of Disney and those endless jejune television comedies, admittedly devised for morons (the famous twelve-year-old mentality of the mass audience). An intelligent person may share with a moron (or twelve-year-old child) numerous primitive perceptions of humor. These perceptions—if they are competently produced—will gain their widest audience by means of the instruments of mass communication. This same phenomenon is true also of serious messages, although no reaction as strong as laughter is elicited from the mass audience by childlike stimuli.[22] Hence, the more sophisticated of the masses become more fatigued and rapidly bored when exposed to serious childlike fare than when exposed to children's comedy.

Freud's psychological theories side-stepped the Bergsonian concept of humor. Repressions are distinctively human phenomena, and, in theory, would exist had men never even discovered primitive mechanics. The transformation of humor to a release of sexual feeling is no more difficult to accept than any other aspect of psychoanalytic theory. It is even easier to comprehend than much of it, because risqué material is present in every type of humor known, from puppet shows to the acts of circus clowns. Dirty jokes are almost invariably the funniest humor on the *sub rosa* (and open) marketplace at any time.[23] The humorous plays of the Greeks have been traced to traditions of satyr plays and Dionysian rites. They indicate that the birth of comedy was apparently an impolite occasion, ribald, and certainly uninhibited. That our polite drawing-room laughter at the latest political joke, or the college professor's anecdotal pun, may somehow relate to libidinal repressions should be less difficult for one to accept than the

[22] Exceptions here would involve reactions to highly charged sexual communications, suspense stories of a primitive nature (some spy stories and westerns are examples) and certain stereotyped domestic situations. *All* low common denominator television programs and motion pictures must therefore—if they are to interest an audience of differing intelligences—either be made up of combinations of primitive themes, or rest upon the humor of childhood. *The Beverly Hillbillies, The Lucy Show, Get Smart* and *Bonanza* are four familiar examples from many of the successful manipulations of childish perceptions for a child-adult public. Their writers, producers and directors are probably themselves, at least emotionally (and perhaps mentally), children. They are thus able to "feel the public pulse" with an accuracy uncanny to those who have never met or worked with them.

[23] Novels recently published abroad by the Olympia Press (and now on the open market in America) are delightful examples of this dark literary tradition in our time. *Lolita* and *Candy* are comparatively mild examples of this art (?) form. More pornographic works like *Who Pushed Paula?* and *The Sexual Life of Robinson Crusoe* have just reached American bookstalls. The wildest and funniest Victorian pornographic book, many believe, is *The Prima-Donna* which purports to be the memoirs of the famous German singer, Wilhelmina Shroeder-Devrient. Copies are now available in the U.S.A., but whether they are genuine and complete copies of the original forgery, it is difficult to determine.

notion that a lyric poet's genius may be motivated by sexual deprivations.

The Freudian construction of the communication of comedy at least locates clearly for us the communality of comic experiences in all three mediums. Eroticism is a ubiquitous phenomenon. Erotic pleasures, whether generalized to include non-erotic activities, or specified by oral, anal or genital stimuli, are, first, the common possession of all humanity, and, second, instruments of the kind of pleasure that turns frequently into laughter.

Margaret Mead has noted, in a perceptive anthropological observation, that the erotic and the humorous, while varying in symbols and specific contexts, seem universally related to human behavior in both primitive and modern cultures. Sexuality and scatology are comic almost everywhere, not just in "modern" culture as some psychologists appear to believe. They are universally scorned by "polite society" and therefore must be repressed. They are censored precisely *because* they are funny and—quite correctly to the modern arbiter of manners—*inappropriately* funny in certain contexts.[24]

Writes Mead:

> The question of regulation . . . comes up in relation to pornography, which manifests itself in some form in every human society—if only in an insistence on a euphemism for the sex organs which, if abandoned, can immediately create sex excitement. *The bawdy laughter* explodes as often in a primitive society where people wear practically no clothes at all at some pictured juxtaposition, for example, of a canoe prow and a human body as it does in a men's smoking room in a university town. The sets of taboos and the requirements of etiquette insure that the unusual or unexpected which in any way involves the human body will be stimulating and will evoke in a group an explosive bawdy response, *usually loud laughter*, and a more-specific bodily response when the individual is alone or with sexual partners. *Every human society has room for the pornographer to operate.*[25]

Starting with the near ubiquitous pleasurable erotic comedy of sexuality and scatology, it is possible to construct a hierarchal ladder of humor on which the gratifications involved in various types of laughter becomes increasingly refined. That is, first "dirty" and/or "black" humor give way to *individual* gratification in comedy addressed to *individual* human situations. These, in turn, are replaced by *social* comedy, derived from the relationships of individuals in society. Finally, humor turns to social-cognitive-

[24] The present tendency to limit the bonds of censorship (and prudery) to a more permissive degree than late Victorian Comstockery appears to be an essentially healthy trend both for our adult population and our children. As the bonds of sexual censorship loosen, however, we may learn painfully William Ernest Hocking's admonition that every exercise of freedom demands an equal exercise of public and personal responsibility—and that sexual matters are not excluded from this tenet.
[25] Margaret Mead, "Sex and Censorship in Contemporary Society" in Kingsley and Eleanor Widmer (eds.) *Literary Censorship* (San Francisco, Calif.: Wadsworth Publishing Company, 1961), p. 141. (Italics added.)

spiritual mirth, as in the humor of parables, or in ironies of spiritual life—
of the kind, for instance, that concerned film maker Ingmar Bergman in *The
Seventh Seal*. The ladder would look something like this (upside down):

1. Scatology (child humor)
2. Pornography (adolescent and adult dirty jokes)
3. Mortality humor (black comedy; sick jokes)
4. Stupidity humor (moron jokes)
5. Man versus mechanics (Bergsonian comedy)
6. Linguistic humor (puns, etc.)
7. Domestic humor (family comedy)
8. Social satire (comedy of manners)
9. Political comedy (celebrity gags)
10. Intellectual anecdotes (professional illustrative stories)
11. Parables (philosophical irony)

If this ladder bears a resemblance to the development of humor in
most fairly complex cultures, what is the common element, from the developmental perspective, running through all the currents of comedy? Is it the
cognitive, social satirical *function* of comedy about which Meredith wrote?
No, since the emotive, individualistic basis of much important and highly
comic communications is apparent. Is it the Bergsonian theses of *man* versus *mechanism*? Obviously not. Do we find anything *other than* the hypothesis of unconscious repression to justify the Freudian sexual orientation? Doubtful.

The common elements center mostly on the *humanity* of laughter.
Our exploration takes us to the poet's confession that ". . . if I laugh at
any mortal thing/ 'Tis that I may not weep." For, on the obverse side of
each of our eleven categories, observe the insistent presence of *futility, vanity, impudence, frailty, avarice, bestiality,* and even *tragedy*.

Wellsprings of Laughter

The discovery of similarities in comic behaviors and laughter situations
involving men, and in similar antics of animals, does not deny the human
nature of laughter. First, the comparison merely illustrates a set of similar,
but not identical, behaviors of warm blooded vertebrates. Second, we may
hopefully shed light and heat on the nature of the strictly human manifestation of laughter.

The noises of a hyena or myna bird, we know, *sound* like human
laughter—may *be* in fact some sort of bestial laughter—and other animal
noises may be direct equivalents of laughter. There is doubt that animal
psychologists will soon produce a lexicon of animal laughter, but certain
animal experts, among them the first man in America to train a camel for
circus performances, *claim* that animals laugh, but that they laugh like animals. Elephant trainers, lion trainers, and dog enthusiasts sometimes make
the same assertions. Cat lovers incline to a belief that cats, under certain

circumstances, laugh quite noticeably (cat-style) at humans. The point is moot.

On the other hand, if we can unmistakably identify behaviors analogous, even slightly, to human laughter in animals, some insight may be gained concerning the function of laughter. Accordingly, the nature of laughter as a quality of communication may also, in some slight measure, be clarified.

Discussing the greeting ceremonies of geese, Konrad Lorenz notices that a number of their behaviors are comparable to "happy" meetings among human groups. Lorenz writes:

> Probably our human laughter in its original form was also an appeasement or greeting ceremony. Smiling and laughing *in my opinion* represent different intensities of the same behavior pattern. . . . In our nearest relations, the chimpanzee and gorilla, there is unfortunately no greeting movement corresponding in form and function to laughter, but it is seen in many macques which, as appeasement gesture, bare their teeth and at intervals turn their heads to and fro, smacking their lips and laying back their ears. It is remarkable that many Orientals smile in the same way when greeting, but the most interesting fact is that, while smiling most intently, they turn their heads a little sideways so that the eyes do not look straight at the person being greeted—but past him. In a purely functional consideration of this ritual, it is unimportant how much of its form is fixed by heredity and how much by the cultural tradition of politeness.[26]

Lorenz continues the discussion with this unusual observation:

> In many respects, the eliciting situations are analogous. When several fairly primitive individuals, such as small boys, laugh together at one or several others not belonging to the same group, the activity, like that of other redirected appeasement ceremonies, contain quite a large measure of aggression directed toward nonmembers of the group. Most jokes provoke laughter by building up tension which is then suddenly and unexpectedly exploded. Something very similar may happen in the greeting ceremonies of many animals: dogs and geese, and probably other animals, break into intensive greeting when an unpleasantly tense conflict situation is suddenly relieved. The . . . analogy lies in the fact that laughter, like greeting, tends to create a bond. *From self-observation, I can safely assert that shared laughter not only diverts aggression but also produces a feeling of social unity.*[27]

He elaborates:

> Laughter produces . . . a strong fellow feeling among participants and *joint aggressiveness against outsiders*. Heartily laughing together at the same things forms an immediate bond, much as enthusiasm for the

[26] K. Lorenz, *On Aggression*, pp. 177–178. (Italics added.)
[27] *Ibid.*, pp. 178–179.

same ideal does. Finding the same thing funny is not only a prerequisite to a real friendship, but often the first step to its formation. Laughter forms a bond and simultaneously draws a line. If you cannot laugh with others, you feel an outsider. . . .

Nevertheless, laughter is in a higher sense than enthusiasm (previously treated) specifically human. The motor patterns of threatening underlying both have undergone a deeper change of form and function in the case of laughter. Unlike enthusiasm, laughter—even at its most intense—is never in danger of regressing and causing the primal aggressive behavior to break through. Barking dogs may occasionally bite, but laughing men hardly ever shoot! And if the motor patterns of laughing are even more uncontrollably instinctive than those of enthusiasm, conversely its releasing mechanisms are far better and more reliably controlled by human reason.[28]

The naturalist, then, pries analogously into the animal sources of laughter. The extensive quotation was reprinted above because of its novelty—and inclusiveness—illustrating the functions that laughter appears to perform as a socio-psychological force. Lorenz's observations lead us to repeat a postulate which others have stated in a less direct manner: *that laughter is an obverse form of aggression.*

The full meaning of this simple statement centers on an assumption that aggression is a universal animal (hence human) trait.[29] In men it is a peculiarly deadly trait, inimical to the welfare of the entire species. Man, the aggressor, is a most fearful killer, not only of other families of animals, but of his own as well.

Aggression was, in pre-history, communicated from individual man-to-man encounters, to families, to tribes. The particular social adaptation required to neutralize this enormous aggressive power probably took the form, eventually, of a primitive type of laughter. It first vitiated aggressive impulses within the individual. Second, it served as rapid-fire communication, from one person to many, similar in nature to the impetus of aggression. Because the aggressive threat in man was obviously many times more deadly—hence more threatening to his survival—than in other animals, its neutralizing force, laughter, was required, perforce, both to be *objectified*, *redirected* and *ritualized* far more specifically than in the lower species. Man therefore laughs both more clearly and explicitly than other beasts.

The naturalistic-evolutionary explanation of the source of laughter does not necessarily contradict the Freudian hypothesis. As aggression is displaced, it is also repressed. So a concept of repression as germane to comedy is logically acceptable to the naturalist. It is doubtful that aggres-

---

[28] *Ibid.*, pp. 293–294.
[29] There are certain animals whose aggressive instincts seem peculiarly weak—for instance, the Koala Bear of Australia—which seems unfortunately unprepared by nature to ward off enemies of almost any kind. The exceptions may be explained, sophistically perhaps, by evolutionary peculiarities which permitted the survival of those few species whose need for aggressive mechanisms was nil.

sion is manifest in as exclusively a sexual context, as Freud assumed; but, in the degree to which social and individual aggression are *motivated* by sexual drives, the *repression* attendant to the laughter produced may also be sexually motivated. The matter is not at issue here; although Lorenz (and other naturalists) deny the primacy of libidinal unconscious drives in aggressive motivation of men. They base their assumptions upon the evolutionary pattern of animal life.

Should we accept Lorenz's observations concerning the wellsprings of laughter, two further curiosities are explained about how comedy is communicated. First, the grotesque physical configurations which laughter evokes from human beings (face forward, head back, neck tense, teeth bared to fangs, excited breathing, increased blood circulation, with spastic motor and nervous involvement) are manifestations of severe rage or anger *blunted*. Their energies have been returned to the organism in sequences of self-generating reflexive spasms that apparently feed with progressive diminution upon themselves, until their power is dissipated, and their aggressive danger vanishes. The individual is also subsequently enervated, less fit than previously for harmful aggression, but particularly vulnerable to the regeneration of more harmless laughter cycles.

Second, aestheticians have frequently been concerned with the so-called "infectious" quality of laughter. The naturalist's explanation tells us *why* laughter is so easily spread socially, although it provides us with little idea of *how*. Throughout most animal life, *aggressive* behavior is communicated to colonized or herded organisms instantaneously, obviously at levels far below (or above) the cognitive capacities of men. Schools of fish, birds and herds of mammals all respond to danger instantaneously and *en masse* in preparation for their "flight or fight" activities that are determined mutually and immediately. Since laughter appears to be a correlative reaction in human beings, it also displays the quality of immediate infectiousness beneath our cognitive threshold, similar to aggressive readiness in animals.

The contagion is manifest in a number of ways. First, laughter itself seems infectious; at times, lacking nearly all cognitive content. Like a number of emotions, it is communicated quickly and immediately from individual to individual across cultural and class barriers. Even sex differences and temperamental abberations often disappear in its wake.

Secondly, the perceptions of laughter (of others and self) enhance the humorous response to comedy itself. In the early days of radio broadcasting, for instance, comedian Ed Wynn found it virtually impossible to sustain the humor of his performance alone in front of a microphone. Before his radio debut in 1922, he accordingly invited to the WJZ studios a pick-up group of electricians, scrub-women, telephone operators and fellow artists who might serve as an audience to perk up his performance.[30] Having at-

[30] See Gleason L. Archer, *History of Radio* (New York: The American Historical Society, 1938), pp. 243–244.

tended a performance of a stage or film comedy without an audience to socialize the humor, one apprehends immediately the social factor so necessary to compound comedy into laughter.[31]

Third, that which is not fundamentally comic may be invested frequently with humor by the contagion that attends it. Much humor (like beauty) lies in the eye of the beholder. The dividing line between laughter and tears is often merely a matter of a perspective that may be shifted reactively. The same play or film may evoke serious reactions on one occasion and hilarious responses on another, and from similar audiences. A serious tenor may have been created by slight (but telling) audience reactions in the first case, and, more important, the infection of laughter may have changed the viewpoint of the audiences in the second. Viewers of old, dramatic, silent films often react in a most unpredictable manner, because, in all probability, one or two members of a group starts a chain of infectious laughter. This response may change the entire viewpoint of hundreds of other onlookers who may have taken a performance seriously *before* they had heard the laughter of others.

Laughing Together

Susanne K. Langer has written:

> Laughter, or the tendency to laugh . . . seems to arise from a surge of vital feelings. This surge may be quite small, just so it be sudden enough to be felt distinctly; but it may be great, and not particularly swift, and reach a marked climax, at which point we laugh or smile with you. Laughter is not a simple overt act, as the single word suggests; it is the spectacular end of a complex process. As speech is the culmination of a mental activity, laughter is the culmination of a feeling—the crest of a wave of felt vitality.

> A sudden sense of superiority entails such a "lift" of vital feeling. But the "lift" may occur without self-flattery, too;[32] we need not be making fun of anyone. A baby will laugh . . . because his wish is gratified. . . . The sudden pleasure raises the general feeling tone, so he laughs.

> In so-called "gallows humor" . . . "the lift" of vital feeling is simply a flash of self assertion. Something similar probably causes the

---

[31] Writers of comic narrative like S. J. Perelman manage to evoke humorous responses from individual readers. So do television performers, acting for small groups of at home viewers. Little experimentation has been done of perception of comedy under these circumstances. Perhaps each individual exposed, by means of whatever instrument he chooses—a book, a painting, a phonograph record, a radio, or a television receiver—is associating himself with a social group. At least he is hypothesizing some sort of relationship with the communicator in much the way one responds to a letter written by another, but imagined, person. Communality is a psychological phenomenon as often, possibly, as it is a physical reality. Psychological communality in the infection of laughter may explain the responses to humor by isolated auditors.

[32] Langer is here referring to the theory of the French film maker, Marcel Pagnol, that laughter, "without exception, betokens a sudden sense of superiority," with which she disagrees.

mirthless laughter of hysterics: in the disorganized response of a hysterical person, the sense of vitality breaks through fear and depression, so that it causes explosive laughter, sometimes alternating with sobs and tears.[33]

If *one* quality of communication is usually caused by the occasion of laughter *in* human communications, as Langer notes, it is *vitality* or the sense of, and zest for, life. Laughter may indeed be in essence a force, the origin of which lay in survival mechanisms which neutralized our evolutionary blood thirst. If so, it was generated as a protector of human life, and it is entirely appropriate that it has been civilized by social experience into a quality embuing with vitality all languages of communication spoken by man.

Despite its utilization by satirists and social comics in our literary tradition from Chaucer to Al Capp, there is little basically "civilized" or "cultured" about humor. Tragedy and drama, of course, demand a civilized setting for their unfolding. In fact, the serious matters in life, as told via the mediums of communications, become increasingly trenchant the more they are impressed with problems arising from social intercourse. Civilized interaction of human beings for common purposes is held against the frailty and futility of individual life in the great fundaments of most of our tragically and dramatically oriented philosophies.

While laughter *may be* a powerful social corrective (or satirists may *think* it is) the humorous spirit will often express itself with extreme antiphilosophical primitivism. Regardless of their pseudo-serious rationales "swinging" hipster parties, "cool" music, formalized drug usage and group sexual promiscuities constitute tame contemporary bacchanatiae, which, by Roman times, were *already* atavistic throwbacks to tribal life. Their most notable content is their uninhibited humor—the Mardi Gras shriek of the Dionysian festival, the fool king and queen and their ritual execution, the shared sexual, drug and alcoholic frenzy. Mostly, it is their primitive vitality that intrigues the student of comedy, because here is laughter without the refinement of high culture and lacking the restraints we call civilization. (When and where these orgiastic rites are performed seriously, in sombre silence, they forebode symptoms of sickness or seem as pointless as the Black Mass.)

For the sheer *act* of meaningful communication, the bonding of man to man, such sub-cultural bestial uproar is, of course, the genuine but raw display of the "instinct" of humor, not the quips of Ambrose Bierce, the parodies of W. S. Gilbert, or the strong ironies of an H. L. Mencken or Malcolm Muggeridge. Certainly their output is funny; and so were (and are) W. C. Fields and the Marx Brothers, George Kaufman, Smith and Dale, Bob Hope, and Jack Benny, *ad infinitum*. These are literary facts, like the list of American presidents we learned as children.

At their wildest and most wonderful, however (and sometimes they

[33] Langer, *Feeling and Form*, pp. 339–340.

are *both* wild and wonderful), they evoke merely, and at best, an echo of the primitive laughter of our forefathers. We are reminded of it particularly on at least two occasions: when we set out to kill, or when we laugh at nothing but the sound of ribald laughter.

Democritus said, "All human affairs are worthy only of laughter," a statement untrue, at least, of comedy.

Conclusion

Humor is potentially integral to all communications. It is a quality which has the power to modify messages of many sorts, in every medium and combination of mediums, and by all instruments of expression known. Many serious thinkers, accordingly, have shown interest in the phenomenon of humor and have found numerous starting places for its systematic discussion. Little, if any, clinical experimentation has been done on humor, or any manifestation allied to it—probably because of its capriciousness. We have, in our tradition, however, a series of more or less organized discussions of what certain people think is funny, why they laugh, and what may or may not be the logical and psychological functions of laughter.

An outstanding—and, in part, satisfying—psychological explanation of humor is derived from psychoanalytic theory. Unidimensional, as first articulated by Freud, the theory accounts for many laughter-producing situations in society. Other, earlier discussions of laughter—particularly the famous discourse of Henri Bergson—were not only inclusive of the social field covered by Freud, but also influenced both the production and analysis of humor up to the present day.

Both Freud's and Bergson's ideas, however, decrease in utility as the social field narrows, and as one regards laughter as an individualistic phenomenon—in the case, for instance, of the laughter of a small baby or as a manifestation of a behavioral disturbance.

The anthropologist and the naturalist, however, remind us that certain kinds of laughter are ubiquitous in human society. By analogy, laughter may be understood also as an organic evolutionary device, through which aggressive impulses were once thwarted or blunted to harmless merriment. Laughter, thus defined, and humor seen as a device for diminishing aggression—not only of individuals but as groups as well—is quickly and efficiently communicated from person to person and, within cyclic limits, becomes the stimulus for more laughter.

Credence has been given also to the "functional" view of laughter as a civilizing force. This perspective, however, has been associated more with the literary aspect of humor than with the generally primitive manner in which laughter itself is communicated. As humor is objectified, as it has introduced into it elements of cognition (and as it serves the cause of satire and social criticism), so does its function as communication appear to be mediated by increasingly complex factors involved in other communications.

Part Five

INSTRUMENTS
OF
COMMUNICATION

Chapter 16

COMMUNICATING
WORDS

VARIOUS FORMS of communication between living organisms had doubt-less reached heights of sophistication long before even primitive speech (or noise) was invented.

One of the many reasons that men have always believed that the act of speech is so crucial to the maintenance of culture is because of its exceed-ingly protean nature. There is literally *no limit* to the number of languages that may be devised. One language, as simple as "pidgin English," may serve a multitude of purposes. Even as technology has advanced to provide new matrices for communication, we are aware of how remarkable it is that *words* have kept abreast (and in some cases ahead) of both the technical and popular aspects of these innovations. Linguistic forms are waiting to be constructed for presently undreamed-of scientific concepts in the natural, social, and behavior sciences. As fast as social patterns change, also, words are modified along with them, sometimes before the change is generally noticeable in culture at large.[1]

In a single chapter of a book of this kind it would be impossible to make a cogent case against the centrality of words in human communica-tion. When one's ideas are committed to print, he is affirming by this act that print is of great significance in the mediation of thought through cul-ture. Nearly all writers agree, if not for psychological or financial reasons, then for logical ones.

[1] The death of the "beats" and the arrival of the "hippies" (and their demise), for instance, produced numerous new linguistic forms in the sub-cultures around us. (In our culture, a significant word gap sometimes exists between the older and younger generations, making communication between the two difficult.) Functionally, language has recently risen to the difficult challenge of meeting the need to articulate how cultural values have changed, are changing, or are likely to change in a relatively short time. The past few generations are probably the first in history to display such universal and wide word gaps between single generations, thus enhancing the apparent significance of the present verbal environment, perhaps beyond its genuine importance.

Experiences with small children and with "alienated" persons, in and outside of institutions, permits a "backstage view" of an eternal performance for which societies appear forever to be dressing-up by means of the costumes and scenery of the verbal environment in which we live. To many, the concept of "communication" and the study of it centers entirely on verbal manifestations. These are the "communication skills" that have replaced older terms like "English," "grammar," "composition" and "rhetoric," to name a few. "Business Communication"—a recent entry into the Bulletins of Colleges of Commerce—is usually concerned mostly with how to handle the verbal environment within and between large corporations and agencies.

In spite of the attention given verbal communications by academicians, there is a possibility that words are by no means of *central* significance to human communication: that other instruments cut more deeply into both our emotional and cognitive lives. How often, for instance, are words employed in modern societies to *cut off* communications or to *blur* their meanings than to facilitate them? One critic has written:

> We speak far too much, far too easily, making common what was private, arresting into the clichés of false certitude that which was provisional, personal and therefore alive on the shadow-side of speech. We live in a culture which is, increasingly, a wind tunnel of gossip; gossip that reaches from theology and politics to an unprecedented noising of private cancers (the psychoanalytic process is the high rhetoric of gossip). This world will end neither with a bang nor a whimper, but with a headline, a slogan, a pulp novel larger than the cedars of Lebanon. In how much of what is now pouring forth do words become word—and where is the silence needed if we are to hear that metamorphosis? [2]

If our currency of words has now been cheapened, we are witnessing a manifestation of three distinct types of cultural change that have occurred since the era of Jacobin democracy, in the U.S.A. particularly. First, education has been spread to the multitudes. The size of the groups we call "masses" have also grown; that is, our middle and lower class quondam nonreaders and writers have increased vastly in the past century. Secondly, a primitive but near universal free education, covering in content at least, the first few years of primary school, *has* expanded the linguistic content of our language. Dictionaries have grown in size since the eighteenth century, less due to the skill of lexicographers than because of the proliferation of words in current use. Third, instruments of human contact—not only technological but also social, like the Pony Express and the Sewing Circle—have put this expanded vocabulary to more uses than were imagined by the most sanguine professors of the Enlightenment. Words (printed and spoken)

[2] George Steiner, *Language and Silence* (New York: Atheneum Publishers, 1967), pp. 53–54.

not only became ubiquitous currency inflated, but currency in a new and variegated market.

The main social factor restraining the trivialization of communication by means of words has been the maintenance, in most societies, of discrete vocabularies within various groups, and the survival of different languages themselves. When (and if) sub-group patois is eliminated, and when (and if) linguistic differences yield to an international language, the currency may well turn up valueless. Mankind may then be forced to destroy its present elaborate mythology concerning the centrality of words as mediators of thoughts and feelings. Hence, if it is realized, the dream of "improved linguistic communications" between the various peoples of the world may become a nightmare, because one homogenous vocabulary will be forced to accomplish too many different sorts of objectives.

The "Tradition" of Print

A sub-myth to the notion of the centrality of words is the supposed cleavage between the "print medium" and other mediums. While differences, of course, exist between them, this is a problem centering on communication of how man articulates what he sees, knows or feels, *not* a problem inherent in the nature of mediums.

The original divisive factor to which words were subject was the invention of the *instrument* of written language. How comforting to remember that ancient philosophers were as disturbed by the supposed power of written (as opposed to the spoken) words as many of us are today with the difference between other instruments of communication and *both* the written and printed word!

Change is always worrisome, and this concern has been exacerbated by a series of dissertations on communications by Harold A. Innis, a Canadian economic historian, and his followers. In his first books, *The Fur Trade in Canada* and *The Cod Fisheries* (said to be classics on the subjects), Innis manifests a concern with the way industry affected environment and environment affected ways of life in Canada. His final work, *The Bias of Communications,*[3] constitutes a series of lectures wherein Innis slides up and down the tree of history to pursue the thesis that the "oral tradition" and the "written tradition" of man represented, as one followed the other, a profound metamorphosis in life style. He claims that responses to the introduction of the "written tradition" caused (sic) innumerable cultural and social minutiae which more or less determined the main cultural thrusts of subsequent history. Innis' mischief lies less in the lack of reasonableness of the rapid-fire cause-and-effect claims he makes without evidence than in the kind of glib historical license he seems to have inflicted upon subsequent Canadian scholarship.

His point is that a symbolic break between the "oral" and "written

[3] Harold A. Innis, *The Bias of Communication.*

traditions" occurred in Ancient Greece during the relatively few years between Socrates and Aristotle. He notes that Socrates was, in his way, the last of the sages in the oral tradition; the dialogues of Plato are mere recordings of oral events. Aristotle, on the other hand, was the first philosopher in the written tradition. He was distinctive because of his break with his immediate predecessor in *choosing* written language for the good reasons he himself notes in the course of his writings. He understood, naturally, that written language was merely an extension of speech.[4]

The subsequent story of the development of instruments for writing, recording and printing is touched upon by Innis. (It has been recorded far more excitingly elsewhere.[5]) To Innis' discredit, he appears satisfied with hasty observations on the relationship between writing and politics, economy, education and materialism. His sentences turn centuries into what is essentially a digest of a pocket history of the world. No major postulate emerges from this work, except the impression that something quite special (and perhaps mystical) was discovered by introduction of the written word to culture.

In regarding speaking and writing as discrete traditions, Innis has, of course, set the stage for the academic discussion which shortly followed his book (mostly in Canada). If, one argues, separate traditions follow the transition of communications from words to written symbols, then transitions to other instruments—particularly those of new technology—must also create new traditions! In accepting this loose logic, we stand at the dawn of a new (and seemingly reasonable) mystique concerning the discrete vocabularies of what are mistakenly referred to today as "media" of communication. The reason that interpretations of these vocabularies are so turgid and difficult to comprehend is, of course, that the premises upon which their articulation rests are spurious.[6]

The division of words into "oral" and "written" categories makes some apparent *logical* sense when held against an artificial background of rapidly changing mores in different nations, as Innis has attempted. But the concept is obviously psychological nonsense, of the same type as the old concern that reading and writing somehow impair man's memory and rhetorical skills. It recalls the unmerited claim of Socrates (in the *Phaedrus* of Plato) that "it (writing) will create forgetfulness in the learners' souls because

---

[4] See Harold A. Innis, *The Bias of Communication*, pp. 9–10, 44.
[5] See S. H. Steinberg, *Five Hundred Years of Printing*, for a fascinating study of the development of this aspect of culture. It includes cogent descriptions of the mechanisms of early printing devices and the technology of later ones. Steinberg wisely sticks to his last and offers few assumptions about the ways in which printing affected the history of the societies in which it developed.
[6] Dr. McLuhan has been credited by numerous contemporary thinkers with being a seminal provocateur who merely serves as "spark plug" for further investigation of these topics. First, he is far from seminal, and in the second place, investigation without the possibility of significant discovery is absurd. Based as these premises are upon dubious assumption, these investigations are leading (and will continue to lead) into blind alleys. There is no shortage of evidence for this claim.

they will not use their memories; they will trust the external written words and not remember of themselves. They will appear to be omniscient and will generally know nothing; they will be tiresome company having the show of wisdom without reality." [7]

Common sense validated this dictum in its time, particularly the implication that pedants make tiresome company. But observation demonstrates also its absurdity, which Aristotle himself recognized almost immediately after it was made. Aristotle's response was characteristically psychological: these fears are simply not justified when one examines the behavior of men and women and how they learn and transmit knowledge.

Innis and his followers have fundamentally, however, based a pseudo-theory on *one* logical fact. Put bluntly, there *is* a noticeable difference between written and spoken language. His followers have been equally as logical (hence the feeling that they "have something") in their insistence upon the self-evident point that there is a difference between most communications when different instruments are used. *That much is all we know, logically*; the entire case for the cleavage between the oral and written "traditions" ends there!

The reader is assured also that there indeed exist certain obvious variable *psychological* functions of different instruments. But these psychological factors are not capable of exact formulation into logical postulates, because they involve numerous variable factors regarding how, why, when, where and for whom the instruments are being employed.

The most significant variable is the *content* of the message. For instance (and simply), the transition of a nursery rhyme from an oral recitation to the printed page of a book is, logically, a sort of modification of a message. Compare the two and you will find *something different*. The change in technique of communication tells us nothing more than this, because we must a) be familiar with the content of the rhyme; b) know how it was handled orally, by whom and for what reason; c) understand the same factors about the printed version; d) appreciate the role of printed words and spoken words in the culture involved; e) determine many factors in the minds of the audiences receiving both messages (including whether they will be the same individuals); f) comprehend the interplay of the *qualities* of the communication in both versions;[8] g) be capable of bringing suitable critical criteria to bear in order to discover the degree of art or artlessness employed in the renditions; and h) remain constantly aware that there are other variables related to the differences between the oral and written pieces. It is doubtful that knowledge of all of these factors would, for even a *simple* oral versus written communication, provide enough data to delineate a meaningful psychological comparison between the two.

In the paragraph above we have been dealing with a comparatively

---

[7] Quoted in J. A. C. Brown, *Techniques of Persuasion*, p. 131.
[8] See Part Four.

elementary transition: the change from spoken to written language. It is so simple that we may teach children its accomplishment quite easily. Let us imagine, now, the psychological complexity of the transition of this same nursery rhyme into the device of the dramatized radio broadcast; or the film (by live-action or animated cartoon); or to any other modern instrument of communication. So numerous become the variables which might re-qualify the change that, psychologically speaking, to look for regularities which might apply to just *two* nursery rhymes each utilizing the instrument of, say, color television would be absurd. There are none,[9] except for the non-variable aesthetic qualities, previously noted, inherent in the mediums of picture, narrative and re-enactment.

Since Innis' idea of the "print tradition" is psychologically impossible, the same drawbacks apply to the claim that we are presently leaving the "print tradition" for another one—presumably "electric" or "electronic." Never having demonstrated that man has *left* the "oral tradition," it is extremely difficult to accept the notion that we are moving into another one. Those who do must deal with the fact that more words are written, printed and read in our culture than in any society in the history of the world.[10]

As for the passage of the "oral tradition, the recent enlargement of individual vocabularies due to free universal education (as well as the spread of topics to talk about by the technological instruments of communication) has produced for us also one of the most verbal societies ever known. That is, we modern Americans probably *talk* longer about more topics with larger vocabularies than any people ever have—including the period of great "conversationalists" of the seventeenth century in England and France! So much, then, for the death of the "oral tradition." [11]

The cause and effect relationships visible in the production, distribu-

[9] Note that, although many nursery stories have been televised, even the successful ones like the American *Cinderella* and BBC's *Alice in Wonderland* have been "translated" to this new instrument in manners extremely different one from the other. Certain fundamental basic aesthetics (of the pictorial and dramatic mediums mostly) were shared in common but little else. Their qualities were at least as different as *television programs* as they were as *narratives.*

[10] In America today, more than 26-million paperback books are sold per year—probably *far* more. About 38,000 hard-cover titles are produced per year, and some 1760 newspapers are printed, which circulate over seventy million copies per day. Other literary periodicals have an estimated total readership of 430-million copies per issue. These statistics were taken from the UNESCO *Statistical Yearbook* (Paris, France: UNESCO, 1966). They prove nothing concerning how much of this output consists of printed words and how much is pictorial, nor do they indicate for what purposes people use these books, newspapers and magazines. They appear, however, to give credence to the argument that the age of the "print tradition," far from being over, is probably now at its all-time zenith.

[11] Concerning education, as previously noted, Martin Mayer writes, ". . . there is one blanket statement which can safely be made about the world's schools: the teachers talk too much." From *The Schools* (New York: Harper and Brothers, 1961), p. 8. As more people spend more time in school, remember, the amount of talk in their lives increases apace.

tion and consumption of consumer goods (including furs and codfish) are irrelevant to cultural interaction when people communicate. Industrial methods will, of course, affect an environment that in turn will affect the people who live in it. To a mind attuned to this sort of causality, it may be difficult to comprehend that, as verbal communication was "replaced" by written words, the overall amount of conversation in a given society *increased*, not decreased, because, along with other factors, the art of writing had provided *more things to talk about*. To the economist, such an anti-arithmetic result seems ridiculous.

In the same manner today, however, electronic instruments of communication are *increasing* rather than decreasing the proclivity to talk and the need to read, just as they are increasing the subjects to talk about and the verbal tools for their articulation.[12] We are not interested here in the *quality* of the talk, its complexity or relevance to life, but merely its *currency*. But, even in qualitative matters, the coming of written language did not mean that there was no longer anything *worth* talking about. Nor did the onset of printing mean that nothing was *worth* writing about in *longhand*. On the contrary, *more* was now worth writing about! And so on, through the progressive inventions of communication technology. This snowball process was neither good nor bad, but inevitable. It is worth noting, however, that this expansion was set against a background wherein the "world population doubled itself twice over in the period between 1650 and 1920, and will have doubled itself a third time by the early 1980's." [13]

Sounds and Noises

Radio, or a device similar to it, is a near-perfect instrument for communication between blind men. If there is a distinctive quality to radio writing, it is an art of the blind communicating with the blind.[14] Instrumental circumscriptions upon the use of sound are therefore elementary: one may communicate only what he may hear.

The major technological devices for communicating sounds today are radio, plastic disc recording and sound tape, all of which make use of common technical principles. All three may be used interchangeably with cleverness and delightful flexibility.

They are (along with the photo-electric process for recording sound on photographic film) similar devices, except for radio which may provide in-

[12] When television was young, two decades ago, predictions were made that it was diminishing the amount of conversation in society. Not one shred of reasonable or definitive evidence has been produced since to substantiate this charge, although a small percentage of television viewers believe that it "interferes with home life." See Garry A. Steiner, *The People Look at Television* (New York: Alfred A. Knopf, 1963), p. 101.
[13] Julian Huxley, *New Bottles for New Wine* (New York: Harper and Brothers, 1957), p. 174.
[14] An author of one of the last and best soap operas on American radio was indeed blind: Hector Chevigney, who wrote *The Second Mrs. Burton*.

stantaneous sound coverage of a live event. The only *essential* difference between radio and recordings is this matter of instantaneous transmission that may or may not be of logical or psychological significance to a listener, depending upon what sound is communicated. As an example, a most attractive feature of a phonograph recording of a symphony is that it is *not* instantaneous, that one may listen to the record whenever and (these days) almost wherever he pleases. The importance of a political speech, on the other hand, may lie in the fact that it is heard simultaneously with its transmission.

The early novelty of radio broadcasting centered largely on its ability to carry sound for great distances instantaneously to a public which was already familiar with "canned" sound on the phonograph.[15] Today, this novelty has worn off, and most radio transmission, except for news and on-the-spot broadcasts, is pre-recorded, frequently in subtle ways of which the listener is unaware.

In the light of spurious ideas concerning the death of the "oral tradition," consider the ways that the modern instruments of sound technology appear to encourage the supposedly moribund "oral tradition" of communication. Most of the programming in words on the more than 4,000 radio stations in the United States is presented in the medium of the vocal *narrative*; small segments, particularly of commercial announcements, comes by means of the *dramatic* medium. The "oral tradition" is thereby continued by the thousands of disc jockeys and news commentators in our nation's radio studios.

Narrative and re-enactment are obviously the only two mediums of communication that may be transmitted by sound devices. The types of material which do not require pictorial dimensions for communicating both cognitions and emotions effectively are broad. The use of sound is not in itself an "art form," as proponents of radio broadcasting have sometimes suggested. Rather, sound may, by virtue of its special qualities, transmit differentially oriented material in narrative and dramatic form, varying in effectiveness first, according to the cleverness and skill of the narrator or dramatist, and second, depending upon what use the particular communication in question makes of the mediums of narrative and drama.

The following chart suggests the potentiality of sound for the transmission of the three mediums of communication *according to the ways in which sound transmission has so far been used in radio broadcasting and recording*. There exists no way of anticipating the future. Note, however, that the list begins with "Silence" and ends with the rich possibilities for the communication of cognitive and emotional content. ("Sounds" as used in the list below include what are generally considered "sound effects.")

[15] For a recently published history of this period see Erik Barnouw, *A Tower in Babel*, pp. 7–188.

FORM	SOUND RESPONSE
a. Pictures	(nothing)
b. Music	(psychological narrative?) [16]
c. Sound	(logical-psychological narrative)
d. Talk	(logical-psychological narrative)
e. Words and Music	(logical-psychological narrative)
f. Monologue (poetic)	(logical-psychological drama)
g. Dialogue (poetic)	(logical-psychological drama)
h. Talk and Dialogue (poetic)	(logical-psychological narrative-drama)
i. Talk and Dialogue (poetic) and Sound	(logical-psychological narrative-drama)
j. Talk and Dialogue (poetic) and Sound and Music	(logical-psychological narrative-drama)

(Note that the assumption is made above that *all* dramatic discourse is in some manner poetic.)

The range, therefore, for the utilization of sound is quite wide, even given the perimeters of two mediums (rather than three) and a limited number of effective relationships, logically, for its employment for dramatic and narrative purposes. Add to these combinations the (possibly) "extra-medium" sound of music, and the possible combinations become even greater.

[16] The question mark is not gratuitous. It represents general bewilderment concerning *what* music communicates, not *how* or *why*. Music obviously has little cognitive content; yet it is directive like narrative, filled with psychological value (for certain people at certain times) and obeys, usually, certain logical aesthetic laws of a complex sort. As a *qualifying device* for either narratives, pictures or re-enactments, its function and its role are quite clear, just as its relationship to dance is obvious. Taken alone, however, it presents even the most skilled critic with innumerable, perhaps insoluable, problems. One of the most sensible discussions of this aspect of music may be found in Langer, *Philosophy in a New Key*, pp. 165–199.
It is worth noting here, at the risk of a slight digression, that according to George Steiner, the literary critic, listening to music is today replacing reading in the United States. "Where library shelves once stood," he writes, "there are proud, esoteric rows of record albums and high-fidelity components. Compared to the long-playing record, the paperback book is an ephemeral, lightly dicarded thing. It does not lead to the collecting of a real library. Music is today the central fact of lay culture . . . the tempo of urban industrial life leaves one exhausted at nightfall. When one is tired music, even difficult music, is easier to enjoy than serious literature. It stirs feelings without perplexing the brain. It allows even those who have had little previous training access to classic masterpieces. It does not separate human beings into islands of privacy and silence as does the reading of a book, but conjoins them in that illusion of community which our society strives for. . . . *In short, the musical sound . . . (is) beginning to hold a place in society once firmly held by the word.*" Steiner, *Language and Silence*, pp. 29–30. Steiner's Innis-like statement may contain a grain of truth. Despite the music craze in its many manifestations that technology has brought us, abstract sound cannot replace words any more than print replaced speech. Many do not therefore share Steiner's alarm, because there are enough tin-eared *music-haters* abroad who have resisted the LP-hi-fi fad, and continue to regard music taken alone either as a background for, or intrusion into, literary experiences. Our present population of *music lovers* have not replaced literary study with high fidelity; they have largely replaced silence with sounds that they have been directed by fashion to feed into their phonographs and tape machines.

In the light of such diversity, one is puzzled by the limited usage to which radio broadcasters and recordists have put their instruments, even during their most ambitious moments in America. There was the period of the nineteen-thirties and forties when Orson Welles and the Columbia Workshop and other "experimental" radio programs were heard on the broadcasting networks. Norman Corwin's much regarded *On A Note of Triumph*,[17] for instance, is a poor attempt at fusing incendiary music with uninspired monologue and dialogue of a pseudo-folk-poetic nature that served its purpose (the celebration of VE Day) but does not stand up today to close scrutiny. One of the best examples of the fusion of these elements is the BBC's famous broadcast of Louis Macneice's radio play, *The Dark Tower*,[18] which, unfortunately, is not presently available for private or public listening in the United States. The script has been given a public reading in America, but lacking the BBC's magnificent cast of voices, Benjamin Britten's score, and its remarkable sound production, it is not a highly effective sound communication when merely read aloud by actors.

The medium of picture is not excluded psychologically by the instruments that transmit sounds to the human ear. Arch Oboler, the radio writer, once made reference to "the wide screen of the human imagination," an ornamental way of saying that, in the normal, human perception processes, sounds evoke images. *All* senses may evoke picture images: taste, smell, pain, etc., may cause certain individual visual concommitants in the perceiver, and sound is no exception. The condition for the evocation is that the individual has already perceived such images (or images like them) before the stimulus is offered. This psychological process may never, however, be relied upon to stir up a complex set of homogeneous visions in a group of intelligent adults. But the "Star Spangled Banner" is likely to produce images of an American flag, and the voice and tap steps of Fred Astaire will probably conjure up his familiar frame for most of us. Such simple and common images—in many instances caricatures and stereotypes of well-known character types or personalities—were once used by radio writers to draw quick, immediately understandable (but shallow) sketches of types of people.[19]

Exceptions notwithstanding, nearly *all* logical meaning and *most* psychological meaning purveyed by sound instruments is accomplished with words. This observation in no way confirms Professor Innis' notion of the "oral tradition" (which was a *word* tradition only, concerned neither with

---

[17] Norman Corwin, *On A Note of Triumph* (New York: Simon and Schuster, 1945). A repeat broadcast of the program has been issued by Columbia Records.
[18] Louis Macneice, *The Dark Tower and Other Radio Scripts* (London: Faber and Faber, Limited, 1947), pp. 20–66.
[19] Note such successful radio figures as Amos 'n Andy, Rochester, the Goldbergs, the O'Neils, Ajax Cassidy, Mrs. Nussbaum, Titus Moody, "Parkyakarkas," Baron Munchausen, "Schlepperman," Bob Burns, "The Mad Russian," Lum 'n Abner, and Dr. Christian, etc.

sound effects nor music), specifically because the instrument of print *also* depends largely upon words for communication. That words, in one degree or another, are verbalized, covertly or overtly, while being read is axiomatic; hence the "print tradition" is, at the outset, a spurious physiological construction. If mankind *has* evolved a tradition upon which it depends for much communication, it might be called simply the "verbal tradition." It has yet to be replaced by another one for certain purposes of efficient communication. That a parallel "pictorial tradition" has also attended culture since pre-literate days, in no manner diminishes the primacy of these sounds we call words (as written or spoken) in the development of civilization.

The close relationship of words themselves to sound is one of the main reasons for the success of methods which teach foreign languages from a spoken rather than written perspective. The concept of teaching conversation, grammar, and vocabulary in this way[20] was developed from the observation that children learn spoken languages far more effortlessly than adults learn written ones. Bi-lingual and even tri-lingual children seem, as well, to have little difficulty with the mastery of their multiple tongues, while efforts to teach foreign languages in a "literary" manner in secondary schools have been near-total failures for generations.[21]

The "audio-lingual" approach to foreign languages boils down to using spoken *words* as the focus in the teaching of other tongues. Certainly, oral instruction by means of tape recordings and discs or, best of all, by a live native teacher who speaks *nothing but* the language, facilitates the process. But the crucial difference between the "old" and "new" methods is that the "new" does away with rules, principles, abstractions, and irregularities of languages and concentrates upon *how words are used for communication.*

Succinctly, it accepts two main points: that words, produced by means of many different instruments, bear a considerable logical, and nearly as great psychological, burden in the transmission of meaning between individuals, but also that their power, when severed from the speech *gestalt* is by no means as critical as was once believed, especially when they are approached in a formal linguistic context, as grammarians and teachers have been doing for generations.

Cold Print

One of the most interesting side products of the development of the mass press was the encouragement of one aspect of the mystique which had already accompanied the production of printed materials. The develop-

---

[20] See Edward M. Stack, "Language Laboratories" in Fred and Corinne Guggenheim (eds.), *New Frontiers in Education* (New York: Grune and Stratton, Inc., 1966), pp. 270–288.
[21] See Jacques Barzun, *Teacher in America* (Garden City, N.Y.: Doubleday and Company, Inc., 1954), pp. 119–132, for an interesting and highly relevant discussion of the difficulties of teaching foreign languages effectively in American schools under conditions of modern schooling.

ments of the elaborate technology of cheap and rapid printing engendered a powerful symbolism which obscured—and obscures to this day—the roles that letters, in fact, play in contemporary life, and their function as instruments of narrative, pictorial and dramatic communication.

The newspaper—and a newspaper may range in quality from a small town weekly, to *The New York Times*, to a racing journal—derives some of its prestige from the unique protection given it (in a constitutional democracy) from governmental interference on the grounds that a "free press" is indispensable to representative government. This relationship is not at issue except to note that the precise role of press freedom in functions of representative government has yet to be determined.[22] What matters here is that, in the United States at least, *only the press* (along with the church, the military and the liquor industry, and excepting governmental organs) is singled out for special attention in our Constitution. Note that "the press" mentioned specifically in the First Amendment, conceivably includes (as has been maintained) *all kinds* of printing presses, including those which stamp out comic books, and perhaps recordings.

Political prestige was (and is) merely one aspect of the magic of the instrument of the printed words. The first books printed throughout Europe in the fifteenth century were bibles and holy documents.[23] Even today, the Bible is publicized as a perennial "best seller," and doubtless it is; new editions and versions of it are continually printed. The Gideons have followed travelers from hotel to motel, and few American homes do not contain a copy of at least *one* holy book.

The actual translation of the sound of language into a written matrix is also frequently regarded as a mystical process, useful in many societies for the preservation of the content and utilization of magic rites and rituals. To generalize this trend so that it applies today to the psychologically powerful process of printing, what is written (and thereby still seemingly magical) increases its power many times by means of a novel sort of technological mysticism *when it is set in type and printed.*

Not only do most of us "believe *what* we read in the newspaper," we believe largely *because* what we read *is* in the newspaper. Further, because certain sequences of words have found their way into print, they represent to us "ideas in the market place of thought," be they brilliant or just nonsense. In addition to the works of the wise, predictions of fortune tellers, the advice of quack psychiatrists, "extra-sensory" psychologists, and crack-pot theories of nutrition somehow manage continually to find their

---

[22] This particular problem has been most rewardingly (if idealistically) discussed in two of the volumes produced by the Luce Commission on the Freedom of the Press, which published its findings shortly after World War II. See William Ernest Hocking, *Freedom of the Press* (Chicago, Ill.: The University of Chicago Press, 1947), and the Commission's one volume summary report, A *Free and Responsible Press* (Chicago, Ill.: The University of Chicago Press, 1947).
[23] Sternberg, *Five Hundred Years of Printing*, pp. 37–80.

way into "reputable" print. Merely because they have been printed they receive, first, the dignity of special protection under law, and second, what is correctly called the "prestige" of the printed word, but may also be described as a functional charisma of the instrument of print.

Statistics of growth of mass literacy are usually employed to demonstrate how effective education is in a certain society, a symptom of a culture increasingly cognizant of social and political issues of consequence.[24] Many new readers probably do develop such awareness, but as they read they are also becoming increasingly vulnerable to the prejudices of editors and reporters, the saleability of gossip and "he-she" jokes, the commercial biases of journalism, and the comfortable feeling of being fed frequent doses of grimy sensationalism.

More important, a larger and larger number of readers (including book buyers, book club members, and digest book club readers) affirm by weight of sheer numbers the mysticism of the print technique for communication of words. Educators have classically worshipped the printed word, just as they have overindulged in the spoken one. Texts and "research papers" are virtuous *per se* in our schools—elementary to graduate—less because of their necessity for either learning or teaching, but because the idea of anything beside a print-based school is inconceivable for conventional educational rituals. Another peculiar aspect, accordingly, of the mysticism of print is that it is most insistently affirmed by extremely influential segments of society: those involved in education and religion, whose status itself *depends upon* the acceptance of the magic of print. Professors and priests thereby verify the mysticism that provides their potency as professors and priests.

Innis, McLuhan and their followers, therefore, become their own worst dupes when they write about the "print tradition" that, they claim, is yielding hegemony to other forms of communication. In the first place, the "print tradition" is, in fact, a "print mysticism," and in the second place, it is yielding ground to nothing.[25]

If the mystique of the printed word is at last falling under a more objective critical scrutiny by the masses than heretofore (which is doubtful), this is due largely to the vast and confusing *amount* of print so easily available to them today, and the ease with which printed material may now be reproduced.

[24] See, for instance, the inferences made relative to the spread of newspapers in a typical book on mass communications as social phenomena such as Melvin L. DeFleur, *Theories of Mass Communication* (New York: David McKay and Company, 1966), pp. 10–21.
[25] That the Innis-McLuhan ideas are presented to the reader in print form is, as noted at the beginning of this chapter, more academic tail-chasing. The concepts in *this* particular volume, have *not*, however, been developed with conventional respects to conventional graduate school print worship—or even *word* worship. Instead, they stem from work with students on highly irreverent and unorthodox projects concerning the use and function of instruments of communication.

Technological visionaries tell us that the concept of modern library, book, editor and publisher is moribund. They note that the enormous centralization at present occurring in the print industries (of which newspapers, magazines and books are just a part) is the economic bugle call for what is to follow. It will be a battle, they say, in the sense that competition for the control of copyrights, patents and servicing of technology will be cutthroat and extensive. Eventually, books as we know them are likely to disappear, and Xerography (or instant, exact replication of written, typed, Vari-typed, or previously typeset documents) will permit any library or bookseller to reproduce quickly—and eventually immediately—any sort of verbal material, translated to written or printed symbols, that has been previously fed to a central bank of data. The bank's appetite for materials will be infinite, and its method of classification (and therefore ability of retrieval) will be perfect.

The "system" for the accessibility of written symbols has not only already been conceived, its design and its production are possible now. Most of the technology (including the requisite facsimile reproduction instruments) is also available. The wedding of the two may take longer than science-fiction enthusiasts in professional education predict,[26] but it will certainly be seen in the West (barring extensive warfare) during the next twenty years. It is an inevitable development of technology, and neither tradition, nor sentiment, nor craft unionism, nor copyright, nor patent law, nor vested economic interests, are likely to do more than delay it for short periods.

The most trenchant effect of this change will center directly on the mysticism of print, not on its utilization or on the economics of the print-dependent industries. There is no reason to believe that the current mystique of print will disappear; merely that it will change. And the transformation will be one that associates the printed with the spoken word more closely than ever before. The study of structural linguistics is currently moving (blindly) towards the study of words and their use as a single facet of culture. In our civilization, these new instruments will bring the fusion between words and culture extremely close and make its study more credible. Structural linguistics may provide for its followers numerous instruments of cultural relevance and control of which they are almost totally unaware, and unprepared for, at present.

The technological-linguistic change has already begun, in that, as one dictates to a tape recorder his day's correspondence, he maintains the psychological image of what his secretary will eventually do to his words by means of her electric typewriter. Not only may he dictate, erase and edit

[26] See The New York Times, Sunday, July 2, 1967, p. 36; also Audio-Visual Instruction, May 1967. An interesting periodical that has kept up with recent possibilities in electronic learning devices and library facilities is Educational Technology, published monthly by Educational News Service, P.O. Box 508, Saddle Brook, New Jersey, 07662.

what he "writes" this way in his office, but in his automobile during traffic jams, as well as at home, or over the telephone when he travels. One's verbal "self"—for purposes of correspondence—is fused to the "cold print" of his letters in exactly the same way in a motel room, aboard an airplane, or when the tired executive is at home sick in bed.

Words written here (by the author) in longhand will eventually (after much revision) be turned into printed images of a photographed plate of machine-set type. Most probably, they will—like most of the ideas that now find their way into print—settle rapidly into the sediment of oblivion. On the other hand, the technical potentiality for their integration into the totality of contemporary letters and chances for longevity are greater than ever before.

This advancing closeness of written words to the rest of culture may breed—like other familiarities—the contempt that we now frequently observe displayed for "just talk." Tomorrow, millions of unread pages may be dismissed daily as "just books," or "just print." The unpublished professor will, by then, perhaps, be of greater value to the administrators of his university (as he is now to his students) than the much-published one. The "power of the press" may also hopefully be reduced to where the power of a healthy rabble-rouser was a generation ago—appreciable, but contingent upon skill, not status; argument, not magic.

Nothing essentially optimistic or pessimistic attends this potential change. Nor must the predictions above be taken to indicate a belief that modern technology is re-creating a tribal community of interactive, sentient masses. What it may forebode simply is a society in which our general incapacity to manage logically verbal symbols, mediated by an infinite number of clever recording devices, will be matched by a similar incapacity to employ logically *written* symbols that, by them, will be as easily manufactured, mediated and reproduced as oral ones are now. Old problems will find their way into newly wrapped packages.

Conclusions

We have examined the major instruments available for conveying words from person to person, including thin air. We began with a skeptical dissection of the common notion that words are the main instruments for man's communication, and a discussion of the forces in culture that have had an effect upon the power of words. We considered, also, how the notion of such power itself has been enhanced by the increase in general word-flow brought about by the numerous phenomena of modernity.

Print was discussed next, primarily in the context of current beliefs in the replacement of an "oral tradition" by a "written" or "print tradition," a notion that appears to have had its origin—in altered form—in ancient Greek thought. The belief has been—and is being—employed to justify many types of societal changes in the past and present. Logical differences between printed and spoken words were, to a degree, granted and discussed for relevance to the "tradition" theory. The psychological differences between the two were examined closely, however, and it was discovered that such a change in "traditions" was most unlikely. The current theory, therefore, that we are leaving the "print tradition" for an "electronic culture" of some sort was dismissed as irrelevant to current communications problems. This is because the "print tradition" itself has, in all likelihood, never existed, and even today, the major currency for the distribution of words remains talk.

Sounds as instruments of communication and their technology were also discussed. Emphasis was placed on the similarity of the different types of hardware employed in this technology and numerous limitations on full use of all three mediums in the communication of sound. In fact, a scale or ladder of techniques demonstrating the relationships of the mediums of communication by means of sound was offered. Conjecture was also raised concerning the psychological evocation of images by means of sounds and the difficulty of making precise logical or psychological statements in this regard. It was noted, however, that such a phenomenon occurs. Words still appear to be the main mediators, by sound, of psychological meaning—and the *only* mediators of strictly logical meaning, with a few exceptions like radio sound effects and symbolic languages (for example, mathematics) constructed for logical purposes.

Lastly, the mysticism of print was discussed, and reasons explored why both the written and printed words appear to evoke a charismatic effect in modern as well as primitive cultures. Sources of this mythology were examined, as well as possibilities for change in the cultural role in our society of writing and printing during the next two decades. Sweeping, but not necessarily perfect, predictions were made about the nature of "publication" of various types by means of the new technologies of print reproduction and data retrieval that appear not only possible today, but inevitable. Logical, psychological, and cultural changes attendant to these changes, and their influence upon the mystique of print, were matters for further unverifiable conjecture.

Chapter 17

POPULAR PERIODICALS

O NE INEVITABLE outcome of popular democracy is a semi-literate population. Countless idealists of the past and present century dreamed of a society that was fully literate, that would, by means of the development of tastes, preferences and life-styles of its citizens, undergo a general cultural uplift from, at least, average to normal.[1] In the words of our outstanding American educational philosopher, "Government, business, art, religion, all social institutions have a meaning, a purpose. That purpose is to set free and to develop the capacities of human individuals without respect to race, sex, class or economic status. And this is all one with saying that the test of their value is the extent to which they educate every individual *into the full stature of his possibility.*"[2]

Optimists at the Office of Education put our illiteracy rate at a figure close to 2%, and this probably is correct, if the criterion of literacy is the ability to read the front of a Corn Flakes box. The back is likely to be more difficult and produce a higher percentage. It is difficult, however, to associate the highly differential reading abilities of our adult population with the quality of American primary and secondary education. Regardless of how they are educated, most people are competent to teach themselves to read whatever it is they must understand in daily life to maintain themselves.

[1] For an interesting discussion of the differences between averages and norms (and average men versus normal men) see Joseph Wood Krutch, *Human Nature and the Human Condition* (New York: Random House, 1959), pp. 75–95. Krutch's point is that by frequently setting our standards or average (or mean) behavior in American life, we have stultified the potential of our culture for normality, the latter by definition almost invariably less often found in a population than the former. The *average* number of legs per person in Hong Kong, for instance, *must be less* than two; the *normal* number is two. Krutch quotes Shaw's occulist who said, "A normal pair of eyes is one of the rarest things in nature."

[2] John Dewey, *Reconstruction in Philosophy* (New York: A Mentor Book, 1955), p. 147. The original edition was published in 1920. (Italics added.)

For recreation and information, the publishing industries produce a plethora of communications regularly using, mostly, the mediums of picture and narration (but often re-enactment as well), designed to meet the differential desires of this variegated audience.[3] The results of this technology of production are our seventeen to eighteen hundred (or so) newspapers which circulate in the neighborhood of seventy million copies daily and multitude of about five thousand periodicals with a per-issue circulation of about 400 million.[4]

Rather than attempt to dissect this mass of pictures and verbiage—which ranges all the way from technical journals to photograph albums for transvestites—according either to style of production (newspaper, newsmagazine, comic book, etc.), or by virtue of dominant appeal (news, entertainment, orientation, etc.), let us examine instead the major and most popular *types* of American periodicals, newspapers excluded. Relating these styles to the mediums of communications employed, their logics and psychologics and the qualities of communication they express, may be of help in understanding the languages they speak and why, if their economic health is to be assured, their entrepreneurs feel that they must continue to operate in certain ways.

Of Men and Playboys

Outside of serious special interest journals (printed more frequently for men than women), two of the prototype masculine magazines published in the United States at present are *Time* and *Playboy*. Each magazine, by virtue of its stylistic consistency and novelty, has tempted its promotion managers to compound its success story to mythic proportions by characterizing the "type of reader" who is likely to subscribe to either—and sometimes both—journals. Both myths have had enormous "spin offs." In the case of *Time*, books and records are sold with the imprimatur of the magazine; they are the kind of literature (fiction and non-fiction) that the stereotyped *Time* subscriber "should" read, the kinds of recordings he "should" listen to etc. The *Playboy* clubs have—with differential successes due to many factors—restyled the older Hollywood-type nightclub into expensive "key club" cabarets,[5] and the *Playboy* insignia is to be found on all

---

[3] Whether or not it meets their *needs* as well is an open question. The flow of the market, at any given time, is determined largely by economic factors and tradition, rather than any specific interpretation of what the requirements of the public are for health, citizenship, intellectual growth or any other cultural *desiderata*. The present societal function of newspapers and magazines is competently explained in Edwin Emery, Philip H. Ault and Warren K. Agee, *Introduction to Mass Communications* (New York: Dodd, Mead and Co., 1960), pp. 161–234.
[4] Theodore Peterson, Jay W. Jensen and William R. Rivers, *The Mass Media and Modern Society*, pp. 65–71.
[5] The "key club," particularly New York's *Gaslight Club*, antedated the *Playboy Clubs* by many years. The older key clubs required (and therefore emanated) greater social prestige than the *Playboy Clubs*, because social attributes other than financial solvency

sorts of consumer goods and services, including neckties and tourist brochures.

Time is the more formidable—and remarkable—phenomenon of the two, in that its close imitator, *Newsweek* displays an apparently more masculine, no-nonsense air stylistically, and it eschews the little puns and minor jokes that gives *Time* prose a somewhat fey tone. Whatever the stylistic qualities of *Time*, sense, feeling and intention overbalance these eccentricities and produce a document of catholic news coverage that is as topical and broad as it is distortive of hard news.[6]

Playboy is virtually alone in its field. Other magazines print neatly airbrushed photographs of nude female 'teenagers. Others deal in randy fiction and "cool" pseudo-philosophy similar to Hugh Heffner's. Others make similar pretenses to instruction on the cultivation of civilized satyriasis, but not one of them contains the amount of this *impedimenta* per issue as *Playboy*. Nor is it usually executed as cleverly. Considering its price, *Playboy* provides for the mental and physical adolescent an economical dose of his particular catnip, just as *Time* in its way does for his self-styled "influential" uncle, older brother—or alter-ego.

Time

What sort of mediums are these magazines?

They are both heavily dependent upon narrative and picture (particularly the latter) in communicating with readers. Why picture in the case of *Time*? First, the context of *Time* is set by its cover: one of three or four types of highly caricatured portraits of the "man (or woman) of the week:" usually a personality whose name is currently in the newspaper headlines or renowned in the world of upper middle-brow culture. This latter group includes high-brow scientists, artists and academicians.

The cover of *Time* is of crucial importance. It employs one superior picture (usually painted, but sometimes a photograph) to communicate the editorial stance of *Time*, the style of *Time*, and the intention of *Time*. It also indicates quite clearly, at the outset, by the treatment of its subject, that a *Time*-style trip through the "news" (including the biography of the cover figure) of the day will be as much a matter of emotional as cognitive

---

were usually required for membership. To be a "Playboy," all a male needs is enough money to join, which entirely is consistent with the magazine's orientation.

[6] While it is not the purpose of the chapter to discuss *Time* techniques of distorting the news under their rubric of "interpretive reporting," the reader may be interested in the following: Ben H. Bagdikian, "Bias in Weekly Newsmagazines," in Reo M. Christenson and Robert O. McWilliams (eds.), *Voices of the People* (New York: McGraw-Hill Book Company, Inc., 1962), pp. 148–164, and the evidence of Phil Kerby in Wilbur Schramm, *Responsibility in Mass Communications* (New York: Harper and Brothers, 1957), pp. 241–242, as well as Schramm's other and frequent references in the volume to the way in which *Time* (and other magazines) "manage" the news to confirm their editorial viewpoints.

involvement.[7] These implications are made before the magazine need be opened. Thus the first few pages' focus on the "hard" news of the week, probably of greater interest to men than women, is slightly feminized by the neatness and rhythm of its prose and the latent emotional power of the cover portrait.[8]

Pictures are also of psychological importance throughout the book. In fact, *Time*'s internal pictures are probably as significant to the emotional tonality of the magazine as *Playboy*'s. In *Time*, nearly every *other* story is accompanied by a photograph which—almost invariably—does not add to our cognitive knowledge of the article accompanying it, but instead, first, makes an emotional comment *on* the story and, second, on the entire page on which it appears. Thus will the commanding presence of a stereotyped military officer lend to a page a sense of authority; a movie star in a wild costume will set the emotional tone for lighter copy; an etching of an old fashioned school scene will provide a nostalgic motif. The exception is *Time*'s frequent use of clearly drawn, consistent and accurate maps and charts.

The masculine appeal of *Time* is therefore both subtle and double-barreled. As a magazine, it promises complete, revealing, virile treatment of whatever during the past week was "news" (which is a difficult matter to determine)[9] in a clear, cognitive context. However, from the minute one examines the cover to the moment he puts down the book, the promise is hedged. The motherly eye of *Time*'s editors are upon you, not so much interpreting the news (which its editors sometimes indirectly admit) or providing a much needed background to understand the stories, but to *steer* you *emotionally* through the non-cognitive landscape from pity to anger to despair to love to laughter, all in the context of the "news of the week" just past.[10] Here is the second masculine appeal: the gentle, mother-

[7] Some years ago, one of my students put together a full gallery of *Time* cover portraits in a class in propaganda analysis. The artistic treatment given Nikita Khrushchev by *Time*'s cover artists during periods of the "cold war," from frost to thaw, was impressive. The magazine's official "editorial attitude," as indicated in the "cover stories," was pictorially (and symbolically) displayed on the cover. These portraits tell the reader immediately who the "good guys" and the "bad guys" are!

[8] When a *Time* cover represents a generalization (the American youth; the scientist; the American woman) the picture is usually highly symbolic, extremely emotional, and clearly oriented towards psychological response, frequently at the expense of logic. It displays a kind of caricature-surrealism *sui generis*. These departures are out of *Time* character, and most *Time* covers are more conservative, symbolically. How interesting, however, that the editors of this enterprise seem willing to experiment with a crucial formula that has been so successful.

[9] The late A. J. Liebling was one of our most adroit recent commentators on the problem of what is and what is *not* news and how a news story can be fabricated out of events that did *not* happen. In *The Press* (New York: Ballantine Books, 1961), a number of his pieces on journalism and newspapers are reprinted. All are astute and enjoyable, but pay particular attention to the section entitled "No News," pp. 225–284, and recall that *Time* is written largely by "experts," in Liebling's sense.

[10] See Schramm, *op. cit.*, pp. 217–265, for a fair discussion of the role of the reporter and editor as guide to the reader through the complexities of so-called "hard" news.

hen editorial staff that massages the bruise of disenchantment and permits an irreverent laugh at the humorous things men do in the subsequent sections headed *Modern Living, Books, Medicine, Education*, and so forth.

The *Time* formulae have been immensely popular in the United States, and have spawned good imitators. While the magazine is widely admired overseas, however, it is not much duplicated by foreign publishers, for a number of possible reasons. First, its sweet-and-sour, hard-soft, masculine appeal may more or less reflect peculiar psychological needs of American men. Second, journals of overt opinion are more the rule than the exception in other nations, where newspapers are more closely related than in America to political life, and where wide differences of political opinion are represented by more than two political parties. A French *Time* might therefore be no novelty, because many daily French newspapers frequently indulge in little *except* interpretive reporting, and its interpretations might necessarily be bewilderingly complex because they stray far beyond politics.

Playboy

As a masculine magazine, *Playboy* appears to be a more cut-and-dried item. Its appeal is immediate and sensual—an emotional double martini delivered monthly to the apparently sex-obsessed subscriber. Unfortunately, the explanation of its popularity is not this simple, nor is the translation of its languages into logical and psychological sense so facile.

Playboy's cognitive content is enormous. The book itself is filled with ideas; simple ideas, pat ideas, neurotic ideas, unpopular ideas, foolish ideas —but ideas. In this sense, it is far more an intellectual journal than *Time*. While it deals with the here and now (cooking, books, recordings, etc.), its editors are essentially *interested* in the ideas they bespeak and *interested* in communicating them to the reader. Mr. Heffner's "philosophy," for all the jokes that have been made about it, is a perfectly legitimate (and relatively harmless) re-expression of the now familiar American "fun morality." Man's state is such, says this sub-ethic, that he will do well to extract as much fun from life as possible. If you are not having fun, there is something the matter with *you*—not with your society or culture or education. This is a familiar cultural stance.[11]

Because Heffner places the burden of his modern hedonism largely on sex, and because the book flays noisily (and mostly) the dead horse of Victorianism, *Playboy* constitutes a virtual masturbatory fantasy-universe in

11 Where does one begin citation concerning the "fun morality"? Erich Fromm, *The Sane Society* (New York: Rinehart and Company, Inc., 1955), and many of the essays in David Riesman, *Individualism Reconsidered* (Glencoe, Ill.: The Free Press, 1954), are basic. Two fairly recent (and different), soft-cover books may be of interest to students of this topic. See Viktor E. Frankl, *Man's Search for Meaning* (New York: Washington Square Press, Inc., 1963), and Hendrik M. Ruitenbeck, *The Individual and the Crowd*, previously cited. Of course, familiar works by Margaret Mead, C. Wright Mills, J. K. Galbraith and others also constitute much of the literature on this topic.

the first instance, and a realistic assessment of the cultural-behavioral status quo in the second. In other words, *Playboy* brings the male reader the best of two possible worlds: slick but false aphrodisiacs (in narrative, pictures and drama) for the purposes of self-stimulation, (inevitably offering grist for the mill of *fantasy* of some kind) and workable instructions, hints and case studies, concerning how to deal with the relatively banal realities of post-Victorian license that obtain now in society which, evidently, cause single (and perhaps married) men no end of concern.[12]

Pictures are, of course, also important in *Playboy*, but, because Heffner uses so *many* of them, they have less relative stylistic importance to his book than the pictures in *Time*, and they probably yield less cognitive content. *Playboy appears* to be highly pictorial—the one characteristic it took intact from its parent *Esquire*—and, despite the degree of selection that the editors purportedly attempt to employ, a shotgun visual approach seems to have been used in each issue. Next to stylized Petty and Varga-type females, one may find an excellent color photography travel spread, fascinating caricatures, or highly suggestive (and emotionally viable) non-naturalistic illustrations for a story: first rate drawings, attitudinally as different from the nude center-spread as Zane Grey from Proust. *Playboy*'s catholicity is enormous in regard to pictures, and because it is eclectic, no *single* picture—as a picture—means much, even the monthly "Playgirl" herself. There are too many similar to, or different from, it—too many alternatives, too many obviously different styles and intentions piled pictorially into one book. While this makes logical sense, it provides psychological confusion that is resolved only when the reader understands the objects of the confusion: first, ammunition for fantasy, and second, hints for "living."

Some of the worst pictorial work technically and stylistically—and the least interesting photographs—occasionally provide considerable cognitive material; when it is Jane Fonda or the latest version of Brigitte Bardot *specifically* who is the victim of *Playboy*'s retouch artists, a cognitive chain of reactions is set up that influences emotions far beyond the pure potential of the photographs, which may be second-rate. When the right amount of spare narrative accompanies a story about a peculiarly "different" *specific* "Playgirl," the psychological appeal to fantasy becomes limitless. The newsstands are cleared of the book thereafter in a matter of a few days. Heffner, however, cannot, it seems, use this device profitably more than (roughly) twice a year.

Magazine Drama

What interests one most sharply about both of these male-oriented publications is their use of the dramatic medium. Here again, they are quite similar, and this phenomenon is probably another symptom of the predom-

[12] For a theologian's opinions of the social and spiritual weakness of this stance see the highly pertinent section in Harvey Cox, *The Secular City*, pp. 199–204.

inantly male appeal. *Time* still lives in the image of radio's ancient *The March of Time*. Each week's developments in history and culture are part of an unfolding *drama of progress*, narrated for us by an unheard Westbrook Van Voorhis, who turns even the most abstruse intellectual developments in Western thought into personalized or institutional conflicts with winners and losers, happy or sad endings. This effect is often most difficult to achieve.[13] It is perhaps most noticeable in the *Time* "Essays," where a current social, cultural or philosophic issue is dramatized and boiled down to about two pages with such consistency as to make the problems and (inevitable) solutions, of homosexuality, foreign trade and air-pollution seem almost identical.

Playboy's god-head is different. The higher pitched tones of Heffner's directives tend to turn life—and particularly one's sex life, although not limited to sex—into one of the many games people play: impromptu dramas that repeat *ad infinitum* simplistic boy-meets-girl, boy-makes-girl and boy-drops-girl plots. The readers find themselves caught in the drama. Writes Harvey Cox, "Obsequiously waiting for the latest signals on what is cool and what is awkward, they are paralyzed by the fear that they may hear pronounced on them that dread sentence occasionally intoned by 'The Playboy Advisor': 'you goofed!' Leisure is thus swallowed up in (the) apprehension . . . (and) self destructive compulsion to consume only what is *a la mode*." [14] The word is given in *Playboy* and, as Cox notes, a highly synthetic doctrine of life is published—a fake little immorality play with the reader as Everyman.[15]

The reader is assured in *Playboy*, deviously but insistently, that the status quo contains little that he cannot manage and that everything will turn out all right. This moment—the present period of our post-Victorian technology—is the apogee of all civilization, and we are now living through

[13] The late Edward R. Murrow embued his nightly news broadcasts with a similar sense of drama, a medium upon which he had evidently learned to draw upon extensively during his World War II experiences in London and Europe. Murrow was nicknamed the "voice of doom." The voice of *Time* is the voice of optimism, essentially the voice of a benevolent god. This is the major intentional and stylistic difference between the two, which accounts for their enormous logical, and less noticeable psychological, variance. For the text of Murrow's news broadcasts see Edward R. Murrow, *In Search of Light* (New York: Alfred A. Knopf, 1967). The dramatization of news presents countless problems, and the similarities and differences between Murrow's virile methods and *Time*'s are interesting variations on the same theme, particularly since Murrow's and Van Voorhis' actual *voices* were similiar.

[14] Cox, *op. cit.*, pp. 202–203.

[15] Cox continues with the probable speculation that *Playboy*'s little dramas are actually most appealing to males who are *afraid* of genuine sexual involvements and help to minimize the terror of sex by keeping it idealized on the one hand, and at a safe distance on the other. Cox contends that the Playboy mystique is "antisexual" (not anti-male), and his point is well taken. There is less genuine extra-curricular sex-play on view at the *Playboy* clubs in America than at the average suburban roadhouse! (Try to proposition a "Bunny," for instance!) What the clubs abound in, is suggestiveness and talk, but rarely does one discover much "action" there, or so the author has been told.

a unique and salubrious liberation in style of life. As in *Time,* all issues are simplified by dramatization, just as they are humanized by it, with the difference that intention and style bespeak what appears to be less emphasis upon contemporary political attitudes in *Playboy* than in *Time.*[16]

Women's Magazines

Because they eventually purchase much of our nation's consumer goods and services[17] and because they have the leisure to read them and the money to buy them, a great part of the periodical market is directed, in one way or another, to a female readership.[18] One may start with *Seventeen* and finally arrive at *Vogue,* stopping off at *Life, Look, Redbook, Mademoiselle, Woman's Day, Family Circle, The Saturday Evening Post,* and numerous magazines like them to justify the assumption that many periodicals have been prepared with a keen eye on the "female market," which is to say that their editors believe they are communicating predominantly with women.[19]

They are apparently effective instruments of communication, whether or not with their intended audience, it is difficult to guess. *The Saturday Evening Post,* for instance, appears to be less capable at present than it once was in serving as a "family" journal, no doubt due to the increasing specialization of magazines. It is doubtless having difficulties in finding for itself a specific, interested *significant* female audience. This, at least, is what the book's advertisers believe, and he who pays the piper calls the tune. The high-style feminine magazines and the homemaker's journals undoubtedly are channelled directly to certain groups of women, and are read almost exclusively by them. *Life* and *Look* are more bi-sexually oriented. *Look,* with its color pictures bled to the margins, specializes, however, in the "exclusive" sort of "inside-dopester" material many women, particularly, enjoy, such as Manchester's *Death of a President* and similar types of personal journalism. *Life* is hardly less sentimental and sensational than *Look,* although its physical format might lead one to think otherwise.[20]

---

[16] *Playboy* is by no means *afraid* of *unconventional* politics. In fact, it probably gives a more complete hearing, in its transcribed tape-recorded interviews with political gadflies, to unconventional political viewpoints than *Time* does. Norman Mailer, the late Lincoln Rockwell, the Black Power people, John Birchers and others have all had opportunities to present their cases in *Playboy.* Whether *Playboy's* political coverage is taken as seriously by its readers as is *Time's,* is another matter. Both books have a conservative political tone when they speak for themselves editorially, although *Playboy seems* more tolerant than *Time* of exponents of social ideas in contravention of accepted values and traditions, including politics.

[17] See Max Lerner, *America as a Civilization,* pp. 253–257.

[18] Outside of a few books and articles written by feminists like Margaret Mead and Ashley Montagu, one of the most realistic and original volumes on the American woman *per se* is the much-hated volume, Eric John Dingwall's, *The American Woman* (New York: A Signet Book, 1957). Dingwall is British and, presumably, had neither an axe to grind nor an American wife to face.

[19] The nature of the female audience—or the myth of it—is discussed in Robert C. O'Hara, *Media for the Millions,* pp. 38–39.

[20] Recently *Life* took open and obvious pride in its pages that it had exposed a dog's

So wide is the spectrum here that there is little point in a close examination of one or two of these magazines. Whatever is "female" in them is highly variable. Women are not spoken to as women as frequently as they are addressed in terms of the *social role* they play: housewife, 'teenager, matron, career girl, etc. Men, as we have seen, do not appear to be classified this discretely by many periodical communications.

As for mediums, there appears to be little question: women's magazines, like many American popular periodicals, rely more fully upon the medium of picture than either narrative or drama. Today, they utilize the technique of photographs primarily. In fact, still photographs for these journals require peculiar technical skills and specialities: high fashion photography, theatre photography, travel photographs, etc. They speak an eloquent, if superficial, language of imagery, usually extremely logical and gratifying psychologically. Most of the photographs make *sense*, even if the things they show us do not. Green nail polish and purple lipstick, "mod" fashions, surgical procedures in color, interior decorations, and many other pictorial subjects appear quite senseless but breathtaking, one imagines, to most female readers. The photographer—the single most important communicator addressing this female audience—is something of a psychologist rather than an artist. He (and the picture editor) calculate the emotive power, less of the photograph itself, than *what is photographed* and *how it is shown*. Much poor photography, stylistically, is in evidence, therefore, in these magazines displaying a countless number of bizarre but arresting subjects.

Narrative is another matter. The most noticeable characteristic of the prose in women's magazines is that, in style tone and intention, it is nearly all identical. Not only is it highly similar when written anonymously, writers who are given by-lines in *Life* and *Look* use similar vocabularies and utilize the medium of narrative in much the same manner.[21] Whether this is the result of conscious imitation or the horizontal professional mobility of middle-class magazine writers and editors in the United States is irrelevant. The important matter is that the female audience appears either to

"concentration camp" (where animals were sold for scientific experimentation), and the proprietor was brought to law. While feeling sympathetic towards abolishing unnecessary cruelty to animals, the sensational coverage (in pictures mostly) of this story impels one to wonder whether its publication was motivated by outrage or the need for circulation, particularly in the light of the immense cruelty to *people* that occurs within a square mile of the Time-Life Building on Sixth Avenue in New York that *Life*'s photographers *might* have shown. The dog problem could have been handled most efficiently by a call to the ASPCA. One formula, however, that *Life* seems to have found successful is to print frequent photographs of animals (many of them laboratory animals) either at work and/or in pain.

21 This observation is not as pertinent to upper-middle-brow publications like *The New Yorker* or *The Saturday Review* as it is to their middle-brow counterparts. Obviously, writers for these publications modify their work according to what they perceive the style of each to be. The editors make numerous transparent changes, but many of their authors maintain, at least, a vestige of their individuality.

have been trained to demand—or accept—*one* type of narrative prose predominantly in their periodicals, even in most of the fiction.

The narrative displays a cognitive bias, rarely to a profound or unsettling depth. This is because the style is glib, superficial, conversational, attitudinally directed to an audience seemingly regarded as quite inferior intellectually to the writers. The author is also frequently *alarmed* (demonstrating definite hortatory qualities) about certain topics, but the alarm is usually tempered with assurances that the problem is, in fact, under control and everything will end happily.

Two nice youngsters, for instance, who look as if they are heading for a date are really dope addicts after a "fix." This emotional jolt is followed by prose which tells us implicitly that these youngsters are, despite contrary evidence, just healthy, clean-cut kids who went astray, down the "path" of heroin addiction. The pictures belie the prose in this famous case, however, not alone by virtue of their photographic clarity exposing a fascinating subject, but because the topic is more cognitively complex and emotionally threatening to the reader than the editors of *Life* were able to control. (Like it or not, the reader of the magazine has to face up to the hard fact that here may be an *insoluble* problem that must get worse before it gets better. And that all the slick talk in the world will not change one jot or tittle the real lives with which *Life* has played.)[22]

That highly superficial material may be so richly emotionally toned is explained by four factors: first, the use of idioms and clichés evoke ready-made responses to sloganlike prose; second, the topics on which the editors center with great care reflect an intense preoccupation with some changing fad or fancy;[23] third, their pictorial accouterments are striking; and fourth, they fuse their narrative discourses with dramatizations. Like the men's magazines, the art of re-enactment is employed in these periodicals, but in a more subtle manner. The writing is frequently directed to "you," the reader, but "you" in a role which the particular article (or magazine) chooses.

The reader's role in this drama is clearer even than the *Playboy* image. It is "you" the mother, "you" the last virgin 'teenager, "you" the home decorator, "you" the cook, "you" the guardian of family morality, "you" the intellectual pace-setter of a household, or some other specific, well-delineated, acceptable female role, current in our culture. Unlike the men's magazines, the roles the readers (the "yous") play are always central parts in *morality* plays, designed to enhance the status and value of the woman reader as *something special*, rarely just a woman, and just as rarely a *person*

---

[22] This particular feature (one of the most shocking ever run in a popular magazine) was published separately in paperback form, so great was its sales potential.

[23] A single copy of a magazine of this kind which is a year old is an antique. While the male-oriented periodicals remain at least amusing for some time after their publication, these women-oriented journals are—except for cooking columns and special features— "dead issues" shortly after their publication.

coeval with men.[24] The "voice of doom" rarely speaks from the woman's magazine. Instead we hear the "voice of reason," asking mom to please her man with an Italian crumb cake, or an Italian bikini, or a morsel of gossip from the Italian Riviera. In fact, it does not even ask. The voice *tells* her that she is already "engaged" in the topic simply because she bought the magazine, and therefore Jacqueline Onassis' mother's problems and prejudices are, in some manner, *hers*, whether she likes it or not.

Erich Kahler brings up another problem[25] that relates to most magazines but is most acute in these particular periodicals. He is distressed by the speed and callousness with which these eclectic journals turn from the tragic or pathetic to the comic and trivial. He is offended by the fact that one may turn, with the flip of a page, from horrible scenes of the destruction of war and grief and death, to the sweet life of Miami millionaires or the mating habits of wild geese or movie stars. Many find these rapid transitions disturbing; it is difficult to concentrate on an article on underground movies immediately after having read about (and seen pictures of) children with brain damage. This concern is valid, but auditors like Kahler may be unnecessarily sensitive to the implications of mere humanism unleashed by the modern techniques of communication on, most particularly, the female American.

In point of fact, this humanistic *mish-mash* need not be felt as more unsettling than the assortment of objects a woman puts into her handbag. A bottle of contact lens fluid will lie beside lethal barbiturates, a good luck charm next to tranquilizers, a driver's license beside a photograph of a friend, and so forth. A woman is likely to jam symbols of the full range of her psychological life into her handbag and regard it as nothing more than an article of dress. Men also fill their pockets and wallets with miscellany. But the American woman's handbag, full of serious, necessary "junk," is an excellent analogy for (and also an accurate equivalent of) the periodicals she reads. Both are representative of a life style that (as Kahler believes) may grow calluses on human sensitivities and encourage superficial relationships with life's significant symbols. He is probably correctly describing a state of affairs about which little can be done.

Comics and Children

Some few years ago the present author wrote a minor essay on the comics in an anthology on the "funny papers," in company with a number of other interested observers of this aspect of American letters.[26] At that

---

[24] This type of communication occurs in *The Reader's Digest* as well as the magazines above. But, in the "little wonder," you can determine the sex of the hero of the drama (the "you") in each article; that is, you can label the pieces "male," "female" or "neuter." The majority appear to be "female."

[25] Erich Kahler, *The Tower and the Abyss*, pp. 94–95.

[26] George N. Gordon, "Can Children Corrupt Our Comics?" in David M. White and

time, connections between his then scattered conclusions concerning the
logics and psychologics of communication had not been developed to their
present state. What the article suggested—and is suggested once more here
—is that the characters of children as portrayed in the comics are more accurate (hence "realer") psychologically, than the children portrayed by any
other middle-class oriented mass communication. The main cause for this,
it was hypothesized, lay in the fact that most comic strip artists who portray
children are themselves relatively childlike or remember the realities of their
own childhood more vividly than many other communicators.[27] They therefore call upon a "direct line" to the world of childhood which they subsequently portray in their supposedly artificial or satirical (but in some ways
quite literal) comic strips. The article produced evidence from the work of
many talented comic strip artists to support this contention.

Since that time, conversations with dozens of cartoonists have revealed
that none of them—even those cited as near geniuses at the portrayal of the
non-innocence of childhood—had read the article or showed the least interest in it! One might suppose that this bears out the contention of the piece.
Children themselves, for instance, rarely read books on child psychology,
and perhaps it is best that cartoonists continue to practice their art without
undue self-consciousness.

Many comic artists are, of course, neither comics nor artists, nor are all
of them experts at communication, logical or psychological. The American
comic strip is an artifact of culture which was developed as a sub-division of
journalism. It manifests, historically, its own cults, mythologies, trends and
schools, largely unrecorded.[28] One of the cleverest cartoonists at work today
(and creator of two adventure strips) cannot draw a line. The "dean of
American cartoonists" has not published a picture in years and is among
the poorest artists in his profession. One of our most popular comic strips is
little more than a reactionary political diatribe. Some of the busiest and
most fully syndicated comic strip artists, whose signatures one sees daily in
the newspapers, have been dead for years, even decades! The world of the
professional cartoonist is one of the last zany outposts of technological communications that has not been despoiled by group-think, conformity, criti-

Robert H. Abel (eds.), *The Funnies, An American Idiom* (New York: The Free
Press of Glencoe, 1963), 158–176.

[27] Novelists are also included here. Mark Twain and Richard Hughes are considered
by some the only recent authors who can hold a candle to the best of our cartoonists
in portraying children. Charles Dickens might be cited, but some of his children are
obvious fakes. Salinger, Golding, Saroyan, and their ilk have created their children in
the mold of the women's magazines, the films and television. They are as "real" as the
Monkees or the Disney kids.

[28] A cultural history of the American comic strip is much needed by serious students
of this communications instrument. But two good histories of the comics themselves
(copiously illustrated) are Coughton Waugh, *The Comics* (New York: The Macmillan Company, 1947), and Stephen Becker, *Comic Art in America* (New York: Simon
& Schuster, 1959). For a complete bibliography of extant works on the comics to
date see White and Abel, *op. cit.*, pp. 293–304.

cal cultism or the tyranny of market research. It is a world of individualists, and much of the cartoonists' work, fortunately, shows it.

Folklore aside, the comic strip, or single panel cartoon, presents to the communications analyst something of an immediate problem because its mediums do not reflect noticeably the previously discussed biases of most other communications techniques. Its aesthetics—or logics—also seem to be dictated in large measure by the conventions of newspaper composition.

The comics are, of course, largely pictorial mediums of communication and thereby respond to the general logical and psychological observations we have made about pictures.[29] The degree of intrusion of the dramatic medium into the comic strip, however, determines how closely the strip itself adheres to a different aesthetic, and how distinctive the particular strip is from other non-serialized types of pictures. The main aspect of drama which the comic strip displays is *action* and, in the degree that the strip is propelled by action, *it* is also dramatic. The now defunct *Toonerville Trolley* panels, for instance, and most political cartoons, are single pictures. Some, like *Our Boarding House*, are almost static tableaus. In these instances, the medium employed is logically predominantly *pictorial*. In an action episode of a serious comic like *Steve Canyon*, or a funny one like *Smokey Stover*, the dominant logical medium is re-enactment or drama, with picture playing a less significant role, logically at least, in the communication.

How much does the comic strip depend upon narrative? Milton Caniff's comment that he thinks of himself neither as a writer, nor as an artist, but as a "journalist," is revealing. Comic themes and comic stories have, since their earliest days, been concerned with matters of morals, ethics, social and political issues (political cartoonists were among the inventors of the cartoon technique). In this sense, *all* comic strips are narrative. That is, they introduce—usually covertly—at least one thematic undertone which rides along with the strip, year in and year out, and which, in a multitude of metamorphoses, replays, in different dramatic formats, reformulations of the didactic-narrative theme. *Blondie*, considered by many cartoonists the "perfect" strip, is an excellent example. Certain concepts of the married American male, his work and home life, his family, his wife, his relationships with others, as well as many aspects of middle-class life, are discussed repeatedly in the "thesis" of the strip. This is artist Chic Young's narrative *raison d'être*, intentional or otherwise, and his work may be studied in these terms for its developments and changes since 1930 when it began.

The psychological side of this particular instrument of communication is another matter, and a bewildering one. It is, of course, a false legend that the comic strip audience is made up of children;[30] more than half the comic

---

[29] See Chapter 9.
[30] See Edward J. Robinson and David M. White, "Who Reads the Funnies—and Why?" in White and Abel, *op. cit.*, pp. 179–189.

strip readers in the U.S.A. are adults, and a good proportion of them are probably well-educated adults. There is no other explanation for the extraordinary popularity of sophisticated strips like the former *Krazy Kat*,[31] *Peanuts, Miss Peach* or *Pogo*. A naïve children's audience is reached on one level of apprehension, while such strips also satisfy interested, educated adults on another. Cartoons pop up on the walls of graduate science departments at noted universities; they have been sent to the author in the mail by professional writers, critics and aestheticians, and he has shared the comic pages of a local newspaper with a Nobel laureate in a "think tank." [32]

Do comic strips appeal to sophisticated and civilized sensitivities in the young or infantile and regressive impulses in adults? Both, one would guess, but more of the latter than the former. Responsible observers doubt [33] that psychological or intellectual damage is done to either children or adults by comics, although a considerable stir was raised a decade or more ago by the noted psychiatrist, Dr. Frederic Wertham. He blamed much contemporary juvenile crime on comic strips, particularly upon serious or "horror" comics which, at that time, were widely circulated in magazine form.[34] The comics have quieted down noticeably since Dr. Wertham rang his alarm bell fourteen years ago. The rate of juvenile delinquency, though, is presently at an all time high! So far, no single set of causal factors—including the influence of violence as depicted on the many devices of mass communication—appear to function as more than contributing agents to the commission of anti-social acts by children.

One may regard with earned charity the unquestionably infantile symbolic appeal at the heart of the popularity of the comic strip. Here is a form, first, of augmented reading which provides dramatic and pictorial zest by means of the technique of printed pictures that words alone cannot provide. Granted that the *Classic Comic* magazines are mere literary shadows of the stories they re-tell, and, as a substitute for reading, such fare is pallid. On the other hand, comics of many sorts obviously serve to introduce the young to more mature reading experiences. They also provide psychological retreat from the fatigue of both the printed and spoken word for adults who live in an overly verbal environment.

So much for their values as augmentation and relief. Comics are but

[31] Connoisseurs of comics consider *Krazy Kat* an artistic achievement unequaled in quality by means of any other mass communication technique—including the cinema—of the past century. Are they over-enthusiastic? The reader is referred to the anthology, George Herriman, *Krazy Kat* (New York: Henry Holt, 1946). A new edition of this book is long overdue.

[32] Adults often admit to severe apprehensions when they see their children devouring comic books, but this particular diet is probably far healthier for them than the equivalent doses of nonsense portrayed on our television screens.

[33] See the essay, "Paul, the Horror Comics and Dr. Wertham," in Robert Warshow, *The Immediate Experience* (Garden City, N.Y.: Doubleday and Company, Inc., 1962), pp. 83–104.

[34] See Frederic Wertham, *Seduction of the Innocent* (New York: Rinehart and Co., 1954).

slightly different from other technological pictorial devices. Most specifically, they are printed, segmented (usually) into panels, sequential, either in story line or by utilizing a set group of characters, from day to day, from Sunday to Sunday, or from magazine publication date to publication date. Their similarity to other communication techniques is illustrated by the way in which they easily cross the barriers of communication technology. *Tarzan* and the *Lone Ranger* are excellent examples of successful comics which were, in the first instance, initially novelized and, in the second, broadcast on radio. Both have also been successful on photographic and electronic screens. At the height of their popularity, many mass communications figures, from Charlie Chaplin to The Beatles, have found their way into comic strips, with good reason. They display a psychological flexibility in the juxtaposition of picture (which provides the illusion of reality) to characterization and dramatic action (which provides gratifications similar to those of the screen or stage).

Psychologically, therefore, the comics may be one of the most potentially protean devices among the languages of communications. Considering the scope of their enterprises—from the political cartoons of Herblock, to the World War II drawings of Mauldin, to the inanities of *Dick Tracy*, to the wildness of the *Katzenjammer Kids,* to the spiritual civilities of the *Peanuts* crowd, and the glorious libidinal Cocomo County of our beloved *Krazy Kat*—the comics may well hold out today's greatest potential of *all* our communication techniques for the giant pragmatic step from popular to fine art.

Or have they already? Definitely not. Although the individual cartoonist (at his best) may ask for special *sympathies* from his audience, he does not require especially sharpened sensibilities or trained perceptions to be fully appreciated. He therefore differs fundamentally from the fine artist. What special qualities of mind are necessary to enjoy *Miss Peach?* None, (although a decade or two as a schoolteacher does no harm in heightening one's sense of the relevance of the strip to real life).

Cartoonists laugh when they are called "artists" and do not like to be taken seriously. They are probably the only group of mass communicators who display this trait almost to a man,[35] except for an occasional political cartoonist, most of whom appear to regard their cartooning more earnestly than their politics.

Conclusions

In this chapter we have first taken cognizance of the enormity of the "communication market" in technological societies, particularly those

[35] Even Rube Goldberg who, at 85, turned from cartooning to sculpture, refuses to discuss seriously either his drawings or his new and delightful statues. His attitude is gratifying and typical of the cartoonist's irreverence toward his own art. See *Rube Goldberg vs. The Machine Age*, edited by Clark Kinnaird and Ralph Hollenbeck (New York: Hastings House, Publishers, 1968).

which have developed semi-literate masses. Relatively new channels of communication were opened by technology, and with the development of these markets, new techniques of reaching publics were also evolved. A few of them, utilizing the technology of the press, were discussed in the chapter, not only in terms of their quality as instruments for the dissemination of cognitions and emotions, but in relation, as well, to the special audiences they appear to satisfy. Recognizing that a review of the entire scope of middle-brow communications is beyond the purview of this book, three classes of communication were differentially discussed: men's magazines, women's magazines and comics.

Publications for men were examined by singling out two distinct types: *Time* and *Playboy*. Attention was called less to the cognitive aspects of these communications than to their emotive and stylistic qualities, which were explained in terms of the many psychological functions each appears to perform, in its own way, for the male reader.

The spectrum of women's magazines was examined more broadly—from *Woman's Day* to *Vogue*—and an attempt was made to find common qualities of communication in them related to the widely variant audiences (including men and children) that they seem to attract. *Look* and *Life*, as pictorial-narrative-dramatic instruments, were given special attention because of their status of "family communications" and the wide range of interests they share. The rapidity with which they move from feature to feature and topic to topic in a single edition was also considered, as well as their tendency to function as immediate exponents of transient environmental values which fall into rapid obsolescence.

Our last look was an admittedly sentimental one at the comics, emphasizing the basically ingenious nature of this communications device: highly dramatic and pictorial, distributed by the same technology (the press) that is responsible for spreading the narrative medium to millions of our population. The adult appeal of the comics was discussed, as well as their psychological relationship to the cognitions and emotions of children. We also noted the way in which comic strip characters and themes have been borrowed from, and used by, other devices of communication. A sanguine future for the comic strip as art was also predicted, although reservations as to its role as *fine* art were entered into the discussion.

Chapter 18

SCREENS

THE BASIC procedure for all kinds of moving pictures centers on a technique of transferring a picture to some kind of plane or screen. The screen may be of almost any size: a square perhaps; the so-called "golden section" with a width 1.33 times the height; or *Cinemascope* in which the ratio of width to height is seven to three. The screen may be a flat screen, a curved screen, a screen of linen or plastic, or the screen found in our television sets consisting of a blown glass surface coated with chemicals. The screen may conceivably take the form of a three dimensional 360° sphere or a section of a sphere.[1] It may also be the retina of an eyeball.

There exist today two fundamental devices for transferring moving pictures onto screens, and two so-called "art forms" have been named after these technologies. They *are* actually differential art forms only to the extent, for instance, that lithography is differentiated from photo-engraving; that is, they represent different technologies requiring different skills, different talents and different knowledges. Some day these devices may (and probably *will*) take their place beside a third, fourth or fifth method of transferring a motion picture to a screen. Or perhaps, employing new instruments of projection, a "screen" of sorts will be created in *thin air* or where two or more "beams" of energy (light or laser) intersect.

One method involves rapid photography of moving images and their transference into sequences of pictures onto perforated celluloid that are projected quickly as discrete images. The other involves a more complicated process by which an image is transferred into electrical impulses, stored as magnetic charges on plastic tape, or translated directly into light and dark and colored lines on a screen or projection device. These two instruments,

[1] For a discussion of various shapes of screens, see Ivor Montagu, *Film World* (Hammondsworth, Middlesex, England: Penguin Books, Inc., 1964), pp. 78–92, and especially his chart of differential aspect ratios on p. 89.

one photographic and the other electronic, we define, first, as cinema (or film or movies), and second as television.[2]

Although they were invented more than a generation apart, they are highly similar *communication* techniques. Except for differences in manners of their distribution and reception (which are rapidly diminishing), they are, in fact, *identical* techniques from a logical point of view for the utilization of the picture medium. They manifest slightly different psychological characteristics, largely because of yet unsolved technological problems and the methods by which they are distributed.[3]

The proportions, size or nearness of a screen to a viewer appear to make less psychological difference to him than was expected by early film and television innovators.[4] Common sense (and logic) provides the limits of the difference, not aesthetics or psychologics. *Cinerama's* scenic films profited, for quite a time, from the giant curved screen that provided a slight illusion of perspective. Television producers tend to confine their films, tapes and live performances to "medium shots" and "close ups" and, wherever possible, stay away from panoramas. They do not use this technique because of any innate qualities of the television camera or recording equipment, but simply because, at present, most viewers observe *this* type of picture on relatively small sceens. The same sort of observation may be made of the use of color in the movies: where and when color is relevant to the dramatic or narrative quality of the pictures, it enhances the qualities of communication—for example, in most of the children's entertainments

[2] *Ibid.*, pp. 11–92 provides a clear explanation of how and why the motion pictures "work" along with a thumbnail sketch of the major historical events that contributed to the near-perfection of certain kinds of motion picture technology. Because television employs electronic (rather than mechanical) methods of transmission, its operation—still something of a mystery even to experts—is more difficult to explain in non-technical language. See Sidney Head, *Broadcasting in America* (Boston: Houghton Mifflin Company, 1956), pp. 42-73, which also contains some material on motion pictures and describes the perceptual processes involved in both cinema and television illusions.
[3] For example, conventional black and white entertainment films shown *in toto* on television are probably perceived psychologically by most people in much the same way they would be in a near empty motion picture theatre. The presence or absence of an audience and differential conditions of performance (home or theatre) circumscribes the limits of psychological differences between the two instruments, in this instance.
[4] There are many good film histories, some illustrated profusely, some mostly descriptive. Among them is Arthur Knight, *The Liveliest Art* (New York: Mentor Books, 1959); and one of its most valuable features is its list of *100 Best Books on Films*, pp. 313–328, a well-annotated bibliography. Comparable works do not as yet exist for television, except for A. William Bluem, *Documentary in American Television* (New York: Hastings House, 1965), and sections here and there in Gilbert Seldes, *The Public Arts* (New York: Simon & Schuster, 1956). Most books on television are either critical, analytic or supportive essays about the instrument as a social, artistic, political or economic force in society. An authoritative, objective history of the instrument of television in the U.S.A. and abroad would fill a gap in the literature of mass communications. Charles Siepmann, incidentally, notes this lacuna in his article "The Missing Literature of Television" in the compendium, *The Eighth Art* (New York: Holt, Rinehart and Winston, 1962), pp. 215-225.

produced by the Disney studios. When color is irrelevant, as in many television programs, or in logically biased films (like *La Strada, High Noon* or *The Spy Who Came in from the Cold*) its absence is irrelevant. Viewing a color film on a television screen in black and white that does *not* profit from the added element of color confirms this immediately.

Multiplicity, shape and manipulation of screens and shapes of the camera aperture[5] appear to make both logical and psychological impressions on audiences, but seem to be less significant than the impression of the very presence of the *screen itself* on the same audience. In other words, a moving picture on a screen is perceived by an audience habituated to television and films for just what it is: a moving picture on a television or fabric screen. At the New York World's Fair in 1965–66, the delightful film *To Be Alive* was projected on multiple screens to achieve a number of interesting pictorial effects. Yet, the audience leaving the performance invariably talked about "the movie" they had seen. Might the effects have been achieved as neatly without the screen acrobatics or by dividing *one* screen into thirds? Possibly. Film demonstrations of this sort were also given at the Expo '67 in Montreal the following year. They raised more questions than they answered, about screens, at least.

At the former exposition, a night-club style "review" mixed live action with pictures on screens. The dividing line between the two was not only obvious, it was utilized for interesting novelty effects. When a filmed character handed a rose to a live performer (who pulled a real rose from behind the screen) the effect was immediately delightful, mostly *because* of the intensive consciousness of the audience of the screen.[6]

Of course, we are seeing pictures of two kinds when we witness such film and live action combinations. We are watching pictures, passed to the retinas of our eyes, of living people, "real" scenery, props and so forth, lit and framed in a certain way by our angle of vision—*and* we are watching pictures moving on screens.[7]

[5] Some experiments in clever variations of these are described in Knight, *op. cit.*, pp. 288–312.

[6] If a critic or historian like Allardyce Nicoll, for instance, claims that the films are *realer* than a real-life theatrical performance, he is taking for granted the basic artificiality of the medium of picture itself. That is, he has subsumed the screen psychologically into his perceptions and thence proceeds to examine the apparent ruthless reality of the camera—its "psychological penetration," in his terms—vis-à-vis the more blurred vision the average spectator receives of the stage in a legitimate theatre. He views incorrectly the theatre, therefore, as a repository of theatrical non-naturalism, while the film, for him, is a naturalistic method of communication. See Allardyce Nicoll "Film Reality and the Theatre" in Daniel Talbot (ed.), *Film, An Anthology* (Berkeley and Los Angeles: University of California Press, 1966), pp. 33–50.

[7] In the case of the so-called three-dimensional films, wearing glasses or without them, we are also watching screens, the images upon which are playing slight tricks on our perceptors and giving us an illusion *more like* our normal vision (but not identical with it) than the two-dimensional pictures to which we are accustomed on conventional screens.

Silent Screens

In 1938, about a decade after the large-scale advent of talking films, Rudolph Arnheim wrote a fascinating (and still relevant) essay about the obvious artistic superiority of silent films over the talking picture.[8] As a psychologist, Arnheim's empirical judgments were sound. "The average talking film today," he writes, "endeavors to combine visually poor scenes full of dialogue with the completely different traditional style of rich silent action. In comparison with the epoch of the silent film there is also an impressive decline of artistic excellence, in the average films as well as in the peak productions, a trend that cannot be due entirely to the ever-increasing industrialization." [9]

Arnheim's argument is based in part upon the "media fallacy," specifically that the silent film is one specific medium and sound film is another, and they cannot—or should not—combine. While *his* distinctions between mediums are sounder and clearer than those of McLuhan and others were to be a decade and a half later, Arnheim arrives oddly at an entirely logical conclusion when he moves from his illogical assumption to conclusions. Granting the assumptions, he makes his case for the concrete reasons *why* the medium of pictures (in motion) is *frequently* most interesting when *not* interfered with by other mediums from a psychological viewpoint.

By no means does this mean that a fusion of sound and picture *cannot* be interesting—more interesting, sometimes, than either pictures or sound alone. What Arnheim observes correctly is one simple curiosity of many technological devices, motion pictures included, that both logically and psychologically, *any aspect of technology (or unit of it) tends to be most interesting when viewed in isolation.* Moving pictures on screens (regardless of how they get there) are no exception. Automobiles are most interesting as technological speed mechanisms in auto races—not on highways or in showrooms, where they perform *numerous* functions. A doorbell is as dull (but not as loud) as a door-knocker, until it is explored in isolation for its fascinating elemental technology. Examples may be cited *ad infinitum.* There is little question that what Arnheim noticed about motion pictures is true; they are generally most interesting when viewed just as *motion pictures,* and his psychological arguments are as relevant to this obvious truth as his ill-advised aesthetic statements are irrelevant.

Might this be taken to mean that one *cannot* therefore produce a great talking picture? What about the unique talkies that *have been* produced? (Some critics would not trade one print of *Citizen Kane* for all the silent footage ever made; and they may well be correct.) Neither Arnheim nor his

---

[8] Rudolph Arnheim, *Film As Art* (Berkeley and Los Angeles: University of California Press, 1957), pp. 199–230.
[9] *Ibid.*, pp. 229–230.

disciples mean anything of the sort. An image of the *picture medium* (in time, in space, and perhaps in color) *must logically be most interesting when it is presented alone and precisely for what it is: visual action.* This action will necessarily be communicated best if communicated alone, just as printed words will be most clearly read if they are printed on blank paper rather than paper with dark scratches on it. The postulate assumes, of course, that our objective here is to communicate visual action efficiently!

When our objective (and here one breaks both theoretically and practically with Arnheim—at least in 1938) is the employment of the pictorial *medium* to communicate, by means of the *device* of moving photographs, on a screen, through the *medium* of re-enactment, sound may not only enhance the effect, it may be necessary for communication. We are not, however, communicating primarily visual action; we are communicating cognitions, emotions, styles, and intentions in the dramatic medium using moving pictures—and one of the technological instruments of their presentation. We are not, analogously, using a racing car (a basic technological mechanism) to take family and friends for a scenic drive and picnic. The objective is now far more complex; the number of logical and psychological elements involved in both operations (projecting the talking dramatic film and taking the automobile drive) increases many times.

Film analysts have, of course, recognized since what Arnheim noted before them: that the introduction of sound to films did *something terrible* to the image on the screen. It destroyed the essential unitary interest in the *moving picture.* But let us remember, in the silent days, the introduction to the pictorial art of movies the dramatic medium with its absurd titles, tacky scenery, stock heroes and villains, and simplistic, artificial plots. These elements, after the movies' first experimental decade, were as great a distracting force as sound would later prove to be.

Interest in motion *pictures* was sacrificed for the greater reward (to most audiences) of the complexities of the dramatic medium with its potential to communicate (mostly) farces or melodramas. The spectrum for communication widened when the films turned to drama and, in documentaries and newsreels, to narrative. This breadth was achieved at the sacrifice of the development of the potential for pictorial artistic elaboration held out by the moving image *alone.* For this reason, when film makers like Griffith and Eisenstein began work, their innovations in pictorial display took them *back* a full decade to the point at which the visual aspect of film technique had been frozen in the early days of the twentieth century by the introduction of drama to movies. How elementary are the close-up, the montage, the fade-out, the dolly shot, and other so-called "innovations" of the pioneers! The early film makers had simply been victims of a technique of pictorial composition which had stopped in its developmental tracks at the turn of the century, mostly by the conjurer, George Méliès, who had the instincts of a good magician and cared less about what his films *communicated* than how many people they might *fool*.[10,11] Many other early film makers unfortunately followed in his tracks.

Not only did later critics naturally feel that sound was an intrusion into a technique which was just in the process of being developed, but film makers agreed also, and probably are still aware of it. John Howard Lawson has written well of his own experiences[12] in Hollywood in the early sound film years reflecting the optimism of many in the USA and elsewhere (including the USSR) concerning the expected "fusion" of the "media" of "the motion picture" and "sound" that would liberate this dramatic "art form" to rival the legitimate stage. He also chronicles the disappointment of the creative artists' discovery of the inevitable. "Hollywood had not so much mastered dialogue as it had been mastered by it. . . . Dependence on speech was magnified by personnel trained in the theatre. Directors, writers and performers did not change their methods of work when they crossed the continent from New York to Hollywood. . . . Their influence helped impose the tyranny of dialogue on the cinema of other countries." [13]

Sound, as actually used by film makers (Orson Welles possibly excepted), at least until World War II, could not help but diminish the former sophisticated techniques of the few masters of the silent screen and their many imitators. In America, in the volatile atmosphere of Hollywood, many of these artists inevitably ended badly, thus accounting in part for the "Hollywood myths" of obscurity to fame and fortune and back again.[14] D. W. Griffith in his later years attempted to direct sound films but died broke and bitter. Chaplin refused to give in to the lure of the sound track, and continued making silent films into the sound era. When he finally employed sound, his work suffered, except for the silent-type sequences interpolated into his films, like the comedy routine with Buster Keaton near the end of *Limelight*.

The silent screen *belonged*, by virtue of its overwhelming presence, to the moving picture—to visual action, and sound in the form of dialogue music and sound effects had almost nothing to do with the technical display of "movies." A piece of film will demonstrate physically this logical statement. The optical or tape track is quite separate physically from the

---

10 The same problem appear to face some movie-makers employing both photographic and electronic techniques today, especially when they play with split-screen techniques.
11 See the sections on Méliès in the bibliography of Knight, *op. cit.*, and also considerable material on him in C. W. Ceram, *Archaeology of the Cinema*, and A. R. Fulton, *Motion Pictures* (Norman: University of Oklahoma Press, 1960), pp. 19–43.
12 John Howard Lawson, *Film: The Creative Process* (New York: Hill and Wang 1964), pp. 97–107.
13 *Ibid.*, p. 106–107.
14 See Ezra Goodman, *The Fifty-Year Decline and Fall of Hollywood* (New York: Simon and Schuster, 1961), for a well-written summary of the rags to riches myths of the film-making capitol. Goodman writes about Hollywood from the points of view both of a lively cultural historian and of a knowing critic of American films.

picture it accompanies. In the earliest days of the commercial sound film, sound was, in fact, coordinated with the visual image manually on a disc. A different part of the electronic spectrum carries sound into our television receivers from that which transmits the video. The two may at times mix, but only in the form of visual or audio static.

The *psychological* non-relationship of sound to the image on the screen is not difficult to demonstrate. As an elementary experiment, simply project a sound motion picture to a group, but locate the sound speaker *behind their heads*. Offer no explanations, but utilize a conventional sound film—with or without music; it is immaterial. For a few minutes the spectators will object, turn their heads, and indicate discomfort at the unaccustomed sound-source placement, but pay no attention. Within ten minutes, perceptions will have accommodated to the situation, and chances are that after the film has concluded (if it is of usual length) they will hardly mention the unaccustomed sound source.

What one discovers is that sound is not necessarily psychologically related in space to the visual action on a screen. Each individual will preserve for himself the integrity of three possible mediums involved. If *moving pictures* are of primary importance (during silent sequences), he will look at the screen. If *narrative* sequences are emphasized, he will psychologically fuse what he sees on the screen to what he hears. If *re-enactment* is the medium of communication employed, he will perform the same operation, in order to receive as full and meaningful a communication as possible, by means of the appropriate medium at the right time.[15]

During a motion picture, some form of visual action is, at most times, occurring on the screen, however, and the techniques of both cinema and television depend heavily upon the medium of picture to achieve whatever uses they make of the mediums of narrative or drama for communications. The screen itself, therefore, remains at the central focus of the technique of the motion picture.

Everything that happens elsewhere involved in the operation of moving picture devices, including the reproduction and amplification of sounds, is of ancillary significance to the still or moving *picture* in theatres and living rooms.

The screen is far more central to the cinema and television devices than the total pictorial image seen by the audience in a legitimate theatre because of the large number of visual options and alternative perspectives one enjoys at a live play, compared to the *single* option for visual viewpoint on a motion picture or television screen. Even when the live theatre and

---

[15] This phenomenon should explain why stereophonic sound seems irrelevant to commercial motion pictures most of the time—except for the first moments of its use, while we are adjusting our perceptions to it. This momentary discomfort (or sense of wonder) was employed skillfully at the end of the prologue to *Around the World in Eighty Days*; the single source speaker was increased to multiple sources as the screen expanded in width. The effect, however impressive, was just momentary.

the screen utilize the dramatic medium in the same way—as in the case of a photographed play, for instance—the difference in options obtains, and the stress upon visual motion rivets focused attention onto the screen to a greater degree than the attention of an audience is forced to *any* single perspective of the living stage.[16]

The medium of drama on the living stage therefore seems to stress more of a balance between the use of the medium of picture and the device of sound than does the motion picture—usually. There are, of course, exceptions. In the Ziegfeld-type theatre musicals of yesterday, one remembers the impact of startling visual displays, apparently as "screen-like" as the visual sequences of Busby Berkeley in the *Gold Diggers* films. Extraordinarily static films like Hitchcock's *Rape* (presented as a single shot with no apparent cuts or dissolves), or Renoir's *La Regle du Jeu*,[17] (a strange and stagey talkpiece), allow one, as he closes his mind's eye to the screen, the same sort of balance between listening and looking that he encounters in a legitimate theatre, but usually under less comfortable circumstances. In front of a television set or movie screen, this is a sign of boredom or fatigue. In the legitimate theatre, it is usually a sign that the medium of re-enactment has been successfully achieved.

Screens, however, must always primarily be regarded, logically and psychologically, as *silent* screens. Sound is something aside from the screen—a technological device that is amplified by a loud-speaker that does not affect at core the visual motion of the picture medium, except in the degree that we think it does, in order to achieve an artistic effect satisfactory to our sense of appropriateness logically, and to our illusions psychologically.

The Screen and Literature

Those who adhere to the notion of the technique of communication by pictures on a screen as an "art form" refer frequently to rough analogies which link the movies or television productions (choosing always the "right" movies and television shows) to the novel as an "art form." The following paragraph by A. R. Fulton presents this viewpoint as clearly as it is expressed anywhere:

It is relevant to observe that the method of the motion picture is more like that of the novel than of the play. The way a novel tells a story—primarily by description and narration—is comparable to the way

[16] Readers who have observed a live television show and seen a tape of it later, or who have been involved in the production of the film, will recognize the startling ruthlessness with which the perimeters of the screen intruded into the sound stage, when memories of "shooting" are compared with perceptions of "viewing." The *new* element brought into the occasion of viewing is, of course, a *screen*. Otherwise, everything is likely to be much as it was when the sequence was "shot"—barring the introduction of dubbed sounds which may not have been present originally.

[17] This particular film classic, considered by many a masterpiece of social comedy, is regarded by others as one of the most static and tedious films ever made.

a film does—primarily by pictures—whereas the dramatic message is primarily dialogue. It is true, of course, that a more literal adaptation can be made of a play than of a novel. A film resembles a play in manner of representation; that is, it can be seen and heard. A play might therefore be so recorded by a camera and microphone as to be almost identical to the play produced on the stage. The more faithfully a film "follows the play," the more like the play it becomes—*and the less cinematic. A novel, on the other hand, is faithfully adapted to the screen by a translation of the novelistic terms into cinematic ones and thus by being different. For these reasons a film adapted from a play is seldom better than, or even as good as, the original novel, and occasionally better.* With a few exceptions, films from novels are better than films from plays. They are invariably better from films adapted from plays literally—and they are better because of the ways in which they are different.[18]

Except for the necessary qualifications concerning *what* play or novel is translated into a film (it is doubtful that Fulton would maintain that bad novels must make better—or more "cinematic"—movies than great, inventive or imaginative plays), this viewpoint has a good deal to recommend it. Hollywood films particularly, and Book-of-the-Month-Club novels notably, have much in common as communications; Hollywood films and Ibsenesque theatrical dramas are *not commonly* "cinematic"—meaning presumably non-static, pictorially. The argument—taken as axiomatic by some film theorists—misses the point of the function of the screen as an instrument of communication with immaculate naïveté.

First, the novel itself is *not* a *medium* of communication. It, like the screen and sound techniques, is an instrument, drawn largely from Italian Renaissance inventiveness, developed (roughly) in the eighteenth century to achieve a distinctive blend of the art of printed narrative (long the classical way of storytelling) and the medium of re-enactment. The printed drama—instead of being played on a stage—was necessarily only *described* in print. Sections of dialogue were presented with and without ascriptions (conventions changed as styles of writing changed, but the form remains in use today), and the whole constituted an instant narrative-evoking device and, for the reader with sufficient imagination, a portable theatre.

In the sense that they are both bastards—with similar genetic backgrounds—one immediately understands the reasons for the apparent similarity between films and novels: namely, the unusually high degree of *narrative medium* they both employ, as opposed to the living theatre which utilizes little.[19] Similar antecedents yield similar results, and, to the novelist

---

[18] Fulton, *op. cit.*, p. 228. (Italics added.)
[19] There are many exceptions in both the classical and modern theatre, from the Chorus in the Greek tragedies and *Romeo and Juliet*, to the narrators who introduce movie-like flashbacks in *I Remember Mama* or the stage version of *Native Son*. Re-enactment, not narration, is the basic currency of theatre, however.

and film maker, this is helpful creative information. It is only of analytic interest to the communications student.[20]

Second, the tendency to associate moving pictures with any single instrument for communication has happily been dispelled by the general format of American television programming. This format, one of the most unusual that any advanced technological nation in the world today accepts from its broadcasters, at least performs the function of demonstrating that no overwhelming aesthetic principles dominate the effective use of pictures on different kinds of screens. It therefore destroys entirely the cinema-novel-nexus fable.

On the American television screen, almost *every* sort of message imaginable is communicated with frequently startling (and jarring) effectiveness. Narrators sit behind desks and gossip for hours with semi-literate movie stars; great dramas are compressed into short sketches; abstract color pictures and Rockefeller Center baritones sell mouthwash; hirsuite hermaphrodites warble Victorian ballads to accompanying close-ups of their pimply faces; and pastoral portraits of mothers and daughters are presented to influence our choice of bathroom tissues. One vista (and accompanying sound) follows another, and this brass and intensity holds millions spellbound for hours. Evidence of the fact that whatever is being shown and said is being communicated effectively is demonstrated by endless viewer statistics and rising sales charts.

What "art form" are we dealing with here? Obviously none. Or many. Films makers producing photographed and taped dramas and commercials for television go about their business in much the same way that they did when film on celluloid was the instrument for the transmission of images to screens. Narrators, be they news analysts or stand-up comics, look at the red light on Camera 2 and talk, on and on and on.

What mediums of communication are involved in these displays? What is the nature of the literature of these images on our screens? Most decidedly, our television screen (in *this* country) is *not* a transliteration of the novel (or even picture magazine) to another "art form." The conventional commercial television screen and sound exhibition provides a potpourri of the three basic media, narrative, picture and re-enactment, in their various emotive, cognitive, stylistic and intentional manifestations (*intentionally* humorous and serious and *unintentionally* humorous and serious) in various intensities and sequences. Some of them are organized and planned to achieve certain effects; but most of them, most of the time, appear to have been scheduled mostly at random.

Because of this latter phenomenon, a sensation of suspense is achieved

[20] See Haig P. Monoogian, *The Film Maker's Art* (New York: Basic Books, 1966), pp. 1–29, for a clear essay on the relationship of film to its debtor arts. Much—or most —of what Monoogian reports may be applied to television, although he himself does not agree with the author's assumption that films and television are almost identical artistic instruments.

from watching the television screen and not knowing, despite the program guide listings of about three-quarters of the material in a single hour, *exactly what sort of communication to expect next.* The effect seems to occur regardless of age, educational or social status, and it demonstrates quite conclusively that an analogy of the screen device to any *single* literary form (most particularly the novel) is spurious. The surface reasonableness of the proposition derives from characteristics which literary forms and types of screen entertainments frequently *lack* in common, rather than those which they *possess.*

One final notation about the supposed literary equivalents of screen techniques. While critics have found similarities in the novel to the conventional fiction film, the form known as the newsreel—or in its more expanded and elaborate form, the documentary—obviously has no equivalent in fiction. The latter, as Roger Manvell notes, is "the use of motion picture photography for 'the creative treatment of actuality.' " [21] The latter term is taken from the writings of John Grierson, a pioneer in both documentary theory and film making,[22] and describes neatly the "non-fiction" concept of the moving picture in its serious manifestation. The documentary might roughly be described as the moving pictorial equivalent of the non-fiction book or article, again too-facile a comparison for practical or theoretical purposes.

There is less difference today between the "documentary" (or "telementary") and the feature film (or "prime time television show") than there appeared to be a generation ago, as methods of pictorial communication on screens. The techniques used are frequently identical, leaving the convention film-as-art-form-critics in confusion as to the "artistic" nature of documentary-style feature films (like *Is Paris Burning?* or *In Cold Blood,* for instance) or feature film-style documentaries like the Japanese opus *The Island.* What they are left with is a basketful of "documentary techniques"—meaning aesthetic styles and tricks of Grierson, Robert Flaherty, Louis de Rochemont, Edward R. Murrow, Henry Salomon and others—somehow "creating actuality" whenever they are used. The *smorgasbord* visible on our television screens again denies the purity of the filmic "art form" of *this* kind of motion picture, because we will view *all* of these styles and tricks repeated *ad nauseam* without evoking noticeable disturbances in our perceptions, and we rarely care if what we see is "created actuality" or not.

When the mediums of picture and re-enactment are overbalanced in a communication experience (utilizing screen and sound techniques) by the

[21] See Roger Manvell, *Film* (Hammondsworth, Middlesex, England: Penguin Books, 1950), pp. 90–95. Although Manvell accepts the "art form" theory of films, his critical writing on movies and television are highly recommended, particularly since they deal as frequently with British communication problems as well as those of the United States.

[22] For his theory in essay form, see John Grierson, *Grierson on Documentary* (London: Collins, 1946).

medium of narrative (in pictures or written or spoken words), we are probably dealing with what is and has been generally regarded in the movies and on television as "documentary." [23] There accordingly are films and television programs of many types, both spontaneous and rehearsed, which rely heavily upon the narrative medium. Call them what you will, they have a quality different from pure pictorial re-enactment, and they differ also in the qualities of communication discussed in Part Three. "Documentary" is as good a name as any other for them.

The Screen and Reality

The perceptual difficulty of accepting moving pictures on a screen as a communication, rather than an actual "event" in time and space, was illustrated clearly by the early audiences of films. They would flinch as a train approached, or they hid their eyes from the real objects that suddenly apparently appeared from nowhere.[24] Probably a good deal of this type of reaction—the magical belief in the films as a *creator* of reality—is involved in both critical and aesthetic discussion one reads on cinema today. It assumes that the screen is a device which in some way must affect or be effected by the real world. In short, the films have been subject for many years to a "reality mystique," and, in the sense that the television screen is almost identical with the cinema screen, the latter has partaken of this mystique as well. The problem is most clearly demonstrated today in "underground" movies and cinematic novelties which are shown at Worlds Fairs and then disappear from the cultural scene. Each type of such "experimental" films asks itself disturbing—but simple—questions about the *reality* of an image on a screen. The questions seem everlasting fresh: how real is an image of a man sleeping for hours, lesbians at love play, the funeral of President Kennedy, or the daring young man on the flying trapeze above our heads? How real *dare* we, the audience, *think* they are?

These questions—as well as the relationship of the film to dramatic and non-dramatic literature—were given extremely clear explanation in a 1934 talk published by Professor Erwin Panofsky,[25] art historian at the Institute of Advanced Study in Princeton. In addition to spinning the yarn that movies are an "art form" and medium of communication, non-theatrical in nature, Panofsky sees the film as a device that might transform all of nature for the viewer into manageable, interpreted reality, much in the way that graphic *art* itself does. A few of his sentences will suffice here. "It is the movies, and only the movies, that do justice to the materialistic interpreta-

---

[23] An excellent study of the televised screen documentary, highly confirmatory of the similarity between cinema and television screens is A. William Bleum's *Documentary in American Television*. It demonstrates the continuum in the development of narrative-pictorial screen communications from celluloid to electronic technology.

[24] See Ceram, *op. cit.*, p. 150. These reactions are noted by almost all film historians.

[25] Erwin Panofsky, "Style and the Medium in the Motion Pictures, in Talbot, *op. cit.*, pp. 15–32.

tion of the universe, which, whether we like it or not, pervades contemporary civilization. . . . The movies organize material things and persons, not a neutral medium, into a composition that receives its style, and may even become fantastic or pretervoluntarily symbolic, not so much by an interpretation in the artist's mind as by the actual manipulation of physical objects and recording machinery. *The medium of the movies is physical reality as such. . . ."* [26]

The confusion that Panofsky articulated dimly has been compounded more recently by Dr. Sigfried Kracauer[27] who seems to offer—in a turgid document—the concept that the film might *redeem physical reality*, particularly reality involving man and his culture. It would thereby serve, somehow, not only as a potent instrument for the re-discovery of the physical world, but of society as well.

Since there is no necessity to indulge in needless cruelty, an attack on Dr. Kracauer's misunderstandings, social optimism, miserable prose or metaphysics is not appropriate here, particularly in the light of Pauline Kael's definitively destructive 1962 essay on Kracauer's *magnum opus*.[28] She recognizes him for the political *agent provocateur* he is, hiding behind a cabal of "reality," that, to critics like Kracauer, is "real" only as long as it strives for an appropriate *social* "truth." Kael's vitriol is justified by Kracauer's instance that the burden for this "truth" be borne exclusively by the delicate device of the screen which, as she notes, can handle communications of subtlety and charm (as well as malice) inconceivable from Kracauer's socio-political viewpoint.

Kracauer occasionally does come to his reader with some interesting oddment of social observation. Take, for instance, his notation: "Startling as it may sound, since the days of Lumière there have been only few cinematic films that would not include a glimpse of a street . . . ," [29] a remarkable observation, except for the fact that it is not true, unless the many films *without* street scenes may not be "cinematic" enough for Dr. Kracauer.

Even this oddity is not so odd, considering that the dramatic medium has, in its history, put to service a great number of simple devices by which the locale of a re-enactment is communicated to an audience simply and efficiently. A charge to Dr. Kracauer: let him find one Shakespearian play-tragedy or comedy—with a vaguely urban setting—that does not have a full

---

[26] *Ibid.*, p. 31.
[27] Sigfried Kracauer, *Theory of Film* (New York: The Oxford University Press, 1960).
[28] Pauline Kael, *I Lost It At the Movies* (Boston: Little, Brown and Company, 1965), pp. 269–292. This collection of essays is one of the best, fairest and clearest works on the film screen. While one may disagree with some of Miss Kael's critical judgments (really judgments of the appropriateness of certain specific re-enactments), she appears to understand the moving image as a technique for the logical and psychological transmission of meaning by means of all mediums of communication and therefore approaches it with a mind unclouded by the "art form" mystique. See also her *Kiss Kiss Bang Bang* (Boston: Little, Brown and Company, 1968).
[29] Kracauer, *op. cit.*, p. 62.

scene *set in a street!* Proving what? That the Bard of Avon re-created "reality" on the stage of the Globe by these settings? Of course not. He was providing a sensible, recognizable background for his actors to communicate their conflicts and stories, through the medium of re-enactment, to the audience for their enjoyment. There was sufficient "reality" in Elizabethan London *outside* the theatre walls.

As long as mystics confuse the film with reality, as long, in other words, as they confuse the mirrors of life with life itself, the Panofskys and Kracauers of the world will attempt to stagger us with their dense metaphysical aesthetics. Their problem, of course, is that they have lost—if they have ever had—a vision of the essential *logical* difference between life and art. In life, *all* stories are either largely tragedies or comedies, depending on how you want to look at them. Either thread of discourse is *logical*; neither, or both, is *real*, depending on who is telling the story and what in particular he desires to communicate. Our every day psychological perspectives of living are similar to the artist's, but they are largely determined by social, genetic, educational, economic and chance influences. We do not possess—unless we are extremely gifted—the artist's power to re-arrange them according, either to our wishes, or to how God might have plotted them in the scenario of our experiences, were He a dramatist. Drugs and alcohol may help us to achieve an illusion that we are masters of reality, but—as Shaw's Don Juan says—we are not masters; we are in the end the slaves of reality.

The artist—especially the artist who speaks by means of images on a screen—has great power to capture facets of reality and, if he is clever, so to combine them that they may be communicated enjoyably and efficiently to his audience. The technical devices made available to him since the days of the Kinetoscope have developed at an astounding pace, and they are growing ever more interesting, inexpensive and elementary to command. They do not alter the immutable fact that the artist himself is limited, in the use of these techniques, to the interplay of three basic means of communication: narrative, picture and re-creation. In the instance of the screen-cum-sound, he has many ways of interlacing these mediums logically to achieve startling effects and to demonstrate his skill as an *artist*—not fundamentally as a film or electronic tape-maker—but as a narrator, photographic artist, and/or dramatist. Like all artists, he succeeds or fails by virtue of the validity of the logic of his approach and the psychological power he generates from *his* unique presentation of thoughts and feelings to his particular audience.

Conclusions

Film and television are profoundly misunderstood today as instruments of communication. Both represent advances in technology of a similar kind that have produced similar results, except for the fact that their techniques employ different methods of information storage and distribution. The end products are nearly identical: a moving picture on a screen with the accompaniment of sound. They will probably be entirely identical before another generation has passed, although screens somewhat different from the fabric and glass variety, with which we are now familiar, may be utilized.[30] Size, proportion and nature of the screen appear relevant to communication itself only in special cases, as does the difference between screens displaying color or black and white pictures.

Communication by means of cinema or television seems to be predominantly visual, and therefore continued credence is given to old arguments concerning the integrity of "visual motion" as the fundamental focus of film and television performances. It was noted, however, that *all* technology stripped to bear essentials is more interesting than various technologies combined. The technology of the screen is no exception. The need for sound in certain kinds of communication also employing visual images was considered, and allowance was made for the still valid claim that the introduction of sound technology to the technique of the screen so altered it as to decrease its artistic value. What sound, of course, accomplished for films was to permit a wider interplay of the three mediums of communication—narrative, picture and re-creation—than the silent screen had previously known. The peculiar balance of these basic mediums determines entirely the nature of the logical and psychological reactions of audiences to what they see on screens and simultaneously hear through loudspeakers. Strictly speaking, the art of visual motion alone remains nevertheless the art of the *silent* screen.

Resemblances between novels and plays were considered, particularly the incorrect, but generally accepted, notion that the screen technique is similar to printed fiction rather than the theatrical medium. The fallacy of this belief was explored, particularly the fact that *both* the novel and the screen are instruments of communications which employ the mediums of re-creation, narrative and/or drama for much the same ends—and therefore *appear* quite similar. It was noticed—on American television particularly—that the blend of mediums crossing the electronic screen daily was nonspecific and largely random. To associate this profusion of impulses, as well as the form of screen journalism called the "documentary," with any single communication technique is an over-simplification of how the device of the screen employs the mediums of communication.

Lastly, the *mystiques* of "film-as-art" and film as the "redeemer of real-

---

[30] In the world of Worlds Fairs (where cinematic nonsense invariably abounds) experiments of various sorts with unconventional surfaces as screens are attempted, including spinning screens, spherical screens, screens built like cubes and other devices which *may* influence the destiny of both film and television screens. But, during the past three generations, they have had little effect upon the development of communication utilizing screens. Their greatest value is as novelties which impress their audiences deeply but are as rapidly forgotten, as is most of the technological moonshine on display at such expositions.

ity" were explored in terms of the considerable confusion experienced by many (more critics than audiences) concerning the difference between "real reality" and "screen reality." In clearing up the linguistic difficulties here, it was also observed that, despite the extraordinary illusion of life offered by the moving image on the modern screen, reality and art are, in fact, entirely separable and probably always will be.

Part Six

THE FUTURE OF
COMMUNICATIONS

Chapter 19

MASS CULTURE

THE TERM "mass culture" as it is presently used by anthologists may refer either to "culture" in the sense of cultivation of excellence of taste
(as in "high culture"), or it may refer, in the anthropologist's sense, to the
folkways of a group or class in society. This latter construction is today
preferred by most students of communication, because there has been no
shortage of anthropological (and/or sociological) speculation on the phenomenon itself. Anthropological study of a culture usually requires, unfortunately, at least a glimpse of the pristine way life used to be before it was
manipulated by "outside influences." [1] In our tradition, a "non-mass" way
of life once indeed existed, but we are extremely uncertain of how and to
what specific facets of culture it is most relevant to the world we live in
today.

Our mass society, so *recent* a phenomenon, burst upon the West as
suddenly as advanced technology itself. The more rapidly change occurs,
the more difficult it is for those living through it to comprehend. The more

---

[1] See Margaret Mead, *New Lives for Old* (New York: William Morrow and Company, 1956), especially pp. 411–434. Mead demonstrates here the influence of a flirta-
tion by a primitive culture with technology by comparing the New Guinea society she
studied in 1928 with the same one in 1953, after the natives had been exposed to the
technology of Western military life. While the new culture she found was anthro-
pologically interesting, it would have been meaningless without the substratum of
reference that she had gained from her previous experience in 1928, chronicled in
Growing Up In New Guinea (New York: A Mentor Book, 1953), first published in
1930. Anthropologists (and others) remarking on much of modern "culture," have
few such clear frames of reference, except written history and contemporary documenta-
tion, neither of which may provide the kind of cultural insights necessary for a clear
view of the culture in which they live. See also the basic anthropological data in the
autobiographical book by Claude Levi-Strauss, *Tristes Tropiques* (New York: Atheneum
Publishers, 1965), pp. 17–64, especially pp. 54–63. It is simply a sad fact, also, that most
anthropological studies of mass (or technological) culture have, to date, left much to
be desired.

difficult it is to understand, the more various and differently oriented the "legitimate" ideas concerning its nature one is likely to discover in the market place of "safe" ideas.

A significant repository of such widely disparate notions about mass communication is found in the familiar anthology *Mass Culture*,[2] in which an attempt is made to bring to the problems of communication "an interdisciplinary focus on problems common to everyone who takes a serious interest in what is happening in this aspect of modern civilization." [3] This it does. It is, of course, not the only book on this subject, or the only anthology devoted strictly to the cultural aspects of mass communications.[4] The nature of *Mass Culture* illustrates, however, a central fact concerning mass culture itself: that it is made up of highly plural phenomena which assault and affect a heterogeneous nation—or society—in many ways. The effect which will be most important to us will depend largely upon the vantage point from which we choose, or are forced, to view it. The variety of the *smorgasbord*, for instance, that Rosenberg and White offer us defies concise description. Why *do* such seemingly competent critics and scholars as are reprinted bespeak such fundamentally different interpretations of the role of mass communication in contemporary life?

The disparity of perspectives one finds in *Mass Culture* helps to explain one other important phenomenon. With opinions as to the *values* of mass culture so various, what can be said with authority about the *effects* of mass communication upon people? The answer is "little," that is, little more than to note their force and power (that nearly all cultural activities display) in *maintaining* myths, legends, and values for a society. Joseph Klapper's clearly constructed compendium of research on the "effects of communications" demonstrates just this.[5] Klapper lists the results of most of the recent studies of mass communications and their effects on children and adults and comes up with an honestly added total, slightly on the positive side of zero.

In the nine years since Klapper's book was published, there have been other studies, but they have not changed the fundamental integrity of his

---

[2] Bernard Rosenberg and David Manning White, (eds.), *Mass Culture* (Glencoe, Ill.: The Free Press, 1957).

[3] *Ibid.*, p. v.

[4] Potentially, the most interesting collection on this subject is Norman Jacobs, (ed.), *Culture for the Millions?* (Princeton, N.J.: D. Van Nostrand Company, Inc., 1959). In this book, a single essay "Mass Culture and Its Society" by sociologist Edward Shils (a piece generally sanguine about contemporary American life) is commented upon by first rate critics from various academic disciplines and professional backgrounds. They include Leo Lowenthal, Hannah Arendt, Oscar Handlin, Leo Rosten, Frank Stanton, Randall Jarrell, Arthur Schlesinger, Jr., and others. Unfortunately, the idea does not bear full sized fruit; Shils' arguments are trivialized in the ensuing discussion, and the points of attack are so variously oriented as to prelude either genuine conflict or enlightenment.

[5] Joseph T. Klapper, *The Effects of Mass Communication* (Glencoe, Ill.: The Free Press, 1960).

conclusion. What has occurred in many well meant attempts at (usually) quantitative display of cause and effect relationships in mass culture—and most have at least been well meant—affirm the sly fact that plural viewpoints yield plural assumptions, which accounts for inconclusive results arrived at by different scholars in different ways. The sensible conclusion, therefore, for social scientists like Klapper, in the face of such chaos, is to suspend judgment. He therefore concludes in the end that the data gathered merely yield concepts valuable for understanding the data themselves. These data, he states in a classic scholarly dodge, are of importance in "indicating avenues of needed research which are logically related to existing knowledge." [6] *Sic transit Klapper.*[7]

That experimental sociologists and social scientists have (mostly) validated null hypotheses concerning the effects of mass techniques of communication does not necessarily imply that these techniques have no effect on people in various contexts of their lives. (By analogy, we cannot isolate the virus which causes the common cold, but this does not mean that colds do not exist!) If our present methods of determining the nature of the effects of television on children, for instance, merely demonstrate that "incidental learning" occurs, as Schramm has noted,[8] or that it had a vague but nonspecific effect upon values, as Himmelweit claims,[9] the issue is not closed. It appears to many parents and teachers, who are familiar with thousands of childrens' responses to video under many circumstances, that what is called for are more accurate and sophisticated experimental devices by which to demonstrate and measure those effects that *both* Schramm's and Himmelweit's researches have clearly missed.

To maintain, as most extant sociological research today does, that mass communications only "facilitate" current social attitudes and behaviors is of course, on its face, absurd—largely because advertisers employing these technologies have *proved* their power for behavioral change beyond doubt. They have spent fortunes demonstrating in numerous ways that commercial messages of many kinds, spread by these techniques, change *all manner* of attitudes, aspirations, customs and even tastes. The commercial

[6] *Ibid.*, pp. 249–250.
[7] Klapper's volume was prepared under the auspices of the Columbia Broadcasting System, which sometimes sponsors studies of this kind when they are almost certain to demonstrate that no one can *prove* that television (particularly) has a harmful effect upon children or adults. As fortunate as Klapper was to find so affluent a patron, it is doubtful that many similar studies will be seen for some time, because at present Professor McLuhan appears willing to absolve *all* communicators (including the CBS, presumably) from *any* responsibility for doing *any* sort of harm (or good) to their audiences, at least so far as content is concerned. With Dr. McLuhan so firmly behind them, why do the broadcasters need mere social scientists like Dr. Klapper?
[8] Wilbur Schramm, Jack Lyle and Edwin B. Parker, *Television in the Lives of Our Children* (Stanford, Calif.: Stanford University Press, 1961), p. 75. Schramm does also call attention to other results as well—most of them trivial.
[9] Hilde T. Himmelweit, A. N. Oppenheim and Pamela Vance, *Television and the Child* (New York: Oxford University Press, 1958), pp. 37–42.

successes of their enterprises rest upon demonstrable cause and effect relationships between mass communications and behavior. The power of today's publicity and public relations organizations (or industrial and philanthropic propaganda arms) is further proof that many specific techniques of communication *work* in the nebulous business of modifying attitudes and opinions—and that they usually work quite efficiently.

There is, accordingly, no possible rational way to evaluate any empirical experimental evidence offered as "scientific" that concludes that the press, radio, television or the films merely enforce present cultural values other than to question at the outset their *validity*.[10] The impact of these facets of technology upon people's commercial, social and political behavior the world over for the past fifty years has been too obvious to write off as mere maintenance of the status quo. One might as well claim that mass transportation or mass production in the international clothing industry have maintained the status quo, simply because we lack measurable evidence that technology has "influenced behavior" in non-ambiguous "before" and "after" contexts that are satisfactory to rigid experimentalists or "scientific" social thinkers.

Mention might well be made here of the work of William Stephenson[11] who has attempted to develop a theory of mass communications—and mass culture—which appears at first glance to effect a compromise between the observational insights of the anthropologist and the rigid large sample techniques of audiences that were relied upon mostly by Klapper.

Using recently developed statistical techniques and uncomfortably small populations (which he represents as typical of given situations), he brings the elaborate device of the Q-sort to bear upon what people have told him, or he sometimes infers they *might say*, about beliefs, attitudes and opinions of the mass communications and matters allied to their functions. Stephenson emerges with a *ludenic* theory which, briefly, regards mass communications in all their phases largely as "play" or "fill," entering into otherwise quietly desperate lives of work and drudgery. "The *important* communication (in the market)," he says, "concerns social matters. The fill serves to maintain status quo positions, since it serves no work purposes. It pleases, entertains. It is basically *aesthetical*, and *amoral, a-ethical* (sic)." [12] It functions both as a social control and as an outlet, he thinks, for expression of individuality within mass behaviors that appear, to the non-Q oriented observer, conformist.

Whether Stephenson's Q-factors are indicative of more than *his* cul-

[10] Such research may be—and usually is—highly *reliable*; that is, the findings may be highly consistent when the experiments are performed with differential groups or subjected to different types of statistical scrutiny. It *tests* whatever it is testing well. The question is whether or not it is testing the right causes or effects.
[11] See William Stephenson, *The Play Theory of Mass Communication* (Chicago and London: The University of Chicago Press, 1967).
[12] *Ibid.*, p. 195. (Italics added.)

tural prejudices must be left to his fellow psychologists and statisticians to determine. His *procedures* appear to defy inductive logic, although he claims both the rigor and precision of science for them, and Q-methodologies are widely used in the social sciences today. His *theory* need not be extenuated upon, or considered in detail in the ensuing section, because it appears to find a middle path—or diversion—from the main arguments that presently face the future of mass culture in technological societies. When one views, as Stephenson does, *all* mass communications essentially as *play*, one must, as Stephenson also does, limn a value judgment of play itself. Stephenson sees what he calls "low culture" as a "normalizer of manners and taste; it developes wants and images and molds social character," which becomes eventually socially ameliorative: for instance, the television viewer's pleasure is somehow transmuted into self-enhancement. "High culture," Stephenson claims, has been, and always will be, replete with pleasure. In effect, he argues that, in *all* communications, he "would like to see more play rather than less, but play directed to cultures which fit the times." [13]

Stephenson's bland compromise gives us much to talk about—particularly the use of the Q-sort as an instrument to find out what, and if, people think—but little of concern directly related to our social, educational and aesthetic problems involving the particular *uses* of the languages of communication. His present work, however, produces the interesting concept of *homs ludens* at a level of social significance in advance of the cruder Freudian "pain-pleasure" principle. This concept will, hopefully, stimulate further and more deeply reflective studies of the role of entertainment in the progress (and decline) of man's cultures.

The Nature of Mass Culture

There are at least two major perspectives by which its critics approach mass culture. One is basically theatrical. Neither employs, nor is much impressed by, the quantitative aspect of the literature, entertainment, drama, music or other culture of communications technology. The first concentrates upon the excellence—or lack of it—displayed by the individual artists involved in using communications techniques and directs its primarily aesthetic criticism at them, utilizing qualitative standards of judgment drawn from "highbrow"—or "class"—culture. The comments about *Krazy Kat* in Chapter 17 were of this *genre*. So is the widely published, culturally astute screen criticism of Judith Crist, the essays of Louis Kronenberger, or the vitriol of Malcolm Muggeridge. Mass culture is rarely called by such critics "mass culture" in this construction, but rather "popular culture." The mass communications technologies are viewed as purveyors of art—"popular" art, "lively" art or "peoples'" art—but rarely "mass" art. In the United States, Gilbert Seldes was probably the first serious critic of popular culture and, by

[13] *Ibid.*, p. 205.

virtue of his articles and books,[14] remains the legitimate father of most of today's criticism of mass art. Seldes kept (and keeps) his eye on what is *best* in this gigantic output (or what should be best but is not), ignoring most of it most of the time, in order to encourage the Bing Crosbys, Edward R. Murrows and Jimmy Durantes of popular culture, rather than castigate our men from U.N.C.L.E., our teenage werewolves and such professional vulgarians as Elvis Presley and *The Monkees.*

The "popular culture" point of view bespeaks an artistic orientation and expresses the notion that popularity does not *necessarily* militate against artistic quality. The plays of Shakespeare were, for instance, popular culture in their own time. The fact that *our* "public arts" (in Seldes' phase) are publicized to a far wider degree than were the Elizabethan's, and that they are intended to please a wider range of tastes for different motives, is irrelevant. Our films, television, radio and publishing industries, it says, have produced an impressive roster of creative talent which is both first rate *and* extremely popular. Their efforts deserve serious, mature critical attention. To deride Ernest Hemmingway, Fred Astaire or Eric Sevareid merely *because* they are popular is snobbery, and—worse—excludes from the marketplace of serious discussion much of the most *meaningful* artistic output of our culture. The reader must by now be aware that the author shares this perspective, to a great extent, with Seldes and his critical offspring.

The sociological "mass culture" perspective, on the other hand, is not much concerned with output. Or, if it *does* examine the contents of the mass communications devices, little differentiation is made between the best and the worst, or few criteria are limned for development of hierarchies of values. When one mentions "movies," for instance, in this context, he is usually understood to mean *most* movies, or the most popular movies, like westerns, pseudo-horror films, sexy spoofs of spy stories, and beach party-rock 'n roll films. "Television" connotes *most* video, daytime quiz programs, *Mr. Terrific,* cigarette commercials and domestic comedies. The "mass press" is associated with books like *Gone With the Wind, Forever Amber, Peyton Place* and *Valley of the Dolls,* frequently written by female novelists. It connotes tabloid newspapers with circulations in the millions and periodicals of the stripe of *The Reader's Digest, Life* and *Look,* as well as others with smaller circulations and displaying less professional publishing skill.

The accent of this perspective of mass culture is upon the *audience* of technological communications and its responses. Ernest Van Den Haag, a psychologist sensitive to this orientation, has listed these generally accurate

[14] Seldes' three books constitute a definitive compendium of the cream of an era of popular culture in the United States. They are so far: Gilbert Seldes, *The Seven Lively Arts* (New York: Sagamore Press, Inc., 1957), published originally in the 1920's; *The Great Audience* (New York: The Viking Press, 1950); and *The Public Arts* (New York: Simon and Schuster, 1956).

characteristics of mass culture (abbreviated here) understood in this manner:

1. Production and consumption of culture are separated; culture is primarily a spectator sport.
2. Mass production standardizes a product to please average tastes and these tastes determine the nature of the output.
3. Power to bestow prestige and success rests with the masses rather than a cultural élite; high culture is interesting only as gossip concerning celebrated artists, i.e., *TV Guide* and *Life* on Horowitz and Picasso respectively.
4. The mass requires distraction from life: thrills, sentimentality and escapism; the bulk of mass culture deals in these qualities.
5. Popularity and popular approval became the dominant moral and aesthetic standards in art and subsequently in life itself.
6. The lure of mass markets diverts potential talent from the creation of art; because commercial artists know this, they lament their "sellout" to the cult of the golden calf.
7. Excessive communication tends to isolate people from one another and from real experience; fabricated experiences (Judy Garland's "concerts," for instance) are "realer" than life—almost spiritual—for many.
8. Since mass culture serves average tastes, it tends to reshape all art—past and present—to meet the expectations and demands of the masses; one discovers hippie *Hamlets* and reads front page articles on fantastic prices paid for "great" paintings.
9. The total effect of mass culture is to militate against the individual's confrontation with a potential life of boredom. The superficiality of the anodyne of mass culture to the problem of boredom only exacerbates the problem.[15]

Notice that Van Den Haag is *not* deeply concerned with the artistic quality of the communications which constitute the fabric of mass culture, merely that it is standardized, average, escapist, etc., all characteristics which relate to the psychologics of the instruments involved rather than their logics or aesthetics. Many ancient Greek comedies were likewise standardized, pitched to an average of tastes, escapist, etc. They were *not* mass culture in Van Den Haag's terms, because they probably did not perform the psychological function (we assume) of insulating the individual from the boredom (or the reality) of his environment, nor did the auditor perceive his environment as necessarily antithetical to the enjoyment of living or, in a word, boring. Neither did the previously defined "mass" exist in those days; so the total socio-psychological result of these vulgar revels could not have been comparable to the currency in our modern, mass produced fun-market.

For Van Den Haag, the *content* of the movies, television shows, novels and recordings that flood our nation is less relevant to mass culture than

[15] Ernest Van Den Haag, "A Dissent" in Jacobs, *op. cit.*, pp. 58–60.

the fact that the market is filled. Neither do cultural arbiters (or individual educational qualifications) stand between the individual's satisfaction of cultural desires and the cultural experiences which *he believes* will satisfy them. The individual may desire a magnificent painting in an excellent reproduction. The quality of *both* the picture and the facsimile process are irrelevant to the psychological use to which the reproduction is to be put. In other words, the Mona Lisa or a Van Gogh self-portrait may *become* mass culture if they are used on a billboard to advertise baked beans, or if they appear on a calendar in a barber shop.[16]

This viewpoint offers to many much to recommend it, providing that one does not relate its assumptions to the total societal spread of mass culture but instead to relevant parts of it. It may represent the greatest *quantity* of modern popular culture, but qualitative factors may be more immediately relevant to the social role of communication technologies in modern life for others.

Germane to both of these perspectives is the concept of "the mass" itself—as distinguished from "the audience," "the public" or "the crowd." We are accustomed to thinking of masses as natural correlates of instruments of mass communication and the systems and personnel who operate them, as well as the technology to distribute their output. But are the latter in fact necessities? Can a mass exist without devices for mass communications, and, conversely, may technologies of modern communications exist independent of a mass? Does Seldes' "popular culture" need a "mass culture" to sustain it? Or are they entirely different phenomena?

While it is not possible to answer definitively these questions, we are able to trace the concept of "mass-ness" as it moved, in the nineteenth century, away from art for its own sake—or even society's sake—towards art as a commodity embued with high utilitarian, psychological value in cutting men off from difficult, individual sources of inspiration and enjoyment. In our century, art took up a new function, as a social palliative insulating individuals either from reality or those meaningful experiences which with it had formerly been associated, namely, the cultivation of the individuality of the sensibilities of, mostly, a leisure class. In recent times, art has become —for better or worse—popular therapy, quite a different matter.

As one result, because today so much popular art is mediated by so many devices of communication to so many people, it has become a statistical probability that *some* of it—if only by accident—rises above the low common denominator of tastes and interests to achieve certain aesthetic distinction. This, of course, is exactly the case at present, a state of affairs rarely appreciated by the mass culture critics of the second type. In their indictment of the *gestalt* as bogus culture, they cut themselves off from

---

[16] Proponents of the "mass culture" perspective would be far more heartened by the sight of a *Playboy* calendar in the barber shop than one that expertly reproduced (and therefore degraded) a great painting by a master.

most of the best of it, which is frequently more interesting than much of the "class culture" presently produced or revived.[17]

At the wellspring of mass culture, according to José Ortega y Gasset, one finds three symptoms so closely related to the nature of contemporaneousness itself that our present brave sociological attempts at differentiating causes from effects appear futile. Ortega observes[18] that mass culture is not at root cause either a technologically or economically determined culture trait, although at first glance numerous analysts associate it mainly with technology and economy. Neither is it a manifestation of materialism itself. Nor is it, by its nature, either a facet of a materialistic ethic, the usual assumption made by a number of contemporary social thinkers whose orientations are economically socialistic.[19]

The three principles that "have made possible this new world," in Ortega's words, "are *liberal democracy, scientific experiment and industrialism.*" [20] The latter two are main constituents of technology but with a vital difference from technology itself. To characterize a society as technological bespeaks for it no established values, no concern with the source of truth, no epistemology. *Scientific experiment,* as historical experience, does. Combine it with industrialism—which is what has occurred in the West—and the result is materialism, or technology *of a distinctive kind:* one the limits of which are bounded by that which is categorizable, testable, and measurable. Since matters of art—even popular art in the way Seldes discusses it— are (at least) non-testable, and since its values are difficult to categorize experimentally, art has become, as we have observed, not *only* a commodity. It is now an *unreal commodity,* tangible only in so far as it yields *results* that can be *quantified.* For instance, one may observe safely that, because one musician has sold more recordings than another, he must be "better" (or at least as good as) the other. Because one television program appears to attract more viewers than another, it too must be distinctive and worthy of recognition, if not superior to the other. Such crude groping after quantity, far from emerging solely for economic impetus or motives, is actually a

[17] Why were a good number—as many as twenty-five perhaps—of the Hollywood films made in the 1930's outstanding examples of the clever and consistent use of the technique of the motion picture? In order to maintain their economic health, Hollywood producers did not *have* to produce fine films. They needed only to follow formulae. Yet, only a fool or pedant would maintain that *all* Hollywood films of this period were artistic trash. The reason for the exceptions was that *some* screen writers, producers and directors were, at *some* stage in their careers, genuine artists who disregarded the demands both of their bosses and of the masses. To ignore entirely the artistic significance of Hollywood films, therefore, means that the critic of mass culture dismisses hundreds of dismal pot boilers at the expense of considering some of the finest films ever made. While this stance is defensible quantitatively, it is indefensible qualitatively.
[18] See José Ortega y Gasset, *The Revolt of the Masses.*
[19] C. Wright Mills was one, and a roster of others, many of whose liberalism is impossible to sever from their socialism, would contain some of our outstanding contemporary social thinkers.
[20] Ortega, *op. cit.,* p. 56.

well-intentioned attempt at the analysis of mass society by *imposing stand-ards of scientific inquiry on the logics and psychologics of art, a technique which has to date, and will tomorrow, inevitably fail.*

The role, mentioned by Ortega, of liberal democracy in mass culture is another matter—and a crucial one. By *liberal* democracy is meant democracy in references beyond its role in the political life of an electorate. It extends democratic idealism to economic affairs, social matters, and cultural matters. It centers on the literal question of how power is used to influence the direction and course of the life of citizens of the state in *all* its manifestations. In the United States, Progressivism or Popularism, as formal movements, are as close as we have come, organizationally, to liberal democracy in Ortega's use of the term. Pragmatically, the drift at first glance—until one discovers how carefully and shrewdly it has been manipulated—of mass culture seems to flow in the direction of ill-organized liberal democracy.

It it has accomplished nothing else, the concept of liberal democracy provided a clarion call for broadcasting network executives (like Frank Stanton of CBS, for instance) who are able to defend their arbitrary displays of poor taste, hypocrisy or downright venality as "giving the public what it wants," the battle-cry of those who call themselves "cultural democrats." [21]

Here is one great failure of liberal democracy, of course: its inability to guide the cultural life of a nation into safe and productive channels. This failure will continue as long as it remains a concept without a working program or concrete objectives, at least until the people have been educated to comprehend what they may rightfully require from society's institutions. Until then, they will be fit only to be led by whomever happens to seize and hold relevant powers at a given time.

Quantitative standards borrowed from science today appear to be very important in accomplishing this conquest. But quantitative standards do not relate to much social reality. Hitler was very popular among the Germans—as popular in his day, at least, as an American movie star. In the absence—for many reasons—of firm critical standards on which to judge *der Fuhrer* in his early days by the relatively well educated German people, his authoritarianism could be concealed under the quantitative mandate of "the will of the people." [22] This "democratic" cover of authoritarian practise, of course, was not new with Hitler. It is as old as the notion of government itself.

The apparent cultural anarchy which evolves from a democracy operating beyond restrained and delimited political and social boundaries is the

---

[21] See Harry J. Skornia, *Television and Society* (New York: McGraw-Hill Book Company, 1965), pp. 136–139.
[22] Hitler, unlike many of our contemporary strongmen, rose initially to power within the genteel parliamentary limits of popular democracy—which he thereupon destroyed within weeks of his election. A number of excellent histories of this period are, of course, easily available in paper editions, one as interesting as the next, all containing lessons that the past so rarely succeeds in teaching the future!

main cause for the apparently tyrannical aspect of mass culture that bothers so many social critics. They speak of a Gresham's law of culture: "Bad stuff tends to drive out good stuff." There is, sadly, no such law. Mass culture, operating with what seems to be a *carte-blanche* socio-political franchise (within the framework of liberal democracy) merely utilizes irrelevant quantitative yardsticks of scientific experimentalism to justify technological growth to industrial dimensions. The results take the form of our modern "communications industries," whose currency by no means "drives out," what is worthwhile in mass or class culture, but instead makes it difficult or impossible to locate amidst the quantitative glut.

Mass Culture and Society

One resultant problem caused by the scope of mass culture is that every essayist who writes criticism about it appears to be discussing something quite different from every other one. We have seen above how vital is the schism between the concepts of "popular arts" and the "mass arts," and we assume in this instance that critics are talking about the *same* aspects of culture. The problem becomes greater when discussion begins concerning *different* parts of the elephant,[23] that is, the industries themselves and their relationships to other social institutions.

Most mass culture industries are centralized in control, a trait that seems inherent to much mass technology. Many of our newspapers are owned by chains. So are our periodicals. In the hey-day of movies, five "giants" dominated their production, distribution and exhibition in the USA. The situation is different today, but the giants are still abroad. Three television networks effectively divide between themselves one national commercial pie. Increasingly, also, communications industries are expanding horizontally: that is, motion picture companies are merging with networks, networks with publishers, publishers with film companies, and so forth. As far as control and direction are concerned, the complex of communications industries in the United States are continually flirting with monopoly laws—getting caught here, sliding past barriers there, in a constant game of tag with the federal Justice Department.

Our mass culture constitutes the images of the sum total of the produce of these industries and the information questionable statistical reports give us concerning our consumption of printed matter, screen exhibits, radio programs, recordings, etc. Against these formidable symbols stands the individual, selecting bits and pieces of the totality according to his economic status, his educational potential, his tastes, his biases and social pressures, in an attempt to consume the appropriate (for him) items. Most of us accept widely various diets from this enormous menu, which, although it

[23] See Joseph Bensman and Bernard Rosenberg, "Mass Media and Mass Culture," in Philip Olson (ed.), *America as a Mass Society*, pp. 166–184, for an excellent survey of extent and nature of the pervasiveness of these industries in our society and their relationships to other institutions.

is standardized and fairly uniform in regard to technical and artistic matters, covers a wide range of content. It runs from kiddies' cartoons to what, to the sensibilities of many, appears to be printed pornographic prose in neat, mass produced pocket editions. Let no one claim that our mass culture is homogenized! Stylistic similarities are the main (and the strongest) elements that bind TV's *Get Smart* to the spiritual pap in the *Reader's Digest* to the glycerin punditry of our TV news analysts.

One discovers also in mass culture an ongoing antithetical force, the source of bewilderment to some social scientists and many artists who condemn mass culture simply *because* it is mass. This is a phenomenon ably discussed by Alvin Toffler.[24] Toffler grants our currency of cultural "kitsch" disseminated by mass communications technology, and appears to take his stand with the mass culture critics who would rate most of it inferior art. But he calls our attention to the manner that mass technology—and the wealth that is the by-product of it—has spread throughout our society. He cites the growth of art museums, libraries, long-playing recordings, symphony orchestras, theatre repertories, FM radio stations, the plenitude on the market place of so-called "better" artistic experiences. His statistics show enormous recent increases in the spread of this sort of culture. He appears certain that a democracy like ours can support the enormous weight of mass culture and, at the same time, encourage the masses, not only to appreciate, but support, high culture. The latter, presumably, will eventually be generally accepted, because of its superiority, by the masses. To critics of his argument he replies, "We are not yet enjoying the exhilaration that perhaps comes of living through a genuine renaissance. But we may well be laying the material and human basis for one." [25]

That mass tastes have not yet been "elevated" in any society, with minor exceptions, is admitted by Toffler, but the historian's pessimism does not seem to discourage him. Even the experience of the British Broadcasting Corporation which, in its radio days, had a virtual monopoly on sound broadcasting in Britain, provided little or no evidence that a substantive change in public artistic preferences resulted from a broadcasting policy designed by expert broadcasters to elevate the taste of the average listener.[26] As bait for the listener, the BBC employed the finest actors, writers, musicians and artists in England to woo the public from its profane Light Program to its more sacred Home Service and Third Programme. But even under these conditions, the people preferred their *panem et circenses.*

In a well-known essay,[27] Dwight Macdonald argues that this burgeon-

[24] Alvin Toffler, *The Culture Consumers*, pp. 211–231 especially.
[25] *Ibid.*, p. 230.
[26] See Burton Paulu, *British Broadcasting in Transition* (Minneapolis: University of Minnesota Press, 1961), pp. 169–190.
[27] Dwight Macdonald, "A Theory of Mass Culture" in Rosenberg and White, *Mass Culture*, pp. 59–73.

ing of high culture in America constitutes, in fact, a *reduction* of what was *once* high (or *avant garde*) culture to the level of mass culture. In other words, many people are exposing themselves to many excellent experiences, but they are enjoying or patronizing them for the wrong reasons. Responding psychologically to a play of Sophocles as if it were a television soap opera (rather than bringing to it to the well-sharpened sensitivities of the individual schooled in the appreciation of fine art) is as debasing a discrete cultural event as enjoying the soap opera itself. Macdonald gloomily sees the technology of mass communications, and the opulence of the masses, as instruments by which high culture is being diluted, simplified and trivialized. Mass culture itself is also unredeemed by its own artists, because they are forced, by the demands of the technology of mass communications, to repeat their own successes to mediocrity.

Macdonald appears on the track of a crucial point in regard to the social value of communications in a technological culture. His argument is fortunately directed not only at the logics of the mediums of communication but their psychologics as well. What Macdonald observes—and Toffler and Seldes and many of the mass culture sociologists miss—is that *raw output* of communications in terms of universality, diversity and conduits of communication means little in calculating their effects upon society. True enough, one cannot obtain at a market a product which is not on sale there, but nearly everything (in cultural *impedimenta*) *is* sold at our market place, and *is* available for nearly everyone, in some form logically acceptable to *him*. Take, for instance, Shaw's play, *Pygmalion*. It is available in numerous editions at various prices for anyone who wants to read it. If you cannot (or will not) read it, repertory companies, stock companies and college dramatic groups are forever performing it. For those of different inclination, a musical version of it was fabricated for Broadway, and its touring companies have crossed the nation. Then the musical became a hit film. (A film of the play itself was made in England and widely circulated a generation ago.) Record albums are available of the scores of the musical or the movie, in various versions, in mono and stereo on records and magnetic tape.

My own psychological reaction to all of this is much the same as one would presume Macdonald's to be: that what was once a charming little cameo re-enactment, Shaw's *Pygmalion* (and many of us treasure one or another favorite performer as Eliza), has undergone a shattering metamorphosis at the hands of the vulgarians—merciful and talented vulgarians like director Moss Hart, designer Cecil Beaton, the singing professor, Rex Harrison, and composers Lerner and Lowe—but vulgarious, nevertheless. Poor little *Pygmalion* has now a vast, new audience; it has entered the world of mass culture. But for those of us who loved it for the unpretentious bittersweet little romantic-social comedy that, for better or worse, it once was, it *can* never be the same again. The *play* is now *My Fair Lady*—without the songs and Ascot costumes!

Mass Culture and Communications

The marketplace is indeed glutted, and it is possible to find there almost *anything* in some form. College students purchase millions of mass-produced review-books, like the universally popular *Philosophy Made Simple*. How long before some enterprising publisher fabricates the rest of the series: *Art Appreciation Made Simple, Playwriting Made Simple, Nuclear Physics Made Simple* and *Surgery Made Simple,* and so forth? Technology today permits the near unlimited distribution of just about every work ever produced in the narrative, pictorial and dramatic mediums. With simple methods of video and sound recording and the development of Xerography, the assortment will grow still wider. Memories of computers will also serve to locate and distribute whatever portion of this output one desires at a moment's notice.

The significant social perspective of these developments, as Macdonald indicates, is *what is done with what is communicated.* How does mass culture relate to the total psychological field of the masses themselves, and how does it bear upon other institutions in society? This question may only be answered in terms of *results.* Macdonald concludes simply that—as far as he can see—neither the wide dissemination of "easy" high culture, or "easier" mass culture, has done much towards humanizing the American masses, either in the intangible civilities of human relationships or in the more noticeable arts and artifacts which historically describe societal enterprise. Toffler's optimism, from Macdonald's view at least, is in no manner justified by simple observation. A meaningful cultural renaissance in the United States appears, at nearest, remotely possible in a good generation or two at its soonest, which puts it well beyond the year 2,000 A.D.

The ultimate test of mass education or any other social control (including the application of any social theory to social problems) is how its techniques have *worked.* In the United States, we have become so accustomed to dodging this social pragmatic test by redefining our tasks in terms of our failures that we are often immune to the evidence of our eyes—or the lack of it. In other nations, for instance, high school children are taught to speak and write foreign languages. Here we alibi our failure at teaching this skill by virtue of the immensity of the job and grab futilely at some form of gadgetry that may hopefully accomplish the task for us. It fails, just as most of our other educational trickery, officially called Audio-Visual Instruction (but nicknamed "Mickey Mouse" education), has, by and large, failed. Nothing is essentially wrong with these devices, but set in the context of our parlous aims and methods of schooling they are administered and communicated in schools of education, and between school systems, by the intellectual dregs of our academic community. And it is difficult to imagine how technological devices, often in the hands of incompetents, will do anything but compound our present problems in the long run.[28]

The results are all around us, and the peculiar nature of American mass culture is one of them, not necessarily the most important. It is, however, symptomatic of *both* a failure of cultural leadership (meaning education and government) and a failure of technology and technologists, which, in this age of technological hegemony, is especially discouraging. It is of no importance that there is today available on the market for the average American technological devices that may potentially be "programmed" for immediate access to the highest cultural achievements of man since the beginning of literacy! Neither is it important that, in the city in which this is being written, the most refined and the most vulgar newspapers in the nation reach the newsstands side by side. It *is* significant that the vulgar one sells many, many times the copies of the other, and apparently its readers are at least as dependent upon it as the readers of the refined one. That daytime television is abominable is almost inconsequential and irrelevant to the total thrust of our mass culture. What should concern our social strategists is the fact that when one of these screen diversions is cancelled in favor of a serious program of *some* value, station managers are literally beseiged by 'phone calls and irate letters protesting the cancellation! Certainly, some of the world's finest museums are located in our American cities; but what does one make of galleries, filled with "op" art, "pop" art and abstractions that would insult the intelligence of a clever ape, attracting dense crowds of spectators who gape at them in admiration simply because they have been *told* to do so?

What *is* also important is that our national magazines (and magazine sections of "better" newspapers) feature articles idolizing "hipsters," "hippies," "teeny-boppers" and professional near-mongoloid singing "groups," many of the members of which could not sing a note if their lives depended upon it! They insinuate and imply that ignorant enthusiasms of the young (justified solely by their youth) represent cultural *desiderata*, wise for their elders not only to condone but to emulate. The problem does *not* lie in the fact that the plurality of our cinema offerings runs from sadistic, neanderthal melodramas to fair-to-middling versions of so-called "classics" like *Tom Jones*. The problem *is* that formularized tripe repeating the *same* stereotypes and the *same* jokes on which our present middle-aged generation was raised attract many times the number of customers (most of them youngsters)

[28] These discontents with American education, based upon twenty-three years as a teacher and teacher of teachers, are by no means unique. For a sound analysis of the problem, read Arthur Bestor, *The Restoration of Learning* (New York: Alfred A. Knopf, 1955), and for the most realistic work on what to *do* about this critical problem, see James B. Conant, *The Education of American Teachers* (New York: McGraw-Hill Book Company, Inc., 1963).

than the few and honest fine films—both American and foreign—that attempt to invest a dose of novelty into that young but tired theatrical technique, the cinema.[29]

What *is* most important about mass culture is not that it is *mass* or that it, effectively, gives the public what it *wants*, especially considering that the public has never been provided with the intellectual or emotional equipment to *want* anything else! The social psychologist's concerns about debasement of taste, isolation of individuals one from the other, or horrors of escapism are not contemporary problems of our greatest concern. *Mass culture is making us no worse than we are!* And if our collective needs for self-aggrandizement, for instance, were not met by television, radio, the press and movies, they would probably be met in other ways. Neither does one take much heart, except momentarily, in the knowledge that *some* of our mass culture may possibly be tomorrow's high culture, and that, even if it will not, some of it is surprisingly excellent.

We live today in an environment fashioned to some extent in the highest ideals of educational aspiration and social idealism. Understood by the progenitors of our American culture was an assumption that the *choices* citizens made—political choices particularly, but not confined to them— were of crucial significance to the welfare and advancement of that culture. This, essentially, is what family life, law, the democratically oriented civilities of social intercourse, and education were—and are—all about, and to these ends did the men who built our country struggle.

For a great part of our society, the illusion is abroad that the apotheosis of Western culture awaits at our doorstep. And the world, past and present, *does* lie at our fingertips. Our great middle class, *including* millions of members of racial and religious minorities, enjoy both wealth and leisure beyond their needs. And what choices *do* we make? We all too frequently choose nonsense over sense, vulgarity over refinement, ugliness over beauty, waste over utility, speed over a sense of direction, "kicks" over pleasure, cruelty over civility, and violence over patience. God may forgive our ignorance, because we have *tried* to prevent it in our schoolhouses. If He is merciful, He will forgive our other frailties as well. But there will be no court of higher appeal to which to refer the verdict of posterity for the choices we have made in the vast marketplace of common experiences we call "mass culture."

No, nothing is necessarily wrong or sinful either in plurality or affluence. The mettle of a people, however, is tested by their exercise of judg-

[29] The "underground cinema" *does* occasionally deal with novelty of a kind. Because it abuses so painfully a technique which employs so well the narrative and dramatic mediums, the novelty is replaced, usually in short order, by tedium. Underground cinema, in fact, *all* experimental movies, hold out hope for the future of the film as a communication device and conduit for the transmission of artistic pictures, narratives and drama to a greater extent than the majority of commercial films. Like youth, the desire to experiment with filmic devices appears unfortunately to be wasted mostly on children. Their efforts are accordingly—and with exceptions—jejune.

ments of *value* in the face of plurality and their sense of *selflessness* in the face of affluence.

Conclusion

In our concern with mass culture, we have noted first, the range and variety of successful popular culture in the United States, explaining in some degree various viewpoints expressed today concerning this aspect of national life by equally competent analysts. We have also noted some of the reasons why experimentalism yields null hypothesis when looking for *specific* effects of various techniques of communication on children or adults. While the abilities of current researchers were not questioned, their objectives, assumptions, hypothesis and methods were, particularly in the light of the *observable* effects of mass communication in the every day contexts of modern life.

The nature of mass culture was next discussed from various perspectives. First, the critical approach of writers like Gilbert Seldes was examined, emphasizing a generally affirmative and constructive attitude towards artists using the modern techniques of communication who had achieved a measure of distinction. Opposed to this point of view was the social psychological perspective which tends to regard mass culture as a single social manifestation, displaying certain societal characteristics. Consideration was given to the nature of what, particularly, distinguishes "mass" culture from "class" culture. The problem of popularizing and spreading wide to the masses an appreciation of class culture was also introduced.

Next, the concept of the "mass" itself was considered irrespective of its relationship to communications, noting that, according to Ortega y Gasset, this phenomenon arose mainly in societies whose value structures had been influenced by concepts of liberal democracy, scientific experimentation and industrialism. The interplay of these factors, their relationship to culture and to communications themselves was noted. Emphasis was placed upon how pseudo-constructions of liberal democracy may lead, not to a widening of popular choice, but rather to the manipulation of the public.

An examination was then begun of the common factors which the output of mass culture displays, patricularly the matter of style, which appears to be the one thread that runs through much of it. Consideration was given spokesmen for the viewpoint that our nation today, by virtue of its cultural riches, is closer to a renaissance of high culture than it has ever been. To this largely quantitative argument were brought the gloomy perspectives of Dwight Macdonald, who sees in the groping after "the better things in life" by thousands of our citizens the vulgarization of art, rather than the elevation of a populace.

Finally, the size of the American marketplace was considered in terms of the relatively few choices consumers make from an enormous variety of goods. Here, the determinism of ignorance, the ineffectiveness of contemporary values, and the futile attempts which educators have made to solve the problem for the average citizen were treated. The vital role of choice was brought up as it influences the future of a society, and attention was centered less upon how full the marketplace is, than what consumers will choose and the bases upon which they are likely to make their choices.

Chapter 20

PROSPECTS

THROUGHOUT THIS BOOK an implicit attempt has been made to show the primacy of content in the languages of communications. It has also aimed at demonstrating the directive power of content in the determination of, first, *what mediums* will be employed for certain communications and, second, *which specific devices* are likely to best utilize these mediums and, third, *how* they may be used. If this approach to the logical and psychological analysis of communications has been adequate, the state of culture, specifically *what people have to say* to one another now and in the future, will necessarily determine the direction and nature of change in *how* people communicate with each other. Since *mass* communications appear at present to hold such immediate relevancies to our institutions, their nature and prospects appear to be major determinants for the future of many other kinds of communications—even those between individuals—in our particular technological society. Hence, the role of the previous chapter in adumbrating an image of mass culture primarily in terms of *what* the languages of communications are saying to us in contemporary western society.

Mass culture is, of course, far from being the sole conduit for communications in a modern culture. But in our time, at least, it seems to have peculiarly pervasive effects, and it appears in some manner to influence nearly all of our major societal movements, including public works, public health, social work (even the direction taken by social problems) and others.[1] Its content so influences general values that few institutions, even

1 Recently, an article appeared in a veterinarian's magazine concerning the relationship between McLuhan's theories and pet ownership ("the dog is an extension of man"). On the same day a frightful television program, in which juvenile narcotic addicts indulged in what might loosely be called "group therapy," indicated how fully speech patterns and sterotyped forms of behavior, responses, dress and motivation are communicated by mass culture, even to these children. What was more disturbing than the addiction of the children was the probability that this session could have taken

our established churches, are beyond its reach.[2] It lends stylistic coloration to nearly every aspect of modern life: our philosophical fashions, the teaching of history in college classrooms, the books we read (or fail to read), financial trends in the stock markets, world trade, international diplomacy and domestic politics. None of these sectors of public activity is beyond the influence of mass communications. This fact is occasionally brought in some manner to public attention, usually to the pseudo-amazement of the mass communicators themselves—for instance, when a national election appears to hinge upon the "television image" of a candidate when he appears on the television tube next to his adversary.[3] We are often reminded, as well, of the ubiquity of the mass communication techniques when an "enemy" nation uses the forum of the United Nations (and its press, radio and television corps) to harangue the world against us.[4]

At the same time, of course, broad cultural influences of mass communications reach into smaller, unlikely places. In some measure they determine how mothers scold their children, and *if* they scold them; how chemistry is taught in high school and, sometimes, *if* it is to be taught; what fashions in research our natural and social scientists follow, and which will be closed to them. The "communications establishment" even provides the rebel with a *specific* mos to oppose, and it offers a whipping post for the iconoclast, the eremite or the snob, as well as the artist or scientist who marches to a different drummer. Rebellion, healthy or unhealthy, against the assumed power of the mass communications industries is a common spectacle today in our literature and in our urban bohemias. Judgments of these rebellions are often hastily announced by Sunday supplement pundits. Either we indifferently, or lazily, encourage psychopaths to inject wild and obviously poisonous nonsense into the bloodstream of society, or, conversely, we reject outright an apparently unworkable "modest proposal" that might

---

place *anywhere* in the United States. On the same day, an "educational" television station presented a number of instructional television lessons prepared by a group of experienced teachers, not one of whom apparently had the slightest notion of the intellectual antecedents of *what* they were teaching, but whose lessons were fouled with the inappropriate use of what are considered television "techniques." This was just part of a normal day's demonstrations of the pervasive influence into unlikely places of mass communications.

[2] See Bernard Iddings Bell, *Crowd Culture* (New York: Harper and Brothers, Publishers, 1952), especially pp. 93–123. The late Canon Bell was a keen social critic of our culture, not only from the vantage point of the Episcopal Church but from the educator's perspective as well. This short book is one of the best yet published on this pervasive quality of mass culture.

[3] See Sidney Kraus (ed.), *The Great Debates* (Bloomington: Indiana University Press, 1962), for a diversified series of analysis of one such particular event—the Nixon-Kennedy "debates"—and the relationships to the techniques of mass communication of the behavior of the voting public in this instance.

[4] See the chapter entitled "We Were Never Lovelier" in George N. Gordon, Irving Falk and William Hodapp, *The Idea Invaders*, pp. 70–91, for example of how, not only the publicity resources of the United Nations, but those of our own open society, were cleverly exploited towards this end by the U.S.S.R. in 1959.

help to ameliorate one of our many social, economic or cultural problems.[5] Whatever their results, they are by-products of our systems of communications.

The cliché artists tell us that we live in an *age of mass communications*. We do: but the observation is as meaningless to *us* as an announcement to the citizens of Nantes in the eleventh century might have been that they were living in an *age of belief*. The label would have been irrelevant to them as is the *age of communications* slogan is to us. Some of the best minds—and the worst—in history have lived through extraordinary periods, quite unaware of what aspect of their particular environments would most trenchantly influence the lives of their own children. Let us not indulge a conceit that we are wiser than they were, or that now, at last, *we* possess *any* scientific, philosophical or technological instrument to predict more accurately *our* destiny than they did. Science and technology have given us *power*, far more power than even our recent ancestors. But they have not given us a single indication of the *direction, place* and *means* we will exercise that power, or how, or to what end, *in any respect*, except for the generally accepted (but doubtful) inference that the future will manifest more "progress" than the present. In the specific matter of the future of communications technology—an ephemeral topic at best—let us, therefore, proceed especially humbly. But let us proceed.

Logic: Narrative

Central to a consideration of the destiny of the logic of narrative is the price that has been paid for contemporary national semi-literacy, a problem previously discussed. Whether the price is worth its consequences is not at issue: merely that the price cannot be underestimated.

In the world of letters, national semi-literacy has produced a form of mass literature unknown before in history, in emotional and cognitive content, in style and tone and intention. Whether this average man, for whom this literature is written, represents the economists' or sociologists' "middle-class man" or "typical bourgeoise" is irrelevant; the only important fact about him is that he is average. Also of little concern is whether he is like the average man of yesterday. What is important is whether he will be like the average man *tomorrow*, and one finds few reasons—upon examination of the two main formative institutions in our society, the home and school—why he will *not* be.

The special literature (in the form of narrative only) that has been created for him, is distinctive in many ways, the most important of which is that it, first, invariably provides reassurance for credence in current social

---

[5] See Robert Lindner, *Prescription for Rebellion* (New York: Grove Press, Inc., 1952), for a well-articulated discussion by a psychoanalyst of the difference between healthy and unhealthy rebellion and the symptoms of each. The late Dr. Lindner, who died in 1956, was himself a rebel among analysts, and his loss has been felt by his admirers from a number of disciplines.

myths and, second, it affirms the excellence of the average man himself, less by virtue of being average than for merely being a man. Its main appeal is to comfort, materialistic success, sexual and sentimental enjoyments. These, in essence, are literature's "American way of life," apple pie and milk, or *impedimenta* of the "swinging" generation.

This form of narrative is by no means as obvious or simple to understand as many, particularly popular critics, seem to think. A great number of Americans are insulated from it by ignorance or wisdom, or because they fancy themselves too "busy" to partake of it. Some are too poor. Others are not able either to concentrate or read well enough. Let us remember, also, that the marketplace overflows with this material, and, if and when one looks beyond the mountains of best known mass circulating books and magazines, the vista is chaotic. Having dealt with *Life*, *Look* and *The Reader's Digest*, one is faced with such an enormous number of alternatives that there is no doubt that many citizens turn away from such a plentitude of literature in sheer confusion.

Convinced, therefore, that *all* narrative should be as culturally affirmative as our new mass literature, narrative artists in other mediums of communication emulate, as closely as possible, this particular literary form. This imitation then becomes the inspiration for more literature, and the cycle spins so fast that we lose sight of both cause and effect.

In the matter of politics, for instance, the introduction of the "columnist" to the daily newspaper focused the narrative aspects of complex political questions into the modest conceptual capacities of the average man. The political cartoonist (in the person of men like Thomas Nast, William Newman and Bernard Gillam in the post-Civil War period)[6] took up the simplistic narrative themes of the columnists' (mostly editors of newspapers) usually negative personal invective and exposé by the latter part of the last century. Before long, these same logical themes had found their way into the theatre in such plays as Edward Sheldon's *The Boss*, and others. The same narrative thrust moved eventually to the movies (even to such "artistic" enterprises as Griffith's *Intolerance*), and into the plots of soap operas[7] more or less intact. Then it moved back to literature again, with such best sellers as *Advise and Consent* and *The Last Hurrah*, and on to the cinema, shown for a while in motion picture theatres, and finally to a more permanent resting-place in repertoire on our home television late shows.

Little of this output had anything to do with more than the marginal

[6] This trend is well covered in Becker, *Comic Art in America*, pp. 288–310.
[7] Memory serves poorly here, but wasn't Mary Marlin's long-lost husband a Senator, and didn't Helen Trent and even Our Gal Sunday and Ma Perkins get involved with the kind of dirty politics that was exposed regularly for the masses in many syndicated newspaper columns? (How unfortunate that neither a definitive library or scholarly analysis of soap opera themes, characters and plots exists. No reputable foundation is, however, likely to underwrite such an enterprise, nor may there exist a competent scholar foolish enough to supervise it.)

aspects of actual American political life![8] Laws and their interpretations, juridical decisions and the actual exercise and distribution of power in a complex (and growing) state were too complicated to reduce to the logical narrative mold to which the public had become, and is, sensitive. For this reason, even contemporary political best-sellers, disseminated by any communications device and employing any of the mediums, are usually expressed in the simplest mode of logical narrative available.

That this mode has also been taken into our textbooks, classroom discussions, and graduate seminars *as well as* by the technological communications devices is relevant to many implications for the future. As a nation, we run one sort of risk when we elect to the office of President the sort of man who refuses to read more than one single page of "boiled down" narrative text. We run another, far graver one, when this same sort of mentality is perpetuated within our entire population for a generation. The result is that even communications addressed to normal or superior minds must be reduced to the level of logic which is most *comfortable* for the mass communications "market."

Logic: Picture

The logic (and here the more commonly used term "aesthetic" is, of course, also appropriate) of picture includes every sight that falls across the human retina, as well as those special visions preserved by paint, print or photography, still or in motion, chemically or photo-electrically generated.

Broadly speaking, therefore, the sights that one sees in a technological society are necessarily sights of technology—so-called "man-made" as opposed to "nature-made" objects. But, as Claude Levi-Strauss stresses,[9] much of what we assume to be the work of nature is simply natural *in spite of* man's continual intervention in natural processes. Today, not only shapes, forms and patterns of movement stem from the technological culture, but colors of peculiar iridescence that are rarely found in nature dazzle our eyes, and we are treated to the optical playfulness of infra-reds and ultra-violets which provide new sensations for visual perceptions. By the last half of the nineteenth century, the re-examination of the discovery of central perspective opened up for artists the insight that, despite their apparent accuracy, pictures of *all* kinds deal in illusions: that oil painting, photography, the motion picture, the television image and the "op art" canvas are *all* illusions, differentiated logically only by the *degree* to which illusion cleaves from reality.

Having examined so intently and frequently technological landscapes

---

[8] When it *did* relate to important political issues, it usually centered on relatively inconsequential aspects of significant themes. For instance, from Nast onward, even our cleverest political writers (with the exception of those who, like Walter Lippmann, addressed themselves to an élite), emphasized "personalities," rather than the issues for which these individuals stood.

[9] See Claude Levi-Strauss, *Tristes Tropiques*, pp. 77–108.

by means of technological devices, we need not be surprised nor soured to discover that the dominant *logical* value apparent in pictures in our culture is that of *technology itself*: man-made objects and—as in the case of Hollywood starlets, "pop art" ketchup bottles and similar items—mass produced, exterior containers filled with organic but (more or less) sterilized natural interiors. That portrait artists and photographers, and little old ladies who paint flower arrangements, are held by this modern pictorial trend in a dilemma with which they can either compromise (as do portrait artists) or bemoan (like old ladies) is inevitable. The version of da Vinci's "Last Supper" that a weekend artist can copy by painting "by the numbers" in Woolworth's window is the prototypical art work right *now*. It is neither better nor worse than abstractions calculated with rulers or achieved by rolling nude women covered with paint on canvas. All of a piece, our *sense of picture* is yielding to the tricks of "know how" that are the basic to the *weltanschauung* of technology.

The future of the logic of picture—of the pictures which the retinas of our eyes will *allow* us to see in the mirror of nature—depends naturally upon the future of technology, not graphic art! Many believe that technological culture is strangling itself by polluting our rivers and air, spreading radioactivity into the seas, poisoning our food supplies with insecticide, putting chemicals in our drinking water (which turn our bones into Delft china), and, in general, creating an environment that none but the heartiest of our progeny will survive. Others are concerned that this same technology is insidiously driving us mad; and still others are convinced that we are on the brink of blowing ourselves to bits. Should *any* of them be correct, the logic of picture will be of little cultural consequence. Whatever of the human race remains after the Armageddon will undoubtedly be hurled back to the symbolism of primitive man and worship of the ruins of former cultures and of nature, like most non-technological people.

Should technology, on the other hand, confound its critics and make good the faith of the common citizen in it, a number of possibilities are present. First, the trend towards the elimination of nature in color, form and movement will probably continue apace. The trend is already dominant in architecture, city planning, industrial design, advertising and the popular arts, and has made numerous inroads into the world of fine art. In twenty years, it may not only be naïve for a still or moving picture to imitate nature, it may be subversive.

Second, movements in the development of realistic illusions may be technically so developed that the conventional laws of perspective will give way to a *technology of perspective*, whereby painting, drawings and motion pictures will all develop three-dimensional illusions similar to those we perceive in life. New kinds of planes, or screens, made up of beams of energy as surfaces for pictures may become commonplace.

Third, the pendulum of culture may swing back—in revulsion *against* technology—towards what is left of the world of nature. We may return in prospect to the garden visions of the eighteenth century; but a cruder nature, as Edward Weston, for instance, saw it with his camera, or as biologists and natural scientists view it, may attract again the attention of our best artists. Some of this curiosity concerning natural processes is visible in the fumbling attempts of today's "underground" movie makers. Their needs seem to be expressed in a desire to explore forms, shapes and subjects which have been hitherto overlooked by motion picture photographers and untouched by editors. What the world of art is waiting for, perhaps, is an Albert Schweitzer (suitably reactionary and self-idolizing) with a paint brush or camera. Perhaps such an individual is aready wandering in the slums of our cities or in authentic jungles, but—although one sees many paintings, pictures and films made in these places—we have not yet seen his work.

Logic: Re-enactment

The logic of re-enactment (to some, the technique of the drama) has, as we have seen, been discovered in every device of communication available today. In many instances, it has worked its way to preeminence, and added distinctive coloration to it. If the utilization of one medium of communication characterizes our culture, our time and our communications devices, it is the medium of re-enactment—in the popular press, on radio, in films, on television and in life itself.

This phenomenon is ironic to many because the professional theatre—the contemporary drama performed in professional playhouses—reaches yearly a new national nadir from the period between Eugene O'Neill and the present. The professional theatre of Broadway has shriveled, while the drama flourishes in such unlikely places as the pages of our magazines, our television commercials and in contemporary novels. Some of the latter constitute little more than stretches of dialogue held together by crudely articulated scene descriptions and stage instructions.

Logically, the drama has remained what Aristotle said it was four hundred years before Christ. And for these reasons, it seems to be *the* ideal medium for the spread of mass culture by means of technological instruments of mass communication. Aristotle noted that the drama was capable of showing *part* of an entire event (he used the illustration of *The Iliad*), while narrative was more suited to encompassing the *entire* event. What coincidences of culture created a technology of communication *and* a public that would be more disposed to accepting simple segments of highly dramatic ideas than complex mosaics of fully articulated constructions, one cannot guess. Such fragmented communications are ideal for our time and place. Modification of narrative and picture by the introduction of dramatic technique—or the illusion of re-enactment—has become a conventional (and stylized) way in which *all three mediums* of communications have been rendered acceptable for distribution by the devices of print, sound and picture transmission. In addition, a public has been trained to expect (and demand) short and dramatic communications that provide the special kind of empathetic impact so easily accomplished by re-enactment.

Our technological culture has emphasized the *digest*—not only of magazine articles, but of operas, novels and almost every other facet of literary culture. For many reasons, we have accepted the canard that ours is a hurried period, when we must believe (quite literally) that time is money, and money paves the road to immortality. In a culture where it is a sin to waste *time*—and where numerous instruments of mass communication bid for our attention at any moment—it is obvious that we will seek out the most dramatic stimuli and those least likely to interfere with our hurry. As Aristotle implies, the individual who has seen a re-enactment of the *part* of a totality is frequently under the impression that he has been exposed to the *whole* experience. Hence, his satisfaction. This psychological phenomenon is of interest here as an inevitable by-product of our contemporary preference for the logics of drama in *all* of our experiences with the mediums of communication.

How pervasive *is* re-enactment? This is difficult to judge, although it is certain, for instance, that the structure of language in "telling" or "reporting" displays a greater dramatic influence than English used for similar purposes a century ago. This is quite simple to demonstrate by comparison of the cognitive, imitative, stylistic and intentional qualities of newspaper stories then to now. We may induce little about differences in face-to-face communication between men in the street, but we *may* roughly judge that, as technology opened up new instruments for communication, the power of re-enactment in sending messages probably increased apace.

We are also living in a period culturally suited to dramatization, whether the cause or result of our technologies of communication, it is not possible to determine. Ours has become the era of the celebrity—the historical or cultural "good guy" or the "bad guy," caught up in the "plot" of time; the "public figure" who plays his role in newspapers and on screens. Individuals may cast themselves as culture comics (like Henry Morgan), tragi-comedy heroines (like Judy Garland), or martyrs (like Greta Garbo). Or they may pretend that fate has somehow placed *them* in stereotyped roles of their own (or fate's) devising (like the Duke of Windsor), providing that the instruments of mass communication are ready to employ the mediums of narrative, picture and drama—but especially drama—to lend credence to their self-characterizations.

Psychologic: Narrative

The future of the narrative medium, from a psychological perspective, unfortunately, is bleak. One is inclined to predict that as the logic of re-enactment increases its hold over the other mediums, as the technological instruments of communications grow in power and ubiquity, and as technology spreads its influence to publics heretofore immune to it by virtue of their economic status, caste or poverty, education for the very *perception* of narrative will diminish. The trend is already evident. The result will be education primarily directed at the perception of drama and picture, if merely by default. Neither words nor print will diminish in their currency, but they will be employed to *say* things in dramatic modes and will increasingly be accompanied by moving pictures. Documentaries on television and the movie screen will become even more fraudulent as mirrors of life than they are now, as they eschew increasingly the realism of narrative for the psychological impact of drama.

The move away from the psychological aspect of narrative is today nowhere more apparent than in our schools, where audio-visual specialists are on the prowl—almost invariably with high motives and sometimes with considerable skill—to translate some verbal or narrative aspect of instruction *from* the narrative medium into pictures or re-enactment, merely by substituting a teaching film or televised lesson for a concept that a teacher once explained in words. There are numerous interesting pedagogical objections to this trend, and some of them have been articulated expertly.[10] But one need be less worried about the trivialization of teaching than the highly contagious assumptions inherent in this tendency. They take for granted that the development of an individual's psychological perceptions in the narrative aspect of communications is somehow less efficient, modern and/or useful than communicating with him in pictorial or dramatic mediums.

In the culture of the last century, the virtue of narrative and the need for the development of powers to assimilate it were understood by educated men as psychological necessities of life. The powers of the printed word were so venerated that university libraries were usually kept locked, lest some sneaky scholar search out corruptive reading matter which might hasten his journey to hell. One had to have permission from a professor to borrow a book. How delightful to imagine the avidity with which nineteenth century scholars drank deep of the heady wines of the narrative medium!

Technology, therefore, influenced the writing, printing and distribution of narrative works—and we may now include also techniques of recorded narrative—in many noticeable and rapid ways. Two generations ago, the delights of narrative were reserved for readers and fortunate listeners to "story tellers" on the Chautauqua circuit and to authors like Dickens and Twain, who read from their own works. With technological change, psychological orientations changed as well. They are still changing. The

[10] See Joseph Wood Krutch, *Human Nature and the Human Condition*, pp. 133–137. Krutch fears that these "new techniques of mass communication inevitably and by their very nature weaken the power to learn at the same time that they make being taught so easy." (p. 136.)

narrative medium is today a stepchild of our educational institutions, except perhaps at the university, where a large and active library is, currently at least, a symbol of status.[11] But what a university regards as a symbol of status, and what a faculty considers "effective teaching" are frequently different. Today's college instructor is likely to pride himself on being a "spellbinder," a dramatist without a stage, who simplifies everything, satisfactory to the comprehensions of his *least competent* students. He frequently measures his effectiveness by the number of films, slides, film strips, television tapes and recordings that he has played in class to "stimulate students' interest." He is almost never aware that he may be but one factor (among many) "deadening the interest" of his class in his *subject* (not in the devices used) and vitiating appreciation of the narrative medium of communication.

These changes may be regarded, for a decade or so to come, as a stylistic modification in letters, inevitable results of the General Semantics movement (and others) to clear our language of its rhetorical haze. They will also be explained as shifts away from the "print media" to the "picture media," moving and still. Interpretations of the metamorphosis may even include explanations involving mind reading and communication by means of a psychedelic vocabulary of sense and feeling to which our perceptions were previously closed.

All such explanations for the decline of the psychological significance of the narrative medium in our time are nonsense! The narrative medium of communication is now being trivialized and extended beyond our public's capacities to comprehend, merely because the basic training of literate men no longer includes—with few exceptions—the development of the power to comprehend narrative connections of ideas in literature, art, history or science. Modern technology simply does not demand that man be trained to partake of these traditions, except crudely and superficially—often *most* crudely and *most* superficially in educational institutions that are considered the most advanced. Prospects for the future are therefore clear.

Psychologic: Picture

When previously discussing the logic of picture, the relationship of man to nature was emphasized. This is a crucial nexus for the future of the psychological aspect of this medium as well. Prior to other considerations, therefore, is the basic observation that no matter how bizarre the *logics* of picture may become tomorrow (in painting, still or moving photography, or some other "art form"), *pictures of the future will be regarded as a move toward realism.* They will be defended primarily as devices for seeing more

---

[11] A large and active library is, of course, *not* a sign of academic excellence! One of the most sophisticated "information retrieval systems" in the nation today is located at a university founded by and named after a faith-healer. Many of us have worked or studied at universities with large and busy libraries where the plagiarism and doctoring-up of term paper bibliographies appeared to be the major ongoing activities.

clearly and deeply into the cognitive and emotional life of man *as he views nature*. This is the psychological starting point for most picture-making at present, and there is little reason to believe that it will change drastically in the next generation. If change does come to this *raison d'être*, it will serve the purpose of keeping certain gods at bay in much the manner that ancestral portraits function now.

Styles of pictures will, of course, follow the developing technology of still and motion photography, and that late-starter with fascinating potentials, television. We may also expect developments of hybrid techniques which utilize both optical and electronic methodologies of taking pictures and showing them on screens. But these styles will change—primarily as they have been changing—in direct proportion to the way in which our picture makers misinterpret the latest findings of experimental psychology, popular psychological and social theory, as well as transient socio-cultural myths that tickle their fancies. The picture maker, unless he is lucky or smart, takes his chances with the psychological fashions of the future. His style may maintain its integrity and meaning for centuries, or it may be passé in a handful of years. The more "modern" he is at one moment, the more "outdated" he may well become the next.

The chances are high that our audiences, generally, will continue to maintain their sanguine attitudes towards pictures. They will continue to believe the wicked lie that a picture is worth a thousand words, and that photography, particularly the moving photography of the cinema and television, gives them a "real" notion of the nature of the subjects it records. They will demand that more and more communications be "illustrated." Especially will the external design of technology, which by its nature they equate with the "useful," continue to fascinate them. Consider, for example, the motor car of today, the exterior design of which has less to do with its function than that of the Model T Ford! To the psychological "mind's eye" it appears more "modern" and "efficient" than the Model T, but it necessitates the removal of a side to fix a dented fender.

Non-truths of this kind will also be encapsulated in the pictures that will influence the costume silhouette of tomorrow's society in quite the same way that they provide the *lingua franca* for today's styles. Were these predictions oriented to the trivial, we might forecast that American women will coat themselves more noticeably with aerosol plastics than at present. They will also bid louder for attention via bizarre makeups, particularly as they paint their eyes, lips and fingernails various colors, accentuating the organs, first, of perception (with which they are incorrectly reputed to experience extraordinarily accurate intuitions), second, of sensual contact and, third, attack, in that order of significance.[12] Men will break away from

---

[12] We will *not* have to live through an era of topless female bathing suits for a number of reasons, but mainly because so many American women frequently tend either to be over-bestowed or flat-chested. What we *will* live to see is spray-on bathing wear in

their nineteenth century dullness in dress, but slowly. While his basic costume will remain dour, the male will, however, gather about him more and more wildly ornamental accessories like eyeglass frames, cuff links, neckties, tiepins, lapel ornaments, etc. Most of them will perform no utilitarian function.

What we will accomplish, of course, is to outfit ourselves psychologically for our technology. If we *think* the technological society deprives us of individuality, our picture mediums will show us how to retrieve characterological uniqueness and be like everybody else at the same time. If technology eliminates the art of cooking (and it may), we will develop new facilities for gourmandism rather than the preparation of foods for eating. If it herds us to urban living centers or mile-high skyscrapers (as Frank Lloyd Wright once predicted), we shall head out into remaining, carefully modernized, woods in droves and live in tents in our spare time, a dreary movement that has already begun. We shall find that all technological change produces psychological reactions, and that every reaction will influence the image that man has of himself in tomorrow's culture. This image, of course, is what we will be shown in our *Life* magazines, our V*ogues*, our films and our television programs. In fact, from a psychological perspective, as we drive today past our ubiquitous billboards, frequently the most beautiful objects on a bleak American landscape, we pass endless self-portraits.[13]

Psychologic: Drama

As we observed when discussing the logics of drama, re-enactment in the past half century has outgrown the theatre. There is no doubt that professional theatres were the best places to nurture the dramatic medium of communication for the first three thousand years of our civilization's life. But technology has torn down theatre walls, and mass literacy and mass communications have introduced the art of re-enactment to new techniques employing printing presses, reproducing still and motion pictures, recording and sound broadcasting.

The legitimate theatre of tomorrow may show occasional moments of excitement for any of three reasons. First, the legitimate theatre performs for us a museum function. When we attend a live play, we associate ourselves psychologically with an ancient tradition which has been more or less continuous through our history.[14] Second, no matter how parlous the state of the drama at any time, the theatre presents a continual forum for revivals of plays of the past. Written for the living theatre, these plays usually

---

aerosol-type bombs. They will cover more epidermis than, say, the current bikinis, but will appear extremely provocative for obvious reasons, and will permit considerable deception in regard to the bust problem.
[13] How disappointing if our future does not include the formation of societies to preserve the highway billboard, which is already disappearing from some of our landscapes!
[14] The author, personally, feels nothing of this sort when he attends amateur dramatic endeavors, which he detests.

maintain a unique investiture of immediate contemporary power on the living stage. Third, it is doubtful that any kind of technology will diminish the peculiar pleasure that an audience takes in watching live performers, particularly celebrated people, perform in person. It matters less how good their performances are, frequently, than how celebrated they are. Often there is no need for them even to perform in a conventional drama; they need just appear, say "hello," sing a song or two, or dance. It is improbable that any amount of technology, no matter how used, will ever vitiate these three qualities, particularly the third, of the living theatre.

Otherwise, the theatre is not dying; it is dead and may only be revived, one suspects, by enforced or accidental extinction of technology. Let repertory companies spring up in mining towns, let brave and idealistic youngsters "pack 'em in" for Shakespeare performances at summer festivals, let troupes of players tour high schools. The end has already arrived. These exceptions exploit the selective sensitivities of few out of millions who have psychologically found their drama in the novels, films, comics, television programs and the rest of mass culture that absorbs much of their lives.

So rapid has been this change—the expulsion of the psychological facets of the dramatic experience from the playhouse—that dramatists themselves are only now beginning to recognize it. But waking up they are, and, as a result, they are not so much deserting the playhouse, as not even bothering to stop there in the first place! At least, this is happening in America, where, since World War II, our three best playwrights are pallid contenders for favors when compared to their predecessors of the previous generation. The drama will die harder on continental Europe and in England, exactly at the rate that Europeans and Englishmen become psychologically oriented to technology, and as drama increases its currency within other mediums of communication.

For the remainder of the present middle-aged generations' lifetime, sentimentalists will offer sufficient encouragement, bolstered by the prejudices of Sunday newspaper drama editors and tricks of press agentry, to keep up psychological steam for the living stage among a small élite audience. This diminishing race may encourage an occasional dramatist to write at least one interesting play before he defects for the greener pastures of the technological world. But this coterie will die out, leaving the legitimate stage to serve its anthropological, museum and curiosity-seeking functions.[15]

Lamentations for the living theatre do not, however, alter the truism that our own individual psychological perceptions of drama are becoming

15 No prediction is made here that large audiences will not turn out to watch celebrities of *all* kinds perform in various sorts of revivals. (*Anything* of this sort is likely to be popular. Why not a State Governor or Senator in a revival of *Roberta*? Can't a hipster version of *The Merchant of Yonkers* be negotiated for some 'teenage stars?) What is moribund is the drama, or the art of the creation of new plays, serious or funny, of contemporary relevance. Tired businessmen will probably seek out lavish burlesque shows for at least the next one hundred years, but even the circus (in a semi-theatrical form) seems at present to be breathing its last gasps.

more and more atuned to the conditions of modernity. What other writers call "anomie" or "alienation" from the environment, and what some psychologists may classify as "neuroses," may often be understood best as circumstantial incompetence at "role playing" in the psychological dramas into which we are cast by life.

Mass communications and mass culture provides us with innumerable stereotypes for the parts we *must* play as parents, children, lovers, workers, etc. Our script is written largely by contemporary myth makers we have discussed in Chapters 5 and 6. Naturally, many millions of us fail—and fail miserably—at playing roles for which we are unsuited. Our recourse to new drugs like LSD, or old ones like alcohol, or to neurosis, is at least understandable and sometimes forgivable.

The words "role playing" are today heard frequently from the lips of sociologists, psychologists and educators. The term is apt, and possibly more broadly applicable to modern life than its glib users intend. Only one major school of psychotherapy, J. L. Moreno's "psycho-drama," utilizes the power of drama in *life* for the diagnoses, treatment or cure of disturbed individuals.[16] There is little doubt, however, that other kinds of therapists have also come to recognize the relevance of the psychologics of drama to the daily lives of most of us and to their own arts and sciences.

Conclusions

To review the predictions for the future of the mediums of communication in this chapter is pointless. They constitute in themselves a synthesis of much that has been written in this book. If one single generalization emerges from these past several pages, it is a simple historical observation: through some kind of cultural inertia of motion, tendencies or trends in the way social institutions develop tend to continue as they have in the past, unless other forces are brought to bear against them. This chapter has centered on those trends and the forces which are likely to oppose the logics and psychologics of communications as they pass into the future.

One point is certain: there is no reverse gear on the instrument of technology itself. It can only continue ahead or stop. As Whitehead says, "Not all your heroism, not all your social charm, not all your wit, not all your victories on land or at sea, can move back the finger of fate. Tomorrow science will have moved forward yet one more step, and there will be no appeal. . . ." and he continues to specify, ". . . from the judgment which will then be pronounced upon the uneducated." [17] Where science shows the way, technology will, of course, follow. And tomorrow's technology will inevitably include those devices which communicate narrative, picture and drama between the billions of people who share their time on earth.

[16] See Jakob L. Moreno and Helen Jennings, *Who Shall Survive?* (Washington, D.C.: Nervous and Mental Disease Publishing Co., 1934).
[17] A. N. Whitehead, *The Aims of Education*, p. 26.

Generations to come will have to make their own peace treaties with these powers. Our *best efforts* to achieve social controls, stability, and the benefits of education for ourselves or our children *by no means guarantee* a life better, in any way than ours, for our progeny. These attempts are only by-products of philosophies by which we live and determine the ways we deploy our material and cultural resources. This book has attempted to make the case that our languages of communication, properly understood, *are* just such resources—if they are realistically and humanely employed.

The achievement of this end will be difficult. This is because the languages of communication are at present victims of exploitation, mysticisms, art cults, "scientific" experimentalists and, worst of all, slick slogans mouthed by false prophets, who have set up their stands in, of all places, the academic community. None are likely to move unless they are pushed. But move they must if we are to use humanely our talents for speaking, writing, drawing and dreaming, as Emerson asked us, ". . . to resist the vulgar prosperity that retrogrades ever to barbarism, by communicating heroic sentiments, noble biographies, melodious verse and the conclusions of history." We can afford to require no less from ourselves, our peers, or our children.

SELECTED BIBLIOGRAPHY

The following books, both those referred to in the text and others, constitute an introductory—and near indispensable—foundation for further enquiry into the logics and psychologics of contemporary communications' problems. The editions cited are, in most instances, readily available at present.

Albig, William, *Modern Public Opinion*. New York: McGraw-Hill Book Co., 1956.

Anonymous (ed.), *The Eighth Art*. New York: Holt, Rinehart and Winston, 1962.

Archer, Gleason L., *History of Radio*. New York: The American Historical Society, 1938.

Arnheim, Rudolph, *Art and Visual Perception*. Berkeley and Los Angeles: The University of California Press, 1965.

———, *Film as Art*. Berkeley and Los Angeles: University of California Press, 1957.

Austin, J.L., *Sense and Sensibility*. Oxford, England: Oxford University Press, 1962.

Bainbridge, John, *Little Wonder*. New York: Reynal and Hitchcock, 1946.

Barnouw, Erik, *The Golden Web*. New York: Oxford University Press, 1968.

———, *A Tower in Babel*. New York: Oxford University Press, 1966.

Barrett, William A., *Irrational Man*. New York: Doubleday Anchor Books, 1958.

Barzun, Jacques, *The House of Intellect*. New York: Harper and Brothers Publishers, 1959.

———, *Science: The Glorious Entertainment*. New York: Harper and Row, 1964.

———, *Teacher in America*. Garden City, New York: Doubleday and Co., 1954.

Becker, Stephen, *Comic Art in America*. New York: Simon and Schuster, 1959.

Bell, Bernard Iddings, *Crowd Culture*. New York: Harper and Brothers, Publishers, 1952.

Bell, Daniel, *Work and Its Discontents*. Boston: Beacon Press, 1956.

Bentley, Eric, *The Playwright As Thinker*. New York: Meridian Books, 1955.

Berelson, Bernard, *Content Analysis in Communications Research*. Glencoe, Ill.: The Free Press, 1952.

——— and Gary Steiner, *Human Behavior*. New York: Harcourt, Brace and World, Inc., 1964.

Berlo, David, *The Process of Communication*. New York: Holt, Rinehart and Winston, 1960.

Bestor, Arthur, *The Restoration of Learning*. New York: Alfred A. Knopf, 1955.

Bluem, A. William, *Documentary in American Television*. New York: Hastings House, Publishers, Inc., 1965.

Blistein, Elmer, *Comedy in Action*, Durham, N.C.: Duke University Press, 1964.

Boorstein, Daniel J., *The Image*. New York: Harper and Row, 1964.

Brogan, D.W., *The American Character*. New York: Time Incorporated, 1962.

Bronowski, J., *The Face of Violence*. New York: George Braziller, 1955.

Brophy, Brigid, *Black Ship to Hell*. New York: Harcourt, Brace and World, 1962.

Brown, J.A.C., *Techniques of Persuasion*. Baltimore, Md.: Penguin Books, 1963.

Burke, Kenneth, *Language as Symbolic Action*. Berkeley and Los Angeles: University of California Press, 1966.

Cassirer, Ernst, *An Essay on Man*. Garden City, New York, Doubleday and Co., 1953.

——, *The Myth of the State*. Garden City, New York: Doubleday and Co., 1955.

Casty, Alan (ed.), *Mass Media and Mass Man*. New York: Holt, Rinehart and Winston, Inc., 1968.

Ceram, C.W., *Archaeology of the Cinema*. New York: Harcourt, Brace and World, Inc., 1965.

Cheney, Sheldon, *The Theatre*. New York: Longmans, Green and Co., 1952.

Cherry, Colin, *On Human Communications*. New York: John Wiley and Sons, Inc., 1961.

Choukas, Michael, *Propaganda Comes of Age*. Washington, D.C.: Public Affairs Press, 1965.

Christenson, Reo M. and Robert O. McWilliams (eds.), *Voices of the People*. New York: McGraw-Hill Book Co., Inc., 1962.

Clark, Barrett H. (ed.), *European Theories of the Drama*. New York: Crown Publishers, 1947.

Conant, James B., *The Education of American Teachers*. New York: McGraw-Hill Book Co., 1963.

Corrigan, Robert (ed.), *Comedy: Meaning and Form*. San Francisco, Calif.: Chandler Publishing Co., 1965.

Cox, Harvey, *The Secular City*. New York: The Macmillan Co., 1965.

Cremin, Lawrence A., *The Genius of American Education*. Pittsburgh, Pa.: University of Pittsburgh Press, 1965.

Davitz, Joel R. (ed.), *The Communication of Emotional Meaning*. New York: McGraw-Hill Book Co., 1964.

De Fleur, Melvin, *Theories of Mass Communication*. New York: David McKay and Co., 1966.

Dingwall, Eric John, *The American Woman*. New York: A Signet Book, 1957.

Dizard, Wilson P., *Television—A World View*. Syracuse: Syracuse University Press, 1966.

Eisenstein, Sergei, *Film Form and Film Sense*. New York: The World Publishing Co., 1963.

Ellul, Jacques, *Propaganda, The Formation of Men's Attitudes*. New York: Alfred A. Knopf, 1965.

——, *The Technological Society*. New York: Alfred A. Knopf, 1965.

Emery, Edwin, Philip H. Ault and Warren K. Agee, *Introduction to Mass Communications*. New York: Dodd, Mead and Co., 1960.

——, and Henry Ladd Smith, *The Press and America*. New York: Prentice Hall, Inc., 1954.

Empson, William, *Seven Types of Ambiguity*. New York: Meridian Books, 1955.

Erikson, Erik H., *Identity: Youth and Crisis*. New York: W.W. Norton Co., 1968.

Eysenck, H.J., *Sense and Nonsense in Psychology*. Middlesex, England: Penguin Books, 1957.

——, *Uses and Abuses of Psychology*. London: Penguin Books, 1953.

Flavell, J.H., *The Developmental Psychology of Jean Piaget.* Princeton, N.J.: D. Van-Nostrand Co., Inc., 1963.

Frankl, Viktor F., *Man's Search for Meaning.* New York: Washington Square Press, Inc., 1963.

Freud, Sigmund, *The Basic Writings of Sigmund Freud.* New York: The Modern Library, 1938.

———, *Civilization and Its Discontents.* Garden City, New York: Doubleday and Co., no date.

———, *The Future of an Illusion.* Garden City, New York: Doubleday and Co., 1957.

Friedan, Betty, *The Feminine Mystique.* New York: W.W. Norton and Co., Inc., 1963.

Friedenberg, Edgar Z., *Coming of Age in America.* New York: Random House, 1965.

Fromm, Erich, *Escape from Freedom.* New York: Rinehart and Co., Inc., 1942.

———, *The Sane Society.* New York: Rinehart and Co., 1955.

Fulton, A.R., *Motion Pictures.* Norman: University of Oklahoma Press, 1960.

Galbraith, John K., *The Affluent Society.* Boston: Houghton Mifflin Co., 1958.

———, *The New Industrial State.* Boston: Houghton Mifflin Co., 1967.

George, Alexander L. *Propaganda Analysis.* Evanston, Ill.: Row, Peterson and Co., 1959.

Gessner, Robert, *The Moving Image.* New York: E.P. Dutton & Co., Inc., 1968.

Ghiselin, Brewster, *The Creative Process.* New York: The New American Library, 1955.

Goodman, Ezra, *The Fifty-Year Decline and Fall of Hollywood.* New York: Simon and Schuster, 1961.

Gordon, George N., Irving Falk and William Hodapp, *The Idea Invaders.* New York: Hastings House, Publishers, Inc., 1963.

Gorelik, Mordecai, *New Theatres for Old.* New York: Samuel French, 1947.

Gregory, R.L., *Eye and Brain.* New York: World University Library; McGraw-Hill Book Co., 1966.

Grierson, John, *Grierson on Documentary.* London: Collins, 1946.

Hall, Edward T., *The Silent Language.* Greenwich, Conn.: Fawcett Publications, Inc., 1961.

Hayakawa, S.I., *Language in Thought and Action.* New York: Harcourt, Brace and Co., 1949.

——— (ed.), *Our Language and Our World.* New York: Harper and Brothers, 1958.

Head, Sidney, *Broadcasting in America.* Boston, Mass.: Houghton Mifflin Co., 1956.

Heilbroner, Robert, *The Future as History.* New York: Harper and Brothers, 1960.

Himmelweit, Hilde, A.N. Oppenheim and Pamela Vance, *Television and the Child.* New York: Oxford University Press, 1958.

Hocking, William Ernest, *Freedom of the Press.* Chicago, Ill.: The University of Chicago Press, 1947.

Hogben, Lancelot, *From Cave Painting to Comic Strip,* New York: Chanticleer Press, 1949.

Hull, Clark L. *et. al.*, *Mathematico-Deductive Theory of Rote Learning.* New Haven: Yale University Press, 1940.

———, *Principles of Behavior.* New Haven: Yale University Press, 1952.

Huntington, Ellsworth, *Mainsprings of Civilization.* New York: The New American Library, 1959.

Huxley, Aldous, *Brave New World Revisited.* New York: Harper and Brothers, 1957.

Innis, Harold A., *The Bias of Communication.* Toronto: The University of Toronto Press, 1951.

Jacobs, Norman (ed.), *Culture for the Millions?* Princeton, N.J.: D. Van Nostrand Co., Inc., 1959.

James, William, *Psychology, The Briefer Course.* New York: Harper and Row, 1961.

Jesperson, Otto, *Growth and Structure of the English Language.* Garden City, New York: Doubleday and Co., 1955.

Jones, Robert Edmond, *The Dramatic Imagination*. New York: Duell, Sloan and Pearce, 1941.

Kael, Pauline, *I Lost It At The Movies*. Boston: Little, Brown and Co., 1965.

———, *Kiss Kiss Bang Bang*. Boston: Little, Brown and Co., 1968.

Kahler, Erich, *The Tower and the Abyss*. New York: George Braziller, 1957.

Katz, Daniel, *et. al.* (eds.), *Public Opinion and Propaganda*. New York: The Dryden Press, 1954.

Kepes, Gyorgy (ed.), *Sign, Image, Symbol*. New York: George Braziller, 1966.

Kerlinger, Fred, *Foundations of Behavioral Research*. New York: Holt, Rinehart and Winston, Inc., 1966.

Klapper, Joseph T., *The Effects of Mass Communication*. Glencoe, Ill.: The Free Press, 1960.

Knight, Arthur, *The Liveliest Art*. New York: Mentor Books, 1959.

Koestler, Arthur, *The Act of Creation*. New York: The Macmillan Co., 1964.

———, *The Sleepwalkers*. New York: The Macmillan Co., 1959.

Kracauer, Sigfried, *Theory of Film*. New York: The Oxford Press, 1960.

Kraus, Sidney (ed.), *The Great Debates*. Bloomington: Indiana University Press, 1962.

Krech, David and Richard S. Crutchfield, *Social Psychology*. New York: McGraw-Hill Book Co., Inc., 1948.

Kronenberger, Louis, *Company Manners*. New York: The New American Library, 1955.

Krutch, Joseph Wood, *Human Nature and the Human Condition*. New York: Random House, 1959.

———, *The Modern Temper*. New York: Harcourt, Brace and Co., 1929.

Laird, Charlton, *The Miracle of Language*. Greenwich, Conn.: Fawcett Publications Inc., 1953.

Lang, Kurt and Gladys, *Collective Dynamics*. New York: Thomas Y. Crowell Co., 1961.

Langer, Susanne K., *Feeling and Form*. New York: Charles Scribner's Sons, 1953.

———, *Mind: An Essay on Human Feeling* (Volume I), Baltimore: The Johns Hopkins Press, 1967.

———, *Philosophy in a New Key*. New York: The New American Library, 1948.

Lawson, John Howard, *Film: The Creative Process*. New York: Hill and Wang, 1964.

Le Bon, Gustave, *The Crowd*. New York: Compass Books Edition, 1960.

Lerner, Max, *America As A Civilization*. New York: Simon and Schuster, 1957.

Lévi-Strauss, Claude, *Structural Anthropology*. Garden City, New York: Doubleday and Co., Inc., 1967.

Levitus, G.B., *The World of Psychology* (2 vols.). New York: George Braziller, 1963.

Liebling, A.J., *The Press*. New York: Ballantine Books, 1961.

Lindner, Robert, *Prescription for Rebellion*. New York: Grove Press, Inc., 1952.

Lippmann, Walter, *Public Opinion*. New York: Penguin Books, 1946.

Lorenz, Konrad, *On Aggression*. New York: Harcourt, Brace and World, Inc., 1963.

Luce Commission on the Freedom of the Press, *A Free and Responsible Press*. Chicago, Ill.: The University of Chicago Press, 1947.

Lynch, William (S.J.), *The Image Industries*. New York: Sheed and Ward, 1959.

Lynes, Russell, *The Tastemakers*. New York: Harper and Brothers, 1955.

McCulloch, Warren S., *Embodiments of Mind*. Cambridge, Mass.: The M.I.T. Press, 1965.

MacGowan, Kenneth, *Behind the Screen*. New York: Delacorte Press, 1965.

McLuhan, Marshall, *Understanding Media*. New York: McGraw-Hill Book Co., 1964.

MacNeil, Robert, *The People Machine*. New York: Harper and Row Publishers, 1968.

Malinowski, Bronislaw, *Sex, Culture and Myth*. New York: Harcourt, Brace and World, Inc., 1962.

Manoogian, Haig P., *The Film Maker's Art*. New York: Basic Books, 1966.

Manvell, Roger, *Film*. Hammondsworth, Middlesex, England: Penguin Books, 1950.

————, *The Film and the Public*. Hammondsworth, Middlesex: Penguin Books, Ltd., 1955.

Maslow, Abraham H., *Toward a Psychology of Being*. Princeton, N.J.: D. Van Nostrand Co., Inc., 1962.

Matson, Floyd W., and Ashley Montagu (eds.), *The Human Dialogue*. New York: The Free Press, 1967.

Mayer, Martin, *Madison Avenue, USA*. New York: Harper and Brothers, 1958.

Meerloo, Joost A., *The Rape of the Mind*. New York: The World Publishing Co., 1956.

Mehling, Harold, *The Great Time Killer*. New York: The World Publishing Co., 1962.

Miller, Merle and Even Rhodes, *Only You, Dick Daring!* New York: Bantam Books, 1965.

Mills, C. Wright, *The Power Elite*. New York: Oxford University Press, 1956.

————, *The Sociological Imagination*. New York: The Oxford Press, 1959.

Milne, Loris J. and Margery, *The Senses of Animals and Men*. New York: Atheneum, 1952.

Montagu, Ivor, *Film World*. Baltimore, Md.: Penguin Books, 1964.

Morris, Charles, *Signs, Language and Behavior*. New York: George Braziller, Inc., 1955.

Muggeridge, Malcom, *The Most of Malcolm Muggeridge*. New York: Simon and Schuster, 1966.

Mulholland, John and George N. Gordon, *The Magical Mind*. New York: Hastings House, Publishers, Inc., 1967.

Nafziger, Ralph O. and David M. White, *Introduction to Mass Communications Research*. Baton Rouge: Louisiana State University Press, 1963.

Ogden, C.K. and I.A. Richards, *The Meaning of Meaning*. New York: Harcourt, Brace and Co., Inc., 1953.

O'Hara, Robert C., *Media for Millions*. New York: Random House, 1961.

Olson, Philip (ed.), *America as a Mass Society*. New York: The Free Press, 1963.

Ortega y Gasset, José, *The Revolt of the Masses*. New York: W. W. Norton and Co., 1957.

Osgood, Charles E., George E. Suci and Percy Tannenbaum, *The Measurement of Meaning*. Urbana, Ill.: University of Illinois Press, 1957.

————, and K.V. Wilson, *Some Terms and Associated Measures for Talking About Human Communication*. Urbana, Ill.: University of Illinois Press, 1961.

Ozenfant, *Foundations of Modern Art*. New York: Dover Publications, Inc., 1952.

Paulu, Burton, *British Broadcasting in Transition*. Minneapolis: University of Minnesota Press, 1961.

Peterson, Theodore, Jay V. Jenson and William L. Rivers, *The Mass Media and Modern Society*. New York: Holt, Rinehart and Winston, Inc., 1965.

Pierce, J.R., *Symbols, Signals and Noise*. New York: Harper and Row, 1961.

Plutchik, Robert, *The Emotions*. New York: Random House, 1962.

Qualter, Terence H., *Propaganda and Psychological Warfare*. New York: Random House, 1962.

Rapoport, Anatol, *Fights, Games and Debates*. Ann Arbor: The University of Michigan Press, 1960.

————, *Strategy and Conscience*. New York: Harper and Row, Publishers, 1964.

Read, Herbert, *To Hell With Culture*. New York: Schocken Books, 1963.

Reik, Theodore, *Jewish Wit*. New York: Gamut Press, 1962.

Richards, I.A., *Practical Criticism*. New York: Harcourt, Brace and Co., 1954.

————, *Principles of Literary Criticism*. New York: Harcourt, Brace and Co., 1947.

Riesman, David, *Individualism Reconsidered*. Glencoe, Ill.: The Free Press, 1954.

————, *et al.*, *The Lonely Crowd*. Garden City, New York: Doubleday and Co., Inc., 1953.

Roback, A.A., *A History of American Psychology*. New York: Collier Books, 1964.

Rosenberg, Bernard and David Manning White, *Mass Culture*. Glencoe, Ill.: The Free Press, 1957.
Rossiter, Clinton and James Lare, *The Essential Lippmann*. New York: Random House, 1963.
Rotha, Paul, *The Film Till Now*. London: Spring Books, 1949.
Rourke, Constance, *American Humor*. Garden City, New York: Doubleday Anchor Books, 1953.
Ruesch, Jurgen, *Non-verbal Communications*. Los Angeles: University of California Press, 1959.
Ruitenbeck, Hendrick M., *The Individual and the Crowd*. New York: The New American Library, 1964.
Ryle, Gilbert, *The Concept of Mind*. New York: Barnes and Noble, Inc., 1941.
Sapir, Edward, *Language: An Introduction to the Study of Speech*. New York: Harcourt Brace and World, 1949.
Sargent, William, *Battle for the Mind*. Garden City, New York: Doubleday and Co., Inc., 1957.
Schramm, Wilbur, Jack Lyle and Edwin B. Parker, *Television in the Lives of Our Children*. Stanford, Calif.: Stanford University Press, 1961.
———, *Responsibility in Mass Communications*. New York: Harper and Brothers, 1957.
Schumach, Murray, *The Face on the Cutting Room Floor*. New York: William Morrow and Co., 1964.
Seldes, Gilbert, *The Great Audience*. New York: The Viking Press, 1950.
———, *The Public Arts*. New York: Simon and Schuster, 1956.
———, *The Seven Lively Arts*. New York: Sagamore Press, Inc., 1957.
Shannon, Claude E., and Warren Weaver, *The Mathematical Theory of Communications*. Urbana, Ill.: University of Illinois Press, 1949.
Shibutani, Tamotsu, *Improvised News*. New York: The Bobbs-Merrill Company, Inc., 1966.
Siepmann, Charles, *Radio, Television and Society*. New York: Oxford University Press, 1950.
Simeons, Albert T., *Man's Presumptuous Brain*. New York: E.P. Dutton and Co., 1961.
Skornia, Harry J., *Television and Society*. New York: McGraw-Hill Book Co., 1965.
Smith, Alfred G. (ed.), *Communication and Culture*. New York: Holt, Rinehart and Winston, 1966.
Snow, C.P., *The Two Cultures and a Second Look*. New York: The New American Library, 1964.
Stanislavsky, Constantin, *My Life in Art*. New York: Theatre Arts Books, 1948.
Stephenson, William, *The Play Theory of Mass Communication*. Chicago and London: The University of Chicago Press, 1967.
Steinberg, Charles (ed.), *Mass Media and Communication*. New York: Hastings House, Publishers, 1966.
Steinberg, S.H., *Five Hundred Years of Printing*. Hammondsworth, Middlesex, England: Penguin Books, Inc., 1955.
Steiner, Gary, *The People Look at Television*. New York: Alfred A. Knopf, 1963.
Steiner, George, *Language and Silence*. New York: Atheneum Publishers, 1967.
Strauss, Anselm, *The Social Psychology of George Herbert Mead*. Chicago: The University of Chicago Press, 1956.
Sullivan, J.W.N., *The Limitations of Science*. New York: The New American Library, 1952.
Swanson, Guy E., Theodore M. Newcomb and Eugene Hartley (eds.), *Readings in Social Psychology* (Rev. ed.). New York: Henry Holt and Co., 1952.
Swartz, Robert J. (ed.), *Perceiving, Sensing and Knowing*. Garden City: New York, Doubleday and Co., 1965.

Sypher, Wylie (ed.), *Comedy*. Garden City, New York: Doubleday Anchor Books, 1956.

Talbot, Daniel (ed.), *Film, An Anthology*, Berkeley and Los Angeles: University of California Press, 1966.

Toffler, Alvin, *The Culture Consumers*. New York: St. Martin's Press, 1964.

Turner, E.S., *The Shocking History of Advertising*. New York: Ballantine Books, 1953.

Vernon, M.D., *The Psychology of Perception*. Baltimore, Md.: Penguin Books, 1962.

Warnock, G.J., *English Philosophy Since 1900*. London: Oxford University Press, 1958.

Warshow, Robert, *The Immediate Experience*. Garden City, New York: Doubleday and Co., 1962.

Waugh, Coughton, *The Comics*. New York: The Macmillan Co., 1947.

Weinberg, Meyer, *TV in America*. New York: Ballantine Books, 1962.

Weiner, Norbert, *Cybernetics*. New York: John Wiley and Sons, Inc., 1948.

Wertham, Frederic, *Seduction of the Innocent*. New York: Rinehart and Co., 1954.

Whatmough, Joshua, *Language, A Modern Synthesis*. New York: The New American Library, 1956.

White, David M. and Robert H. Abel (eds.), *The Funnies, An American Idiom*. New York: The Free Press of Glencoe, 1963.

———, and Richard Averson (eds.), *Sight, Sound and Society*. Boston: Beacon Press, 1968.

Whitehead, A.N., *The Aims of Education*. New York: The New American Library, 1949.

———, *Symbolism*. New York: The Macmillan Co., 1958.

Whorf, Benjamin Lee, *Language, Thought and Reality*. Cambridge, Mass.: The M.I.T. Press, 1956.

Whyte, William H., *The Organization Man*. New York: Simon and Schuster, 1958.

Widmer, Kingsley and Eleanor (eds.), *Literary Censorship*. San Francisco, Calif.: Wadsworth Publishing Co., 1961.

Wilensky, Harold L., *Organizational Intelligence*. New York: Basic Books, 1967.

Wolfenstein, Martha and Nathan Leites, *Movies, A Psychological Study*. Glencoe, Ill.: The Free Press, 1950.

INDEX

Abstract art, 132
Adler, Alfred, 62
Advertising, and relationships between mass communications and behavior, 289–90
Aeschylus, 116
Aesthetic distance, 147
Aesthetics, 12, 13, 98, 127; *see also* Art
Aggression, as human trait, 229–30
Alcoholism, 93, 107
Allport, Gordon, quoted, 212
Alzheimer, Alois, 20
American Revolution, 70
Analogy, symbolism as, 63, 64, 65, 66
Anthropology, 87, 112, 113, 287, 290
Antonioni, Michaelangelo, 214
Arent, Arthur, 207
Aristophanes, 116
Aristotle, 7, 8, 10, 14, 15, 16, 23, 117, 144, 145, 146, 150, 151, 240, 241, 311, 312
Arnheim, Rudolf, 114, 115, 138, 272, 273; quoted, 71, 110, 114, 133–34, 138, 272
Art, 132, 138, 140, 144, 173, 202, 208, 209, 210–11, 217, 282, 291, 294, 301, 311; *see also* Aesthetics; Pictures
"Artlessness," 207
Attitude Inventories, 193
Attitudes, and styles in communication, 192–201 *passim*
Audience psychology (Le Bon), 98
Audio-visual instruction, failure of, 300, 313
Austin, J. L., 67; quoted, 67
Ayer, A. J., 67

Bacon, Francis, 7, 9, 20
Barrett, William, quoted, 10
Bartlett, Edna, xii
Barzun, Jacques, 29, 141; quoted, 141
Beardsley, Aubrey V., 197, 198
Belgium, education in, 90
Bennett, Arnold, 193
Bergman, Ingmar, 52, 53, 170, 227

Bergson, Henri, 222, 223, 224, 225, 227, 233; quoted, 222
Berkeley, George, 4
Berlo, David, 14, 15, 16
Bertalanffy, Ludwig von, 3, 5, 52; quoted, 3–4, 51–52
Bias of Communications, The (Innis), 239
Bible, as best seller, 248
Bierce, Ambrose, 232
Birth control, 86 (table), 91
Blanchard, Fred, xii
Blistein, Elmer, 220; quoted, 220
Book clubs, 249, 277
Books, 250
Boorstein, Daniel J., 61, 62
Boss, The (Sheldon), 308
Breuer, Joseph, 21
British Broadcasting Corporation, 246, 298
Bronowski, J., 5
Brophy, Brigid, 155, 212
Brophy, Mary, xii
Bureaucracy, 77–78, 88; and mythological symbols, 85, 86, 86 (table), 88
Burke, Kenneth, 51, 52, 58, 59, 60, 61, 212; quoted, 53, 61

Campbell, Josef, quoted, 124
Canada, 98, 239, 240; education in, 90
Canniff, Milton, 265
Cartoonists: comic-strip, 201, 264, 265, 267; political, 308
Castro, Fidel, 69, 186
Cellini, Benvenuto, 193
Cervantes, Miguel de, 64–65
Chaplin, Charles, 151, 223, 224, 274
Character, as factor in logical and psychological entropy, 45
Charcot, Jean M., 20
Cherry, Colin, quoted, 130
Chomsky, Noam, 162
Churchill, Winston, 125, 191